Political Science: Looking to the Future

Volume Four

Political Science: Looking to the Future
William Crotty, General Editor

Political Science: Looking to the Future

Edited by William Crotty

Volume Four
American Institutions

Northwestern University Press

Evanston, Illinois

Northwestern University Press
Evanston, Illinois 60201

Copyright © 1991 by Northwestern University Press
All rights reserved. Published 1991
Printed in the United States of America

First printing, 1991

ISBN: 0-8101-0953-0 (cloth)
      0-8101-0954-9 (paper)

Library of Congress Cataloging-in-Publication Data

Political science : looking to the future / edited by William Crotty.
    p.   cm.
    Includes bibliographical references.
    Contents: v. 1. The theory and practice of political science — v.
2. Comparative politics, policy, and international relations — v.
3. Political behavior — v. 4. American institutions.
    ISBN 0-8101-0922-0 (v. 1 : alk. paper). — ISBN 0-8101-0923-9 (v.
1 : pbk. : alk. paper)
    1. Political science. 2. International relations. 3. United
States—Politics and government. I. Crotty, William J.
JA37.P75   1991
320—dc20   91-7988
                                                                 CIP

Contents

Acknowledgments

A project of this magnitude involves the efforts of a large number of people. Among those contributing in significant ways to the publication of these volumes have been Alan D. Monroe, Richard P. Farkas, Ruth S. Jones, Catherine E. Rudder, Molly Crotty, Dale D. Vasiliauskas, M. L. Hauch, Lucille Mayer, Laura Olson, and Ada W. Finifter, whose advice in the preliminary stages of the undertaking was of great assistance. The evaluations of the entire manuscript by Jonathan D. Caspar, Leon D. Epstein, and Joseph M. Schwartz were deeply appreciated.

Those at Northwestern University Press who were particularly helpful include: Jonathan Brent, the press's director; Susan Harris, Managing Editor, who oversaw the editorial process; Nan Crotty, Jill Shimabukuro, Amy Schroeder, Rina Ranalli, and Rachel Inger.

To all, we are grateful.

Introduction: Setting the Stage

William Crotty

Political science, like much of academia, is at a crossroads.[1] The causes are many.

First is the problem of generational change. Estimates vary, but one-half or more of the practicing political scientists in the United States are expected to retire roughly by the year 2000 (give or take five years or so). A new generation of academicians will take over, with consequences uncertain. The loss of the postwar giants that shaped the modern era of political science will be keenly felt. It is always tricky to select a few names to illustrate a trend, but the legacy of those such as William H. Riker, Robert A. Dahl, Warren E. Miller, Gabriel A. Almond, Harold Guetzkow, Richard F. Fenno, Jr., Donald R. Matthews, Samuel J. Eldersveld, Dwaine Marvick, Philip E. Converse, Donald E. Stokes, Heinz Eulau, David Easton, Joseph LaPalombara, Harry H. Eckstein, and their colleagues is compelling, as the papers published in these volumes make clear. The list of names is obviously incomplete; yet it does illustrate the magnitude—in terms of intellectual force and disciplinary impact—of those for whom replacements must be found.

Where the discipline is to go, who are to be its intellectual patrons, and what concepts, theories, problem areas, or approaches are likely to dominate its collective consciousness—these are some of the questions that led to the explorations contained in these volumes. The aim is not to answer these questions with a degree of certainty: intellectual dogmatism serves no good purpose, and no one point of view (as will become readily apparent) guided these efforts. The idea was to explore options, ask questions, sort through subfields, and attempt to separate that which may be useful and productive from that which may be old, worn-out, or misleading. Each author had license to do this in the manner he or she found most appropriate. There were no preconditions concerning the points to be raised or the intellectual forces to be addressed. The intent was to raise issues and advance ideas, to force people to think. What does the future hold? How should we in political science prepare for it? What is the best we have to offer, and what can most conveniently be left behind?

Generational concerns are also reflected in the balance of authors chosen to write the subfield essays. Most significantly, each was a scholar of stature in his or her subfield. In addition, however, the likelihood is that most of the contributors should be around for the next several decades to help set in broad relief the future directions the discipline will pursue. Thus, there is a heavier reliance than otherwise might be the case on respectable scholars from middle-level age groups who have already made substantial contributions to their particular specialties. Clearly, many who could have qualified have not been included. This is not the point. Those who were chosen must wrestle in the near future with precisely the types of concerns they address in their papers. The selection strategy was intentional.

These essays will be controversial—some more than others. Each, however, represents an author's (or authors') perspective on the broader questions raised as exemplified by his or her subfield. Each author, in turn, is considered an expert in his or her field with something of importance to say concerning its present condition and its likely future course of development. Their ideas are worth considering; they are meant to stimulate, to serve as a basis for discussion and contention, and to force a reexamination, however modest, of a discipline entering a critical phase in its development. If they accomplish these ends, they will have served their purpose.

Social science, like all of academia, has gone through a difficult period. Support for education, funding of original research, and an emphasis on the qualitative development of knowledge have not been priorities in American culture and politics since at least the late 1960s. The predictable result has been a drop-off in the initiation of research and a stabilization, and even decline, in the number of students seeking Ph.D.s. Teaching and research have not been prized career objectives over the last several decades. It is also probable that, with scholarship support decreased and many universities severely restricted in their hiring, graduate schools have not only had fewer applicants, but the quality of those seeking entrance has not been of the caliber it might be. Law, medical, and business and professional schools may be proving more attractive to the abler undergraduates. Little of this can be directly and quantifiably proven. Still, the difficult times faced by the academic community have been real, and the fears expressed about the long-term consequences reflect those heard on campuses throughout the nation.

In more specific relation to political science, there has also been a mood of disenchantment. The unity, cohesiveness, and commonalities of the field seem to be in eclipse; perhaps they have already been abandoned.[2] This is a common theme in many of the essays that follow. Frequently, the approaches or substantive concerns that have held a subfield together and contributed to its distinctiveness are now in doubt. There is change in the redefinition of boundary areas, in what is significant and should continue to be so in contrast to what has been considered important in the past. The subfields are in flux: some are assuming greater importance; the interest in others is declining. Political science is a discipline in transition.

The question of seeking a broader identity for the field is raised in varying contexts by a number of authors. What distinguishes political science as an integrative whole, a bounded and coherent intellectual pursuit? What makes the discipline distinctive? What constitutes its particular problems? What should be the central focus and common bonds among its practitioners? These concerns are addressed in differing contexts and, in particular, served as the basis for those contributing to Volume 1, *The Theory and Practice of Political Science,* arguably the most contentious of the four. These questions are the mega-issues, the ones that concern all of us as practicing academicians. Whether it is preferable to achieve the coherence, stability, and self-assurance that some found in the past, or whether a more eclectic, exploratory, and innovative practice is preferable is debatable. Whether conceptual approaches ("power," "politics," "markets," "representation," "democracy"), subject matter (the study of government, institutions, political behavior), or definitional guides ("the authoritative allocation of values," "who gets what, when, and how") are the best indicators of relevance is also arguable.

Both approaches have their costs: in one, smugness, perhaps, and a hint as to what can or "should" be done, contrasted in the other with a disparate, shotgunlike scattering of interests that raises questions about the interests or bonds that political scientists share. What distinguishes political scientists from sociologists, economists, historians, or anthropologists (or, for that matter, from those who work in professional schools of law, journalism, management, or policy)? Should distinctions among them be made? Can they communicate intellectually with each other? What do they have to share, borrow, or contribute that is distinctive to their respective disciplines? Or, conversely, are those valid concerns? Some believe that each subfield should follow its own road. Eventually, they argue, all—or at least knowledge writ large—should prosper. The role of graduate education—what skills and perspectives are transmitted to future generations of practitioners—in such a scheme is unclear—a further sign of a discipline's indecision. Many believe that this indecision typifies the mood that has been progressively enveloping the discipline over the last generation.

The questions raised in the essays that follow are basic. No effort has been made to supply answers—should they even exist at this point in time—on which the balance of contributors might agree. The purpose is to encourage critical thought at a convenient summing-up point in a discipline's development.

Finally, a note on what the essays that follow are not. They are not intended to be comprehensive reviews of the literature in any given area.[3] In fact, the authors were specifically asked not to do this. These instructions, however, did not exclude the compiling of bibliographies to many of the essays that might provide a reasonable starting point for serious inquiry into the subfield being discussed. Many of these are extensive.

The authors were also asked not to restrict themselves to the need to present a balanced or thorough examination of their respective fields. This type of directive is a little unusual in academia. One result may be the intentional omission of works of stature, the contributions of major scholars. The editor, not the authors, takes full responsibility for such deficiencies. Rather than comprehensiveness, fairness, or balance, we wanted ideas—a freshness of perspective, a personal signature on the observations made. The goal has been to raise issues of significance for discussion and debate. Where are we? Where are we going? What could prove useful to us as we move toward an uncertain future? These are the comments that unite the chapters.

The papers were commissioned for a special series of theme panels held at the 1989 annual meeting of the Midwest Political Science Association. At that time, William Crotty was serving as president of the association and assumed the principal responsibility for organizing these panels. Alan D. Monroe served as program chair for the meeting. In addition, significant support was provided by Richard P. Farkas, then executive director of the Midwest Political Science Association, and Catherine E. Rudder, executive director of the American Political Science Association.

The idea behind the theme panels was to have a distinguished practitioner in a field prepare a paper on his or her specialty written in the context described above. A panel was then built around each paper and included three to four discussants, also individuals of prominence in the subfield, who commented on the paper, challenging its assumptions and often advancing alternative explanations, relevant criteria, or scenarios for future exploration. Most of the individuals who contributed in these ways are acknowledged by the authors in their essays.

The papers were then read before a group presumed to be expert in most cases, or at least interested enough as teachers or researchers in the area under discussion to participate in such a specialized critique. In general, the sessions were well attended. Surprisingly, perhaps, many of the panels had standing-room-only audiences, and in a few cases the meeting rooms were unable to accommodate all those wishing to attend. In most cases, too, the exchanges were lively, perhaps indicating that the issues being addressed and the questions raised reflected generally felt concerns in the discipline.

The authors were asked to incorporate into their essays the points they considered most relevant from the resulting exchanges and, specifically, to address in some fashion any issues that might appear to have been deficiencies in their original presentations. In some cases, the editor also advanced suggestions, but always with the understanding that the author's judgment as to relevance and importance, and the issues and themes that he or she preferred to emphasize, took precedence. No two essayists address the same questions within the same format. Some of the papers are lengthy; others are relatively brief. Some are opinionated; others preferred to mute their approach while allowing their personal preferences to remain clear. Some are cautiously optimistic; others are not. Some attempted to document their arguments extensively; others opted for a simpler thematic presentation. All in all, though, we trust that the essays taken together serve to highlight many of the most significant issues facing the discipline today, and that they provide a starting point for a serious discussion about where we as political scientists now are, what we have to contribute, and where we, as a discipline, may be headed.

IN THIS VOLUME . . .

The study of legislatures has traditionally been a central preoccupation of political scientists. Legislatures provide good laboratories for testing theories and methodologies of significance in the discipline and, more broadly, for contributing to an understanding of how representative government works.

Legislatures are intrinsically interesting; information on their operations is easily accessible; and they are critically important institutions of governance. Their traits reflect those of a human group, thus accommodating a wide diversity of research interests. All these characteristics contribute to their popularity as objects of research attention among political scientists.

Roger H. Davidson ("Legislative Research: Mirror of a Discipline") makes these points in assessing the thematic continuities and conceptual and methodological approaches to legislative research. Davidson reviews the rise of legislatures and the manner in which these have been studied traditionally. There have been many approaches: legal and historical, reformist, and institutional-bureaucratic assessments of policy-making, to mention a few of the more prominent early ones. None proved totally satisfactory. More successful were the behavioral studies of the 1960s and early 1970s, exemplified by the research of Ralph K. Huitt, Donald R. Matthews, and John C. Wahlke and associates. The body of work produced at this time has provided much of the core for the present understanding of legislative operations.

In the postbehavioral era, no one theme or approach has dominated legislative studies. In fact, the field is characterized by diversity. The perspectives employed range from a renewed interest in historical analysis and qualitative case studies to formal modeling and a continuing emphasis on a behavioral orientation. The focus of research concerns has diversified: presidential-congressional relations, congressional campaigns and elections, and the operations of the committee system being among the leaders. Davidson critiques promising developments in each of these areas.

As a future research agenda, Davidson advocates the following: careerism in legislative bodies and, comparatively, other political institutions; constituency relations with representatives; the roles legislative parties and partisanship play in institutional decision-making, problem-solving and policy-making in legislatures; longitudinal changes in legislative structures and functions; the comparative analysis of legislative operations; and the need for broader theoretical explanations of legislative behavior. Theory combined with observation would serve the needs of the field well. Its future course may not be clear; nonetheless, the study of legislatures is at the heart of an understanding of democratic representation. For this reason and the others cited, it will remain both an important and attractive focus for political science interest.

Paul J. Quirk ("What Do We Know and How Do We Know It? Research on the Presidency") looks at the most powerful of modern institutions, the presidency. Research on the presidency has been criticized—legitimately, some would say—for doing less in a less sophisticated way than should be expected of efforts to understand the critical center of decision-making in a democratic order. As Quirk points out, the more recent research on the presidency holds significant promise of producing a more penetrating and multifaceted appreciation of how the institution operates.

Research in the area is diffuse and fragmented, a condition not unknown in a number of other subfields in the discipline. Sustained investigations of many problems have been rare, resulting at times in a cursory and superficial knowledge of how things work. Quirk indicates, however, unlike in some of these other areas, the research on the presidency may be assuming a more cohesive and cumulative orientation.

Quirk identifies topics for research attention that focus on the president's role in the policy-making process. Each has its own set of concerns, but all are related in the opportunities they offer for the investigation of significant research questions and for accumulating a body of relevant knowledge for assessing the functioning of representative government. Each also directly exploits concerns of traditional importance to political scientists. Quirk initially examines six topics: policy planning and program development in the executive branch, and particularly the organizational influences that affect these; explanations of policy decisions in terms of the personal, political, or social goals sought; the executive-congressional relationship; presidential influence on the administrative process, an area much neglected by political scientists; the cultivation of public support for presidential initiatives; psychological and biographical assessments of individual presidents; and change in the institution and operations of the presidential office.

In each area, Quirk evaluates the research now being done, the quality of the knowledge available, and the most plausible prospects for further investigations of broad significance. He makes these assessments in terms of the substantive issues to be addressed and the way in which they might best be approached. The critiques are tough-minded and insightful.

Quirk argues that political scientists have been overly concerned with power outcomes and zero-sum resolutions in policy analyses. The consequence has been a corresponding deemphasis on issues relating to the broad deliberative processes involved in the framing of policy options and the use of bargaining and mediation to advance conflict resolution through policy-making.

Quirk, like a number of other authors in these volumes, suggests that specialists on the presidency become more comfortable with diversity. More controversially, he advises scholars of the presidency to define themselves, and approach their subject matter, in broader field perspectives (leadership studies or administrative behavior analyses are examples). Such orientations might lead to the more theoretical and methodological sophistication the field needs. They might also result in clearer standards for evaluating what constitutes success in the presidency. There are certainly tendencies in these directions, as Quirk makes clear. It may well be that the future course of the field will reflect the main outlines of the advances he has indicated. If so, and judging by this essay, the study of the presidency could emerge as one of the more stimulating problem areas.

"Schizophrenic," "distinctive," "old," "multidisciplinary"—these are a few of the adjectives Elliott E. Slotnick ("Judicial Politics") uses to describe the study of judicial politics. This area is basically different from others because its principal subject matter has a clearly identifiable focus and the freedom of actors within the system (for example, judges) is circumscribed. There is also a tension in the field between emphases such as those implicit in the term *judicial politics* and the structurally more prescribed *public law*. In addition, a political scientist often must justify his specialization in law; a legal researcher or law school professor encounters no such demand.

Social scientists conceptualize questions differently from those who teach in law schools, and the results of their research often challenge the founding myths that law schools promulgate. Most of the students who eventually move on to law school and law careers receive their preprofessional training at the hands of political scientists, who teach an orientation that most law schools do not choose to pursue. For these reasons, there are strains implicit in the study of law and politics not found in other subfields of the discipline. Compared to other specializations, it is a well-bounded unit of inquiry and, like many others, one with a great deal of diversity.

Slotnick traces the history of the field from its heavy legalistic orientation in its earlier periods, through the realism of scholars such as Robert K. Carr and Alpheus T. Mason, up to the quantitative analyses that marked the behavioral era. At the same time, researchers moved from a fascination with the Supreme Court and the evolution of constitutional law to studies of the behavior of judges and to predicting the outcomes of judicial decision-making. The judicial process, what influenced it, and how it impacted on other aspects of American politics have become the focal points of attention. At the time those developments were taking place, curiously, public law as a subfield was declining in prestige, the number of its practitioners falling, and its contribution to mainline political science was deemphasized and underappreciated.

Since the 1960s, there has been a greater diversity in the problems and processes explored by constitutional scholars and in the ways they approach them. The traditionalist-behavioral split, with its attendant self-conscious evaluations of methodologies and their role in delimiting research outcomes, came to the judicial field later than others; not until the 1960s and 1970s was the battle fully joined. Eventually it was to give way to a basic stability in research and a tolerance for an eclectic mixture of approaches and substantive concerns, hallmarks of research on judicial politics in the contemporary period. In an area that has relied on description, case studies, and legalistic analyses, the development of theoretical perspectives to explain observations—especially inclusive theoretical orientations—and the application of controlled-hypotheses testing and comparative analyses have been slower to emerge than in most other fields.

As to future research, Slotnick points to the need for a broader conceptualization of the politics of court processes. He advocates research focusing on trial and lower court operations, decision-making, and litigation processes, topics now receiving greater attention; examination of the public perceptions of the courts and their influence on judicial decision-making; analyses of the role of the courts in influencing policy outcomes; and, perhaps surprisingly, a return to an emphasis on more traditional normative studies.

The study of judicial processes and public law is an old and esteemed pursuit in the discipline. Yet it is one that actively worries about its ties to mainstream political science and the threat of the increasing insularity of its concerns and its practitioners from their disciplinary brethren. Considering the clear interdisciplinary interests, the promise provided by increasingly robust and accessible data banks, and the challenge implicit in an eclecticism of approaches and focuses, the future looks attractive. The subfield may well develop confidence in what it does and an assertiveness as to what it has accomplished. Its position within the discipline is secure; the likelihood is that it will receive increasing recognition for its contributions.

Interest groups have played a major role in policy-making since the beginning of the Republic, a fact observed and justified by James Madison. Some of the most influential ideas in political science (the group theory of politics, pluralism, interest group liberalism, redistributive policy allocations) have roots in interest group representation, and some of the discipline's most honored work has resulted from interest group-based investigations (David B. Truman's *The Governmental Process* in 1951 is illustrative). But, as Allan J. Cigler ("Interest Groups: A Subfield in Search of an Identity") indicates, the research in the field has not been especially systematic, comprehensive, or plentiful. The reasons are many: the absence until recently of large data repositories; cost; access; the attractiveness of alternative, related organizational areas (such as political parties); and the ambivalence with which many attach to interest group ends. Nonetheless, since the mid-1970s the field has experienced a rebirth of interest, a sophistication of theorizing and experimentation in the analytic strategies applied to data. These developments have coincided with an increasingly productive, empirically-based research.

Cigler looks at the two main thrusts of interest group research: demand aggregation, or how interests are organized and represented, the category of studies with the more pronounced theoretical insight; and group impact, or how groups achieve political influence, their role in elections, and the consequences for policy-making. Cigler explores both areas in depth.

Since the 1960s, there has been a substantial increase in the number of groups concerned with influencing national policy. The extent of citizen, public interest, and voluntary group lobbying has increased substantially, as have corporate and trade association efforts to benefit from governmental policy. Overall, interest group leverage is skewed decisively toward the financially better-off, a finding that has remained consistent over time. Results such as these have served to cool an earlier infatuation with explaining American politics in terms of a balance among competing organized interests. The same pattern appears at both the national and, to the extent the data are available, the state levels. The topography may change by time period or locale; the balance of power does not.

Organizationally, the nature of groups has changed, with the more traditional mass membership groups giving way to those with Washington-based, personalized staffs purporting to speak for national coalitions of citizens whose only contribution to the "group" is financial. Studying such groups and their membership ties has forced a rethinking of concepts of representation and participation.

Cigler devotes particular attention to the collective action problem in group-based research: the motivations for group membership and the reasons for interest group proliferation. This is the single most frequently investigated area of interest group studies, and in theoretical terms the most provocative. As an example, Mancur Olson's (*The Logic of Collective Action*, 1965) depiction of the "free rider" problem in large-group formation has contributed to a series of "incentive theory" investigations into the reasons underlying the appeal of a given group for prospective members that challenges several of his basic assumptions. Economic self-interest, it would seem, is only one reason for collective group action. Many of these efforts have attempted to modify Olson's assumptions to reflect the reality of multiple motivations and imperfect information about the formation of group ties.

Robert H. Salisbury's development of "exchange theory" helps to explain group mobilization and adaption through a mutually satisfying and dynamic exchange of leadership incentives for membership backing. Groups can also solve their participation difficulties, as many environmental and public interest groups do, by finding a patron, an individual or institutional financial sponsor, to supply the bulk of the organization's capital. While much remains to be done in relation to the collective action of groups, and Cigler indicates the types of questions that remain underexplored, the advances made in theorizing and understanding in this particular area within a short period of time have been impressive.

The campaign finance laws of 1971 and 1974 have, for the first time, made extensive data available on the financial involvement of groups in elections, one measure of their impact on the policy-making process. Studies of the Washington-based representatives of a variety of organizational interests, a population that has expanded considerably in recent decades, emphasize the continuity and stability of the group goals over time and the professionalization of the advocates. What has changed is the increase in interest group activity since the early 1970s.

In relation to policy development, Cigler makes the point that the more recent scholarship concerning interest groups discredits the old "iron triangle" description of governmental policy-making. This joining of administrative agency, congressional subcommittee, and interest group in deciding policy has given way to a more fluid, open, and competitive process. The result is a less predictable, less stable policy climate, but one in which even the most powerful of interest advocates (the American Medical Association, for example) face the possibility of challenge in seeking their legislative ends. There has been a redefinition of concerns and a broadening of the number of actors and interests involved in determining policy outcomes in most arenas, developments that markedly change our perception of how decisions are made and resources allocated. The results are not necessarily better; the context of policy-making is, however, different.

Cigler concludes that while knowledge in the field has been substantially advanced in recent years, the potential foci for interest group research is vast and much remains open to investigation. Many who work in the area see themselves as other than students of interest groups, a fact that lends it a diversity of perspectives and approaches. The likelihood is that diversity, as well as expansion of subject-matter interests, will continue as the hallmarks of this subfield.

The study of political parties is a sprawling enterprise. It is a traditional area of political science inquiry and, as William Crotty shows ("Political Parties: Issues and Trends"), one with an uneven development. It is also one that, like interest groups, legislative research, and presidential studies, has many readily available and persuasive critiques of its achievements.

Political parties research lacks any particular thematic unity or intellectual cohesiveness. Investigations in one aspect of the subfield can have little in common with those in another. Given this condition, Crotty chooses to focus on selective areas: the quest for theoretical direction in parties research; the party as vote mobilizer; party activists; the nomination function of political parties; and the party as organization. The latter perspective offers promise as a potential unifying force for party concerns, although research in the area has not been as extensive as earlier work of consequence might have warranted.

In each subarea, the concerns are different and the quality of effort variable. Several, such as the research into activist motivations and professionalization and efforts to model nominating processes, while limited in number, hold promise of the guided, systematic, and cumulative exploration the field needs.

It may be symptomatic of the state of the research that one of the more significant questions facing party specialists is the overall health and vitality of the institutions they are studying. This has been a perpetual question of concern. Yet it is difficult to establish commonly accepted criteria as to what constitutes a viable or stronger or more representative party system in responding to issues that have pervaded much of the debate over party developments. One thing is clear: political parties are undergoing change. Their importance as instruments of democratic governance, long recognized by political scientists, is now apparent to layman and politician alike in countries undergoing the transition from authoritarian to more open and competitive rule. There is ferment in the field, and the future holds promise for innovative, comparative research of consequence.

The study of federalism and intergovernmental relations has enjoyed renewed popularity in recent years. As Susan A. MacManus ("Federalism and Intergovernmental Relations: The Centralization versus Decentralization Debate Continues") reports, however, the issue that has attracted the most attention remains much the same: at what level of government should the responsibility for various services be placed? Related to this question are fundamental concerns: How much centralization is good? What should be private and what should be public responsibilities? Are smaller, decentralized agencies with greater local control preferable to larger, more centralized institutions? Which is more economical or more efficient in service delivery? What values and priorities should the distribution of authority within the federal system take? Where should policy programs be initiated, managed, or assessed? How should they be funded? These are a few of the problems that have spurred research. The questions raised are not substantially different from those which have engaged government officials and political observers since the creation of the federal system.

The research in the field has been less systematic, comprehensive, and empirical than in many other areas. Rather, there has been an overreliance on case studies and descriptive accounts whose findings are difficult to generalize; and there is little cohesion or compatibility in the problem areas investigated or in the way in which they are addressed. Nonetheless, the fifty states provide a natural laboratory for social science investigation. A number of the studies that have chosen to take advantage of these conditions have resulted in research that ranks among the discipline's most creative.

Federalism students have had a strong interdisciplinary orientation, borrowing from related fields such as policy studies, public-choice modeling, public administration, law and politics, presidential and legislative studies, administrative behavior, political parties, and electoral systems. Research into intergovernmental relations is a significant contributor to the discipline's mainstream interests.

The recent research holds the power of introducing more powerful conceptual tools, as it does of recasting our thinking on federalism. For example, an outgrowth of the interest generated by efforts in Washington to return policy responsibilities to the states are indications from recent scholarship that such changes may result in programs most responsive to constituent groups and more equitable in allocating resources than many had believed to be the case. In a dynamic field, the long-run consequences of such transferences, as well as the debate over the privatization of public services, remain to be assessed.

Research interest appears to be moving toward cross-national studies of economic development and management issues within a globalized world economy. At the same time, a number of nations are beginning to confront in earnest the issues raised by the centralization-decentralization debate long familiar to American political scientists. The delivery of social programs within the federal system, the competition among governmental units to attract industrialization and an enlarged tax base, assessments of state government programs and administration, and the next cycle of modeling over reapportionment, with its political and economic consequences, should appear as significant items in future research agendas.

The federal system is constantly in flux. The best of the existing research acknowledges this fact of life and capitalizes on it. One consequence is that no one orthodoxy dominates inquiry. It is a subfield responding in creative ways to an ever-changing political universe.

Ronald E. Weber ("The Study of State and Local Politics: A Preliminary Exploration of Its Contributions to Empirical Political Theory") believes that, with the methodological tools developed over the last generation, and given the variation in units of analysis and the variety of data available, few subfields can equal the study of state and local politics for the systematic testing and exploration of empirical theory. Using research that takes as its focus state and local institutions, Weber examines the contributions to theory-building in six problem areas: political participation, vote choice, recruitment, representation, decision-making, and policy-making. The approach is inclusive and the research contributions reviewed impressive.

Both aggregate data and survey analytic approaches have been used to study voter turnout. Researchers have been able to estimate the effects of financing and registration practices on participation. Studies of voter decision-making have attempted to isolate the impact of state and/or local contextual factors on the vote choice or to combine these with national-level influences to explain outcomes. Economic conditions, electoral structures, incumbency, performance while in office, and campaign spending all have shown relationships to voting results in different circumstances. The combination of local influences with national concerns is a newer thrust of this type of inquiry.

The study of recruitment for political office, one of the staples of research in the area, has focused on such factors as opportunity structures, the process of recruitment, incentives to hold office, and the representativeness of those who do. Issues of representation in state and local research look at such dimensions as styles of representation, policy responsiveness, and electoral structure as it influences social group representation. In such areas of pursuit, there are significant needs to expand the available pool of knowledge and to investigate questions (such as constituency-legislator interactions) which, while explored in national politics, have received little attention at the state level.

Decision-making studies of state and local institutions have concentrated primarily on legislatures and the courts as the objects of their investigations. Less developed than explanations of the actions of collective decision-making bodies has been individual decision-making by, for example, state legislators, a topic more thoroughly explored in the congressional research.

State and local studies may have contributed more research of quality to an understanding of policy-making than any other area. Topics that have received attention include the determinants of fiscal and redistributive policies; the impact of electoral, legislative, and executive structures in policy decision-making; service delivery; and regulatory practices. The work has been among the most productive in the discipline.

State and local politics hold promise for the development of a quality of comparative theorizing of benefit to political science, broadly conceived. The road has at least been preliminarily mapped. The areas needing attention have been indicated by Weber, as have the approaches that have proven productive. The field is broad, in one way or another allowing for the investigation of a variety of issues of central concern to political scientists.

Kenneth R. Mladenka and Bryan Jones ("Urban Politics and Political Science") conclude the volume by looking at the issues of contention in the study of urban politics. Urban research, despite a strong tradition of important work, at present appears to have little influence on the rest of political science. To consider one indicator of impact as an example, articles on urban research appear infrequently in the discipline's major journals.

The authors offer a number of reasons for the current state of urban research: the emphasis on grand explanatory themes to the neglect of empirical investigations and the testing of carefully constructed propositional inventories; the absence of carefully drawn, tightly constructed empirical studies; a thinking and writing in the field characterized by vagueness and generality, rather than rigor and precision; an inability to identify for investigation distinctively political questions of relevance to the city; and a tolerance of, and even dependence on, a diversity of multidisciplinary orientations, many at best of indirect value to the political scientist. Combine these factors with a quickly changing menu of interests, and even faddishness, in the topics singled out for investigation, and the subfield's state of ill health is understandable.

Urbanists tend to focus on whatever constitutes the latest urban controversy: crime, drugs, the impact of federal programs, housing, fiscal crises, schools, the need for economic development and an expanded tax base, racial problems. The issues are not insignificant. The problem is to develop cumulative, replicable, and empirically verifiable explanatory theories that have academic utility beyond the immediate need to understand the latest challenge to the civic fiber. The demands placed on the urbanist are severe: the production of knowledge that helps in governing and problem-solving yet at the same time serves the cause of a cumulative, systematic, and lasting political science. Events move quickly; the urbanist runs to catch up. The authors would opt for a commitment to building a foundation of knowledge relevant to the issues and approaches that are seen as important in the broader discipline.

The study of urban politics has great potential. The test for the future will be to tie performance to the promise implicit in the subject matter. Too frequently, issues of concern to the political scientist have not received the attention they merit.

The volume concludes with brief biographic sketches of the authors.

NOTES

1. William G. Boyer and Julie Ann Sosa, *Prospects for Faculty in the Arts and Sciences: A Study of Factors Affecting Demand and Supply, 1987 to 2012* (Princeton, N.J.: Princeton University Press, 1989).

2. Gabriel A. Almond, *A Divided Discipline* (San Mateo, Calif.: Sage Publications, 1989), and idem, "Separate Tables: Schools and Sects in Political Science?" *PS* 21:828–42. See also Kristen Monroe, Gabriel A. Almond, John Gunnell, Ian Shapiro, George Graham, Benjamin Barber, Kenneth Shepsle, and Joseph Cropsey, "The Nature of Contemporary Political Science: A Roundtable Discussion," *PS: Political Science and Politics* 23 (1):34–43.

3. These are needed and welcome. See, as examples, Ada W. Finifter, ed., *Political Science: The State of the Discipline* (Washington, D.C.: American Political Science Association, 1983), and Fred I. Greenstein and Nelson W. Polsby,

eds., *Handbook of Political Science*, 4 vols. (Reading, Pa.: Addison-Wesley Publishing Company, 1975). See also Herbert S. Weisberg, *Political Science: The Science of Politics* (New York: Agathon Press, 1986). A guide to the relevant literature critiquing the discipline can be found in Donald M. Freeman's "The Making of a Discipline" in volume 1.

REFERENCES

Almond, Gabriel A. 1989a. *A Divided Discipline*. San Mateo, Calif.: Sage Publications.

———. 1989b. "Separate Tables: Schools and Sects in Political Science?" *PS* 21:828–42.

Boyer, William G., and Julie Ann Sosa. 1989. *Prospects for Faculty in the Arts and Sciences: A Study of Factors Affecting Demand and Supply, 1987 to 2012.* Princeton, N.J.: Princeton University Press.

Finifter, Ada W., ed. 1983. *Political Science: The State of the Discipline*. Washington, D.C.: American Political Science Association.

Greenstein, Fred I., and Nelson W. Polsby, eds. 1975. *Handbook of Political Science*. 8 vols. Reading, Pa.: Addison-Wesley.

Monroe, Kristen, Gabriel A. Almond, John Gunnell, Benjamin Barber, Kenneth Shepsle, Joseph Cropsey, George Graham, and Ian Shapiro. 1990. "The Nature of Contemporary Political Science: A Roundtable Discussion." *PS: Political Science and Politics* 23 (1):34–43.

Weisberg, Herbert F., ed. 1986. *Political Science: The Science of Politics*. New York: Agathon Press.

1

Legislative Research: Mirror of a Discipline

Roger H. Davidson

An otherwise unremembered United States Representative once observed that "Congress is a mirror in which the American people can see themselves." Whether he was correct or not—and I think he was—it is surely true that legislative assemblies are mirrors for the political science profession. Since the advent of political science as an organized discipline, researchers have regarded legislative institutions as laboratories for developing their methodologies—empirical, conceptual, or theoretical—and for refining their theories about politics and politicians. As a result, the overall picture of legislatures drawn by political scientists is something approaching a portrait of political scientists themselves—their concerns, their skills, and their prejudices.

Legislative institutions and processes have long been central concerns of the political science profession—both in its traditional phases and, especially, in the "scientific" research enterprise that emerged in the decades following World War II. Legislative assemblies, in particular the United States Congress and state legislatures, were, and are, unique experimental settings for applying and testing a wide variety of quantitative and systematic research tools. Moreover, legislatures are superb strategic sites for viewing the wider political system and for rais-

I want to thank Keith Hamm and Matt McCubbins, who made many useful criticisms and suggestions during the Midwest Political Science Association panel at which the paper was discussed. I am grateful also to Christopher J. Bosso, whose 1987 survey of congressional and presidential scholars provided me with "hard data" concerning current research trends.

ing basic empirical and normative questions. Finally, legislatures are intrinsically fascinating: how could it be otherwise, with so many elected politicians under one roof?

The ease of gaining information about legislative bodies makes them uncommonly useful to scholars and students. Compared with other types of government agencies, legislatures are singularly open to the probings of outsiders. Executive officials typically work under the cloak of anonymity or secrecy; their complicated vertical and horizontal relationships make access and data gathering difficult. Judges deliberate behind closed doors, rarely talking for the record about how they arrive at their decisions. In contrast, legislators are generally accessible and are accustomed to talking with strangers about the things they do and the decisions they reach. Indeed, many of their actions—notably the positions they take—are framed in terms of how they can be explained to others (Mayhew 1974, 61–73). Even the voluminous printed record itself has been known to stimulate innovative and insightful research. Like journalists who cover Congress or the state legislatures, political scientists are justified in regarding legislative assemblies as "the best beat in town."

Equally important for scholars, legislatures exhibit the entire range of traits of human groups; they possess leaders and followers, roles and norms of behavior, learning processes for new members, patterns of communication and influence, and sanctions for deviant behavior. It is significant that legislatures are composed of numbers of individuals, elected in a similar manner, serving parallel (if dissimilar) constituencies, and responding to what are essentially the same stimuli. These conditions yield comparative data on the responses of politicians that are far richer than would be the case for a single politician acting alone. One has only to think of the problems inherent in studying chief executives—the president and state governors, for example—to appreciate the advantage that sheer numbers lend the legislature as a research subject.

Little wonder, then, that legislatures have proved irresistible to generations of American scholars harboring widely differing research agendas and analytical perspectives. The present chapter is intended as a review and analysis of the themes and character of this enterprise, and a contemplation of possible directions for future research. My objective is not a comprehensive review of the subfield, nor a catalogue of major researchers and their contributions to the literature. A few years ago, I collaborated in an extensive effort to organize and take an inventory of the legislative research subfield and to produce a handbook for researchers and practitioners (Loewenberg et al. 1985). My purpose here is more modest: to outline the continuities and developments in legislative research; to highlight the substantive, conceptual, and methodological trends of greatest contemporary significance; and to speculate upon those concepts, substantive orientations, and methods that may hold promise for future research.

TRADITIONAL LEGISLATIVE RESEARCH

Scholarly interest in legislative institutions by no means began with Woodrow Wilson and his generation, who led the discipline of political science from its infancy into its healthy if awkward adolescence. Philosophers and historians had in fact devoted much attention to legislative assemblies from the time of the Middle Ages, when clashes between popular assemblies and the Crown became the fulcrum for intellectual debate over the proper structure of government. Thomas Hobbes, John Locke, James Harrington, and the authors of *The Federalist* were just a few of the noteworthy participants in this dialogue, which occupies a justifiably large place in the history of Western political thought. The rise of mass-based legislatures in the nineteenth century naturally engaged the attention of emerging scholarly disciplines both in this country and abroad.

From the outset, historians took the lead in legislative research, bringing with them their profession's preconceptions, perspectives, and techniques (Thompson and Silbey 1985, 701–2). In Europe, the leitmotiv of much of this research was the rise of parliamentary authority, usually in opposition to centralized executive power—no doubt the residue of nearly a millennium of theoretical and political disputes over parliaments' origins, legitimacy, and proper role. In the New World, where legislative institutions had been entrenched since colonial times, historians pursued a variety of topics perhaps less fundamental in character. They undertook "highly detailed studies of great leaders, individual bills, and momentous confrontations among legislative blocs— efforts that have produced a stunning corpus of work" (Thompson and Silbey 1985, 702). A 1977 bibliography compiled by the Historian of the United States Senate listed more than eight hundred books, articles, and dissertations reflecting such traditional concerns (Baker 1977). Among these were numerous biographies and autobiographies, works especially valued by traditionally minded scholars and practitioners.

Early political scientists tended to embody the public-law tradition, whose venerable roots could be traced to such diverse sources as German university scholarship and the compelling symbolism of the United States Constitution. When public-law scholars examined legislative bodies, they naturally emphasized formal structures—rules, precedents, and procedures. It was this legalistic, formalistic approach, typified by the works of such scholars as John W. Burgess, that the young Woodrow Wilson sought to replace with a more realistic assess-

ment of political institutions. "The Constitution in operation," he asserted (1885, 30), "is manifestly a very different thing from the
Constitution of the books." In place of the "literary theory"—exegesis
of the Constitution and such authoritative sources as *The Federalist* and
Story's *Commentaries*—Wilson proposed to analyze American government in its "rough practice," to discover (1885, 30) "the real deposito-
ries and the essential machinery of power. There is always a centre of
power: where in this system is that centre?" Wilson's quest led him inevitably to Congress, even if he was not persuaded to visit Capitol Hill in
person. Because Wilson chose not to go beyond secondary (and even
tertiary) analysis, his *Congressional Government* describes conditions of a
bygone era, the so-called "Gilded Age," that had already changed profoundly by the 1880s (Thompson 1985, 23–25). This essentially obso-
lete account was framed in the language and assumptions of Anglo-
American reformism. It survives by virtue of a felicitous literary style
and an acerbic attitude toward legislative foibles that strikes a responsive chord among present-day scholarly critics.

While the bulk of scholarship adhered to the earlier public-law can-
ons, growing numbers of political scientists followed Wilson's lead in
studying the "rough practice" of American politics. Some (for example,
Follette 1896; McConachie 1898) went so far as to examine legislative
leaders, parties, and factions. Others found legislatures to be ideal bat-
tlegrounds for observing "the group basis of politics" (Herring 1927;
Schattschneider 1935; McKean 1938). Still others took up reformist
topics, after the fashion of the era's Progressive publicists and "muck-
raking" journalists. Electoral defects, lobbying abuses, biased procedures, and partisan manipulations—all manifesting the "rough
politics" of the age—were obvious targets of scholarly attention.

Whatever their topic of focus, political scientists in the first half of
the twentieth century borrowed their research methods mainly from the
traditions of historical and legal studies, which emphasized data drawn
from the public records of hearings, floor deliberations, precedents, and
legislative enactments, with the addition of biographies and memoirs.
Although much early scholarly writing about legislatures was either
hyperfactual or anecdotal or both, the best of these studies (among
them the works cited above) were of transcendent quality and can be
fairly judged to have withstood the test of time.

Traditional scholars, like their modern counterparts, approached
legislatures (national and subnational) with descriptive or normative
models that were sometimes explicit but frequently implicit. That is,
they tended to view legislatures through the lenses of particular conceptual frameworks.

One model of legislatures—that of *arenas of two-party debate and
confrontation*—has been a special favorite of American political scien-

tists. Viewed from this standpoint, legislative bodies were arenas for a pervasive system of representation based upon two program-oriented, disciplined, responsible, and competitive political parties. Their primary functions would be to clarify policy alternatives and to represent majority and minority factions, each lined up behind explicit party platforms. The model was drawn from the British party system (or, rather, a caricature of that system), which attracted the fervent devotion of generations of political scientists. Woodrow Wilson (1879, 147) pronounced it "by far the best . . . ," while James Macgregor Burns (1949, 38) called it "an almost ideal form of representative government." For a time, the "responsible parties" model enjoyed the status of the official doctrine of the American Political Science Association through the reports of its Committee on Congress (1945) and its Committee on Political Parties (1950), both of which had a strong reformist flavor. Although today's political scientists seem less reform-minded than their predecessors, they are still intrigued by "responsible parties." Fifty-five percent of the respondents in a 1987 survey of congressional and presidential specialists agreed that the United States should have "a party system which fits more the 'responsible party' model" (Bosso 1988).

By such standards, American legislative bodies were, and are, easily faulted. More attuned to constituencies back home than to party organizations, platforms, or leaders, lawmakers oftentimes seem to wear their party labels lightly or not at all. As soon as the legislative chambers are organized, party labels cease to provide unambiguous cures to voting records. Bargaining for ad hoc majorities blurs lines of party and policy. Decentralized power and decision-making, coupled with rules that offer a veritable armory of weapons for delay and obfuscation, prevent the kind of two-party confrontation and clear-cut issue resolution that used to be commonly ascribed to the British system. Thus, Congress and other American legislatures have been judged to be imperfect imitations of the Mother of Parliaments.

Another approach adopted by political scientists was to view legislatures as *policy-making instruments*. Here the analogy drawn was usually (although not always) to formal bureaucratic structures as prescribed by scientific management and interpreted by traditional doctrines of public administration. Perhaps the foundation for this approach lay in the box-and-string notions of organizations that were designed to reach an agreed-upon goal through "the one best way"; perhaps it rested in some scholarly penchant for simple organizational categories and neat hierarchies of control; perhaps it flowed from the fact that, to the extent that political scientists of that era enjoyed firsthand experience with government, it was likely to be in administrative agencies and consultancies. Whatever its origins, the policy-making approach tended to stress an institution's capacities for identifying public problems, clarifying alternatives, gathering and processing cost-benefit data, and designing or invoking coherent policy directives.

Legislative performance, need it be said, can be quite disappointing when judged by standards of rational problem solving. To be sure, many individual lawmakers labor over substantive policy problems with a devotion and grasp for detail that would surprise cynical outsiders; and the specialized consideration given to issues by standing committees can be as searching as any comparable review mechanism inside, say, a large business firm or public bureaucracy. But legislative policy-making is uneven and discontinuous: individuals and work groups possess varying levels of expertise; committee hearings and floor debates can seem superficial or beside the point; and, perhaps above all, there is an absence of the neat hierarchy of command or even the precise delegation of specialized authority that would lend managerial coherence to the process. What is more, the calculus of democratic politics may produce no positive solution to the problem at hand. For politicians, "doing nothing" may be the most rational way of "doing something." But legislative nondecisions are especially contentious and visible, in part because the disappointed interests are directly represented and frequently vocal.

Nor do legislatures behave as model *boards of directors*. Policy analysts usually conceded that, insofar as representative assemblies are incapable of solving policy problems on their own, they should accept the chief executive's agenda and ratify or modify alternatives developed by the executive bureaucracy. Again referring to the organizational analogy, the relationship is that of a board of directors (the legislature) to the management of a firm (the political executive). This analogy led to one of the most common assumptions in scholarly writing: namely, that legislators are "generalists" while executives are "specialists." As Arthur Macmahon (1943, 414) wrote of the appropriations process, "The hazard is that a body like Congress, when it gets into detail, ceases to be itself; it acts through a fraction which may be a faction."

The bulk of evidence indicates that American legislatures, at least, do not invariably fit this mold. For one thing, many of them—including Congress and state legislatures—frequently delegate decisions to their specialized subunits. Decisions are made de facto, not by the full assembly, but by separate chambers, committees, subcommittees, or less formal work groups, and by parties or more fluid factional alignments. In dealing with complicated or perplexing issues, lawmakers (like the rest of us) frequently abandon "general principles" in order to "get down to cases"; they are continually meddling in details ("micro-managing," in current terminology) where the generalist-specialist dichotomy dictates they should keep hands off. Hence legislatures, at least in the American mold, fail to measure up to the standards implied by the model of a board of generalist directors.

Perhaps because legislatures fell short of the conditions implied by these models, American political scientists for a long time exhibited considerable ambivalence toward homegrown legislative institutions. Where the U.S. Congress was concerned, this ambivalence often betrayed outright hostility. (My assumption is that this attitude extended to state legislatures as well.) Woodrow Wilson, as everyone knows, expressed contempt for Congress long before he had occasion as president to encounter its obduracy firsthand. Quoting Walter Bagehot's caustic description of Parliament, Wilson wrote (1885, 49) that Congress was "nothing less than a big meeting of more or less idle people."

In the post–New Deal period, it was not legislatures but executives who were most likely to embody the policies and values favored by the liberal intelligentsia—internationalism, foreign aid, civil rights, civil liberties, social planning, and welfare programs. Malapportioned and dominated by rural interests, legislatures, in contrast, remained bastions of conservatism, parochialism, and obstructionism.

At least since the Progressive era early in the twentieth century, political scientists have exhibited reformist tendencies. When Senator Clifford P. Case (R-N.J.) canvassed the profession in 1963, he found overwhelming sentiment that "Congressional reform is long overdue." At the state level, scholars were long associated with the legislative reform movement. The clash of values and policy preferences served to exacerbate the gaps between political scientists and political practitioners. Neil MacNeil, veteran Capitol Hill correspondent for *Time* magazine, observed (1965) that Congress reacted toward its academic critics the way the catfish must have felt toward the fisherman: "Hold still, catfish," the fisherman said. "I only want to gut you."

THE BEHAVIORAL REVOLUTION

The "behavioral revolution" overtook political science in the post–World War II era. With concepts and methods borrowed from sociology, social psychology, and anthropology, behavioralist researchers found legislative assemblies to be ideal research sites. No doubt this explains why so much attention began to be paid to the United States Congress; at the same time, state legislatures, municipal councils, and representative assemblies in other nations were also objects of research.

Although quite varied in perspectives and methods, the new generation of studies veered away from the earlier emphasis upon formal rules and procedures. Favored subjects were those that illustrated human interactions and group dynamics (for example, role orientations, decision-making, communications, committees, and factions) and those that permitted statistical comparisons of behavior (voting studies, most

particularly). Preferred research techniques included personal observations, audits of communication, statistical analyses of floor votes, structured questionnaires, personal interviews with legislators and staffs, and
mass-opinion surveys. Nor should I neglect participant observations,
described by Richard F. Fenno, Jr. (1978, 249–95) as "soaking and pok-
ing—or just hanging around." Unlike Woodrow Wilson and the earlier
generations of scholars, behavioralist political scientists tended to place
high value on close-range observation and interaction with the subjects
of their research—even though not all behavioralist studies were conducted in or near legislative halls. Research funding and internships at
all levels of government were guided by this objective.

The legacy of behavioral research is impressive both in quantity and
in quality. The 1960–75 period, in particular, yielded an enormous
body of solid and sometimes brilliant research findings; much of our
knowledge about legislative assemblies and the behavior of their members dates from that period. In a brief essay such as this, it would be
futile as well as pointless to attempt a review even of the highlights of
this research, which is being constantly updated and extended by a sizable number of scholars. Fortunately, others have attempted to describe
the movement, its objectives and its accomplishments. The behavioralist agenda was explained by Robert L. Peabody in an essay (Huitt and
Peabody 1969, 3–73) written at a time when the behavioralists and the
traditionalists were still grappling in full combat in many of the nation's leading academic departments of political science. Assessments
of the findings and results of behavioral research can be found in the
essays commissioned for the *Handbook of Legislative Research* (Loewenberg et al. 1985). As someone originally associated with the behavioralist research perspective, I can perhaps do no better than cite three early
landmarks that influenced my own thinking and subsequent work.

The first landmark was an article with the modest title "The Congressional Committee: A Case Study" (Huitt 1954). It was written by
Ralph K. Huitt, who gathered his data in the library of the University of
Wisconsin from the published hearings held by the Senate Banking and
Currency Committee in the spring of 1946 on the question of ex-
tending price-control programs. Drawing hypotheses from the literature of interest-group politics, Huitt was able to identify a number of
roles played by committee members and to derive generalizations and
new hypotheses about committee behavior. His substantive conclusions intrigued me and later proved helpful in my own research; but
even more important was his fresh, imaginative use of the public record
to derive insights that were at the same time behaviorally consistent and
politically relevant.

The second landmark in my personal journey was Donald R. Matthews's *U.S. Senators and Their World* (1960). Matthews's subject was
the 180 men and women who served in the 1947–57 decade, "who they

are, how they behave, and why they behave the way they do" (vii). His technique was an ingenious blend of data derived from a variety of methods: biographical data; 109 focused interviews with senators, staff, and others; and extensive use of qualitative data and inventive statistical indices. But while the work displayed methodological rigor and quantitative sophistication, it was the author's insight and common sense that made it the standard work on the post–World War II Senate. It is more insightful if not quite as colorful as William S. White's much-quoted account (1956) of the same period. And while Matthews's Senate has long since passed from the scene, his work was sensitive to the underlying sources of subsequent change and has yet to be replaced as the standard full-length portrait of the institution.

The final landmark was *The Legislative System* (Wahlke, Eulau, Buchanan, and Ferguson 1962), a comparative study of four state legislatures. The conceptual point of departure for the study was the notion of role orientations: legislators' attitudes toward their tasks and the expectations others hold for their performance of those tasks. Wahlke and his colleagues concluded that the role concept (Wahlke et al. 1962, 8):

> yields a model of the legislator as an acting human individual which is consistent with the basic understandings of individual and group psychology. At the same time, it yields a model of the legislature as an institutionalized human group which logically incorporates the model of the individual legislator and which relates the behavior of legislators to problems of legislative structure and function which are the traditional concern of students in the field.

The comparative aspect was important, for it promised to free legislative research from the prison imposed by single-case analysis. Equally important was the strategy of approaching large samples of lawmakers with a lengthy, complicated survey instrument. Considering the backgrounds and prejudices of legislators of a generation or more ago, this kind of heavy-bore social scientific research was a risky, controversial enterprise. Nonetheless, the conceptual clarity and empirical richness of the four-state study persuaded my colleagues and me to replicate portions of the interview schedule with a sample of 116 members of the United States House of Representatives (Davidson 1969). Many similar studies of state legislatures and assemblies throughout the world were undertaken.

THE POSTBEHAVIORAL ERA

Legislative research in the years since 1975 has retained its central place for political scientists, even though the pace of the research appears to have slackened off somewhat. Yet with each passing year it becomes more difficult to discern a dominant theme or organizing concept that would be accepted by all or most researchers in the field. Rather, scholars seem to be following a multitude of paths, utilizing a wide array of methods and conceptual frameworks. Contemporary research seems bent on realizing the scholarly equivalent of President George Bush's "thousand points of light."

Behavioral analysis continues to exert a powerful influence over current research, as shown in table 1.1, which reports results from Christopher J. Bosso's 1987 survey of specialists in the subfield (Bosso 1989, 3). Yet the frequency of other approaches—from such "conservative" techniques as case analysis and historiography to more avant-garde approaches (formal modeling, "new institutionalism")—is impressive. No doubt the interaction and synthesis among categories is greater than table 1 indicates.

The *topics* currently being studied by researchers are shown in table 1.2. The popularity of legislative-executive relations problems flows from the fact that the survey included presidential as well as congressional specialists. Campaigns and elections, the committee system, representation, and political parties are also frequently mentioned.

Legislative elections have always attracted lively interest, but until recently scholars have lacked the data necessary to study voters' behavior in subnational election contests. Of course, presidential elections received early and intense attention from researchers; analyses of nationwide sample surveys yielded, by the 1960s, a coherent theory of presidential voting, a plausible definition and explanation of partisanship, and a typology of elections.

By contrast, congressional, state, and local elections exhibit characteristics that differ markedly (and increasingly) from nationwide patterns; the study of these elections entails complicated and expensive sample surveys and analyses of voting results. Increasing numbers of reliable statewide (and occasionally countywide or citywide) surveys have made this task somewhat easier. Legislative districts, however, pose a special problem for survey research: because their boundaries often parallel no other political or natural divisions, it is difficult and expensive to draw adequate voter samples from enough of them to permit statistical comparisons. It was not until 1978, for example, that a nationwide sample of United States House of Representatives districts was undertaken. Since then, there has been a veritable explosion of literature on House elections. The picture of congressional elections that has emerged, while very different from that gained from presidential contests, is no less interesting (Jacobson 1987). As state election data are compiled and refined, similar interest in subnational elections ought to be forthcoming.

One problem with studying legislative elections is that the vast majority of them are never in any doubt. That is, relatively few contests are

Table 1.1
Primary Research Approach of 262 Political Scientists (1987)

Approach	Percent
Behavioral analysis	35.5
Case studies	14.9
"New institutionalism"	11.4
Organizational theory	10.3
Historiography	9.2
Democratic theory	6.0
Formal modeling/game theory	9.1
Other (e.g., policy studies)	9.9
Total	100.3*

Source: Christopher J. Bosso, "Research on Congress: Current Emphases and Future Directions," paper delivered at the annual meeting of the Southwest Political Science Association, Little Rock, Arkansas, 1989.

*Total does not equal 100 percent because of rounding.

competitive. Over the 1946–88 period, 92 percent of all U.S. Representatives who ran for reelection were in fact successful; the figure for U.S. senators over the same period is 75 percent. These low levels of competition have led researchers to turn their attention to other aspects of the "recruitment process," including the kinds of considerations that lead some people to become candidates and others to refrain from entering the fray. Second, the success of sitting members in winning repeated reelection has produced a sizable literature on various aspects of so-called incumbent advantage—for example, the extent to which ombudsmanlike activities on behalf of constituents translate into votes at reelection time (Johannes 1984; Cain, Ferejohn, and Fiorina 1987).

The individual and collective behavior of legislators continues to fascinate scholars, especially those of a quantitative bent. A major problem for behaviorally oriented investigators, however, is the mounting difficulty at the national level of doing extensive interviewing of members. Spread thin because of demanding schedules and protected by cadres of staff aides, senators and representatives are less accessible than they once were to requests made by disinterested scholars. Interviews with large samples of members are virtually out of the question these days; researchers must be content to interview staff or to rely on nonintrusive measures of behavior. Or one can turn to state or local legislatures, where access is easier to achieve.

The early emphasis on roles, norms, and folkways has subsided—partly because it has been found difficult to link these attitudes to con-

Table 1.2
Aspects of Congress Currently Being Studied

Aspect	Percent
Relations with executive branch	20.9
Campaigns and elections	14.8
Committees, committee system	11.5
Representation	10.1
Parties and party leadership	9.6
Floor activity/roll calls	8.0
Rules and norms	6.6
Budget process	5.6
Oversight	3.3
Other (e.g., media, policy areas)	8.9
Total	99.3*

Source: Christopher J. Bosso, "Research on Congress: Current Emphases and Future Directions," paper delivered at the annual meeting of the Southwest Political Science Association, Little Rock, Arkansas, 1989.

*Total does not equal 100 percent because of rounding. Respondents selected one or two items; percentages are of total mentions.

crete behaviors, and partly because many of the norms themselves have proved unstable. The way in which individual legislators reach decisions on floor votes is a complicated question that has attracted a number of scholars, among them Clausen (1973) and Kingdon (1989). Notwithstanding the inherent difficulty of investigating these topics, they remain a challenge that could perhaps be pursued more fruitfully in state and local bodies receptive to interviewing and participant observations.

Like other political entities, modern legislatures have become big, complex institutions whose members are supported by large cadres of staff aides. Whereas earlier students could afford to treat legislatures simply as gatherings of interacting individuals, this view can no longer be held with confidence. A collection of interacting bureaucracies would be a more accurate picture of the United States Congress and at least some state and foreign legislative bodies (Salisbury and Shepsle 1981). Only recently have scholars started to take staff politics seriously, and much research remains to be done.

Committees and subcommittees are so important in American legislatures that a huge literature has grown up surrounding them. In addition to descriptions of individual committees, there have been a number of comparative committee studies within a single chamber. Fenno (1973) and Smith and Deering (1990) have examined congressional committees at different points in time. On Capitol Hill, the decentralization of the 1960s and 1970s produced what some have called "subcommittee government" (Davidson 1981), which, though difficult to study in detail, nevertheless continues to permeate much of the operations of the current Congress.

At another level of comparison, researchers have focused attention upon interchamber and interstate differences among committee systems. Surveying all ninety-nine state chambers, Francis and Riddlesperger (1982) found sharp differences in the centrality of committees, depending on such factors as chamber size, party domination, and procedural characteristics. Another study, by Hamm and Moncrief (1982), compared committees not only among states but over time, measuring the effects of certain structural changes upon committee performance.

Another intriguing cluster of questions concerns how committee members are selected for their assignments—the "giant jigsaw puzzle" that can yield clues about individual lawmakers' motivations and the intraparty influence structure (Shepsle 1978). Ironically, however, just as soon as political scientists seemed to have pieced together the jigsaw puzzle, the importance of assignments declined markedly in Congress because of the rise of decentralization, multiple-committee memberships, and cross-committee handling of measures. In state legislatures, however, committee assignment remains a lively topic.

Formal structures, work loads, and processes have become the objects of renewed emphasis. Policy agendas—their origins and maturation—are one focus. Another is the legislative work load, which varies over time in ways that cannot be ignored—for example, as legislatures shift between activism and passivism, or as policy-making initiatives shift between the federal government and the states. Other researchers employ the concepts and methods of organizational theory, searching for forces that drive the overall institutional behavior of the legislature (Cooper 1981).

A new wave of formal analysis, called the "new institutionalism," has refocused our attention on the formal attributes of legislatures and their procedures, though with theoretical premises quite different from those of pre–World War II political scientists. Using models borrowed from political economy and game theory, theoretically minded political scientists have turned to the question of how legislative structure dictates certain decision sequences and policy forms. As stated by the editors of one compilation of works (McCubbins and Sullivan 1987, ix), the central problem had become: "How do institutions evolve in response to individual incentives, strategies, and choices; and how do institutions affect the performance of political and economic systems?" Such questions can be raised in any legislative setting; nearly every legislative body has distinctive rules or practices that can be used to test broader theories.

In yet another way, the cycle of research interest has repeated itself in recent years in the examination of historical data to find out more about the evolution of legislatures and to compare present forms with previous ones. This surge of interest on the part of political scientists comes at the very time when many historians have abandoned such pursuits, preferring to study everyday citizens rather than political or governmental elites. On Capitol Hill, the Senate and House of Representatives have established historians' offices, which endeavor to preserve historical records, to compile information on sources and repositories, and to encourage further research. Legislators themselves became acquainted with historical themes in connection with their celebration of the 200th anniversary of the federal government in 1989.

Cross-national comparative studies are, as might be expected, distressingly rare. Part of the problem stems from the difficulty of mastering the factual background needed to understand more than a single legislative body. Another problem, at least for U.S. observers, is the difficulty of comparing legislatures operating within a separation-of-powers systems with those operating under a parliamentary scheme. Still, some pioneering efforts at generalization have been attempted (Loewenberg and Patterson 1979; Olson 1980). The *Handbook of Legislative Research* (1985) includes one chapter on research into Third World legislatures but none on state and local legislatures, and none on the broader subject of legislative comparisons. Comparative studies apparently occupy a secondary place in scholarly journals, presumably because few truly comparative studies have been undertaken.

Even though legislative studies have not sustained the rapid growth they enjoyed in the era of behavioralist ascendancy, they have in recent years solidified their place in the scholarly community. The American Political Science Association's Congressional Fellowship Program enables interested scholars to spend a year on Capitol Hill, working and learning as "insiders." In 1976 the journal *Legislative Studies Quarterly* was founded; the following year the Legislative Studies Group became the American Political Science Association's first organized subsection. Publication of the *Handbook of Legislative Research* (Loewenberg et al. 1985) was the culmination of a sustained effort by many scholars to provide landmarks and directions for research—a sign that the subfield had truly come of age. Although the dynamism of research served to make the *Handbook* out-of-date almost from the moment it appeared, the volume did underscore the systematic and cumulative nature of legislative research. It also served to identify gaps in knowledge, which would constitute a future research agenda.

SOME THOUGHTS ON FUTURE DIRECTIONS

As a stimulus for discussion about the future directions for legislative research, I offer these suggestions for renewed or continued emphasis in seven topic areas.

1. *Legislators and their careers.* By now we have a reasonably clear picture of the overall historical trends in legislative careers, as well as the causes and some of the consequences of rising careerism. We need to compare levels or stages of careerism as found in different legislatures. At the same time we ought to give attention to the career linkages (or lack of them) among different levels of our political system—among Congress, state legislatures, other public offices (judicial, for example), and nonpublic-sector activities. While every evidence points to the fact that these careers have become more insulated from one another, the career "tracks" are nonetheless related, among other things because they affect the same pool of potential candidates or elected officials. We ought to examine the phenomenon and inquire into its consequences for our political institutions.

2. *Legislators and constituents.* Some major questions surrounding representation—demographic, attitudinal, and functional—seem to have been answered. But we still know relatively little about constituency relationships as seen from the grass-roots level; too few researchers have taken up Fenno's (1978) challenge to view representation from the perspective of direct interactions between officeholders and the represented. In particular, we still know relatively little about public perceptions and assessments of legislators and legislative assemblies.

3. *Political parties and party leadership.* Following the profession's flirtation with the "party government" doctrine in the 1940s and 1950s, there was a flurry of research on the relative importance of party and constituency in legislative voting and activity. Once that set of questions appeared to have been answered, however, political scientists paid relatively little attention to the role of parties and party leaders in legislative bodies, seemingly accepting the thesis of "party disintegration." However, party leaders have long wielded impressive power in many state legislatures, and more recently in Congress as well. Institutional and behavioral studies are needed to probe the role of legislative parties and the persistence of partisanship on the part of individual members. Leadership selection needs renewed attention, both in Congress and in the state assemblies where cross-party coalitions have appeared. Indeed, the influence of party leaders and caucuses is very different at the national and state levels.

4. *Legislatures and public policy.* Despite a surge of interest in legislative policy-making in the 1960s and 1970s, much remains to be

learned. Skillful case studies are always needed; even more, we need comparative studies that will combine and integrate the knowledge gained from individual cases.

5. *Change in legislatures.* With historians having apparently abandoned this field, political scientists ought to be ready to take up the slack. Historical analysis, of course, implies more than factual richness, biographical details, or chronological precision. Framed correctly, historical analysis can help us address some of the most fundamental questions about legislatures: why do they function as they do? Why do they enact the policies they do? How and why do they change over time? As with other topics, state and local assemblies may provide the most fruitful subjects of analysis, inasmuch as many of them have modernized their operations or experienced profound party or factional changes.

6. *Legislatures in comparative perspective.* American political analysts are all too often deterred from cross-system analysis by their uncritical acceptance of what might be termed the "myth of American singularity." United States legislatures, it is said, resemble few others in the world because they operate in a separation-of-powers framework rather than a parliamentary system. At a superficial level this is certainly true. Beneath the surface, however, there certainly exist functions and behaviors that are distinctively legislative in character, whatever their institutional or systemic setting. Moreover, the theories developed by legislative analysts need to be tested rigorously in a variety of arenas. Theoretical propositions that seem to apply to Congress, for example, ought to be tested in the statehouses, where accessibility is less of a problem. Imagination and sensitivity—not to mention collaboration among knowledgeable scholars and observers from the disparate political cultures—will be required to achieve the goal of truly comparative legislative analysis.

7. *Theory Development.* Systematic political science requires the development and refinement of theories about political events, behaviors, and outcomes. In earlier periods, the theoretical underpinnings of research were more or less understood, sometimes quite explicitly and other times by implication. The behavioral research of the 1950s and 1980s was often used to illustrate a system of patterned interactions in which subsystems of structure and function normally worked in rough equilibrium. In the 1970s, research into the activities of individual lawmakers seemed to embody the currently popular scholarly paradigm, drawn roughly from economics (Mayhew 1974). Lawmakers were seen, not as role-players in a complex system of interactions in equilibrium, but as individual players in a vast open marketplace that rewarded self-interested competitiveness with little or no regard for the welfare of the whole. Today, a fashionable view of the legislature conceives of it as a game of incentives and rules that constrain players and help to determine outcomes.

The ongoing course of theoretical development is difficult to predict. I tend to view theorizations not only as abstractions from objective reporting but also as reflections of trends within the discipline. Also, I sense a diminished enthusiasm among political scientists for general theories and a retreat to middle-range or limited theories. Whatever one's judgment of specific theories, it is imperative that scholars continue to strive toward broad generalizations and statements of causal relationships. Often, perhaps most often, theorization will be developed by those who are not themselves engaged in close observation or empirical research. But close collaboration between theorists and empiricists (or experimentalists) is essential if legislative scholarship is to advance.

Theory must be informed by empirical observation; in turn, observation without theoretical development is a dead end. What the precise relationship will be between theory and observation I cannot predict with precision; but this relationship is central to the future development of legislative research. We must never forget, no matter how specialized our investigations may be, that they must ultimately, and collectively, illuminate the age-old questions of politics: What is government? How is it organized? What are the purposes of political institutions? How well do they achieve these purposes? Are democratic assemblies possible or viable?

REFERENCES

American Political Science Association. 1945. *The Organization of Congress*. Washington, D.C.

————. Committee on Political Parties. 1950. *Toward a More Responsible Two-Party System*. New York: Rinehart and Company.

Baker, Richard A. 1977. *The U.S. Senate: A Historical Bibliography*. Washington, D.C.: Government Printing Office.

Bosso, Christopher J. 1988. "The Congress Project: Summary." Preliminary summary of a survey of 361 members of the American Political Science Association's Legislative Studies Section and/or Presidency Research Group, March.

————. 1989. "Research on Congress: Current Emphases and Future Directions." Revised version of paper initially delivered at the annual meeting of the Southwest Political Science Association, Little Rock, Ark., June.

Burns, James Macgregor. 1949. *Congress on Trial*. New York: Harper and Brothers.

Cain, Bruce, John Ferejohn, and Morris Fiorina. *The Personal Vote: Constituency Service and Electoral Independence*. Cambridge, Mass. Harvard University Press.

Clausen, Aage. 1973. *How Congressmen Decide*. New York: St. Martin's Press.

Cooper, Joseph, 1981. "Organization and Innovation in the House of Representatives." In Joseph Cooper and G. Calvin Mackenzie, eds., *The House at Work*, 319–55. Austin: University of Texas Press.

Davidson, Roger H. 1969. *The Role of the Congressman*. Indianapolis: Bobbs-Merrill.

———. 1981. "Subcommittee Government: New Channels for Policy Making." In Thomas E. Mann and Norman J. Ornstein, eds., *The New Congress*, 99–133. Washington, D.C.: American Enterprise Institute.

Fenno, Richard F., Jr. 1983. *Congressmen in Committees*. Boston: Little, Brown.

———. 1978. *Home Style: House Members in Their Districts*. Boston: Little, Brown.

Follett, Mary Parker. 1896. *The Speaker of the House of Representatives*. New York: Longmans, Green.

Francis, Wayne, and James W. Riddlesperger. 1982. "U.S. State Legislative Committees: Structure, Procedural Efficiency, and Party Control." *Legislative Studies Quarterly* 7 (August): 453–71.

Hamm, Keith E., and Gary Moncrief. 1982. "Effects of Structural Change in Legislative Committee Systems on Their Performance in the U.S. States." *Legislative Studies Quarterly* 7 (August): 383–400.

Herring, E. Pendleton. 1927. *Group Representation Before Congress*. New York: Russell and Russell.

Huitt, Ralph K. 1964. "The Congressional Committee: A Case Study." *American Political Science Review* 68 (June): 340–65.

———, and Robert L. Peabody. 1969. *Congress: Two Decades of Analysis*. New York: Harper & Row.

Jacobson, Gary C. 1987. *The Politics of Congressional Elections*. 2d ed. Boston: Little, Brown.

Johannes, John R. 1984. *To Serve the People: Congress and Constituency Service*. Lincoln: University of Nebraska Press.

Kingdon, John W. 1989. *Congressmen's Voting Decisions*. 3d ed. Ann Arbor: University of Michigan Press.

Loewenberg, Gerhard, and Samuel C. Patterson. 1979. *Comparing Legislatures*. Boston: Little, Brown.

———, Samuel C. Patterson, and Malcolm E. Jewell, eds. 1985. *Handbook of Legislative Research*. Cambridge, Mass.: Harvard University Press.

McConachie, Lauros G. 1898. *Congressional Committees*. New York: Crowell.

McCubbins, Mathew D., and Terry Sullivan, 1987. *Congress: Structure and Policy*. Cambridge: Cambridge University Press.

McKean, Dayton D. 1938. *Pressures on the Legislature of New Jersey*. New York: Columbia University Press.

Macmahon, Arthur. 1943. "Congressional Oversight of Administration: The

Power of the Purse." *Political Science Quarterly* 63 (March): 161–90; (June): 380–414.

MacNeil, Neil. 1965. "Congress and Its Critics." *New York Herald Tribune*, August 17, 18.

Matthews, Donald R. 1960. *The U.S. Senators and Their World*. Chapel Hill: University of North Carolina Press.

Mayhew, David R. 1974. *Congress: The Electoral Connection*. New Haven: Yale University Press.

Olson, David M. 1980. *The Legislative Process: A Comparative Approach*. New York: Harper & Row.

Salisbury, Robert H., and Kenneth A. Shepsle. 1981. "U.S. Congressmen as Enterprise." *Legislative Studies Quarterly* 6 (November): 559–76.

Schattschneider, E. E. 1935. *Politics, Pressures, and the Tariff*. New York: Prentice-Hall.

Shepsle, Kenneth A. 1978. *The Giant Jigsaw Puzzle: Democratic Committee Assignments in the Modern House*. Chicago: University of Chicago Press.

Smith, Steven S., and Christopher J. Deering, 1990. *Committees in Congress*. 2d ed. Washington, D.C.: Congressional Quarterly Press.

Thompson, Margaret Susan. 1985. *The Spider Web: Congress and Lobbying in the Age of Grant*. Ithaca, N.Y.: Cornell University Press.

———, and Joel H. Silbey. 1985. "Historical Research on Nineteenth-Century Legislatures." In Loewenberg et al., eds., *Handbook of Legislative Research*, 701–32. Cambridge, Mass.: Harvard University Press.

Wahlke, John, Heinz Eulau, William Buchanan, and LeRoy C. Ferguson. 1962. *The Legislative System*. New York: Wiley.

White, William S. 1956. *Citadel: The Study of the U.S. Senate*. New York: Harper and Brothers.

Wilson, Woodrow. 1879. "Cabinet Government in the United States." *International Review* (August): 148–63.

———. 1885. *Congressional Government*. New York: New American Library/Meridian Books, 1956.

2

What Do We Know and How Do We Know It? Research on the Presidency

Paul J. Quirk

Two tough questions occasionally asked about a president are: What did he know? And when did he know it? The issue is always whether he knew more about some disreputable activity than he admits. One can also ask tough questions about research on the presidency: What do we know? And how do we know it? As many others have pointed out (King 1975; Heclo 1977b; Pika 1981–82; Thomas 1983; Rockman 1986), we know less, through less substantial investigations, than one would expect in view of the importance of the subject. In recent years, however, there has been an outpouring of new research on the presidency, and the field has made noteworthy strides. In this essay I offer a fresh appraisal of its achievements.

To make the task less formidable, I have adopted certain expedients. I discuss only a handful of research issues, which, I argue, however, represent the core topics of the presidency field. For each of these issues, I consider only a few recent works that in my view are noteworthy or representative. The result is neither a comprehensive review of the current literature nor an account of how the field has developed. It is a

I am grateful to Lawrence Baum, James MacGregor Burns, Martha Derthick, Doris Graber, Andrew McFarland, Bert Rockman, and Norman Thomas, who provided helpful comments on an earlier draft of this paper; to George Edwards, Joseph Pika, and Steven Shull, who gave especially detailed criticism and bibliographic advice; and to many others who sent me reprints, page proofs, or manuscripts that I had asked for. Those named are entitled to be presumed innocent of any errors, omissions, or misjudgments that remain.

commentary on the current state of the literature and prospects for further progress in what I think are the central areas of presidency research.

In each area, I try to assess whether and by what means important understanding has been gained. How far, for example, have the theories or methods of academic political science produced knowledge that is more precise, penetrating, or reliable than that of sophisticated lay observers of the presidency? I also try to identify the mistakes, omissions, or unfavorable circumstances that have retarded progress and to suggest promising avenues for further research.

In the course of discussing the several areas of research, I make few pronouncements about the field as a whole. The state of the literature varies radically across areas. Indeed, I suggest that the presidency is not a single, coherent field, even potentially, and point out some consequences of its fragmentation. Nevertheless, I also suggest that the field should have a more definite agenda, which should focus mainly on the president's role in policy formation.

THE PRESIDENCY AND PUBLIC POLICY

The presidency is a massively complex institution, with a differentiated internal structure, relationships with a multitude of other actors and institutions, and involvement in nearly every area of public policy. It offers an almost unlimited array of potential topics for research, and political scientists have addressed a large number of them. As a result, unfortunately, the literature is diffuse, touching upon numerous topics but containing sustained investigation of very few. This is one reason why the field lacks the refinement of some other areas of political research. There is no escaping this condition. The difficulty could be mitigated, however, if the field were to select a manageable list of core topics and, without abandoning other inquiries, devote a preponderance of effort to investigating them.

The most attractive way to identify such core topics, I would argue, is to select those (issues of presidential behavior and influence that are central to the president's role in the formation of public policy.) There are other conceivable ways to orient presidential research, but none has comparable potential to elicit a coherent effort. Purely from the standpoint of scientific procedure, for example, the preferred approach would be to choose research questions with a view toward developing a theory of the presidency. But there is currently no such theory to occupy this role, and for reasons I will discuss below, virtually no likelihood of one emerging (Rockman 1986; Edwards 1983b). Another possible approach would be to organize research to address the presidency's effects on procedural or foundational aspects of the political system: the stability and legitimacy of the regime; popular participation; or the integrity of constitutional principles. Such effects are obviously worthy of investigation; but in a stable, relatively democratic political system like that of the United States, researchers inevitably are more interested in immediate issues of public policy. The most plausible way for the literature to become more coherent is therefore to devote concerted attention to the president's role in policy-making.

If the principal focus is policy-making, then a handful of topics constitute the core of the field. The central issue is obviously how presidents make policy decisions. This question has two largely distinct aspects: how presidents use information and what goals or interests they respond to. A second major issue is how presidents get their decisions put into effect. More specifically, how do they lead Congress and control the bureaucracy? Because the president's influence depends on his public support, two further key issues are how presidents obtain public approval and how they lead public opinion. Finally, two additional issues have important bearing on all the others: how presidents' individual attributes affect their performance and how the presidency changes. (I leave out the question of how presidents are recruited, which also has such general bearing, only because the literature on recruitment is so large that it constitutes a field in itself.) Not surprisingly, much of the literature already treats these issues.

Decision-Making Information

For analytic purposes, we can distinguish two dimensions of presidential decision-making: information and objectives. The dimension of information, broadly defined, concerns how intelligently presidents and their staffs design policies and how accurately they anticipate the consequences. Research on this dimension therefore seeks to learn how presidents obtain and use information, and with what consequences for the outcomes. The work in this area has not made notable advances beyond the casual theorizing of sophisticated participants. Nevertheless, some of it has made a modest contribution to presidential capabilities.

Most of the work by political scientists on presidential use of information has concerned the organization and management of advisory processes. A number of researchers have examined the organization of the White House staff or the machinery for making economic policy, domestic policy, or, especially, foreign and national security policy.[1] Indeed, these issues are the principal focus of literature on the presidency in foreign policy.

On the whole, the research has relied on much the same methods of observing and interpreting events as those employed by participants. Researchers have carried out detailed studies of decision-making in par-

3

ticular cases (Destler 1980; Porter 1980), or they have relied on judgments by participants and lay observers to reach conclusions about performance (Hess 1976; Campbell 1986). Their analytic frameworks have consisted largely of conventional administrative doctrine modified by a few apparent lessons of recent presidencies. Lacking any distinctive theoretical or methodological tools, students of advisory processes have debated the same organizational issues and used the same arguments as practitioners—disagreeing about the proper roles of the secretary of state and the national security adviser, for example, just as those officials themselves have disagreed (Rockman 1981).

The main obstacle to progress has been the one Herbert Simon (1949) described in his critique of traditional public-administration theory. Organizational design is a matter of striking the right balance between conflicting objectives—for example, reducing the burden of coordination versus increasing the flow of information. In the absence of genuine experimentation, the influences on organizational performance are too complex for analysts to determine the consequences of alternative structural arrangements with any precision.

Despite the resulting limitations, the research in this area has been useful. Salamon (1982) has laid out the major organizational options facing a president along with their strengths and weaknesses. George (1972, 1980) has articulated the advantages of an organizational technique, multiple advocacy, with enough persuasiveness to inspire its adoption by at least one president (see Porter 1980). With the advantage of an international perspective, Campbell (1986) has pointed out the exceptional weakness of the mechanisms for policy coordination in the executive branch of the United States.

The main contribution of political scientists with respect to advisory processes, however, has been to make up for the lack of institutional memory in the White House by preserving accounts of what has been tried, and with what results. Knowledge has accumulated as successive presidents have adopted new organizational strategies and succeeded or failed in novel ways. On some points a degree of consensus has emerged. Recent discussion has favored a White House organization with some combination of the hierarchical and spokes-in-a-wheel models (Campbell 1986; Weatherford 1987). For economic policy-making, it has called for a collegial system centered on the Council of Economic Advisers (CEA) and the cabinet and for treating economic policy as a distinct function with its own structure (Weatherford 1987; Campbell 1986). Even if mainly as repositories of the collective memory, political scientists have played a role in designing the advisory processes of several presidents.

Conceivably, research on presidential advisory processes could become decisively superior to lay opinion through the development of better methods. That would require, above all, a method of gathering usable data about the quality of presidential information and judgment in a large number of decisions at feasible cost. Despite the risk of a certain amount of inaccuracy, the most promising approach is probably to do limited interviewing and other data gathering on each decision and rely on the respondents to make relatively complex, interpretive judgments about performance.

Unfortunately, the research has largely neglected factors other than the organization of advisory processes. In a penetrating essay, George (1980) noted that obstacles to effective use of information arise at three levels: the beliefs and personality of the president; the small-group interactions among the president and his principal advisers; and the organizational functioning of the executive branch. Students of the presidency have given almost all their attention to the organizational level, neglecting the individual and small-group levels. Among the few exceptions, Janis (1972) has discussed the dynamics of small decision-making groups. Buchanan (1987) has explored the implications for presidential decision-making of basic findings on heuristics and biases in human judgment. Two studies of decision-making on the Vietnam War (Gelb and Betts 1979; Berman 1982) have traced the rigidity of the American response to a pattern of basing foreign-policy decisions on overly generalized strategic doctrines. Recently, Greenstein and Burke (1989) have revisited the Vietnam case to explore the interaction of advisory systems and personality in shaping presidents' ability to test reality.

Researchers have overlooked the effects of the circumstances of decision or the issues at stake. There are a few studies on the effects of crisis, pointing out that information gathering and analysis deteriorate when decisions must be made quickly (Herman 1969). In a study of the Social Security program, Derthick (1979) shows that the design of a program may hinder recognition of its effects. A comprehensive inquiry into presidential use of information will have to go beyond organizational issues and explore a wide range of other factors.

Decisionmaking: Objectives

The objectives pertinent to presidential decision are both the personal goals that presidents pursue (such as reelection or a place in history) and the societal interests to which they respond (such as group benefits or economic efficiency). These two kinds of objectives play different roles in explaining decisions and present different tasks for research.[2] Although many studies of particular presidencies, policy changes, or areas of policy contain some discussion of presidential objectives (Reichley 1981; Hargrove 1988), few have addressed such objectives in general. In contrast, the corresponding issues about Congress, administrative agencies, and the judiciary are treated in substantial literatures.

There seem to have been two contradictory reasons for this omission. On the one hand, presidency researchers have considered presidential objectives to be unproblematic. In the 1960s many analysts took it for granted that, because of the importance of large industrial states in presidential elections, presidents were inherently inclined toward liberal social policies (Burns 1963). That notion was discredited by the Nixon, Ford, and Reagan presidencies. Less restrictively, many now assume that presidents are primarily responsive to broadly based national interests and are largely responsible for government's capacity to serve such interests (Fiorina 1984). In an extreme formulation of this view in the context of foreign policy, Krasner (1979) virtually defined national interests as those which presidents pursue. To identify presidential policy in any simple way with broad interests, however, is unfounded. Indeed, as the beginnings of airline deregulation in a highly publicized congressional investigation demonstrate, it is sometimes Congress or a congressional committee that takes the initiative on behalf of such interests (Derthick and Quirk 1985).

At the same time, researchers may have doubted that efforts to explore presidential policy objectives would produce significant findings. They may have suspected that presidential policy goals would turn out to be relentlessly idiosyncratic. They also may have feared that research on presidential policy choice would recapitulate the work on Congress. With some modifications, most of the incentives and constraints that affect members of Congress undoubtedly also affect presidents.

Whatever the reasons, research that explicitly addresses presidential objectives in policy-making is scattered and uneven. The most substantial work is on the politics of macroeconomic policy—an area of research that, although not conventionally identified with the presidency field, is largely about the behavior of presidents.[3] One branch of this literature, concerned with the hypothesis of a political business cycle, proceeds from an explicit motivational assumption—namely, that presidents use economic policy to pursue electoral success for themselves or their parties. Indeed, they are willing to sacrifice economic stability for electoral gain. From well-established assumptions about the electorate, it follows that presidents will try to manipulate the economy to ensure prosperity in election years. Despite the fanfare that greeted this analysis in the mid-1970s, however, the political business-cycle hypothesis has largely failed in empirical tests (Weatherford 1988). According to the weight of the evidence, neither the performance of the economy nor even fiscal or monetary policy tracks the electoral cycle.

Nevertheless, more attention should be paid to the influence of electoral incentives and the electoral cycle on presidential decisions. Even if they do not go so far as to manipulate macroeconomic performance, presidents probably respond to electoral considerations in less dramatic ways. Kessel (1974) has shown that presidents emphasize different policy areas in State of the Union addresses at different stages of their terms.

Another branch of the macroeconomic policy literature explores the effects of political party, in particular, the differences between Democratic and Republican presidents in their responses to inflation and unemployment.[4] Because such differences may reflect either ideological or electoral interests, this work has no definite bearing on presidential motivation. Rather, it confirms and elaborates conventional views of the effects of party. Nevertheless, it is the most substantial body of research that assesses presidential response to interests with some degree of generality.

Apart from the macroeconomic policy literature, a handful of other studies have focused broadly on presidential policy choice. Light's (1982) study of the president's agenda, probably the most frequently cited work on presidential policy choice, is most useful in explaining how the stages of a president's term affect his decisions and effectiveness. His analysis of presidential objectives and criteria of choice, however, is rudimentary. Light argues that presidents select issues for attention so as to maximize political benefits; that they choose policies for serious consideration to minimize political costs, and finally, that they adopt measures as presidential proposals on the basis of political feasibility. Such segregation of benefits, costs, and feasibility into different phases is implausible; to avoid serious irrationality, a president must consider all these criteria throughout the process. More important, neither Light nor anyone else has investigated how presidents judge benefits, costs, and feasibility.

Two studies (Ostrum and Simon 1985a; Kernell 1986) have analyzed presidential policy choice as a trade-off between policy achievement and popularity. These studies assume that presidents are interested in both achievement and popularity, and that proposing controversial policies is generally costly in public support. Presidents therefore alternate between promoting significant policy change at a cost to their popularity, and stressing noncontroversial campaignlike appeals and public-relations techniques to restore their popularity to acceptable levels. This analysis, although interesting, has difficulties. For one, policy achievements are not a luxury for presidents but an important source of their popularity. In addition, there is presumably a point of diminishing returns in campaigning for popularity, and presidents (or the astute ones) may always operate at that point. Neither simple trade-offs nor opportunities for variation over time may exist. In any case, these studies at least begin to investigate presidents' policy choices in light of explicit analyses of their objectives.

Doing the same thing in another way, Weatherford (1987) looks at the interplay of electoral and policy objectives to account in some detail for the weak findings on political business cycles. Contrasting economic policy in the Eisenhower and Nixon administrations, he argues that electoral objectives compete with the president's economic ideology and the influence of his economic advisers. Reelection is the dominant goal only when that ideology is absent and those advisers are weak. Eisenhower was committed to budget balancing and limited government and had defined a strong role for his economic advisers. Accordingly, he refrained from attempting to manipulate the economy for electoral ends. In contrast, Nixon, concerned mostly with foreign policy, evinced little interest in economic policy and had a disorganized system for economic advice. His successful efforts to boost the economy before the 1972 election is the prime example of electorally inspired manipulation.

In future work, there may be several ways to get some purchase on presidential objectives. As we have seen, one way is to analyze presidential decisions in light of the conflict between electoral success or popularity and other objectives like ideology or policy achievement. Another is to analyze presidents' electoral strategies in more detail—for example, by considering the conflict between serving party constituencies and appealing to independent voters or marginal groups.

A third approach is to explore more systematically differences between presidents' policy tendencies and those of other officials or institutions. For example, we should assess systematically how presidential action or refusal to act in conflicts between general and special interests compares to that of the whole Congress, congressional committees, and entrepreneurial members of Congress. We also should analyze the substantive and political basis of presidential conflict with the bureaucracy.

Finally, it would be useful to explore the contents of the president's policy agenda as a whole. This could tell us, among other things, whether presidents balance out the distributive effects of their entire agenda, whether they limit their efforts on behalf of general interests to relatively visible issues, and whether they select most of their initiatives to fit their central rhetorical themes.

Influence: Legislative Leadership

With certain limited exceptions, a president's policy decisions are consequential only if he can induce other decision-makers to endorse or execute them. The most difficult task usually is to gain congressional consent. For a long time political scientists have traced the fluctuating relationships between the president and Congress (Sundquist 1983), debated the adequacy of the structural conditions for presidential leadership (Burns 1963), and described the organization of presidential lobbying activities (Wayne 1978). More recently, a substantial body of research, much of it quantitative, has directly addressed presidential influence in Congress.[5]

Unfortunately, that influence is hard to measure with any precision.

To produce conceptually sound, reliable findings about presidential influence in Congress, research should identify and weigh legislative outcomes that occur only because the president acts to bring them about (see, however, Bond and Fleischer, 1990). To do so, it should take into account: the relative importance of different bills, the correspondence between the president's substantive goals and legislative outcomes, and the prior disposition of Congress to pursue the same objectives. The analysis should include cases where Congress rejects a proposal without voting on it. As an indication of the strength of the president's preferences, it should take note of his effort to shape the outcomes.

The quantitative research has made impressive advances, but it still falls short of these requirements. The early work (Edwards 1980) used Congressional Quarterly's Presidential Support Scores to measure congressional support and made no effort to consider the importance of votes or the degree of presidential effort. Recent work has used CQ's Key Votes (Edwards 1989) or votes identified as important in White House records (Covington 1986; Sullivan 1988). But either set of roll calls is selected, inappropriately, for controversy,[6] and there has been no attempt to weight votes by their substantive importance or to measure presidential effort. Considering that each administration has a mere handful of proposals of highest priority (Light 1982), this is a major limitation. A few studies have tried to control for Congress's prior dispositions by estimating baseline models of congressional voting (Sullivan 1988; Mouw and MacKuen 1989), but they have succeeded only partially in isolating presidential effects. Apart from taking into account the numerical strength of the parties, the research has failed to control for nonpresidential influences on Congress, such as economic conditions or public opinion on specific issues. In a useful analysis that extends and refines the approach of CQ's Presidential Box Scores, Peterson (1985) has brought the attributes of individual issues into the analysis. But there has been no systematic attempt to consider bills that the president blocks without a floor vote or, on the other hand, that he tries to bring up without success. Researchers understandably have avoided attempting to measure the correspondence between legislative outcomes and presidential goals.

The findings of this literature generally have been plausible and interesting. The principal finding is that the president's influence is above all a function of his party's numerical strength in Congress. Most of that relationship, however, undoubtedly represents ideological harmony more than presidential influence. There has been an illuminating, even though inconclusive, discussion of how the president's public approval affects his influence (for varying assessments, see Edwards [1989], Rivers and Rose [1986], and Bond, Fleischer, and Northrup [1988]). The research has deflated the "two presidencies" thesis: special congressional deference to the president in foreign policy has been limited to Democratic support for internationalist Republican presidents (Edwards 1989).

Yet because of the limitations of the research, such findings must be regarded as highly uncertain. Some of the potential for error is suggested by Covington's (1986) comparisons between roll calls identified as important by internal documents of the Kennedy-Johnson White House (about fifty per year) and CQ's Key Votes, one of the standard data sets, during the period. Support for the president was substantially more partisan on the White House's set of votes than it was on CQ's. It seems likely that votes more important to the White House would also show a greater effect of presidential approval. And there may be even larger discrepancies between findings on the standard support scores and those on, say, the ten roll calls per year most central to the president's agenda.

The most provocative findings of the quantitative research, those concerning presidential legislative skill, are particularly subject to challenge. From comparisons of the support scores of presidents with varying reputations for legislative skill, Edwards (1980) concluded that such skills "are not a prominent source of influence," a view he has only slightly modified in later work (Edwards 1989). These methods have limited bearing on this issue, however. They can test only for one possible form of presidential skill: the ability to change votes in large enough numbers to affect support scores. Yet it is doubtful that presidents even try, except casually, to change that many votes; they apparently reserve their major lobbying efforts (in which they phone congressmen, make national television appeals, and so on) for a handful of crucial votes. In any case, a president's main skills probably have less to do with changing votes than with getting the right issues to the floor (Shull 1989).

Legislative skill has been treated more convincingly in case-study literature. In a perceptive study of one major initiative by each of six presidents, Kellerman (1984) links success to energetic and intelligent persuasive effort on the part of the president and his staff. In a study of the White House Office of Congressional Relations, Bowles (1987) portrays the complexity of the lobbying function and demonstrates wide variation in the precision and coordination of that function. Robyn's (1987) account of the Carter administration's efforts to deregulate the trucking industry analyzes skill in four aspects of policy promotion: the strategic use of policy analysis, the organization of a lobbying coalition, the design of measures to reduce opposition, and negotiation with opposing forces. Although such studies cannot directly demonstrate the effect of skill, they provide strong indirect evidence of its significance. The evidence reveals, among other things, the sheer complexity of the lobbying task as presidents and their staffs conceive it.

Ironically, nearly all the research has neglected what is probably the single most important presidential skill. A president's legislative success often will depend on the ability to design proposals that serve his objectives and yet provide the basis for winning coalitions in Congress. In view of the typical indeterminacy of majority preferences, there presumably is often a wide scope for shaping the outcome through the appropriate design of a proposal (see Riker 1986). In contrast, as the quantitative research rather convincingly indicates, there is usually limited scope for changing votes on a given measure. To be able to use the design of proposals as an effective tool, a president and his staff must have flexibility and a capacity for intelligent strategic judgment. One insightful study of this capacity is Nelson's (1988) analysis of President Roosevelt's 1937 court-packing plan.

Neither the quantitative nor the case-study literatures have looked carefully at the effects of changes in the structure of Congress. It is often claimed that the decentralization of Congress in the mid-1970s increased the obstacles to such leadership (see, for example, Jones 1983). But there has been little research to document this and it is by no means self-evident. Decentralization requires the president to deal directly with numerous individual members of Congress. Yet because he can deploy White House and agency staff in large numbers for that purpose, the additional work may not pose a great difficulty. Moreover, the loss of a few people with the power to say *yes* is also the removal of a few people with the power to say *no*, and it leaves the president by far the most powerful actor in the legislative process. To reach well-founded conclusions about the effects of congressional structure for presidential leadership will require close study of the president's strategic opportunities under different conditions.

The literature on presidential influence on Congress has steadily improved. To continue to achieve greater depth and realism, however, it eventually will be necessary to go beyond analyzing roll-call votes and to look directly at the president's impact on public policy, weighing that impact in light of his objectives and the other forces acting on Congress.

Influence: Control of Administration

Compared with his legislative influence, political scientists have hardly noticed the president's influence in the administrative process as a subject for research. The literature consists of scattered studies on several aspects of the topic. Among the more significant works, Randall (1972) studied welfare administration under Nixon to assess the president's ability to control a specific program. Moe (1982) analyzed enforcement actions of the National Labor Relations Board to test the effect of presidential administrations on agency performance. More broadly, Aberbach and Rockman (1976) and Cole and Caputo (1979) measured the president's ideological support among agency officials. Rose (1976) evaluated Nixon's attempt to introduce management-by-objectives, and Greenstein (1982) and Redford and McCulley (1986) described the administrative strategies of two presidents.

An important point sometimes overlooked in the research is that presidents, although often depicted as struggling vainly to get the bureaucracy under control, in fact have been relatively uninterested in administration. They have used management initiatives like program budgeting and management-by-objectives mainly "to create an image of leadership, without making a sustained effort to expand their discretion and control" (Randall 1982). As Derthick (1990) shows for the Social Security program, they also have ignored the administrative consequences of policy decisions.

Despite the fragmentation of the literature, there has been an interesting debate about the utility of the management approach, used especially by Nixon and Reagan, of politicizing the bureaucracy and centralizing control in the White House. In a sympathetic account of the Nixon administration, Nathan (1976) described and largely endorsed the "administrative strategy" that Nixon adopted for his second term. In contrast, Heclo (1975) criticized Nixon's politicization of the Office of Management and Budget (OMB), arguing that it undermined the agency's capacity to provide competent, politically neutral service, and Hess (1976) denied that the president should even attempt to be the general manager of the executive branch. The debate was renewed in response to the Reagan presidency, with its unprecedented degree of White House intervention and emphasis on ideological conformity and political loyalty in selecting political appointees. Most of the commentary on Reagan's approach was critical (see, for example, West and Cooper 1985). But Nathan (1983) found Reagan's methods appropriate and effective, and in a influential essay Moe (1985) argued that politicized administration is probably desirable and, in any case, virtually inevitable.

The merits of the debate are, at this point, impossible to resolve. It arises from the conflict between the president's interest in controlling administrative policy and his interest (shared with future presidents and the citizenry) in maintaining competent performance in the bureaucracy. Moe's argument boils down to a few points: to be successful, electorally and otherwise, presidents must manage to secure both responsive and competent performance from the bureaucracy. As the pronounced trend toward greater centralization and politicization of the bureaucracy under recent presidents demonstrates, however, they find the need for responsiveness the more compelling. Inasmuch as presidents have incentives to make a careful decision, that judgment is presumably warranted, at least from their standpoint. The extreme point to which Reagan took the pursuit of responsiveness is thus no aberration, but rather the culmination of an underlying process of institutional development.

Moe's argument, though certainly plausible, is not compelling (for a useful critique, see Aberbach and Rockman 1988). For one thing, it requires a strong assumption that presidents are accurate, unbiased judges of their own interests in regard to management strategy. In fact, there are reasons to suspect that they will overvalue central control. There is a fundamental cognitive bias toward overconfidence (Kahneman, Slovic, and Tversky 1982) that may lead the White House to undervalue independent advice. For whatever reason, overcentralization is apparent in business corporations, which sometimes accumulate large headquarters staffs only to end up cutting them, with good results. The argument for politicization also assumes that presidents are unable to control the bureaucracy by less drastic means. This, however, is also doubtful. Heclo (1977a) found that political appointees who start out being suspicious of civil servants usually come to regret it. "What is truly surprising about asserting the near impossibility of managing the bureaucracy," Randall (1982) argues, "is that recent presidents haven't attempted it in a sustained manner." Finally, Moe does not address the consequences of politicized administration for future presidents or the political system.[7]

As Moe points out, the debate needs to be adjudicated through empirical research on the consequences of presidential management strategies for administrative performance. Such research must look at the actual outcomes, both substantive and political, in particular agencies. To my knowledge, the only such study (Lynn 1985) is a casual investigation of the performance of six Reagan-appointed bureau chiefs. Lynn found that, with one exception, Reagan's loyalist appointees performed adequately and advanced the president's political objectives.

For the literature on presidential control of the bureaucracy to become substantially more informative and reliable, there will have to be several improvements in the research. First, it should use more comprehensive criteria to evaluate control. It is inadequate to ask only whether an agency complies with the president's demands or implements his announced policies. Presidents do not want merely to impose certain policy changes regardless of the consequences. They also want the changes they introduce to be widely accepted, at least after the fact, and actually to produce certain benefits. An adequate evaluation of presidential control therefore must also ask whether an agency translates the president's objectives into politically viable and workable policies. Second, the research should examine large enough numbers of programs, agencies, or decisions to estimate the frequency of different outcomes. A management strategy that fails in, say, one program out of twenty is highly effective; a strategy that fails in one out of four is not. To be of much use, research on presidential management must be able to detect such differences. Just as for research on presidential use of information, the key to attaining this capacity is the development of methods to reach complex judgments at a low cost for each case.

Finally, research should not seek mainly to resolve practical debates like the one about politicization; it should aim primarily to develop a general analysis of presidential control of administration. In a rare such effort, Garand and Gross (1982) have outlined a theory of bureaucratic compliance with presidential demands. Despite their narrow definition of the relevant performance as compliance, they provide a valuable starting point for such an analysis.

Public Support

A president's ability to influence public policy depends on his ability to elicit support from the general public. It seems likely, despite the empirical ambiguities, that his influence in Congress is in some degree a function of his public approval or "popularity." His influence in the administrative process probably is too. Even more clearly, however, the president's influence depends on his ability to elicit public agreement with his policies. Both aspects of public support are important, but because of the availability of superior data, research on approval is more advanced.

Consistent data on presidential approval is available, for longitudinal analysis, in a time series with over five hundred data points spanning about forty years and, for cross-sectional analysis, in most of the recent Center for Political Studies National Election Studies. Exploiting this advantage with increasing sophistication, research has made rapid progress and clarified some central issues.[8] It has demonstrated that approval is not somehow a mechanical function of the president's length of time in office, but rather responds to conditions and events. Thus it is important whether the news is dominated by stories favorable or unfavorable to the president (Brody and Page 1975; MacKuen 1983). Contrary to common expectations, public approval does not reflect individuals' reactions to their personal experience, but mainly their broader judgments about governmental or presidential performance, especially the management of the economy (Kinder and Kiewet 1981; Kiewet 1983; Edwards 1983a).[9] The findings in some areas are highly refined. There is evidence that Americans employ consistent criteria to evaluate presidents' personalities (Kinder and Fiske 1986); that the public's response to events varies with the salience of the issues to which they pertain (Ostrum and Simon 1985b); and that prospective judgments about economic performance are more important than retrospective ones (MacKuen, Erickson, and Stimson 1988).

Although impressive progress has been made, the literature on presidential approval still has important limitations. It has difficulty sorting out the effects of slowly changing variables, such as the president's style or the nature of the leading issues in a given period. There is disagreement, for example, about whether Eisenhower's sustained popularity resulted from his strategy of avoiding controversy (Greenstein 1982) or from the prominence of consensual foreign-policy issues during his administration (Ostrum and Simon 1985b). The research also has difficulty clarifying some important interactions, such as those, likely to be important, between the president's public-relations efforts and other circumstances that affect his popularity. Thus, several authors have described presidents' use of direct appeals to the public and considered the typical effects of those appeals on public approval (Lowi 1985; Kernell 1986; Ragsdale 1984). But none has carefully examined whether such appeals lose effectiveness with frequent use or whether they require certain conditions to be productive.

The president's ability to elicit public agreement with his policies is more elusive because it turns on changes over a short period in opinions that are not measured on a regular basis. In one-shot surveys, individuals express more support for a policy if they are told it is a presidential proposal (Edwards 1983a). (Toward the end of his administration, Jimmy Carter was an exception [Sigelman and Sigelman 1981].) This would suggest a substantial presidential capacity for leadership of public opinion. However, in studies that compare opinion on an issue before and after a presidential effort to change it—which provides a more demanding and realistic test—presidents appear much less persuasive. Using a carefully assembled body of such before-and-after data, Page and Shapiro (1985) found no general disposition to follow the president. Rather, presidents were able to change opinion only if they had high approval ratings, and then only by a few percentage points. Unfortunately, usable before-and-after data is in short supply (presidents do not give advance notice of their attempts to change public opinion), so findings in this area are crude and tentative.

In the future, research on presidential approval undoubtedly will become increasingly sophisticated and informative. By comparison, in the absence of a large-scale project to generate appropriate data, the literature on opinion leadership is likely to remain sparse and primitive.

Presidents as Individuals

Two further areas of investigation—presidents as individuals and change in the presidency—have bearing on all of the preceding issues. Important recent work has been done in both areas. The literature in each, however, is disorganized; there is little agreement about the central questions, let alone the most promising avenues of inquiry.

Research on the psychology of the presidency probably was set back by the appearance of James David Barber's *The Presidential Character*

(1972), which, though highly influential, was widely and severely criticized. Other researchers seem to have kept their distance from the subject as if to avoid guilt by association. Nevertheless, the presidency clearly offers exceptional opportunity for the play of individual attributes. The only question is how to investigate them.

There is little justification for studying presidents in order to construct general theories of personality development or psychodynamics (Rockman 1986); almost anyone else is a more accessible and equally pertinent subject for research on that topic. Rather, psychological research on presidents should aim to understand how personality and related attributes of presidents affect their performance, and how the career ladders and election processes leading to the presidency select for those traits.

Issues of abnormal psychology, even if suspiciously dramatic, are pertinent (cf. Tulis 1981). Considering the prolonged period of extraordinary effort and risk-taking required of a politician seeking the presidency, it would hardly be surprising if presidents were often driven by needs associated with fragile or unstable personalities. Nevertheless, most individual differences among presidents seem to involve dispositions well within the bounds of normality. Kellerman (1984) suggests, for example, that a president's political skill depends on a particular combination of outer-directed and inner-directed traits—extroversion and a tendency to be guided by strong convictions. Leaving the underlying personality aside, several studies have shown the importance of skills, beliefs, and dispositions acquired by a president from prior experience in his professional career. Jimmy Carter may have had a strong need for achievement all his life; but it was mainly while he was governor of Georgia that he came to define himself as a moral leader who served the public by insisting on principled solutions to difficult problems (Hargrove 1988).

For the most part, research on presidential psychology has been improving with respect to both theory and methodology. Much of the improvement is due to the contributions of psychologists. In contrast to Barber, who invented a good deal of his psychological framework, they have employed theories and typologies with validation in mainstream psychology.[10] They have distinguished among presidents with respect to their needs for achievement, power, and affiliation (Simonton 1987); explained presidents' foreign-policy behavior on the basis of interpersonal generalization theory (Etheridge 1978); and linked presidents' adaptability and success to their explanatory style (Zullow et al. 1988).

Perhaps because psychologists are accustomed to the convenience of experimenting with student subjects, however, they sometimes have fallen short of the methodological requirements for credible research in natural settings. Some of the best work has used painstaking, objective measures to assess presidents' personalities; in an especially elaborate effort, for example, Simonton (1987) had professional historians review presidents' biographies to score the items of standard personality instruments. But other work has used dubious evidence of presidential personality, such as content analysis of inaugural addresses. Most of the psychological research has ignored problems that arise from the multiple sources of presidential performance. The typical approach has been to compute simple correlations between measures of personality and, say, the occurrence of wars or historians' rankings of presidential greatness.

Ideally, research on presidents as individuals should combine the strengths of psychology with those of political science. It should employ concepts and theories from general psychology, combine substantial behavioral data with well-validated instruments to assess personality, and test the effects of personality on performance by methods that control for other influences. For some purposes, it is less productive to study *actual* presidents, who are too few in number for reliable findings, than past or current *aspiring* ones, who undoubtedly resemble actual presidents and yet are available in quantity.

Change in the Presidency

The changes in the presidency that most warrant attention, by our criteria, are those that affect the president's impact on public policy. There have been relatively durable changes with such effects in presidential roles, activities, and practices; in the size and structure of the presidential bureaucracy; and in the president's relations with other actors and institutions. There is a good deal of literature about such changes. Because of the several features subject to change and the difficulty of tracing the causes of long-term developments, however, the conclusions are generally quite speculative.

Most of the analysis has focused on several kinds of linear or cyclical change. To explain the expansion of the presidency's role and resources, researchers have pointed to the increasing size and complexity of the federal government, growing American involvement in international affairs, and presidential dominance of the media (Greenstein 1988; Rose 1988). To explain presidents' increasing use of public speeches and other mass appeals to promote their policies, they have pointed to the same dominance of the media along with the decline of political party organization (Kernell 1986; Lowi 1985). The more cyclical factors producing change are public moods, party realignments, and the rise and fall of party coalitions. Nelson and Hargrove (1984) suggest that such changes produce a cycle of presidencies of preparation, achievement, and consolidation; and that each kind of president requires distinctive strategies and skills. Combining linear and cyclic factors in a provocative analysis, Skowronek argues that presidents who take office upon the demise of a preceding governing coalition have exceptional discretion to alter basic commitments and coalitions, but that such discretion narrows with the gradually increasing complexity and rigidity of the political system. This view contrasts with Sundquist's (1983) account of cycles of party politics overlaying a long-term increase in congressional deference associated with the growth of government.

Such studies, though certainly useful as far as they go, face the difficulties of drawing inferences from a rather short series of presidencies—fewer than ten, if one views the so-called modern presidents as the relevant universe (cf. Skowronek 1986)—and a single historical sequence of events. They cannot easily develop reliable, discriminating causal findings. For the most part, they report gross relationships (such as that between party realignment and the president's ability to produce dramatic policy change), suggest associations between whole sets of underlying developments and resulting features of the presidency, or go out on a limb with more specific speculation. We have little precise knowledge, for example, about the relative importance of governmental growth and media attentiveness in the expansion of the president's role; or about whether the rise of the strategy of "going public" reflects an increase or a decrease in presidential power. For better or worse, moreover, studies of the development of the presidency rarely have been grounded in explicit theories of institutional change.

To improve this state of affairs will not be easy. But researchers should at least aspire to greater precision and generality. Instead of consorting with sweeping conceptions of the presidency, they should focus on explaining specific features, such as the organization of the White House (Walcott and Hult 1987), the functions of the cabinet (Cohen 1988), or presidential methods of policy promotion (Kernell 1986). They should look closely at the timing and processes of change to tease out the separate effects of various underlying conditions. Finally, they should explore the potential for grounding explanation in general theories of institutional change (Moe 1985) or accounts of American political development.

THE PRESIDENCY AND NEGLECTED DIMENSIONS OF POLICY-MAKING

Beyond the strengths and weaknesses in specific areas, I want to point out a limitation of perspective in the presidency field as a whole. Without taking the space for a full discussion, I will suggest that the literature reflects a largely unrecognized preoccupation of the entire discipline with the zero-sum aspects of political conflict (Quirk 1989).

Like most research on political institutions and policy-making, research on the presidency has sought fundamentally to explain who wins and who loses in policy conflict. At least implicitly, the central question has been the distribution of power among competing actors, interests, or institutions. That orientation, though obviously pertinent for political analysis, tends to overlook two further dimensions of policy-making that I shall call deliberation and conflict resolution. Students of the presidency accordingly have failed to explore the president's performance with respect to these dimensions.

The dimension of deliberation concerns whether or not policy decisions are reached intelligently, on the basis of adequate understanding. Thus it involves the character and adequacy of information gathering, analysis, and consideration of alternatives (Bessette 1981). A highly diffuse process in our open and fragmented political system, deliberation ranges from formal debate on the Senate floor to private reflection by ordinary citizens. Notwithstanding the cultivated cynicism of journalists and political scientists, policy-making arguably consists largely of deliberation about how to advance goals, or comply with norms, that have widespread support. The effectiveness of that deliberation, however, is far from unproblematic. On the contrary, it is a crucial variable in the performance of government.

Unlike students of Congress, who have ignored deliberation almost entirely, students of the presidency have addressed it quite extensively, as we have seen, in relation to advisory processes for White House decision-making. Besides deliberating over their own decisions, however, presidents participate in broader processes of deliberation that include Congress, other elites, and the general public. An important aspect of the president's performance, barely touched upon by political scientists, is the degree to which he enhances or undermines those processes.

The principal study of how presidents affect public and congressional deliberation, Jeffrey Tulis's *The Rhetorical Presidency* (1987), takes a dim view of their performance. Tulis shows that in a profound change beginning with Theodore Roosevelt and Woodrow Wilson, presidential policy rhetoric has become not only more public (directed to mass audiences) but also more intellectually impoverished (relying on simplistic arguments and symbolism).[11] Indeed, Page and Shapiro (1989) have shown that presidential rhetoric is often essentially deceptive, reflecting several identifiable forms of bias. It is hard to determine the effects of simplistic or misleading presidential rhetoric on public and congressional deliberations or on policy outcomes. Tulis has explored such effects in brief case studies of some major policy choices, including the Johnson administration's War on Poverty, but further efforts along these lines are needed.

The dimension of conflict resolution concerns whether or not policy conflicts are decided cooperatively, on the basis of agreement and joint gain. The processes central to this dimension are bargaining and, in some cases, mediation. In many important policy conflicts, the opposing groups or factions have both complementary and conflicting interests. They thus have an opportunity, in principle, to achieve joint gain by reaching agreement and bringing about cooperative policy change (Quirk 1989). However, as the inability to act constructively in relation to budget deficits, welfare reform, environmental regulation, and many other conflicts demonstrates, they often fail to exploit such opportunities.

In a recent paper (Quirk 1989), I outlined a theoretical framework for research on the cooperative resolution of policy conflict, and suggested issues and hypotheses about the effects of several features of the policy process: issue content, the structure of conflict, party politics, institutions, and leadership. With respect to leadership, and thus the presidency, the principal task from this perspective is to understand leaders' contribution to the prospects for cooperative outcomes. In other words, research should assess presidents' performance from the standpoint of the requirements for integrative bargaining and effective mediation. Under what conditions, for example, do presidents adopt mediating roles? What methods of presidential policy formation and advocacy best preserve the potential for reaching agreement with opposing factions? To my knowledge, there is no substantial study of the presidency that seeks to answer such questions.[12]

THREE PRESCRIPTIONS AND A PROGNOSIS

Apart from these brief remarks about the neglect of deliberation and conflict resolution, I have mainly offered observations about several discrete literatures concerned with different aspects of the presidency. I will conclude with a few comments about the field as a whole. Secure in the knowledge that I have no significant exposure to malpractice liability, I will offer three prescriptions and a prognosis.

The first prescription is that students of the presidency should learn to live with the fundamental diversity of the field. Some reviews of the presidency literature have speculated about whether the field will someday achieve coherence through the development of a general theory of the presidency. That will never happen. Indeed, considering the range of issues addressed in the field, it is hard to understand what it would mean. One of the few works advocating discussion of general models of the presidency, an essay by Seligman (1980), demonstrates the limited prospects for such models. It actually outlines several obviously limited conceptions of the office (majoritarian leader, administrative leader, and the like), and presumes that most of them will remain prominent.

Indeed, as the research develops it becomes increasingly dubious to think about the presidency as a distinct and independent focus of specialization. The development of the field almost surely will be better served if researchers consider themselves primarily students of leadership, decision-making, public opinion, administrative behavior, the legislative process, or political development—that is, of the broader fields that provide relevant theories or methods—and only secondarily students of the presidency. A researcher whose primary field is the presidency will be, in regard to theory and methods, a dilettante.

A second prescription is that theory, whatever its subject, should seek a general comprehension of the behavior it seeks to explain. Some areas of presidency research have been overly confined to practical issues—such as how the president should organize the White House, or how he should seek to control the administrative process. Adopting such a practical focus restricts attention to a narrow range of factors that the president can manipulate. Broader theoretical inquiries—which instead would address, for example, presidential use of information or bureaucratic implementation of presidential policy—would certainly produce better social science. In the long run, by putting the manipulatable factors in context, they may also improve the capacity to give practical advice.

Similarly, research and commentary should use comprehensive criteria to evaluate presidential success. A definition of success is often implicit in presidency research: for example, in discussions of whether Eisenhower's "hidden hand leadership" worked (Greenstein 1982; cf. Kernell 1983) or whether Reagan's loyalist appointees served him well. The tendency is to choose a least-common-denominator criterion—reelection, popularity, or the sheer amount of policy change—in the apparent belief that it avoids imposing the analyst's values. As Ceaser (1988) points out, however, presidents have complex objectives. In addition to popularity or reelection, they want their beliefs and policies to be adopted; they want the policies they put in place to be accepted and to endure; and they want to feel they have helped solve the problems of the country. At any rate, these are surely requirements for the success of a presidency as judged from the public's standpoint. Research that purports to evaluate presidential success should take all of these elements into account.

Finally, I want to prescribe (as if it were so simple) methodological innovation. The presidency literature has become richer and more sophisticated as a result of methodological developments in recent years—especially the wider use of quantitative analysis and the exploitation of archival records. Methodologically sophisticated researchers have attempted to develop dynamic models of presidential popularity and to ground analysis of presidential influence in baseline models of congressional voting. Innovative in a different way, Lynn's (1985) brief case studies of administrative performance by six Reagan subcabinet appointees and Heclo's (1977a) broader study of political leadership in the executive branch both rely on participants to provide complex, interpretive information at low cost.[13] With regard to the logistics of generating evidence, a project at the University of Virginia has produced an oral history of the Carter presidency and made some of the information available for research without the usual delay.[14]

At the same time, a note of caution about some of the recent enthusiasms is appropriate. Detailed research in presidential documents, oral histories, and so on will be most useful when it has a reasonably narrow focus. Notwithstanding the "shroud of secrecy" supposedly surrounding the White House, there is voluminous and generally accurate journalistic coverage of many aspects of presidential activity. Primary research can illuminate, for example, decision-making on a particular subject or the performance of a particular White House function, where journalistic coverage is inevitably superficial. But it rarely will hold surprises about the general dimensions of a presidency: no one is going to find out in a library, for example, that President Reagan had a strong grasp of policy debates or that the Carter administration was well coordinated. Seemingly at odds with this suggestion, the most prominent presidential study based on archival research, Greenstein's 1982 book on Eisenhower, is a general treatment of presidential management and decision-making. It is the kind of exception that proves the rule: the study's thesis is, after all, that Eisenhower's political role was kept hidden from the public by extraordinary, and presumably very unusual, deception. Of course, the need for discriminating application of methods pertains equally, if not more, to quantitative analysis. Indeed, a presidential study of whatever variety that is advertised or cited primarily for methodological virtues rather than new or persuasive findings probably is not much of an advance.

Finally, a favorable prognosis is in order. In almost every area touched upon here, I have been able to describe major research projects—often conducted with improved methods or more thorough research than previous studies—and to report findings that have enhanced our understanding of the presidency. No longer are students of the presidency, as Anthony King (1975) once complained, merely taking in each other's laundry. It is time to pronounce the presidency field, though not yet exceptionally strong, certainly in good health.

NOTES

1. Some of the useful studies include: on the White House staff, Hess (1976), Campbell (1986); on national security, Allison and Szanton (1976), Destler (1982), and George (1980); on economic policy, Porter (1980) and

Anderson and Hazelton (1985); on domestic policy, Salamon (1982). For a study that uses organization theory to explain stable features of the White House, see Walcott and Hult (1988).

2. Societal objectives are proximate causes of a president's policy decisions, often tantamount to the decision itself. To avoid triviality, research must not simply stipulate but rather seek to explain those objectives. Personal objectives are more remote causes. It thus is defensible in principle either to assume variation in those objectives, to attempt to explain such variation, or to specify certain objectives as a starting point.

3. For a brief review of this literature, with citations to several lengthier reviews, see Weatherford (1988).

4. See, for example, Hibbs (1977). For more citations, see Weatherford (1988).

5. The principal early work was Edwards (1980). There is now a substantial literature. See, in particular, Edwards (1989), Rivers and Rose (1985), Covington (1986), Peterson (1985), and Sullivan (1988).

6. On Congressional Quarterly's Key Votes, see Shull and Vanderleeuw (1987). The bias toward close votes should suppress variation in presidential success and attentuate all sources of variation in presidential influence.

7. Nor is the issue preempted (as he implies) by the difficulty of constraining the president's methods: keeping officials from doing what they may want to do is, after all, the very essence of constitutionalism.

8. For general treatments, see Edwards (1983), Kernell (1986), and Kinder and Fiske (1986).

9. There is a puzzling loose end here. Over time, national economic conditions powerfully affect a president's approval ratings. Yet, in cross-sectional research, neither individuals' perceptions of their own economic circumstances nor their perceptions of the nation's overall economic performance are strongly associated with their approval of the president. This leaves a troubling question of the mechanism of the longitudinal effect.

10. For a discussion and thorough review, see Simonton (1987).

11. Kernell (1986) covers some of the same ground, but contrasts public rhetoric with bargaining rather than deliberation.

12. Although both deliberation and conflict resolution are associated with nonzero-sum conflict, they are distinct phenomena and depend on substantially different conditions. For example, the failure to achieve cooperation with respect to federal budget deficits is not the result of failing to understand the consequences of deficits.

13. They use interview subjects not only as sources of hard evidence but also as expert judges of influence or causation. This violates traditional notions of rigor, but it permits relatively reliable interpretation of a large number of cases. For a useful discussion of several varieties of case study, see Thomas (1983).

14. The project, organized by James S. Young, so far has produced two useful books: Hargrove (1988) and Jones (1988).

REFERENCES

Aberbach, Joel D., and Bert A. Rockman. 1976. "Clashing Beliefs within the Executive Branch: The Nixon Administration Bureaucracy." *American Political Science Review* 70:456–68.

———. 1988. "Mandates or Mandarins: Control and Discretion in the Administrative State." *Public Administration Review*, March/April, 606–12.

Allison, Graham, and Peter Szanton. 1976. *Remaking Foreign Policy*. New York: Basic Books.

Anderson, James E., and Jared R. Hazelton. 1985. *Managing Macroeconomic Policy: The Johnson Presidency*. Austin: University of Texas Press.

Barber, James David. 1972. *The Presidential Character*. Englewood Cliffs, N.J.: Prentice-Hall.

Berman, Larry. 1982. *Planning a Tragedy: The Americanization of the War in Vietnam*. New York: Norton.

Bessette, Joseph M. 1981. "Is Congress a Deliberative Body?" In *The United States Congress*. Proceedings of the Thomas P. O'Neill, Jr., Symposium on the U.S. Congress, Boston College.

Bond, Jon R., Richard Fleisher, and Michael Northrup. 1988. "Public Opinion and Presidential Support." *The Annals of the American Academy* 499: 47–63.

———, and Richard Fleisher. 1990. *The President in the Legislative Arena*. Chicago: University of Chicago Press.

Bowles, Nigel. 1987. *The White House and Capitol Hill*. New York: Oxford University Press.

Brody, Richard A., and Benjamin I. Page. 1975. "The Impact of Events on Presidential Popularity." In *Perspectives on the Presidency*, ed. Aaron Wildavsky. Boston: Little, Brown.

Buchanan, Bruce. 1987. *The Citizen's Presidency*. Washington, D.C.: CQ Press.

Burns, James MacGregor. 1963. *The Deadlock of Democracy*. Englewood Cliffs, N.J.: Prentice-Hall.

Campbell, Colin. 1986. *Managing the Presidency: Carter, Reagan and the Search for Executive Harmony*. Pittsburgh, Pa.: University of Pittsburgh Press.

Ceaser, James W. 1988. "The Reagan Presidency and American Public Opinion." In *The Reagan Legacy: Promise and Performance*, ed. Charles O. Jones. Chatham, N.J.: Chatham House.

Cohen, Jeffrey E. 1988. *The Politics of the U.S. Cabinet*. Pittsburgh, Pa.: University of Pittsburgh Press.

Cole, Richard L., and David A. Caputo. 1979. "Presidential Control of the Senior Civil Service: Assessing the Strategies of the Nixon Years." *American Political Science Review* 73:399–413.

Covington, Cary. 1986. "Congressional Support for the President: The View from the Kennedy-Johnson White House." *Journal of Politics* 48:717–28.

Derthick, Martha. 1979. *Policymaking for Social Security*. Washington, D.C.: Brookings Institution.

———. 1990. *Agency under Stress: The Social Security Administration in American Government*. Washington, D.C.: Brookings Institution.

———, and Paul J. Quirk. 1985. *The Politics of Deregulation*. Washington, D.C.: Brookings Institution.

Destler, I. M. 1980. *Making Foreign Economic Policy*. Washington, D.C.: Brookings Institution.

———. 1981. "National Security II: The Rise of the Assistant, 1961–81." In *The Illusion of Presidential Government*, ed. H. Heclo and L. Salamon. Boulder, Colo.: Westview Press.

Edwards, George C., III. 1980. *Presidential Influence in Congress*. San Francisco: Freeman.

———. 1983a. *The Public Presidency: The Pursuit of Popular Support*. New York: St. Martin's Press.

———. 1983b. "Quantitative Analysis." In *Studying the Presidency*, ed. George C. Edwards III, and Stephen Wayne. Nashville: University of Tennessee Press.

———. 1989. *At the Margin: Presidential Leadership of Congress*. New Haven: Yale University Press.

Etheridge, Lloyd S. 1978. "Personality Effects on American Foreign Policy, 1898–1968: A Test of Interpersonal Generalization Theory." *American Political Science Review* 78:434–51.

Fiorina, Morris P. 1984. "The Presidency and the Contemporary Electoral System." In *The Presidency and the Political System*, ed. Michael Nelson. Washington, D.C.: CQ Press.

Garand, James C., and Donald A. Gross. 1982. "Toward a Theory of Bureaucratic Compliance with Presidential Directives." *Presidential Studies Quarterly* 12:195–207.

Gelb, Leslie, and Richard Betts. 1979. *The Irony of Vietnam: The System Worked*. Washington, D.C.: Brookings Institution.

George, Alexander L. 1972. "The Case for Multiple Advocacy." *American Political Science Review* 66:751–85.

———. 1980. *Presidential Decisionmaking in Foreign Policy: The Effective Use of Information and Advice*. Boulder, Colo.: Westview Press.

Greenstein, Fred I. 1982. *The Hidden-Hand Presidency: Eisenhower as Leader*. New York: Basic Books.

———. 1988. "Toward a Modern Presidency." In *Leadership in the Modern Presidency*, ed. Fred Greenstein. Cambridge, Mass.: Harvard University Press.

Greenstein, Fred I., and John P. Burke. 1989. *How Presidents Test Reality: Decisions on Vietnam, 1954 and 1965*. New York: Russell Sage Foundation.

Hargrove, Erwin C. 1988. *Jimmy Carter as President: Leadership and the Politics of the Public Good*. Baton Rouge: Louisiana State University Press.

Heclo, Hugh. 1975. "OMB and the Presidency—The Problem of 'Neutral Competence.' " *Public Interest* 38:80–98.

———. 1977a. *A Government of Strangers: Executive Politics in Washington*. Washington, D.C.: Brookings Institution.

———. 1977b. *Studying the Presidency*. New York: Ford Foundation.

Herman, Charles. 1969. "International Crisis as a Situational Variable." In *International Politics and Foreign Policy: A Reader in Research and Theory*, ed. J. Rosenau. New York: The Free Press.

Hess, Stephen. 1976. *Organizing the Presidency*. Washington, D.C.: Brookings Institution.

Hibbs, Douglas. 1977. "Political Parties and Macroeconomic Policy." *American Political Science Review* 71:1467–87.

Janis, Irving L. 1972. *Victims of Groupthink*. Boston: Houghton Mifflin.

Jones, Charles O. 1983. "Presidential Negotiation with Congress." In *Both Ends of the Avenue*, ed. Anthony King. Washington, D.C.: American Enterprise Institute.

———. 1988. *The Trusteeship Presidency: Jimmy Carter and the United States Congress*. Baton Rouge: Louisiana State University Press.

Kahneman, Daniel, Paul Slovic, and Amos Tversky, eds. 1982. *Judgment under Uncertainty: Heuristics and Biases*. Cambridge University Press.

Kellerman, Barbara. 1984. *The Political Presidency*. New York: Oxford University Press.

Kernell, Samuel. 1983. Review of Fred I. Greenstein, *The Hidden-Hand Presidency*. In *Congress and the Presidency* 10:251–56.

———. 1986. *Going Public: New Strategies of Presidential Leadership*. Washington, D.C.: CQ Press.

Kessel, John H. 1974. "Parameters of Presidential Politics." *Social Science Quarterly* 55:8–24.

Kiewiet, D. Roderick. 1983. *Macroeconomics and Micropolitics*. Chicago: University of Chicago Press.

Kinder, Donald R., and D. Roderick Kiewiet. 1981. "Sociotropic Politics: The American Case." *British Journal of Political Science* 11:129–61.

———, and Susan T. Fiske. 1986. "Presidents in the Public Mind." In *Political Psychology: Contemporary Problems and Issues*, ed. Margaret G. Hermann. San Francisco: Jossey-Bass.

King, Anthony. 1975. "Executives." In *Handbook of Political Science*, vol. 5, ed. Fred Greenstein and Nelson Polsby. Reading, Mass.: Addison-Wesley.

Krasner, Stephen. 1979. *Defending the National Interest: Raw Materials Investments and U.S. Foreign Policy*. Princeton, N.J.: Princeton University Press.

Light, Paul C. 1982. *The President's Agenda*. Baltimore: The Johns Hopkins University Press.

Lowi, Theodore J. 1985. *The Personal President: Power Invested, Promise Unfulfilled*. Ithaca, N.Y.: Cornell University Press.

Lynn, Laurence E., Jr. 1985. "The Reagan Administration and the Penitent Bureaucracy." In *The Reagan Presidency and the Governing of America*, ed. L. Salamon and M. Lund. Washington, D.C.: Urban Institute.

MacKuen, Michael B. 1983. "Political Drama, Economic Conditions, and the Dynamics of Presidential Popularity." *American Journal of Political Science* 27:165–92.

————, Robert S. Erickson, and James A. Stimson. 1988. "On the Importance of Economic Experience and Expectations for Political Evaluations." Paper presented at the annual meeting of the American Political Science Association, Washington, D.C. September.

Moe, Terry M. 1982. "Regulatory Performance and Presidential Administration." *American Journal of Political Science* 26:197–224.

————. 1985. "The Politicized Presidency." In *The New Direction in American Politics*, ed. John E. Chubb and Paul E. Peterson. Washington, D.C.: Brookings Institution.

Mouw, Calvin, and Michael MacKuen. 1989. "The Strategic Configuration, Political Influence, and Presidential Power in Congress." Manuscript. University of Missouri, St. Louis.

Nathan, Richard P. 1975. *The Plot That Failed: Nixon and the Administrative Presidency*. New York: Wiley.

————. 1983. *The Administrative Presidency*. New York: Wiley.

Nelson, Michael. 1988. "The President and the Court: Reinterpreting the Court-Packing Episode of 1937." *Political Science Quarterly* 103:267–93.

————, and Erwin C. Hargrove. 1984. *Presidents, Politics, and Public Policy*. New York: Knopf.

Ostrum, Charles W., Jr., and Dennis M. Simon. 1985a. "The President and Public Support: A Strategic Perspective." In *The Presidency and Public Policy Making*, ed. George C. Edwards III, Steven A. Shull, and Norman C. Thomas. Pittsburgh, Pa.: University of Pittsburgh Press.

————. 1985b. "Promise and Performance: A Dynamic Model of Presidential Popularity." *American Political Science Review* 79:334–58.

Page, Benjamin I., and Robert Y. Shapiro. 1985. "Presidential Leadership through Public Opinion." In *The Presidency and Public Policy Making*, ed. George C. Edwards III, Steven A. Shull, and Norman C. Thomas. Pittsburgh, Pa.: University of Pittsburgh Press.

————. 1989. "Educating and Manipulating the Public." In *Manipulating Public Opinion*, ed. Michael Margolis and Gary Mauser. Chicago: Brooks-Cole.

Peterson, Mark. 1985. "Domestic Policy and Legislative Decision Making." Paper presented at the annual meeting of the Midwest Political Science Association, Chicago, April.

Pika, Joseph A. 1981–82. "Moving Beyond the Oval Office: Problems in Studying the Presidency." *Congress and the Presidency* 9:17–36.

Porter, Roger B. 1980. *Presidential Decision Making: The Economic Policy Board.* New York: Cambridge University Press.

Quirk, Paul J. 1989. "The Cooperative Resolution of Policy Conflict." *American Political Science Review* 83. In press.

Ragsdale, Lyn. 1984. "The Politics of Presidential Speechmaking, 1949–1980." *American Political Science Review* 78:971–84.

Randall, Ronald. 1979. "Presidential Power versus Bureaucratic Intransigence: The Influence of the Nixon Administration on Welfare Policy." *American Political Science Review* 73:795–810.

———. 1982. "Presidential Use of Management Tools from PPB to ZBB." *Presidential Studies Quarterly* 12:186–94.

Redford, Emmette S., and Richard T. McCulley. 1986. *White House Operations.* Austin: University of Texas Press.

Reichley, A. James. 1981. *Conservatives in an Age of Change: The Nixon and Ford Administrations.* Washington, D.C.: Brookings Institution.

Riker, William H. 1986. *The Art of Political Manipulation.* New Haven: Yale University Press.

Rivers, Douglas, and Nancy L. Rose. 1985. "Passing the President's Program." *American Journal of Political Science* 29:183–96.

Rockman, Bert A. 1981. "America's Departments of State." *American Political Science Review* 75:911–27.

———. 1984. *The Leadership Question.* New York: Praeger.

———. 1986. "Presidential and Executive Studies: The One, the Few, and the Many." In Herbert F. Weisberg, *Political Science: The Science of Politics*, 105–40. New York: Agathon Press.

Rose, Richard. 1976. *Managing Presidential Objectives.* New York: The Free Press.

———. 1988. *The Postmodern President: The White House Meets the World.* Chatham, N.J.: Chatham House.

Salamon, Lester. 1982. "The Presidency and Domestic Policy Formation." In *The Illusion of Presidential Government*, ed. Hugh Heclo and Lester Salamon. Boulder, Colo.: Westview Press.

Shull, Steven A. 1989. *The President and Civil Rights Policy: Leadership and Change.* Westport, Conn.: Greenwood Press.

———, and James M. Vanderleeuw. 1987. "What Do Key Votes Measure?" *Legislative Studies Quarterly* 4:573–82.

Seligman, Lester. 1980. "On Models of the Presidency." *Presidential Studies Quarterly* 10:353–63.

Sigelman, Lee, and Carol K. Sigelman. 1981. "Presidential Leadership of Public Opinion: From 'Opinion Leader' to 'Kiss of Death.'" *Experimental Study of Politics* 7:1–22.

Simon, Herbert A. 1960. *Administrative Behavior*. New York: Macmillan.

Simonton, Dean Keith. 1987. *Why Presidents Succeed*. New Haven: Yale University Press.

Skowronek, Stephen. 1984. "Presidential Leadership in Political Time." In *The Presidency and the Political System*, ed. Michael Nelson. Washington, D.C.: CQ Press.

———. 1986. "The Presidency in the Political Order." *Studies in American Political Development* 1:286–302.

———. 1989. "The Paradoxes of Presidential Leadership." Paper presented at the Conference on the Founding and Development of the Presidency, Smith College, February 24–26.

Sullivan, Terry. 1988. "Headcounts, Expectations, and Presidential Coalitions in Congress." *American Journal of Political Science* 32:657–89.

Sundquist, James L. 1983. *The Decline and Resurgence of Congress*. Washington, D.C.: Brookings Institution.

Thomas, Norman C. 1983. "Case Studies." In *Studying the Presidency*, ed. George C. Edwards III and Stephen Wayne. Nashville: University of Tennessee Press.

Tulis, Jeffrey. 1981. "On Presidential Character." In *The Presidency in the Constitutional Order*, ed. J. Bessette and J. Tulis. Baton Rouge: Louisiana State University Press.

———. 1987. *The Rhetorical Presidency*. Princeton, N.J.: Princeton University Press.

Walcott, Charles, and Karen M. Hult. 1987. "Organizing the White House: Structure, Environment, and Organizational Governance." *American Journal of Political Science* 31:109–25.

Wayne, Stephen. 1978. *The Legislative Presidency*. New York: St. Martin's Press.

Weatherford, M. Stephen. 1987. "The Interplay of Ideology and Advice in Economic Policy-Making: The Case of Political Business Cycles." *Journal of Politics* 49:925–52.

———. 1988. "Political Business Cycles and the Process of Economic Policymaking." *American Politics Quarterly* 16:99–136.

West, William F., and Joseph Cooper. 1985. "The Rise of Administrative Clearance." In *The Presidency and Public Policy Making*, ed. George C. Edwards III, Steven A. Shull, and Norman C. Thomas. Pittsburgh, Pa.: University of Pittsburgh Press.

Zullow, Harold M., and associates. 1988. "Pessimistic Explanatory Style in the Historical Record." *American Psychologist* 43:673–81.

3

Judicial Politics

Elliot E. Slotnick

INTRODUCTION

The subfield of judicial politics is, perhaps, the most schizophrenic of the recognized sub-areas within our discipline. If that overstates my premise, few, I think, would dispute the fact that we have the earmarks of multiple personalities and that the internal tensions abounding in the field in which we labor are more substantial than in those areas mined by our colleagues. Our roots are multidisciplinary, and we owe a great deal to fields as diverse as history, psychology, statistics, literature, philosophy, anthropology, economics, sociology, and others. At the same time, we are in no sense simply a result or a residual of these other disciplines. Indeed, within political science, we predate most other areas of study, as our work was generally pursued under the label "public law." Our self-image is clearly defined in terms of our "distinctiveness," and our self-studies have clearly informed us that our field is "unusually distinctive in that it is both more isolated and closer to unique in its characteristics than are most other fields" (Baum 1983, 197).[1]

I would like to thank Linda Hamilton for her superb job in preparing this manuscript. Ann Peyser of the American Political Science Association provided me with useful information about judicial politics panels at the American Political Science Association conventions during the past decade. Karen O'Connor of Emory University provided much information about the 1989 American Political Science Association judicial politics panels and also sent me some very useful data about judicial politics journal submissions. An earlier draft of this chapter was presented at the 1989 annual meeting of the Midwest Political Science Association. This revision owes debts to several colleagues. Karen O'Connor and Charles Johnson of Texas A & M made several valid observations in responding to my paper. In addition, my interaction with my colleagues at Ohio State, Larry Baum and Greg Caldeira, has had a substantial impact on my own thinking. Naturally, I alone am responsible for the brew that remains.

What, fundamentally, makes the brand of politics that we study different from that studied in other areas of political science is the linkage of judicial politics to the concept of law. As Pritchett stated it so well two decades ago when referring to judicial decision-making:

> (P)olitical scientists who have done so much to put the "political" in political jurisprudence need to emphasize that it is still "jurisprudence." It is judging in a political context, but it is still judging; and judging is something different from legislating or administering. Judges make choices, but they are not the "free" choices of congressmen. . . . There is room for much interpretation in the texts of constitutions, statutes, and ordinances, but the judicial function is still interpretation and not individual policy-making. It is just as false to argue that judges freely exercise their discretion as to contend that they have no policy functions at all. Any accurate analysis of judicial behavior must have as a major purpose a full clarification of the unique limiting conditions under which judicial policy-making proceeds. (Pritchett 1969, 42)

Tensions within our field flow, in part, from the need to reconcile the realities of "judicial politics" with the demands of "the law." Often, such tensions have been manifested in debates over appropriate research strategies and methodologies, appropriate data sources, and questions to study. We are prone to a great deal of self-analysis, and there have been few, if any, resolutions regarding what we see as "our problem." As noted by Helm, "Public law is clearly one of the more self-conscious of the subfields in political science constantly meditating on 'Whither Political Jurisprudence,' . . . congratulating itself on their break from the past and announcing a bold advance into the future . . . only to fall back into doubts as to whether they are taken seriously both in the professions of law and political science" (1987, 10).

In taking note of the existence of a parallel profession, legal academicians, whose focus of interest (albeit *not* research agendas, methodologies, and the like) often mirrors our own, Helm has identified a unique reference point in the environment for judicial politics scholarship that has considerable impact on our self-perceptions and seeming quest for external legitimacy as well as respectability within our own profession. As noted by Murphy and Tanenhaus years ago, "the question most frequently asked of any social scientist interested in public law is, What are you doing studying Law? Unlike the attorney, the social scientist must constantly justify his research in the legal processes, and he often envies his colleagues in the law schools who can do their own thing without having to reiterate its relevance or their own competence." Such a need for justification can, however, have its salutary affects, "since it serves to remind the social scientist that he is not a lay lawyer but a professional with special interests of his own" (1972, 7). Clearly, the academic lawyer need not labor long or hard to justify an interest in studying law. There is, however, a tendency "to view all other people, whether laymen or social scientists, who proclaim an interest in law as poachers on a private hunting preserve" (Murphy and Tanenhaus 1972, 8–9).

In a sense, the difficulties facing political scientists who study judicial processes range beyond the question of legitimacy per se. It is the nature of our enterprise that our analyses will often serve to raise questions about the legalistic myths surrounding judges and judging. Yet for many in the law school professoriate, such myths constitute the guiding premises from which their doctrinal studies flow. In this respect, the political scientist studying judicial politics is twice damned. Our legitimacy and credentials are at issue before we begin, and our inquiries into judicial processes and behavior often result in observations and findings that few want to hear.

The "Fellini-esque" nature of our calling has other dimensions as well. Although not often articulated, our subfield has, perhaps, a somewhat unique teaching mission as well: students passing through our classes view them as an entrée into the parallel world inhabited by the legal academicians. Thus, we do a significant amount of preprofessional training (unlike most other areas of our discipline and, perhaps, against the wishes of the law schools!), teaching predominantly in the most traditional corner of our field of study—constitutional law and civil liberties. (Parenthetically, it should be noted that, outside of introductory American government courses taught by countless political scientists, many of whom are not even in American politics, our teaching responsibilities touch more closely upon the "civics training" sorely needed by most college students than any other experience they are likely to have in their academic careers. In a weak moment I am certain that many—most?—of us would admit that teaching civil liberties, for example, may be the most "important" thing we do as professionals.) If we are schizophrenic, need anyone wonder why?

The nature of the predicament facing our field can be glimpsed from the playing out of the scenario surrounding a visit to Ohio State made by Harold Spaeth several years ago prior to the Supreme Court's decision in the Bakke case. Spaeth was to deliver a lecture on predicting Supreme Court decisions. The visit was jointly sponsored by Ohio State's School of Law and Department of Statistics. It would be covered by a student journalist reporting for the OSU newspaper. We in political science were lucky to learn of the visit. The Spaeth presentation was quite a curiosity for the students and scholars in attendance from all camps, none of whom seemed to know what to make of it all.

Among the law students there was considerable indignant snickering and nervous laughter. They seemed unwilling to entertain the possibility that the decision-making of the likes of a Frankfurter or a Black could reflect, in part, their political preferences. Among the statisticians there appeared to be much awe and reverence. Clearly taken with the "magic" that Harold was spinning, several statisticians huddled and chattered in the back of the room until one was brave enough to ask a question that went something like this: "What you are doing seems quite impressive. Yet so much of it seems to be based on using the number nine. Is there some special significance to that number? Would your calculations work as well if you had based them on another number?"

I had hoped that the student journalist's coverage would moderate between these two extremes. The next day, however, it was duly reported that, according to Professor Spaeth, a renowned expert, unless the Supreme Court were to decide the pending Bakke case the way he predicted it would, the case would be decided "wrongly."

At bottom, there were three groups present in Spaeth's audience. First were the professional functionaries of the law who did not want to listen to what we had to say. (I should, however, underline the obvious. Based on an experience I had when making a presentation at OSU's School of Law on judicial selection during the Carter years, it is clear to me that there is a great deal legal academicians do *not* know and much that we can tell them!) The second group present, the statisticians, had the tools to follow what Spaeth was doing but lacked the substantive knowledge to truly understand it. The lay journalist (and, perhaps, the general public) might have had some modicum of interest in our message, yet we might be fundamentally failing them in terms of getting that message across in a language they could understand. While it clearly overstates the point (and certainly does not accurately describe Harold Spaeth's excellent and clear presentation at OSU that has served as my springboard), Dixon's intemperate critique of judicial behavioralism, written years ago, strikes a chord still worthy of close attention.

> Pritchett has said that recent trends in "political science" public law have provided it "with a vocabulary which makes discourse possible with the more methodologically sophisticated sectors of the profession." Fine. But perhaps the word "only" is creeping in, and then the line will read . . . "discourse only with the more methodologically sophisticated sectors of the profession." How abstract can a profession become, and still serve society? (1971, 25)

As frustrating as the Spaeth visit was for me and, undoubtedly, for Harold, it is important to recognize that it could have been worse. Indeed, a few decades ago the perspectives I have outlined could easily have corresponded to the views expressed by various scholars in judicial politics teaching at different institutions or perhaps even within the same department! Clearly, this is not the case today, and, in this sense, we have come a long way.

My introductory comments should not be taken as counsels of despair. Rather, they are aimed at portraying the environment in which we operate and underlining the influences of that environment upon what we do. As political scientists we must realistically understand the constraints under which we labor, yet we cannot abandon the thrust of our inquiries. As Murphy and Tanenhaus have noted, "A political scientist has to be concerned with the activities of judges because the consequences of what judges do may vitally affect both specific policies and the general conditions under which polities operate. And if judicial decisions do have such effects, how judges make up their minds, how they are selected, and how they can manipulate their power, all become matters of fundamental importance" (1972, 12). In pursuing our work, our unique and complex setting must serve as a backdrop, for "Ours is a place within political science where questions of fact and values go together: empirical and evaluative or prescriptive analysis both find a home where the concern for state responses to specific cases is so central" (Sarat, in Stumpf et al. 1983, 555).

A HISTORICAL OVERVIEW OF THE SUBFIELD

My introductory remarks have suggested that our subfield is somewhat isolated from the mainstream of political science while at the same time being characterized by a significant amount of internal diversity. Neither circumstance has necessarily always been the case. Indeed, there was a time when a focus on legal institutions, and in particular their substantive decisions, occupied center stage in the emerging discipline of political science. As noted by Baum, "early in this century, judicial politics by its various names was somewhat near the center of the study of politics, because of the legalistic approach that pervaded so many fields" (1983, 197). Over time, the rest of the discipline's concerns grew less legalistic—a transformation that could never occur as completely in our own domain.

The roots of scholarship in our field have, from the start, been heavily interdisciplinary. Murphy and Tanenhaus point out that Edward Corwin, for example, "the greatest American scholar in the field," received his training as a historian. They add that, "Both before and after Corwin, anthropologists, economists, historians, journalists, lawyers, philosophers, political scientists, psychologists, and sociologists have contributed to understanding the work of judges. And like Corwin, these writers have themselves often been educated in several intellectual disciplines" (1972, 4).

Despite such eclecticism in where we came from, early scholarship tended, for the most part, to remain heavily tied to a legalistic mode.

Pritchett has argued that "mechanical jurisprudence and the myth of the nonpolitical character of the judicial task" served to constrain political scientists from thinking about the courts in any other terms. The only way to pursue one's judicial interest was "by acting like a lawyer, a philosopher, or an historian" (1969, 29). Vines adds that, "the field of public law was tied to the elements of the legal subculture in a way characteristic of no other field, not even political theory in its relationship with philosophy" (1970, 125). The shoe fit, however, "since the first professors to call themselves political scientists were in fact lawyers, philosophers, or historians in their training and interests" (Pritchett 1969, 29). What may indeed be most noteworthy about early efforts in our subfield is what ultimately emerged out of them given their formalistic roots. As noted by Vines, "Political scientists in the field of public law had claimed an important area of political science, including one of its major institutions (the judiciary), a group of its most important decision-makers (judges), and one of its leading political processes (the judicial process), and perceived it in terms largely suitable for the training of legal professionals. . . . Given the immersion of public law in legalism, it is remarkable that any research emerged that was concerned with political behavior, power, or the political process" (1970, 125).

The legalistic tradition in our subfield has certainly not been without substantial consequences. To be sure, the movement toward legal realism that emerged in the legal academy during the first decade of the twentieth century took hold within our subfield and discipline as well. Clearly, our leading scholars were realists. Nevertheless, the impetus for legal realism was primarily its status as "an intellectually powerful movement among judges and academic lawyers. It has served as a far more influential counterweight in the courts to the mechanistic myths than has the work of social scientists" (Murphy and Tanenhaus 1972, 13).

According to Murphy and Tanenhaus, the "realists" in our subfield between 1920 and the end of World War II (such as Robert Carr, Charles Fairman, Alpheus T. Mason, and Carl B. Swisher) shared several fundamental assumptions. These included the notion that the Constitution does, however vaguely, mark the boundaries of governmental authority among institutions and between the political system and its environment. The Supreme Court was viewed as an integral part of the political system because of its interpretive role. The Court, however, could be affected by actors who had the ability to select judges, alter judicial authority, and "sanction" it in many ways. Consequently, Supreme Court decisions could be seen as "a mixture of law, politics, and policy. The background, training, personality, and conscious as well as unconscious value preferences of individual judges influence the manner in which they decide cases. Judges, however, are not completely free agents. To some extent their choices are restricted by the wording of the

Constitution, precedent, fear of sanctions, and systemic and environmental forces" (1972, 16–17).

While this view of courts was a refreshingly realistic one, research
accomplished in the wake of this new perspective had substantial limits.
Among them could be counted an almost exclusive focus by judicial
politics scholars on the United States Supreme Court, with little comparative interest or, indeed, any interest in lower federal courts or state
court systems. Even at the Supreme Court level, the highest degree of
concern centered on the institution's "boundary defining decisions"
and the possible influences of the judge's personal values on decisions
in this area. Limited analytic tools correspondingly limited efforts to
explore diverse questions about decision-making in an intellectually satisfying manner. Although there were some exceptions, like most political scientists, judicial politics scholars "did not take great advantage of
techniques of quantitative analysis that had been available since the
1920s. Instead, they basically relied on judicial opinions, on the writings of judges . . . and on their own informed intuition to demonstrate
the influence of personal values" (Murphy and Tanenhaus 1972, 17).

In a similar vein, Vines has argued that the research conducted between 1920 and 1948 did not "furnish the creative basis for the development of a judicial politics." Studies tended to be discrete efforts
generating little subsequent research in their wake. Contributing to the
subfield's movement away from the core of the discipline, studies "did
not serve as the basis for a reorientation of the concepts taught and cited
in the political science of that day." The studies had little theoretical
orientation and, "when findings and conclusions were not justified by
reformist apologia or normative reference to a better judiciary, they
were stated in largely descriptive terms" (Vines 1970, 129).

Such criticisms were not made to devalue early public-law research
efforts but, rather, to underline their limitations. In fact, as Murphy and
Tanenhaus argue, "What they did they did superbly," and the work of
later scholars served "to demonstrate in a more orderly, quantitative
way the insights of these earlier students" (1972, 18). One of the
legacies of the early work that does, however, still have problematic
consequences for the judicial politics subfield was the use of the
nomenclature "public law" to label what we studied. The rubric underlined our "separation from other fields of study in American politics
and suggested an orientation toward law rather than political science"
(Baum 1983, 198). To the extent that the term remains in vogue within
our subfield (which, happily, is not great), it "fails to capture the mood
and the substance of the new scholarship in judicial politics that has
made such pronounced progress and recalls, instead, a legalistic past"
(Vines 1970, 139–40). Becker adds that "we must drop the label 'public law' immediately. It is not particularly euphonious; it hardly evokes

nostalgia; it misleads the uninitiated; and it has absolutely no relationship to the development of any theory whatsoever" (1970, 145).

In the discussion by several analysts of the roots of contemporary work in our field, it is no accident that 1948 continues to emerge as the end point to what has been broadly characterized as "early" research efforts. As accurately noted by Grossman and Tanenhaus: "Major watersheds in the development of a field of inquiry are often hard to identify, even in retrospect. Yet there is a watershed in the area of political science concerned with judicial research so imposing as to be unmistakeable" (1969, 4). That watershed, of course, was the publication in 1948 of Pritchett's *The Roosevelt Court*. Pritchett's book aligned judicial politics research more closely with other behavioral work in American politics, and its decision-making focus clearly resonated with what other political scientists were doing. As noted by Grossman and Tanenhaus: "Pritchett . . . foreshadowed and stimulated two new research emphases. One was methodological in character—the utilization of quantitative techniques. The other represented a shift in target from 'what do judges say?' to 'what makes judges behave as they do?' " (1969, 4).

The "behavioral mood" that characterized Pritchett's effort was soon broadened beyond a concern with judicial decision-making (although this certainly remained a dominant focus) to the Court's external environment. Here, the classic breakthrough came in Peltason's 1955 study, *Federal Courts in the Political Process*. Peltason's process orientation spawned numerous efforts that moved judicial politics research in several directions simultaneously, and numerous case studies of facets of the judicial process would follow.

> Some focused on the activities of pressure groups in fostering their interests by sponsoring law suits, while others investigated the actual impact of Supreme Court decisions on specific facets of public policy and the feedback from those decisions into Congress, the presidency, state politics, and again into the judicial process. Other scholars were expanding their jurisdiction to include at least portions of a far wider range of problems than had men like Corwin and Cushman and were using as laboratories state, local, foreign and lower federal courts. (Murphy and Tanenhaus 1972, 20)

Thus, by the late 1950s many scholars (such as Danelski, Jacob, Kort, Nagel, Spaeth, Ulmer, Krislov, Schubert, and many others) were moving the subfield in the directions that Pritchett, Peltason, and others had pointed them toward. Their work would greatly extend the quantitative techniques that Pritchett had pioneered. The broad liberating implications of work such as his, as well as that being accomplished by Peltason and others, allowed Pritchett appropriately to conclude that, "The major development in public law since 1948 has been the shift of attention from the court as enunciator of legal doctrine to the Court as instrument for the resolution of political conflict" (1968, 486).

The decade of the 1960s was one of great consolidation favoring the judicial process/judicial behavior approach to "doing" judicial politics research. As Schubert aptly noted, "In 1959 it was still possible for public lawyers to debate whether the then upstart work in judicial process and behavior should be tolerated; by 1969 the shoe seemed to be on the other foot" (1972, 7). While the 1960s seemed, on the one hand, to move judicial politics back toward the mainstream of political science with the dominance of a process/behavior orientation, it is curious and somewhat ironic that the rest of the discipline did not seem to notice. Indeed, if anything, the field grew more isolated and saw its relative status in the profession decline. Thus, while they sensed a nascent change in the trend, Murphy and Tanenhaus nevertheless opined in 1972 that, "In the 1950s and early 1960s . . . it seemed to many observers that public law had drifted out of the mainstream of American political science" (1972, 3). Pritchett took note that we had become the smallest field in the profession: "At the time the 1953 Directory of the American Political Science Association was prepared, 18.1 percent of the membership claimed an expertise in public law, but in the 1961 Directory the figure was 16.4 percent. . . . Only one other field, public administration, experienced a decline in its attractiveness to the profession during the eight year period" (1968, 480). Perhaps the "unkindest cut of all" was that noted by Helm: "Perhaps the real nadir was reached when Somit and Tanenhaus (both students of the law) reported in the 1963 study, *American Political Science: A Profile of a Profession*, that in the eyes of the discipline public law was making only a minimal contribution to the growth of a science of politics" (1987, 10).

Actually, more than one irony may be at work here. First, vast changes occurring within judicial politics research were not altering perceptions of the "public law" field—at least not in any timely fashion. Second, the changes in what we were "doing" were not, for the most part, being translated into what could be characterized as equally radical changes in our classrooms. Thus, according to Stumpf, "Whatever the merits of judicial behavioralism . . . it is fair to say that the movement never really took root as a mainstay in classroom approaches to the study of the judiciary" (1983, 538). While this may overstate the case, I think that it is fair to conclude with Pritchett that, "Since 1948 the substantive law announced in Supreme Court opinions has continued to be the basic content of most public law courses." Pritchett adds, however, "that in comparison with law professors doing the same thing, political scientists have tended to fare less well than in the pre-1948 period. . . . Today it is the leading figures in the law schools . . . who are called before congressional committees and quoted by the press on constitutional issues"

(1968, 483). This, too, may go too far. For though judicial politics scholars maintain a substantive interest in law, most of us are no longer willing to play the legal academician's game. And when public and media attention focuses on the relationship between judicial processes and the law, one is just as likely to see reported the wisdom of a Sheldon Goldman, Henry Abraham, David O'Brien, Harold Spaeth, J. Woodford Howard, and numerous others as one is to see the musings of Laurence Tribe, Arthur Miller, or A. E. "Dick" Howard. Perhaps, in this sense, we have not "lost" as much as Pritchett suggests.

Our historical overview has been suggestive of significant changes in the core of what we, as a subfield, studied between the turn of the century and the late 1960s. The nature of this core, as we have seen, has undergone several changes. While the central concerns of constitutional law and judicial processes and behavior remain with us, we now study many more things in many more different ways than ever before. As much of the remainder of this essay will illustrate, "the period since the 1960's has seen a great expansion of subject matter and a subtle movement away from a central theme. The field has taken with a vengeance C. Herman Pritchett's advice to 'Let a hundred flowers bloom'" (Baum 1983, 190). This characterization, for good or ill, well defines judicial politics as we approach the twenty-first century.

DATA, METHODOLOGY, AND THEORY IN JUDICIAL POLITICS

Concerns about data, methodology, and theory have never strayed far from center stage in the judicial politics subfield, particularly in the wake of the advent of behavioralism in the study of judicial decision-making. Indeed, as a graduate student in the early 1970s, it was easy to sense a rift in the subfield over the issue of method as that concern focused on the single dominant research issue of the day, the judicial decision. In a sense, such division was to be expected. For one thing, the traditionalist/behavioralist battles were fought out somewhat earlier in other subfields but emerged in judicial politics only after the pathbreaking research efforts of the 1960s. Second, both traditional and behavioral scholars were predominantly concerned with understanding judicial decision-making, a relatively narrow turf to be occupied and a "natural" setting in which division could flourish.

The importance of methodology in judicial politics and, indeed, some of the inherent problems characterizing the methodological state of some of the research in the subfield have been well outlined by Gibson.

A myriad of implications flow from the reliance on epistemologies supporting methodologies within which reproducibility is difficult. Without adherence to a common method, it is hard to determine whether hypotheses have been supported by empirical findings. . . . Because . . . nonscientific methods rely so heavily on the . . . assumption that each court is unique . . . it is difficult to draw generalizations across different systems and across different research projects. There is also an inordinate emphasis given to description, in contrast to more analytical research. . . . [E]xploration and induction must ultimately give way to deduction and confirmatory research requiring scientific methodology. (1986, 145–46)

Yet for every voice arguing for greater sophistication in and greater attention to be placed upon methodological concerns in our subfield there has remained a contrapuntal call for "reason" and a substantive focus. Indeed, in the early 1970s, a time in which behavioral approaches had clearly found their place in judicial politics scholarship, Dixon asserted that "The dedicated, extreme behavioralist . . . is distinctly nonempirical. . . . He builds models and talks about role playing and games, but the only game that really holds his interest is the methodology game. The game becomes an end in itself, the method becomes the message, ever more divorced from the real world" (1971, 24).

The "real world" state of methodology, data, and theory in the "big picture" of judicial politics has, I think, been a relatively healthy one— not suffering unduly from the methodological maladies identified by Gibson nor succumbing to the lack of substantive concern suggested by Dixon. Research designs utilizing statistical measures clearly increased in the wake of Pritchett's early efforts and, during the 1960s, both their ambitiousness and their ultimate purpose grew more complex. As noted by Tate, "The transition from the use of statistical methods and measures in support of description to their use in hypothesis testing was subtle" (1983, 55). If there was a turning point that signaled the trend it was the publication in 1965 of Glendon Schubert's *The Judicial Mind*. Schubert's work "marked the end of the pioneering and the beginning of the modern era because it represented the first full scale, completely behavioral, methodologically sophisticated effort to develop a theory of judicial decision making in the world's most celebrated court. . . . It also served as a reference point for later inquiries" (Tate 1982, 10).

By 1972 Murphy and Tanenhaus could predict increased reliance on quantitative methodologies in the future and note that "Those who denigrate numbers as evidence of flashy but unsound scholarship have shrunk to . . . minority status. . . . Quantification is now not only accepted, it is respected." Yet as evidence of our collective health, Murphy and Tanenhaus could also add that, "as a sign of their maturity, most political scientists are becoming impatient with unsophisticated data analysis and intolerant of quantification for its own sake" (1972, 216–17). Certainly in the last two decades, tolerance has been the predominant watchword regarding methodological choices in judicial politics research. Indeed, "most scholars are content to demand only that a research target be professionally interesting and that the methods employed are appropriate for marking its outer ring" (Grossman and Tanenhaus 1969, 20).

Trends in the utilization of various methodological techniques and data sources have marked the judicial politics subfield during the past three decades, and several of these trends have been examined by Hensley and Rhoads (1988). The study was limited to examining judicial politics research published in four "general" political science journals between 1960 and 1987, and it served to underline graphic changes taking place during the 1960s and the relative continuity since. "Research in the field has changed dramatically during the period from 1960 to 1987, but by far the most significant changes occurred between the sixties and seventies in response to the behavioral revolution which gripped the discipline; the decades of the seventies and eighties have seen basic continuity in the field" (Hensley and Rhoads 1988, 26).

Thus, for example, Hensley and Rhoads found that 44 percent of the studies published during the 1960s could be classified as "quantitative," whereas 73 and 77 percent could be so classified in the 1970s and 1980s, respectively. The domination of the judicial decision as a data source is revealed in all three decades—with 70 percent of the studies published in the 1960s and 1970s and 68 percent of the studies published in the 1980s relying on it. Interestingly (and happily), "other court materials," never utilized in published research analyzed for the 1960s, were utilized in 14 percent of the articles published in the 1980s.

The Hensley and Rhoads study further underlined the increased diversity in judicial politics data sources, as the residual "other" data source category was coded for more than half of the articles published in the 1980s. Further, it should be noted, many studies now utilize multiple data sources, a considerably rarer phenomenon in the past. Thus, during the 1960s, 64 percent of the published research under analysis used only one data source, and no analyst used more than four data sources in any published study. During the 1980s, however, only 43 percent of the articles analyzed used only one data source, whereas 20 percent of the studies utilized four or more. Clearly, the trend toward utilizing multiple data sources enriches our substantive knowledge while lending greater legitimacy to our theoretical insights. Also of interest, the use of questionnaires mailed to judges decreased as a data source over time, while obtaining personal interviews with judges has been on the rise (Hensley and Rhoads 1988). This finding is suggestive since, it appears, numerous scholars have been able to gain direct access to judges when they make the effort to penetrate the "purple curtain." If that indeed is the case, renewed efforts toward utilizing mailed surveys to judges at different levels of the judiciary might prove to be a fruitful line of inquiry.

It should be noted that the finding that a particular datum, the judicial decision, for example, has been used extensively over time should not be taken to mean that it has always been used in the same way. Thus, just as we have witnessed increased diversity in data sources, so we have seen greater sophistication in the way in which individual data sources have been utilized. As Schubert has noted of judicial decisions, for example, "Research in the fifties tended to extract from . . . case reports only codes of outcomes and of individual or group judicial voting; in the sixties much more attention was given to the content analysis of briefs and opinions associated with judicial decisions, and to coding variations in individual opinion (as distinguished from voting) behavior" (1972, 9).

In addition to focusing on trends in data sources, Hensley and Rhoads also characterized the methodologies that researchers were employing. If there was one particular methodology associated with the rise of behavioral research in judicial politics it would clearly be scalogram analysis. Indeed, "in the first half of the 1960s, it was used in 35 percent of all quantitative studies that were published in four major political science journals" (Tate 1983, 65). Hensley and Rhoads well document the decline in the use of Guttman scaling in the research they surveyed. Thus, while 27 percent of the articles used scalogram analysis during the decades of the 1960s, 18 percent of the studies used such a technique during the 1970s, and cumulative scaling was only used in 9 percent of the published studies during the 1980s. Similarly, less powerful bloc analytic techniques were used in 18 percent of the studies surveyed in the 1960s, 8 percent in the 1970s, and 7 percent in the 1980s (Hensley and Rhoads 1988). These findings suggest several possibilities. For one, they may reveal that the theoretical limitations of such techniques have given analysts some pause about using them. Further, and equally likely, more powerful and sophisticated methodologies are increasingly attracting researchers, and scholars are increasingly examining questions for which scalogram and bloc analyses may not be appropriate.

In focusing on data sources and research methods it has not been my intention to underemphasize the importance of constructing variables with validity, imagination, and sensitivity to the limitations of the data that we do have. As Tate has opined, "There is a regrettable tendency among social scientists to focus too much attention on statistical analysis, which often is or should be relatively straightforward, and too little on creating appropriate variables to submit to that analysis"

(1983, 65). As the scope of judicial politics research has expanded, the problem of variable construction may have been exacerbated. Thus, when our collective gaze tended to be focused almost exclusively on federal appellate courts, "fairly arbitrary decisions have become widely accepted as conventions, thus contributing to reproducibility. . . . Largely as a function of the expansion of judicial politics research to the study of trial courts, a significant amount of work today is characterized by much weakened ties to scientific epistemology, especially insofar as the key issue of reproducibility is concerned" (Gibson 1986, 144). Of equal importance, whatever the level of the judiciary being examined, while official records may contain a wealth of potential data for the analyst, they are not easily or automatically transformable to fit the needs of social science research. As Tate has aptly noted: "The data that may be derived from . . . records is complex and rarely self-representating. It almost always requires laborious coding (of votes, outcomes, policy or legal issues, etc.) by a sophisticated investigator before it is useful" (1983, 58).

One data problem that has historically plagued judicial politics scholarship has been the tendency for scholars to duplicate their efforts, often coding the same cases and the same or similar variables for different research efforts. Archiving of judicial politics data has lagged far behind the efforts made in other areas of American politics, most particularly voting behavior and legislative studies. Disparate projects utilizing different coding systems for different time periods have resulted in the judicial politics subfield, and the consequences have not been trivial. "At best, this means that at least some scholarly effort is wasted through unnecessary duplication. At worst, it means that the timeliness of the . . . data set suffers and that the discipline is subjected to idiosyncratic and non-comparable research" (Tate 1982, 25). This appears to be one problem area where movement in the right direction has perhaps been evident. Thus, for example, the Federal Judicial Center has recently made available, through the Inter-University Consortium for Political and Social Research at the University of Michigan, data for every federal district court case between 1969 and 1987 and every federal appellate court case between 1970 and 1987. Further, in recent years the National Science Foundation has proven to be quite receptive to prodigious efforts to generate data archives in the judicial politics domain. Thus we have witnessed (or soon shall) the creation of several highly articulated and painstakingly collected data sets, including the Civil Litigation Research Project Data Archive (Kritzer), the U.S. Supreme Court Judicial Data Base (Spaeth), and the U.S. Supreme Court Judicial Data Base: Phase II (Gibson). In addition, Songer has examined the possibility of establishing a Multi-User Data Base for the U.S. Court of Appeals (through an NSF grant) while, in recent years, Rowland and

Carp have developed an extensive data set for U.S. District Court decisions.

It must, of course, be recognized that the standardization of data inherent in the creation of massive data archives can be a double-edged sword. Analysts must be wary of taking a "codebook" approach to research that could impose rigidity and stifle creativity among scholars. The greatest value of the newly created data bases may lie in their contribution to reliability in research. They do not, of necessity, guarantee validity of measurement and thereby remove ultimate responsibility from the individual analyst. It should be underlined, however, that widespread access to massive data sets will, at a minimum, serve as useful tools for the training of graduate students in the research enterprise as well as an added research resource for those already laboring in our subfield.

The potential for the use of data archives is great, and perhaps in another decade we shall know what fruits they have borne. All told, the data sources and data generation methods available for judicial politics scholarship remain quite extensive. As Tate (1983) has copiously outlined, judicial politics analysts have available multiple existing written sources (including official published records, archives, docket books, and so on), the possibility of conducting survey research and interviews, content analysis, direct observation of some legal proceedings, simulation, experiments, and numerous other research techniques.

To this point I have focused on data and methods in judicial politics research without addressing the issue of theory in our subfield. In some respects this has been to put the cart before the horse. My approach, I fear, flows from the recognition that it has been data and methodology which have raised debate in the subfield, while a lesser focus has centered on judicial politics theory.

> When traditionally oriented public law scholars discuss judicial behavior, it is clear that they usually are thinking more of the use of quantitative methods to study courts and judges than of the theoretical propositions about individual and group political behavior that judicial behavior scholars have striven to develop. This is not entirely appropriate. Methodology should always be the servant of theory, not even its coequal, much less its master. (Tate 1983, 51)

Clearly, it goes without saying, political scientists in judicial politics should bring a theoretical orientation to their work in all areas where the state of our data and substantive understanding warrants it. As judicial politics scholars have expanded their gaze, the need for theoretically rich research has similarly expanded. As Murphy and Tanenhaus have noted, "The shortcomings of relying on description and anecdote when assessing a single court in a single country quickly multiply when one begins to discuss two or three levels of courts in five or more countries" (1972, 218).

Theoretical strands of many stripes have been prevalent in much judicial politics work through the years, clearly reflecting our eclectic roots. Indeed, if advanced graduate students in our subfield were given a sample list of theoretical approaches used in political science writ large (such as systems theory, small groups theory, role theory, dissonance theory, attitude theory, organizational theory, probability theory, game theory, group theory, and so on), they could undoubtedly recite numerous examples of research designs in our subfield that utilize an identifiable theoretical framework. As Gibson has noted:

> In the past three decades, palpable progress has been made in the development of theories of judicial politics. There is today a greater awareness of the need for and value of theoretical research, and prominent examples of highly developed theoretical areas can be found, as, for example, in research on judicial decision-making. The accumulation of theory in the last thirty years has been a slow process, but there have certainly been discernible advances. (1986, 146)

Thus, Hensley and Rhoads found that only 13 percent of the studies they analyzed in the 1960s had an explicit theoretical framework, whereas 30 percent of the published research in the 1970s and 1980s was theoretically oriented (1988).

In his own work, Gibson has argued that theory in our field has been "balkanized," with little effort being made to integrate different approaches within a comprehensive theory that is more complex than any one of its parts. Thus, regarding judicial decision-making (where a myriad of theoretical frameworks has been utilized), Gibson hypothesizes that "Judges' decisions are a function of what they prefer to do, tempered by what they think they ought to do, but constrained by what they perceive is feasible to do. Individuals make decisions, but they do so within the context of group, institutional, and environmental constraints. Thus, in order to understand decision-making, not only are multivariate models necessary, but the models must also be capable of incorporating effects operative at varying levels of analysis" (1983, 7). Obviously, in areas where it is warranted (such as judicial decision-making) such a wholistic approach can be most theoretically promising and powerful.

For his part, Gibson feels that theoretically guided efforts in the subfield have been wanting. There has been "an excessive reliance on description, to the detriment of hypothesis testing; an overreliance on induction as a means of developing theory; an aversion to theoretical complexity; a commitment to idiographic theory; and a lack of cross-level (macro-micro) theory" (1986, 146). He adds that, "as in so many areas of political science, much of existing theory is of suspicious generalization. This is not simply a limitation on extant empirical findings . . . but instead reflects rather weak commitment to the development of nomothetic theory. Judicial institutions and processes (especially at the lower court level) are too often perceived as in some unspecified sense unique, with differences among different court systems, the lower and appellate courts, and judicial and nonjudicial institutions being so great as to render them virtually noncomparable" (1986, 153).

Unfortunately, however, wishing for greater comparability may not make it so. Too often, I fear, courts are *not* simply courts—nor are they legislatures. Further, as O'Brien has argued, "The absence of major theoretical advances seems neither particularly remarkable nor disturbing given the inevitable pluralism and the complex, lengthy process of consensus building within any scientific community; and especially, within a subfield with roots in law, history, and philosophy and now increasingly drawing on the resources of other social sciences as well" (Stumpf et al. 1983, 563). Baum correctly notes that our explanations "generally remain fragmentary and imprecise" (1983, 202). He adds, however, that "some special characteristics of this field do retard the development of explanation. The breadth of the field means that in most areas relatively few scholars are doing research, and the continuing need for description draws the attention of some of those scholars. As a result, the efforts devoted to explanation of particular phenomena tend to be relatively limited" (1983, 202).

Thus, *a* theory of judicial politics does not appear to be on the horizon. There are many areas, however (such as judicial decision-making, agenda setting and docketing, impact and implementation, and so on), where theoretically oriented research can be expected and where such research should yield continued results. Hopefully, in the not too distant future, more areas of judicial politics research will reach a stage where they will benefit from added theoretical rigor. In addition, it is hoped that in areas where theoretically oriented models already exist they will undergo more conscious empirical testing than may currently be the case.

TRENDS IN JUDICIAL POLITICS RESEARCH

Any discussion of the substantive directions that research in a subfield is taking or commentary regarding where such research should be heading must, of necessity, be a highly subjective enterprise. Starting with the broadest brushstroke, one can readily agree with Murphy and Tanenhaus's contention in the early 1970s that research in the field has become more "cosmopolitan" in its outlook than during the 1960s

(1972, 216). Up until that time much of the doctrinal work that was done in judicial politics greatly resembled the work of legal academicians. While behaviorally oriented research pointed us back in the direction of work going on in other areas of political science, as Baum has aptly noted, new approaches in the subfield strengthened our interdisciplinary links and resulted in the emergence of numerous new research questions.

> A continued focus on judicial behavior in appellate courts would have limited interdisciplinary ties, because this is not a subject of central interest in other social sciences. When political scientists became more interested in subjects that were of central interest in other disciplines, particularly subjects related to civil litigation and criminal court processes, a basis for closer relationships was established. (1983, 196)

Unfortunately, and perhaps somewhat ironically, however, establishing closer relationships with other disciplines has not necessarily served to better integrate judicial politics research into the broader political science domain.

Historically, behavioral judicial politics research first focused on the United States Supreme Court, and most would likely argue that this unique institution remains the subfield's central concern. This does not mean, however, that scholars continue to address the question of Supreme Court voting behavior solely through the oversimplistic and reductionist ideological models associated with the 1960s, to the virtual exclusion of other concerns. Rather, added complexity has been brought to the study of judicial behavior, and one can sense increased attention being placed on ancillary facets of Supreme Court decisional processes and decisions on matters beyond the merits of cases, such as oral argument and opinion development. The process of Supreme Court litigation, including the role of interest groups and briefs, has clearly attracted increased scholarly attention as well. Thus, analyses of the Supreme Court cannot simply be characterized as old wine in new bottles. More to the point, however, it should be underscored that increased focus on trial courts has been an important theme in judicial politics research in recent years, and this area of inquiry will probably continue to blossom in the foreseeable future, reflecting both the dearth of knowledge about such courts and the relative degree of accessibility to them. It may indeed be the case, as Baum has argued, that "By far the most important move towards diversity in the field of judicial politics has been the growth of trial court research" (1983, 193).

Although a growth in trial court research was accurately predicted by Murphy and Tanenhaus in the early 1970s, their expectation that "accurate, detailed, and widespread dissemination of knowledge about the work of constitutional courts" would "generate more and more truly comparative research" has not been met (1972, 216). Tate has noted that even less ambitious and powerful single-country studies comparable to much work on American courts have not been widespread, and he attributes the problem to several causes.

> For one thing, data collection and/or generation is typically a much more difficult proposition in non-American research settings. More importantly, and less excusably, American judicial behavior scholars continue to be overwhelmingly U.S.-focused in their research designs, while non-American scholars either remain heavily traditional in their approaches to courts and judges and/or simply consider them to be politically irrelevant institutions and actors. (1983, 56)

In their survey of four political science journals, Hensley and Rhoads found only nine published studies of non-American courts (out of 330 articles) between 1960 and 1987. Four of these studies were published during the 1960s (1988, 18–19).

It is commonplace for "state of the art" surveys in political science to issue calls for more truly comparative work, and certainly scholars who pursue such research warrant our commendation. Our collective substantive competence for comparative work, however, is quite limited and, given how much remains to occupy the attention of judicial politics scholars in the American context, the impetus for comparative work must come from comparativists before such research becomes a priority for our subfield.

A host of questions that engage judicial politics scholars have clearly emerged from a broadened "law and society" focus during the 1970s and 1980s, and often such research takes the analyst away from the domain of courts and judges: "Political scientists used to see themselves as students of courts. They must now begin to see themselves as students of the whole continuum of triadic dispute processing running from go-between to mediator to arbitrator to judge and including many bargaining and less than fully adversary proceedings" (Shapiro, in Stumpf et al. 1983, 546). As part of the added emphasis that judicial politics scholars are placing on alternative forms of dispute resolution, much needed attention will be focused on potential litigants and the choices they make. As Sarat has noted, scholars have begun "to explore the pre-history of litigation. . . . What is at stake is an understanding of the social processes through which grievances are acknowledged and claims of right emerge. . . . Litigation is but one response to a situation of trouble and conflict. We should . . . acknowledge that litigation is but one type of a larger category of social behavior, what might be called individuated claims for redress engaged by the experience of injustice. In order to understand litigation . . . we must examine the reasons and

situations in which individuals or groups . . . choose one or another
mode of response" (Stumpf et al. 1983, 555). In viewing resort to judicial processes as, perhaps, the result of many prior events and individual
choices warranting our study, Sarat has clearly and appropriately broadened the judicial politics scholar's field of inquiry. It is important, however, that we remain sensitive to the role of governmental actors in
initiating litigation, and focus on the litigation strategies of these players remains an important research concern as well.

Naturally, every scholar's "wish list" of the direction in which he or
she would like to see the field move in its collective research agenda may
be highly personalized and idiosyncratic. We have touched upon the
trial court interests and broad law and society concerns that are engaging many scholars. One can point to numerous other concerns, however, where many scholars in our field would agree that more work is
needed and likely to occur.

One broad area necessitating increased inquiry concerns the relationship between judicial policy-making and numerous environmental
factors that touch upon the judiciary's operation. A prime topic for additional research remains the relationship between courts and public
opinion. Existing research has tended to view this issue on a grand scale
in an effort to assess the judiciary's role in assuring regime legitimacy.
Clearly, such questions are important ones, but they may be asked at
too high a level of abstraction or sophistication to tap into the true level
of public feelings toward the Court. Considerably more effort must be
devoted to gleaning the more mundane descriptive knowledge of the
courts held by the citizenry. Can the public actually name the Supreme
Court justices? Do they know the basics of judicial selection processes?
Are they aware of the term of judicial office? Do they know anything
about the Court's jurisdiction? Much of the information the public has
on questions such as these is derived from the media. Here again we find
a considerable research vacuum. What can we expect the public to
"know" based on the information at its disposal? How do newspapers
and television cover the Court? Are majority opinions cited? Dissents?
Are justices' names given? How likely is a Supreme Court case to be
reported? Questions such as these have primarily engaged journalists,
and much is to be learned by political scientists seeking to link public
knowledge of the judiciary to the nature of the media coverage it receives.

Another area that continues to warrant additional study includes
various facets of lower court decisional processes and a focus upon the
relationships among lower courts. In the federal district courts the realities of the judicial process call for added attention to the role of U.S.
magistrates. As in the past, judicial selection concerns will remain a focus of much inquiry; yet perhaps because of the current actuarial state of

the Court, greater efforts are being made toward empirical analysis of Supreme Court recruitment. For the policy-minded student of judicial politics, questions of judicial impact and implementation remain areas where theoretically oriented work holds much promise.

If pressed to make one summary generalization about what I see as the major current trend in the subfield, I must say it is ironic (and, I think, disappointing to many) that, above all else, we may be heading back in the direction from which we came—toward doctrinal analyses with normative roots in the concerns of democratic theory. Talk of a "counterrevolution," however, may overstate the case. For one thing, doctrinal analysis has never really left the subfield, and some scholars have foreseen its renewed vigor. Indeed, Murphy and Tanenhaus wrote over a decade and a half ago that, "although development is less certain here than in other areas, political science is approaching a renaissance of serious work in normative . . . jurisprudence" (1972, 223). More recently, Baum has taken note of "the resurgence of an interest in judicial outputs and normative questions" (1983, 190). Most broadly, Pritchett has opined that, "A primary task for public law since 1948 . . . has been development of a theory of democratic government and judicial review, and a corresponding frame of reference for research, which would accommodate the participation of an activist court in the making of public policy" (1968, 488).

Clearly, such questions have engaged legal academicians for a long time, and such work has proliferated in the wake of Harlan Stone's famous Footnote Four in the Carolene Products case and the extraordinary controversies surrounding Supreme Court rulings such as *Brown v. Board of Education* (1954) and *Roe v. Wade* (1973). While many of us, however, have read the work of Ely, Perry, Choper, Tribe, and many others on these questions, there is a sense in which they all, I think, tend to strike us as *politically* naive, thereby necessitating the judicial politics scholar's perspective. Further, two events in recent years have, I think, served to strengthen the impetus in judicial politics for more "traditional" work. These are the bicentennial of our constitution's framing (when traditional writing, sometimes under the guiding hand of Project '87, became more acceptable and, indeed, more "fashionable") and the entire scenario surrounding Robert Bork's aborted Supreme Court candidacy, when the entire country was engaged in a seminar on constitutional law and the stakes seemed to be so high.

Movement in the normative directions outlined above clearly engenders controversy. One naysayer is Helm. "The task of empirical political science is explanation not advocacy and, as a consequence, normative questions of judicial review in a democratic society are best reserved for the political theorist or philosopher" (1987, 6). Shapiro points us in the same dubious direction:

[F]or better or worse the kind of old-fashioned con law . . . is, thanks to the new emergence of the jurisprudence of values, no longer old-fashioned. An increasing proportion of the political jurisprudence of the eighties will be more normative than positive. While fully acknowledging that courts are part of the political process, this work will be less concerned with the process than with the doctrinal outcomes which it will treat as a declaration of public values that must survive ethical scrutiny. The danger is, of course, that much of the work will contain no distinctive political analysis—that the new jurisprudence of values will serve as a cover for slipping back into playing "little law professor" for undergraduates, writing conventional case law doctrinal analyses of the same sort that the less bright academic lawyers do and engaging in seat-of-the-pants social judgements. (Stumpf et al. 1983, 543)

The potential consequences of such movement within our subfield could be striking, and again, Shapiro warrants citation at some length.

I do not know the cure for this problem. . . . If political scientists now move to the style of doctrine cum values analysis always common among lawyers, the challenge will be to define some distinctive and useful role for political scientists engaged in the study of law. Political scientists were experts at process. They are not experts at values. The eighties may be a period in which the lawyers win again. They have absorbed the political science they needed to know. The jurisprudence of values will turn law toward moral philosophy. And political scientists are even less well equipped to do moral philosophy than are lawyers. . . . One thought that I resist because I believe strongly in the need for empirical work in this area is the following: The jurisprudence of values is . . . really a branch of normative political philosophy. A certain kind of political scientist is expert at normative political philosophy. Thus we might expect that . . . the old ties between "political theory" and "public law" will be reestablished, political scientists trained in the empirically oriented "American politics" field will be shoved to the edges of "public law," and political jurisprudence will be converted to "legal and political theory." (Stumpf et al. 1983, 543–44)

Clearly, if the problems posed by Shapiro are to be avoided, the doctrinally focused work in our subfield must offer a unique social science orientation. Thus, for example, research utilizing a technique such as content analysis could lend a new and useful perspective to the more traditional doctrinal work associated with legal academicians.

The potential for increased isolation of the judicial politics subfield within political science is a real one, and it stems both from the interdisciplinary interests of judicial politics scholars underlined throughout my comments and from the normative trend discussed above. Throughout this essay I have taken note of the findings of Hensley and Rhoads regarding publication of judicial politics research in four major general journals of political science. It is instructive to note that only 6.7 percent of the articles published in the journals under analysis between 1960 and 1987 qualified for inclusion. There has been little variation in the publication rate over time, and a lesser tendency for judicial politics research to see print in what are, arguably, the two most prestigious general journals: *The American Political Science Review* (4.3 percent of its articles) and *The American Journal of Political Science* (6 percent of its articles). By way of contrast, 7.5 percent of the articles in the *Western Political Quarterly* and 9.1 percent in the *Journal of Politics* qualified for inclusion in the Hensley and Rhoads study (1988, 10–12).

Although we have grown more eclectic and diverse, this has not necessarily served us well within our own discipline. As Baum perceptively noted: "In the 1970s and early 1980s political science journals reflected little of the expertise of the judicial politics field, concentrating instead on areas of traditional interest and those relatively close to the mainstream of American political research. . . . This pattern of publication has had an interesting and rather important effect: political scientists are increasingly likely to be unaware of the state of the judicial politics field on the basis of their reading of the discipline's own journals" (1983, 200). Hensley and Rhoads substantiate this point. Indeed, they find that of the 417 articles cited by two contemporary judicial politics texts (authored by Glick and Stumpf), only 67 (16 percent) were articles identified in their survey of political science journals (1988, 25).

Data collected by Karen O'Connor shed further light on the relationship between judicial politics research and political science journals. Thus, for example, in the 1987–88 fiscal year of eighteen judicial politics manuscripts submitted to the *American Political Science Review*, two (both focusing on the Supreme Court) were accepted for publication. Six submitted manuscripts (33.3 percent) focused on some facet of constitutional law. While the numbers are obviously quite limited, it should be noted that in 1988 six judicial politics manuscripts were submitted to the *American Journal of Political Science*, with four rejected, one accepted, and one remaining under consideration. During 1988, the *Journal of Politics* accepted 8.3 percent of the judicial politics submissions as compared to an overall acceptance rate of 23.7 percent in American Politics. Writ large, the data collected by O'Connor, as well as that examined by Hensley and Rhoads, demonstrate that we do not publish a great deal in political science journals, nor do we submit a great many manuscripts to such journals. Indeed, any political scientist interested in seeing what judicial politics scholars are "doing" would be best advised to consult a large number of journals outside of our discipline. These would include, among others, numerous publications of the American Bar Association and the American Bar Foundation, *Judicature, Jurimetrics Journal, Justice System Journal, Law and Society Review, Law and Policy Quarterly, Supreme Court Review*, and a number of law journals that have a social science orientation.

Of additional interest, I have compiled a gross rendering of what judicial politics scholarship has "looked like" through the eyeglasses of the topics covered on APSA convention panels since 1980. While my categorization of panel topics summarized in table 3.1 would make a first-year graduate student cringe in horror, the broad brushstrokes revealed there are instructive. If one can overlook the overlapping categories and the mixture of concerns identified as "topics," a number of interesting observations can be made. Foremost is the dominance of traditional doctrinal studies, even when the "banner year" of 1987 is discounted. Note, in a similar vein, the recent interest in the topics of democratic theory and judicial review. Policy analyses of some persuasion more than hold their own, and a surprising number of panels have a comparative orientation.

An aggregate view of the convention proposals submitted to Karen O'Connor for the 1989 APSA meetings is also illustrative. Of the 62 proposals received, 17 were doctrinally focused, 36 were process-oriented (broadly defined), and only 9 could be characterized as judicial behavior or decision-making. Perhaps most telling, another look at the proposals reveals that 41 utilized traditional constitutional interpretation or case-study methodologies. Only 19 proposals appear to have been quantitative in their orientation. Finally, of the 62 paper proposals submitted, the majority (36) were submitted by graduate students and assistant professors.

As another crude indicator of our subfield's direction, I have examined and attempted to categorize the dissertations completed in judicial politics between 1980 and 1987 as annually compiled by *Political Science*. The results of my coding are found in table 3.2.

Once again, the data is illustrative and should be taken with a full measure of salt. Nevertheless, the predominance of two concerns among our subfield's young is quite evident. Dissertations prevailingly focus on doctrinal concerns or on some facet of criminal justice. In the first instance, the approach is likely to be traditional; in the second, interdisciplinary. Neither focus, it seems to me, is likely to be welcomed warmly by the discipline as a whole.

JUDICIAL POLITICS AND POLITICAL SCIENCE

Scholars in the field of judicial politics have, as we have seen, cast a wide net over the multitude of concerns related to the place of law in the political system. If, as Shapiro has noted, "the orthodoxy of the profes-

Table 3.1
APSA Judicial Politics Panels (1980–1989)

Topic Area	1980	1981	1982	1983	1984	1985	1986	1987	1988	1989	Totals
Doctrinal/Legal language	2	4	1	1	3	3	4	10	5	5	38
Democratic theory/Judicial review	0	1	0	0	1	1	0	3	3	0	9
Criminal justice	1	0	0	1	1	0	1	0	0	1	5
Trial courts	0	1	0	0	0	0	0	0	0	0	1
State courts	0	0	0	1	0	1	3	1	0	1	7
Lower federal courts	0	1	0	0	0	0	0	0	0	0	1
Special federal courts	0	0	0	0	0	0	0	0	0	0	0
Appellate courts	0	0	0	0	0	0	1	0	0	0	1
Supreme Court: Decision-Making/Behavior	0	0	0	1	1	1	0	1	0	0	4
Supreme Court: Leadership, Small group, Biography	1	0	0	0	1	1	2	0	0	1	6
Judicial process	1	1	0	1	0	1	0	1	1	2	8
"Uncourt" legal issues	0	0	0	0	0	1	1	0	0	1	3
Court-Congress	0	0	1	1	0	0	0	0	0	0	2
Court-Public opinion	0	0	0	0	0	1	1	1	0	0	3
Judicial selection	0	0	0	0	0	0	0	0	1	0	1
Judicial policy: Impact and implementation	2	1	1	2	3	1	0	1	3	1	15
Theory/Data/Methods	0	0	1	1	0	1	1	1	1	1	7
Administrative law	0	0	0	0	0	0	0	0	1	0	1
Judicial administration	0	0	0	0	0	0	1	0	0	0	1
Comparative judicial politics	1	2	1	0	1	1	0	2	1	0	9
Public service panels	0	0	1	0	0	0	0	1	1	0	3
Uncoded	0	0	3	0	0	1	1	1	2	2	10

Table 3.2
Dissertations Completed In Judicial Politics (1980–1987)

Topic Area	1980	1981	1982	1983	1984	1985	1986	1987	Totals
Doctrinal/Legal language	3	7	2	3	2	3	2	5	27
Democratic theory/Judicial review	0	2	1	1	1	2	0	1	8
Criminal justice	0	9	5	1	2	1	2	2	22
Trial courts	0	1	0	2	0	0	0	1	4
State courts	2	0	0	1	0	0	0	3	6
Lower federal courts	1	0	1	0	0	1	1	1	5
Special federal courts	1	0	0	0	0	0	0	0	1
Appellate courts	0	0	0	0	0	0	0	0	0
Supreme Court: Decision-making/Behavior	0	0	3	1	3	0	1	0	8
Supreme Court: Leadership, Small group, Biography	1	0	0	0	0	0	1	3	5
Judicial process	0	1	0	1	1	0	2	1	6
"Uncourt" legal issues	1	1	0	0	0	0	0	0	2
Court-Congress	0	0	0	0	1	0	0	0	1
Court-Public opinion	0	0	1	0	1	0	1	0	3
Judicial selection	0	0	1	0	1	0	0	2	4
Judicial policy: Impact and Implementation	0	1	1	1	2	0	1	1	7
Theory/Data/Methods	0	0	0	0	0	0	0	0	0
Administrative law	0	0	0	1	0	0	0	0	1
Judicial administration	1	0	0	0	0	0	0	0	1
Comparative judicial politics	0	2	0	0	0	0	0	1	3
Public service	0	0	0	0	0	0	0	0	0
Uncoded	0	1	1	1	0	0	0	0	3

sion today is . . . that the political scientist is primarily concerned with the authoritative allocation of values" (Shapiro 1972, 412), then there is great reason for political science, as a discipline, to be concerned about work in judicial politics. Thus, "it is almost impossible to discover any body of law that does not authoritatively allocate values. . . . [N]early all law is an instrument of value allocation (Shapiro 1972, 412). Somewhat paradoxically, however, much of what judicial politics scholars have studied may be viewed as inappropriate by the broader discipline since, at least on the surface, private law concerns might be involved. For example, "as long as the judges were making the law protecting consumers, no political scientist was allowed to study it, because it was private law they were making; but as soon as the legislature passes statutes requiring the manufacturer to build in greater consumer protection, then political scientists could study them because these are public laws and 'government regulations of business.' The ultimate paradox is that once the statute is passed, the judicial specialist could study court decisions interpreting the statute because those are public law decisions. . . . [T]he judicial specialist requires a legislative intervention to allow him to study courts" (Shapiro 1972, 413).

Such concerns about boundaries are, of course, bogus. Our legitimate domain is appropriately wide, and when "we admit that political science is the study of public policy then the public in public law automatically disappears" (Shapiro 1972, 413). Helm is indeed on target when he asserts that our subfield's group boundaries are "only moderately strong," that we identify ourselves clearly as social scientists, and that we are "almost passionately committed to interdisciplinary research" (1988, 11). We utilize numerous methodologies and call upon the skills of a myriad of disciplines. We are "egalitarian and individualistic in terms of research agendas and substantive findings." We "study everything related to the law—so long as the appropriate methodology and standards of relevant research are applied" (Helm 1987, 29). The three trends identified by Baum and alluded to throughout this essay (our diversity, interdisciplinary interests, and normative concern about judicial outputs) have, collectively, limited our subfield's integration into the field of American politics and, more generally, the broader political science discipline (Baum 1983, 199). Our eclecticism is further revealed in our own collective insecurities and is "also manifest in the need to clarify, explain, and justify the enterprise so frequently" (Helm 1987, 11).

Clearly, we are less constrained in what we do than we were two decades ago, more willing to talk to people beyond ourselves than we ever have been, and more committed than ever before to talking in terms that people who are not certified political scientists can understand. As noted at the outset, the coexistence of a parallel profession has tended to exacerbate our communicative failings. "[P]olitical scientists do not do . . . well if they are trying to communicate with lawyers, law professors, judges, and others outside their own garden. What profiteth a man, if he writes the most profound truth in a new language, and then finds that neither the King nor any adviser to the King will learn the new language?" (Dixon 1971, 21). Our diversity of publication outlets beyond the journals examined by Hensley and Rhoads (1988) and the continuing interdisciplinary focus in our work both suggest that we are doing considerably better on this score than at the time Dixon wrote. Perhaps the one interface where we need to build stronger interdisciplinary bridges remains the law schools themselves, where joint teaching and research could productively coalesce. The barriers and mutual suspicions here are real, however, and much mutual commitment will be needed. It is instructive, however, to note that legal academicians may be, in fact, a valid reference group for us.

> For someone trained in a great middle-western university at the start of the 1970s it surely comes as a surprise to find . . . that it is indeed appropriate to measure the significance and stature of work . . . by its reception in law schools. . . . (W)hat we did was neither understood nor appreciated by them. We, after all, aspired to a scientific study of legal phenomena, they were merely technicians. As a graduate student I was given the sense that the true measure of my work would be its reception by political scientists in Ann Arbor, Michigan, not academic lawyers in New Haven. Perhaps it is because we have failed as scientists or maybe because we have matured as scholars that we can take some pride in having educated them, who, for so long, denied the significance of us. (Sarat, in Stumpf et al. 1983, 512–13)

While the educational process that Sarat alludes to may not have proceeded as far as he thinks, the enterprise is clearly a worthy one and, I think, more professionally "acceptable" than in the past.

In looking to the law schools as potential audiences, colleagues, and collaborators, we have come, in a sense, full circle to the starting gate where "public lawyers" were viewed with some degree of suspicion. We were told as graduate students that our audience were political scientists and that there were problems we would face.

> First was the identification of . . . "public law" with traditional, doctrinal, constitutional law. When the scientists of our discipline thought of what we did, they thought of constitutional law. We were for them the fake lawyers who serviced a traditional, some surely felt marginal, concern of political science, and who taught large undergraduate courses to students more interested in law school than social science theory. Our second problem was precisely that we were not lawyers, that there were other academics who, because they had degrees in law, somehow seemed to have a more legitimate claim to the

intellectual terrain of legal analysis. (Sarat, in Stumpf et al. 1983, 551–52)

As Sarat recognizes, these problems were, and in some respects still are, "real" ones, although "the pretensions are . . . significantly diminished" (Sarat, in Stumpf et al. 1983, 551–52). We have learned, I think, that there is, at bottom, little for which we have to apologize. Sarat develops the point quite well.

> Political scientists who study law are, in the aggregate, about as scientific as other political scientists: yet leaving the pretense of science behind has opened and enriched our study. Historical, doctrinal, descriptive, institutional, normative approaches all seem relevant. Indeed, one can hardly imagine good graduate training today that ignored any approach. This pluralism combined with the proliferation of objects of study means that we have more to say about a considerably broader range of legal subject matters than we did ten years ago. Pluralism . . . has, in the case of political jurisprudence, had an enriching effect. (Sarat, in Stumpf et al. 1983, 552)

We are less concerned and preoccupied with methodological battles for their own sake than we were two decades ago, and we have continued to identify interesting questions that appeal to traditionalists, have implications for substantive case law, and can be examined in empirical ways. Graduate students and junior colleagues have received the various wisdoms of many schools of thought from faculties where once-strong battle lines have somewhat dispersed. We have, I think, been concerned for too long with what political science, as a whole, thinks about us. We have, I think, reached a stage where we can begin to feel comfortable with ourselves. If we in judicial politics can accomplish that, the discipline of political science will surely follow our example.

NOTES

1. It should be noted at the outset that a mark of our schizophrenia may, in fact, be our collective inability to reach a consensus on whether or not we are indeed distinct. This issue, in fact, raised the greatest amount of discussion and controversy when this paper was originally presented. One commentator, Charles Johnson, took issue with the importance I placed on our coexistence with the parallel profession of legal academicians. He correctly pointed out that international relations scholars coexist with diplomats, political theorists with philosophers, students of public administration with bureaucrats, and so on. The reader can be the judge of whether such parallel worlds to other subfields have the same implications as those discussed below have to ours. In a similar vein, Karen O'Connor suggested that perhaps the road to our subfield's integration with the broader discipline would be through our demonstrating that we

"do," in fact, much the same thing as other political scientists. For example, our concerns and concepts focus on issues such as the recruitment and selection process for institutional actors, decision-making and conversion processes, leadership and collegial behavior, implementation and impact, and so on. It should be pointed out, however, as Micheal Giles did from the panel audience, that one domain in which we are clearly "different" is our analysis of legal doctrine. One could not imagine, for example, a legislative scholar viewing the "logic" of a legislative text. In addition, many of the issues that we examine (such as criminal justice) could easily lead colleagues outside of our field to ask, "What does this have to do with politics?"

REFERENCES

Baum, Lawrence. 1983. "Judicial Politics: Still a Distinctive Field." In *Political Science: The State of the Discipline*, ed. Ada W. Finiter. Washington, D.C.: American Political Science Association.

Becker, Theodore L. 1970. "Judicial Theory." In *Approaches to the Study of Political Science*, ed. Michael Haas and Henry S. Kariel. Scranton, Pa.: Chandler Publishing.

Dixon, Robert G. 1971. "Who Is Listening? Political Science Research in Public Law." *PS* 4:19–26.

Gibson, James L. 1983. "From Simplicity to Complexity: The Development of Theory in the Study of Judicial Behavior." *Political Behavior* 5:7–49.

———. 1986. "The Social Science of Judicial Politics." In *Political Science: The Science of Politics*, ed. Herbert W. Weisberg. New York: Agathon Press.

Grossman, Joel B., and Joseph Tanenhaus. 1969. "Toward a Renaissance of Public Law." In *Frontiers of Judicial Research*, ed. Joel B. Grossman and Joseph Tanenhaus. New York: Wiley.

Helm, Charles. 1987. "The Problem of Judicial Review and Judicial Activism: Disciplinary Boundaries and the 'Rule of Law.'" Paper presented at the annual meeting of the American Political Science Association, Chicago.

Hensley, Thomas R., and James C. Rhoads. 1988. "Studying the Studies: An Assessment of Judicial Politics Research in Four Major Political Science Journals, 1960–1987." Paper presented at the annual meeting of the Southern Political Science Association, Atlanta.

Murphy, Walter F., and Joseph Tanenhaus. 1972. *The Study of Public Law*. New York: Random House.

Peltason, Jack W. 1955. *Federal Courts in the Political Process*. New York: Random House.

Pritchett, C. Herman. 1948. *The Roosevelt Court*. New York: Macmillan.

———. 1968. "Public Law and Judicial Behavior." *Journal of Politics* 30: 408–509.

————. 1969. "The Development of Judicial Research." In *Frontiers of Judicial Research*, ed. Joel B. Grossman and Joseph Tanenhaus. New York: Wiley.

Schubert, Glendon. 1965. *The Judicial Mind*. Evanston, Ill.: Northwestern University Press.

————. 1972. "Judicial Process and Behavior during the Sixties." *PS* 5:6–15.

Shapiro, Martin. 1972. "From Public Law to Public Policy or the 'Public' in Public Law." *PS* 5:410–18.

Stumpf, Harry P., and Martin Shapiro, David J. Danelski, Austin Sarat, and David M. O'Brien. 1983. "Whither Political Jurisprudence: A Symposium." *Western Political Quarterly* 36:533–69.

Tate, C. Neal. 1982. "The Development of the Methodology of Judicial Behavior Research: A Historical Review and Critique of the Use and Teaching of Methods." Paper presented at the annual meeting of the American Political Science Association, Denver.

————. 1983. "The Methodology of Judicial Behavior Research: A Review and Critique." *Political Behavior* 5:51–82.

Vines, Kenneth N. 1970. "Judicial Behavior Research." In *Approaches to the Study of Political Science*, ed. Michael Haas and Henry S. Kariel. Scranton, Pa.: Chandler Publishing.

4

Interest Groups: A Subfield in Search of an Identity

Allan J. Cigler

The nature and role of organized political interests have been core concerns of observers of the American polity, from Madison through Tocqueville to George Will. Political scientists have been among these observers, and interest groups have been a central focus in scholarly work on representation and interpretations of political behavior and policy-making. Some of the discipline's most broadly influential works have had interest groups as their focus (Bentley 1908; Truman 1951; Lowi 1969; Dahl 1961).

Yet as a subfield within the discipline of political science, interest group politics is often considered "undertilled," with a perceived gap between the presumed importance of the subject and the quantity and quality of research upon which firm generalizations can be based (Arnold 1982). Generalization is often based upon scanty evidence from narrow case studies or historical examples, rather than upon large, systematically collected data sets, which presents a problem for a field that commands a healthy respect for complexity and offers tentative answers to difficult questions.

There are a number of explanations for the paucity of interest group research. Like the public at large, political scientists have often viewed interest groups with ambivalence, recognizing their inevitability but uncomfortable with their impact. One consequence may be that scholars interested in political organizations have been drawn to the study of

I would like to thank Paul Johnson, Burdett Loomis, Larry Rothenberg, Robert Salisbury, and John Wright for their helpful criticisms and other suggestions.

99

political parties rather than interest groups. In part this derives from their fascination with and commitment to the functions of parties to aggregate and articulate broad interests, in contrast to the narrow, selfish, and predominantly upper-class concerns of most interest groups (Leon Epstein 1983; Walker 1983a).

The difficulty and expense of doing systematic empirical field research on interest groups have also discouraged scholarly inquiry. Unlike research fields such as elections or legislative behavior, which receive "large automatic subsidies that defray most research costs" (Arnold 1982, 101), those who would study interest groups, until quite recently, have not had easily accessible data sets comparable to election statistics, census statistics, or roll-call votes. Interest group researchers often must travel at their own expense (usually to the nation's capital) to engage in projects involving personal interviewing and extended periods of observation (Arnold 1982). Research is often made difficult because interest groups and associations are semiprivate or private entities sensitive about their visibility, and because access to the main actors is by no means assured. The "hard" data that do exist in the interest group area are often nominal or ordinal in scale and hold little attraction for a generation of scholars looking to apply advanced data analysis techniques. Unlike some other subfields in American politics, the behavioral revolution did not swell the ranks of political scientists studying interest groups.

Nevertheless, research in the interest group area has increased markedly in recent years, and in this essay I shall concentrate on developments in the interest group subfield since the mid-1970s, when several comprehensive reviews were presented (Greenstone 1975; Salisbury 1975; Garson 1978). My sense is that the mid- to late 1970s marked a major shift in focus and direction in the study of interest group politics, not so much in terms of the questions asked, but in the nature of the theory and evidence that have been brought to bear on the subject matter. In recent years interest group theory has been substantially refined, and a growing number of empirical studies have given us new insights into the contemporary group universe. The group politics data base, which had previously limited research, has expanded, and new opportunities for interest group research have arisen. In addition, various analytical techniques, such as probit and logit regression, have been developed that encourage the multivariate analysis of interest group data, and a number of methodologically sophisticated researchers have been attracted to the enterprise.

Although "the empirical phenomena which fall within the scope of a concern with organized interest groups are of huge proportions" (Salisbury 1975, 176), it seems appropriate to separate the subject matter broadly into concerns of demand aggregation and group impact. The demand aggregation literature focuses on questions of the scope and representativeness of the group universe, how political groups organize, attract, and retain members, and the internal workings of political interest groups. It is in the demand aggregation area that interest group theory is most developed. The group impact literature focuses on the role and tactics of groups in the political influence process, both in terms of electing candidates and formulating public policy.

DEMAND AGGREGATION RESEARCH

A Portrait of the Contemporary Interest Group Universe

The nature and scope of the interest group universe, and the possibility of representative bias, have long been of interest to political scientists and appear to have drawn attention in direct proportion to concern that the government was not functioning well. For example, in the immediate post–World War II era, when the nation appeared to have a strong domestic economy and a hegemonic foreign-policy influence in the world, pluralism was the dominant view among students of interest groups (Truman 1951; Latham 1952). Groups were viewed as nonthreatening, self-correcting, and making positive contributions to the workings of democracy. Politics was conceived largely as the resolution of conflict among contending groups, and the political process was depicted as reasonably "representative," in that interests would virtually arise automatically to protect themselves when threatened.

The turbulence of the 1960s, coupled with greatly expanded government activity, proved to be the catalyst for renewed attention to interest groups. A number of authors focused on the distorted policy outcomes of "interest group liberalism" (Lowi 1969) and on obvious biases of the interest group universe (Schattschneider 1960; Olson 1965). The implication was that the public interest may not be well served by unrestrained group competition.

Concern over the role of special interests accelerated in the 1970s and continued into the 1980s, particularly in the popular press. The tremendous expansion of the group universe, both in numbers and in scope, the decline of political parties as aggregators of mass interests, and the heightened visibility of groups in the policy and electoral processes, appeared to parallel the diminished capacity of the government to deal with economic and social problems. Some political scientists came to see special interest groups as lying at the heart of the problem of contemporary governance: specifically, "how to formulate solutions for complex policy questions in an environment characterized by numerous diverse interests—many passionately expressed—yet with few means to aggregate them" (Cigler 1985, 319).

It was not until early in the 1980s that a number of empirically based studies appeared to paint a detailed picture of the new group universe and how it had changed since the early 1960s. A mail survey, conducted in 1980–81, of voluntary associations listed in the *Washington Information Directory* (business and labor organizations were excluded), open to membership, and interested in national public policy, found that there had indeed been a proliferation of political groups on the Washington scene since 1945, a trend that had accelerated since 1960 (Walker 1983b). Particularly impressive was the growth in the number of nonoccupational groups. Although almost 80 percent of the groups in the survey were occupationally based, 20 percent were citizens' groups, open to membership without special occupational qualifications. Half of the citizens' groups in the survey had been formed since the 1960s, 30 percent since 1975, and the citizen group category had grown at double the rate of the occupational group category. Other research has documented the great growth in the number of citizen and public interest groups, particularly in the 1970s (Berry 1977; McFarland 1976), as well as the growth of citizen involvement in such organizations (Michell 1979). While the group growth rate has probably leveled off in the 1980s, a study conducted in 1985 suggests that "the system still seems to be expanding briskly" (Peterson and Walker 1986, 165).

The growth in the number of membership groups in recent decades, while impressive, may not be the most important feature of the new group universe. Particularly striking has been the expansion of political activity of individual corporations (Vogel 1978; Ryan, Swanson, and Bucholz 1987; G. Wilson 1981, 1986; Humphries 1988). Corporations and business organizations now lobby through more than interest-wide coalitions or peak associations, such as the National Association of Manufacturers or the American Petroleum Institute. The number of individual corporations with Washington offices had increased over tenfold between 1961 and 1982 (Colgate 1982), and companies increasingly send their own corporate officials to lobby in Washington or hire professional lobbyists to represent their interests.

The last few decades have also witnessed the increasing involvement of other institutions in Washington political activity; these represent both the profit and nonprofit sectors and include churches, state and local governments, hospitals, foundations, think tanks, public interest law firms, and universities (Salisbury 1984). A large number of factors underlie the great proliferation of interests in the recent decades (Berry 1988; Salisbury 1984; Loomis and Cigler 1986), but particularly important has been the expansion of government activity in virtually all aspects of business, cultural, and social life.

These trends in special-interest representation have led some political scientists to wonder whether or not the term "interest groups" is really the proper one to reflect the subfield's concerns. To capture the essence of today's special interest process in Washington one must focus on all "organized interests," not simply membership organizations (Schlozman 1984; Schlozman and Tierney 1986; Salisbury 1983; Salisbury 1984).

Using such a broad organized interest perspective, Kay Schlozman and John Tierney (1986) examined the general background of nearly 7,000 organizations listed in *Washington Representatives—1981* that had a Washington office or retained Washington counsel or hired representatives, and they surveyed an additional 175 of the organizations in some depth. Their findings essentially confirm those of Walker in terms of the proliferation of voluntary associations since 1960, but they offer additional insights into our understanding of the influencing process in the nation's capital and of bias in the representative system.

They find that the number of groups representing broad public interests and the disadvantaged in society has increased in recent decades, with well over half of such organizations having been founded since 1970. But the most distinctive growth in Washington representation is evident in the case of business. Over 45 percent of all organizations having a Washington presence are corporations, compared to less than 5 percent representing public interest and disadvantaged interests. Although baseline comparisons to 1960 are difficult to draw, it appears that the proportion of public interest groups among interests represented in Washington has actually declined. Public interest organizations also appear less stable than other types of organized interests, in that only one-third of such groups listed in 1960 were still active in 1981. The public interest group growth was concentrated in the consumer and environmental areas. Labor representation was one instance in which a sector did not produce growth in terms of absolute representation. Overall, the findings suggest that, in spite of the proliferation of interests in recent decades, including in the public interest and disadvantage sectors, "the pressure system is tilted heavily in favor of the well-off, especially business" (Schlozman 1984, 1029).

An ongoing research project at the state level, involving over seventy political scientists studying each of the fifty states, suggests that the great proliferation of interests active in Washington mirrors activity in the nation's state capitals (Hrebenar and Thomas 1987). While the public interest and occupational representation sectors have grown markedly at the state level, so too has the expansion of political activity by individual corporations and institutions, particularly cities and localities. The growth of local political groups has rapidly expanded during the past quarter of a century as well, especially among elements of society previously not represented organizationally (Langton 1978; Knoke and Wood 1981; Schumaker, Cigler, and Faye 1989).

The increasing acceptance of "organized interests" as the proper subject matter for interest group scholars has implications for future research. Social movements (usually studied by sociologists) and corporations (usually studied by economists) could well become important subjects of political scientist concern, as could "institutionalized" personalities such as Ralph Nader, Jeremy Ripkin of the Foundation on Economic Trends, or Arthur Simon of Bread for the World. And institutions, be they private-sector hospitals or public-sector universities, are fundamentally different representative entities than membership groups, since they do not necessarily speak for their employees or need to consult with them (Salisbury 1984); these large entities pose new challenges for researchers attempting to understand their role in the representation process.

The traditional membership group, relying upon mass contributions and face-to-face interactions among members, appears to be the exception rather than the rule among contemporary groups (Hayes 1986). Many groups have no members at all; others rely on "checkbook participation" or funding from outside sources and are essentially "staff" organizations. This is particularly true in the public interest sector (Berry 1977; McFarland 1976) and raises a number of questions about the elite character of such groups and their representative function (Hayes 1983).

Nor is citizen participation in the new group universe well understood at this time. Some researchers have suggested that we must fundamentally alter our conception of group membership, especially since for many members a financial contribution may be their only involvement with the group (Baumgartner and Walker 1989). They find in a pilot study, using a revised version of the standard group affiliation question in the American National Election Studies, and allowing for multiple memberships and for financial contributions, that membership in voluntary associations is far greater than previously thought. Gains in voluntary group involvement were particularly evident in the charity group category. Such groups—the American Cancer Society would be a good example—are often not thought of as political groups, and are probably more "institutions" in terms of organizational form; but they are increasingly active politically, and involvement in them often translates into involvement in other political entities.

It seems reasonable to conclude this section by noting that we have just begun to comprehend the nature and meaning of changes in the complexity of the group universe. We now have an empirically based portrait of Washington-based interest groups—something seriously lacking before this decade. But representation is more than merely recognizing the number and diversity of groups; it should involve the comparative assessment of group resources, including intangible assets such as experience, skill, and tenacity. For example, though public interest groups are a relatively small proportion of the overall group universe, some of the literature on groups in the policy process to be later presented suggests that their involvement in governmental decision-making is far in excess of what might be predicted by numbers alone. At this stage, we understand "scope" far more than "bias" in the interest group universe. The most difficult research tasks still lie ahead.

The Collective Action Problem

Explaining why people join groups and clarifying the reasons for the recent proliferation of groups have perhaps drawn more attention from interest group scholars than any other research challenges. For many political scientists, the evolving body of theory and research on the collective action problem gives the interest group subfield its main identity and, incidentally, its reputation as "theory rich and data poor" (Arnold 1982, 97).

Until the 1960s, pluralist notions dominated explanations of group formation, membership, and the continual expansion of the group universe (Truman 1951; Latham 1952). From the pluralist perspective, individuals can recognize the existence of common needs and develop a group identity or consciousness; in the face of a common problem or threat, spontaneous organization for political purposes will take place. Although pluralists recognized that individuals sharing a common interest might lack resources or remain too isolated from each other to mobilize easily, these theorists shared a fundamental optimism that organization would eventually take place (Truman 1951; Latham 1952).

Pluralists believed that the group universe would continually expand as society became increasingly differentiated due to economic and social changes. The "latent" interests would become organized in the face of "disturbances" in the existing order, which threaten the balance within the system, and groups would arise both to improve their position and/or to protect existing advantages. From this perspective, the interest group universe was inherently unstable, as group formation "tends to occur in waves" (Truman 1951, 59), being more frequent in some periods than in others. Groups formed from an imbalance of interests in one area induce a subsequent disequilibrium, which acts as a catalyst for individuals to form groups as counterweights to the new perceptions of inequity.

Economist Mancur Olson (1965) effectively challenged the basic pluralist assumption that individuals will organize spontaneously in behalf of their common interests. In so doing, he reoriented the direction of theory and research on groups by political scientists. Using a "rational economic man" model as his framework, based on individual cost-benefit assessments, Olson posited that even individuals who have common interests in a political goal are not inclined to join organizations that attempt to address their concerns. The major barrier to group organization in pursuit of political goals is the "free-rider" problem: "rational" individuals choose not to bear the participation costs (time, dues) because they can enjoy the group benefits (such as favorable legislation) whether or not they join it.

The size of the group in question is fundamental to Olson's formulation. Large groups, particularly those pursuing "collective" benefits, which accrue to all members of a class or segment of society regardless of membership status, will have great difficulty forming and surviving. According to Olson, it would be economically irrational for individual farmers to join a group seeking higher farm prices when benefits from price increases will be enjoyed by all farmers, even those who contribute nothing to the group. Small groups are more likely to be "privileged," however, and are able to overcome the "free-rider" problem more efficiently, because personal efficacy is greater (members can see how their contribution may make a difference), social pressure is more powerful, and bargaining and organization are easier to undertake.

For Olson, other than coercion, the key to group formation and maintenance (his major focus) is the provision of "selective" benefits. These rewards, such as travel discounts, informative publications, inexpensive insurance, and the like, go only to members. Organizations in the best position to offer such benefits are those initially formed for some nonpolitical reason, which ordinarily provide material benefits to their members. In the case of unions, for example, membership may be a condition of employment. In professional societies, membership may be a prerequisite for occupational advancement and opportunity. Political activity of the leaders of such organizations, then, is the "by-product" in certain "organizations that obtain their strength and support because they perform some function in addition to lobbying for collective goods" (Olson 1965, 132).

Olson's theory challenged not only pluralist assumptions concerning the basis of collective action, but the normative implications of pluralism as well. Olson's group universe was skewed in favor of narrow economic interests, and his collective action logic noted the great disadvantages faced by social and political interests composed of broad constituencies. Unlike the pluralists, Olson's interest group system does not foresee the representation of virtually all interests.

Olson's economic theory of collective action, which attracted scholarly attention during the very period of time when public interest groups were developing and/or expanding their membership during the 1970s, sparked a number of critiques and extensions of the rational-man model. By the late 1980s, a loosely integrated body of "incentive theory" literature had largely supplanted the pluralist model as the subfield's main paradigm to explain group mobilization and development. This literature ranges from the highly formal models of the public choice theorists, to empirical tests of why individuals join groups; it is difficult to summarize, given the variation in how scholars define "rationality" in their theories and the difficulty of constructing empirical tests of the formal models.

In general, however, this body of literature suggests that while the "free-rider problem" does indeed exist, it may not be as delimiting to group development as Olson suggests. There are apparently a number of solutions to the collective action problem, aside from coercion and the development of selective benefits, that enable even large group constituencies to organize in pursuit of collective political goals. There is strong theoretical and some empirical evidence to suggest that Olson's concentration on tangible economic motives underestimates the potential for collective action, and that cooperation among citizens in pursuit of collective goals can occur under a variety of different circumstances.

Much of the debate among scholars has focused, less upon the notion that individuals engage in a cost-benefit analysis as they decide whether or not to pursue collective action, and more upon the range of motives and their weights in the calculation. As an economist, Olson was most concerned with material benefits, tangible rewards of participation, such as income or services that have monetary value. But solidary incentives, the socially derived, intangible rewards created by the act of association—such as fun, camaraderie, status, or prestige—are also significant, as are expressive or purposive rewards derived from advancing a particular cause or ideology (Clark and Wilson 1961; Salisbury 1969; Gamson 1975; J. Wilson 1973).

It has been argued that intangible factors such as a sense of fairness, duty, and moral obligation override "rational" economic calculations by individuals and cause them not to "free ride" (Hardin 1982a). In addition, some persons "care about the rightness of their actions, regardless of what others do and regardless of individual or collective practical effect" (Nagel 1987, 33–34). Others have argued that individuals have in effect two utility curves, one reflecting their self-interest, and another that "incorporates a taste for having other people better off" (Margolis 1984, 21).

There is also some debate over whether certain factors are benefits or costs in the participation calculus. Hirschman (1982), for example, argues that many individuals derive personal enjoyment from the time and effort expended in collective action, and that the pursuit of collective action itself has positive value and should be considered a benefit in the calculus. Others have wondered whether individuals even engage in a meaningful cost-benefit calculus in some participation situations, since "there seems to be a general threshold level of involvement below which free rider calculations pose few inhibitions for purposive commitment from moderately affluent citizen supporters" (McCann 1989, 385).

In general, although the empirical literature on why individuals join groups is not large, it does indicate that individuals join and participate in groups for many reasons beyond narrow economic self-interest, including collective goals, even without the availability of meaningful selective benefits (Cigler and Hansen 1983; Tillock and Morrison 1978; Berry 1977; Godwin and Mitchell 1982; Cook 1984; Moe 1980a; McFarland 1984; Rothenberg 1988a). Even in economic groups with significant selective benefits, groups that best fit Olson's theory, many members join for collective reasons and pay little attention to selective benefits (Marsh 1976).

Olson's underlying logic of collective action has also been challenged by a number of game theoretic and experimental studies. Hardin (1982a), for example, argues that collective action might be best viewed as an iterated Prisoner's Dilemma game, since in "social contexts we typically face ongoing collective action problems rather than once-only actions that are isolated from other interactions" (3). In Hardin's view, "coordination by convention" can occur because the interaction process itself teaches individuals to cooperate. Axelrod (1984) argues that cooperation in pursuit of collective action can be learned, largely through the system of rewards and punishments that results from the operation of tit-for-tat decision rule in the collective action situation. A number of experimental efforts also suggest that Olson has underestimated the potential for collective action, even in situations where individuals have no face-to-face contact (Marwell and Ames 1979, 1980; Frolich and Oppenheimer 1984).

It has also been argued that, in opposition to Olson, large groups are not necessarily disadvantaged in the pursuit of collective action, and the influence of group size on the potential for collective action is conditional. The key factor is the existence of an "efficacious subgroup" (Hardin 1982a, 48–49). Larger groups can also "exploit economies of scale in establishing and maintaining awareness of their activities" and can "create a larger pool of organizational resources to be flexibly deployed in conflict situations, as well as attracting better leadership personnel" (Dunleavy 1988).

Research in the last decade on the collective action problem has increasingly focused on making Olson's basic rational-man model more "realistic" in terms of underlying assumptions, particularly in questioning the notion that individuals are perfectly informed as they engage in the cost-benefit considerations, and in asserting that subjective considerations are crucial (Frohlich and Oppenheimer 1978; Frohlich et al. 1971; Moe 1980b; Smith 1985). Particularly important may be individuals' overall sense of "subjective efficacy," "which, regardless of its justification in the objective context, gives them every rational incentive to contribute" (Moe 1980b, 602). Given the American socialization process, many citizens may face collective action situations with certain "efficacy predispositions" that make them feel their contributions to a group may be far greater than the objective context may indicate, which helps to explain why economic models often overestimate the tendency of individuals to free ride (Moe 1980b).

Rothenberg (1988a) has further extended the imperfect information model by adding a learning component to the decision to join and remain in a political group. Realistically, often individuals have little information about the costs of group membership (other than dues) and are unaware of many of the potential benefits of group involvement. Once they have joined the group, however, they engage in an "experiential search" and "reevaluate their decision in accordance with what they have learned about the costs and benefits of participating" (1133–34). Applying this model to retention decisions among Common Cause members (based on a 1981 survey of over 1,200 group members), he found that members do indeed learn, many tending to drop out of the organization if they have made a "mistake." The author's findings suggest that entrance motivations and retention motivations may be quite different: individuals often join for vague collective and purposive reasons, yet make retention decisions when specific solidary and selective reasons are crucial.

Evidence also suggests that the context in which individuals assess group membership and participation is also crucial, since "people in different contexts have different preferences and resources and hence different subjective weightings of the benefits and costs of group participation" (Hansen 1985, 80). For example, people obviously can bear certain costs like dues better in some economic contexts than others; they are more willing to take risks under certain circumstances than in others, especially when threatened; and in certain contexts they have more information about their choices than in others.

Hansen (1985) posits a "context-sensitive" model of interest group membership and examines the effects of expected political benefits, selective benefits, and costs on the changes in aggregate membership numbers over time in three national organizations: the American Farm Bureau Federation, the League of Women Voters, and the National Association of Home Builders. His findings suggest that, contrary to Olson's claim, individuals do join political interest groups in response to the provision of collective benefits, particularly in periods when groups are threatened by adverse conditions. Hansen offers that groups can claim "credit" for successes in the political arena (like increases in farm subsidies), later seeing their membership rolls expand by the joining of individuals who are impressed by or grateful for government action. A related study, which explored the effects over time of context and selective benefits on changes in membership of five state Farm Bureaus, did not confirm Hansen's national-level findings (Brown 1989).

While much of the literature in the "incentive theory" area considers group involvement from the perspective of the individual thinking about becoming involved, a much smaller body of literature approaches the collective action problem from the perspective of group organizers (entrepreneurs) involved in stimulating organization formation and in maintaining the group (Salisbury 1969; Moe 1980a, 1980b; Berry 1978). Since group formation, even in the face of demand, cannot occur unless benefits are supplied, group entrepreneurs are the catalysts of organizations, as they search for potential members and resources, design an organization to provide benefits to members, and manage the affairs of the group (Salisbury 1969; Hansen 1985).

From the "exchange theory" perspective, the development of a political group involves a "mutually satisfactory exchange," with both leaders and followers experiencing a net gain from organizational involvement, as leaders offer incentives to members in exchange for support (Salisbury 1969). In the mobilization stage, entrepreneurs are often able to launch their recruiting efforts when conditions or events make particularly salient the incentives they offer and when potential members have the capacity and willingness to bear costs (Salisbury 1969).

Exchange theory is a particularly useful framework within which to examine group development from a dynamic perspective. For example, after group mobilization, group institutionalization and maintenance often necessitate a different kind of test for the leadership. Because the demand for benefits and the willingness to bear costs among group populations may change in response to varying conditions and circumstances, a group's survival may depend upon the skill with which its leaders tailor and adapt group incentives to the changing context. For many groups, long-term survival is problematic (Salisbury 1969).

In the mobilization stage of a political group, clever entrepreneurs can often achieve some success with little in the way of tangible resources. The development of the American Agriculture Movement (AAM), founded as a protest group in the late 1970s, provides a good example. A skillful group of entrepreneurs were able to mobilize a large group of farmers in the short run by collective material and expressive appeals (through the use of symbolism, emotionalism, and rhetoric), as well as through clever organizational arrangements that provided solidary benefits (Browne 1983; Cigler and Hansen 1983). But collective and material appeals are often enhanced by certain circumstances (like a period of low farm prices), and more stable incentives must often be developed if a group is to survive in the long run. In the case of the AAM, when the group attempted to moderate its message in order to broaden its appeal to less radical farmers (lower expressive costs for some), group leaders attempted to develop a number of selective incentives as well as opening a Washington office with a lobbyist and a political action committee. Such actions so alienated many of the group's original expressive activists that the AAM split, and survives today largely as a "staff" organization with few members and a narrow founding base (Cigler 1986). The attempt to institutionalize the women's movement experienced similar difficulties (Costain and Costain 1981a).

The bulk of the literature dealing with the collective action problem focuses upon the relations between individuals and groups, but groups can also overcome the free-rider problem by finding a sponsor who will support the organization, thus reducing its reliance on membership dues, and "patrons of political action play a crucial role in initiation and maintenance of groups" (Walker 1983b, 402). This seems to be especially true of citizens' groups (such as environmental and consumer groups) that seek noneconomic collective benefits. Jeffrey Berry's (1977) study of eighty-three public interest organizations found that at least one-third received more than half their funds from private foundations, while one in ten received more than 90 percent of its operating expenses from such sources. Jack Walker's (1983b) survey of Washington-based interest groups confirmed many of Berry's earlier findings, indicating that foundation support and individual grants provide 30 percent of all citizens' group funding.

Walker (1983a, 1983b) further suggests that patrons are more than merely passive sponsors responding to group requests for funds. Group mobilization often comes from the top down rather than from the bottom up. The patron—which can be an individual, an institution, another group, or a governmental entity—may be the initiator of group development, not merely contributing funding, but seeking group entrepreneurs and providing a forum for group development. The role of the government as patron may be especially crucial, since public-policy enactments themselves are often catalysts for group development, rather than the reverse, as is demonstrated by studies of the hunger lobby (Berry 1984) and disability rights groups (Scotch 1985). According to Hansen (1985, 94), "The key to understanding which organizations form, then, is understanding which groups get subsidized and when."

While we are far from an empirically grounded theory of organizational formation and maintenance, our understanding is far greater than even a short time ago. Many of the important elements have been identified, and both theoretical and empirical work continues at a faster pace than previously.

Still, we know relatively little about key aspects of group participation decisions and the role played by group entrepreneurs and patrons. Little research, for example, has been undertaken about the basic manner in which people first learn about shared interests and how this affects the group participation decision (Dunleavy 1988). With the exception of Wilson's (1973) general discussion of "organizing cadres" in the public interest sector, and Berry's (1977) survey of entrepreneurs in the same sector, there are no recent systematic studies of group entrepreneurs, their backgrounds, and their recruitment. Even less is known about group patrons, their relationship to group entrepreneurs, and the important question of how patronage relationships affect a group's political agenda.

Given the subfield's resource investment in the collective action problem and its case study orientation in the policy impact area, it also seems strange that few in recent years have comprehensively studied even single political organizations in detail. The one notable exception is McFarlan's 1984 study of Common Cause. Evidently, the long-term, in-depth study of a political organization has deterred scholars, perhaps because of the time investment and the difficulty of organizational access.

There are some hopeful signs, however. Scholars in the late 1980s are increasingly turning to the internal aspects of organizations and the way in which various allocation and strategic decisions are made. Studies investigating the use of direct mail as a device to recruit members (Godwin 1988), how organizations design their benefit packages and set membership dues (Johnson 1987, 1990), how members become activists in organizations (Rothenberg 1988b), and how groups decide upon the level of both electoral and legislative influence strategies (Delancy, Fiorito, and Masters 1988) all have contributed to our understanding of intraorganizational decision-making. Others have studied how outside consultants have affected internal group development (Cigler 1986).

The research task facing us in the collective action area is substantial. While some might argue that empirical work should not proceed until theory is more developed (Hardin 1982b), most would probably agree that what is needed is more empirical research on a wider-ranging set of groups and other organized interests than is currently the case, especially since the empirical work to date focuses almost entirely on public-interest groups. Studies surveying members as well as nonmembers would lend additional insight into why a certain few decide to become involved in groups. Trade associations and institutions as political entities have been particularly neglected. Just about any well-crafted study of an organized political interest would make a much needed contribution to the collective action data base.

GROUP ACTIVITIES AND IMPACT

Groups in the Electoral Process

Groups have long played a prominent role in American elections, their activities ranging from simple endorsement of candidates through participation in the nomination and platform writing processes, to mobilizing voters and supplying candidates and campaigns with money and other resources. Such activities have often been viewed with alarm by a suspicious press and a distrustful public, who have perceived groups as attempting to buy influence, and candidates as pandering and selling out to special interests. Still, the tangled relation between group involvement in elections and the subsequent behavior of public officials has been difficult to determine. Candidate and group interactions have often escaped the public eye, and laws concerning the relationship either nonexistent or easily evaded.

One effect of the 1971 and 1974 campaign finance reform laws has been to make the role of groups in the electoral process more visible, by requiring that their sources of funds and campaign contributions be available for public scrutiny. The result has been a "bull market" in research on group activities in an election, especially the activities of political action committees (PACs). PACs are "either the separate, segregated campaign fund of a sponsoring labor, business or trade organization, or the campaign fund of a group formed primarily or solely for the purpose of giving money to candidates" (Sabato 1984, 7). Federal Election Commission reports provide interest group scholars with large reliable data sets from which to assess many questions surrounding contributions to candidates, election outcomes, and the linkage between "interested" money and public policy.

The availability of funding data has not automatically produced good research or clear results. PAC money is analytically difficult to separate from all other sources of money in terms of its impact on elections, and money itself is only one of many political resources in a campaign. Not all PAC contributions are financial, and "in kind" contributions such as shared poll results or help for the candidate's staff are difficult to evaluate and hard to assess in terms of the campaign effort.

Judging the impact of PAC contributions on later political behavior of election officials is even more fraught with analytical difficulties. Statistical associations between contributions and legislative behavior, usually measured by roll-call votes, tell us little about causal relationships. Contributing PACs and public officials insist that money follows votes rather than determining them. Legislative decisions are often complex: an official's constituency, party, ideology, peer influence, and considered judgment are all potentially important. The groups themselves use other influence tactics such as direct or grassroots lobbying, and it is hard to assess precisely separate impacts. To derive definite findings about the impact of special interest money on legislative behavior, given the probable reciprocal nature of the relationship and the large number of other factors that must be measured and controlled for, is no mean task.

Perhaps the one thing researchers who study PACs can agree upon is the diversity of the organizational subject matter. Some PACs, especially independent, ideological PACs such as the National Committee for an Effective Congress (NCEC), are essentially interest groups in their own right. Others, like union or corporation PACs, are typically divisions within an organization (ranging from an elaborate separate unit to an informal committee that meets on an ad hoc basis) and are merely one among many sources of political influence within the sponsoring organization. Candidates and elected public officials can create PACs separate from their campaign organizations, such as Senator Robert Dole's Campaign America PAC. Although there are over 4,000 registered PACs at the national level, roughly one-third contribute no money at all in elections (Sabato 1984), 70 percent give an aggregate of $20,000 or less (Sorauf 1988), and very few of even the largest PACs contribute the maximum allowed by law (Sorauf 1988). Finally, many of the most powerful organizations in American economic and political life have elected not to form political action committees, itself a decision worthy of study (Andres 1985; Ryan, Swanson, and Buchholz 1987).

Unlike the collective action research, most of the research on PACs as organizational entities is simply descriptive, focusing on such issues as how they raise funds, the nature of the PAC as an organization, and internal decision-making within the PAC, including allocation decisions and resultant spending patterns. Research findings from this literature tend to destroy the myth that has equated the amount of money raised (or spent) with groups' political efficiency and unity of purpose.

Clearly, the most important distinction among PACs is between those with parent organizations and those without them (Sorauf 1988). Independent PACs tend to raise funds by direct mail or telephone, have relatively small staffs to determine political strategies, use the bulk of their funds on overhead rather than on campaign spending, and pursue more ideological and nonincumbent-giving strategies. Such features have caused some political scientists to worry about exactly whom PACs represent and to whom they are accountable (Sorauf 1983). Affiliated PACs, on the other hand, solicit money from within the organization and have administrative and overhead costs provided for by the parent organization. Such PACs often do not have total control over their campaign contribution strategies and may experience tensions with the local affiliates and/or the lobbying arm of the parent organization

(Wright 1985; Sabato 1984). Other organizational factors may affect PAC behavior as well, including the size of the PAC, the nature of its connected organizations, and whether or not it is based in Washington (Eismeier and Pollack 1984).

PAC contribution behavior has been a special focus of political scientists, since PACs face a number of strategic options, including whether to support incumbents or challengers, the amount of the contribution, the role of party versus ideology, whether to concentrate resources on the House or the Senate, and how many candidates should receive aid. Researchers find that strategic patterns depend on the type of PAC under study (Latus 1983, 1984; Gopoian 1985; Wilcox 1988; Wright 1985; Handler and Mulkern 1982; Welch 1979; Ryan, Swanson and Buchholz 1987). Independent PACs appear to be willing to take the "risk" of supporting challengers and often make decisions on an ideological basis. Corporate and association PACs most often follow the more pragmatic strategy of supporting incumbents and strategically placed legislators. But even here generalization is tenuous and PAC types are hardly monolithic in their behavior. Oil company PACs, for example, appear to behave more like the nonaffiliated PACs, contributing much more to nonincumbents and Republicans than other corporate PACs (Handler and Mulkern 1982; Evans 1988). Organizational features, especially in groups like organized labor with its strong tradition of local involvement, may "constrain the strategic choice" of some PACs (Eismeier and Pollack 1986, 197), and in some powerful economic lobbies where money is raised at the local level, "the organizational arrangement that allows PACs to raise and allocate large sums of money also restricts their ability to influence roll calls" (Wright 1985, 411). It must also be remembered that most PACs are small, are based outside of the Washington area, and are "remarkably unsophisticated" in their contribution behavior (Eismeier and Pollack 1984).

As has been widely reported, the bulk of PAC contributions goes to incumbent legislators, but such aggregate figures can mask the diversity among the various types of PACs (Malbin 1984). Organized labor, for example, almost never contributes to Republicans and traditionally gives a substantial portion of its contributions to challengers. In contrast, corporate PACs overwhelmingly contribute to Republican incumbents and give nearly as much to Republican challengers as to Democratic incumbents, although the pattern has been somewhat altered in the most recent elections. Associational PACs tend to contribute to incumbents of both parties. Only among ideological PACs is there a preference for challengers. Overall, while PAC contributions go largely to incumbents, probably helping them ward off serious challenges, if a race is genuinely competitive, challengers do quite well in terms of raising PACs funds (Malbin 1984).

Besides attempting to affect electoral outcomes, PACs contribute to candidates for a myriad of reasons (probably including to avoid angering a legislator who has requested a contribution), but it seems reasonable to assume that the other major reasons for such contributions are either to reward those who have acted on the group's behalf or to attempt to gain access and influence legislative behavior. Although "access" is a very elusive concept and difficult to measure (Sorauf 1988), it is the word most often mentioned by PAC officials when explaining their actions (Sabato 1984; Grenzke 1989).

What is the effect of PAC money? When one turns to the research literature on the relationship of PAC contributions to congressional voting, one finds that it "is filled with ambiguity and apparent contradiction" (Wright 1985, 401). Studies dealing with such issues as the B-1 Bomber (Chappel 1982), minimum wage legislation (Silberman and Durden 1976), the debt limit, windfall profits tax, wage and price controls (Kau and Rubin 1982), trucking deregulation (Frenreis and Waterman 1985), legislation of interest to doctors and auto dealers (Brown 1983), and gun-control legislation (Cleiber, King, and Mahood 1987), have concluded that special interest money does appear to make a substantial difference. Others find no simple, direct relationship between contributions and issues such as the Chrysler loan guarantee program (Evans 1986) or dairy price supports (Welch 1982). Two studies, each of which examines a large number of issues, make virtually no common generalizations (Ginsberg and Green 1986; Grenzke 1989). Generalization from this literature is obviously very risky, but it does appear that, while PAC contributions are far less important in roll-call voting than constituency, partisan, and ideological factors, such funding may have an influence under certain circumstances. When issues are not widely visible and when legislators have no strong preferences, PAC contributions may make a difference (Evans 1986; Denzau and Munger 1986; Malbin 1984).

PACs have also been criticized for contributing to the decline of political parties because they potentially erode the role that parties play in funding campaigns and in promoting candidates "with little sense of obligation to their state and local parties" (Bibby and Huckshorn 1982, 91). The evidence suggests that while parties and PACs competed vigorously for campaign funds in the early years of PAC growth, parties seem to have adapted to the PAC threat, and "the institutionalization of the national parties . . . transformed the hostility that surrounded early party-PAC . . . relations into a less conflictual and, in many ways, highly cooperative set of relationships" (Herrnson 1985, 7). Although Republicans remain far ahead of Democrats, both national party organizations have formed loose fund-raising alliances with some prominent

PACs. In their emerging role as brokers, the national parties regularly assist PACs in directing contributions to particular campaigns and aid candidates by soliciting funds from potential donor PACs (Sabato 1984; Sorauf 1988). Parties have even been involved in new PAC creation (Frantzich 1989). Finally, the little empirical research that exists on the subject leads one to conclude that PAC contributors are not necessarily antiparty, and even ideological and single-issue PACs have not altered American politics in fundamental ways (Green and Guth 1986). The business-labor division among PACs roughly follows the New Deal divisions that continue to differentiate the parties.

PAC research in the future will likely move in a number of different directions, including basic investigation of types of PACs that have been neglected (such as candidate PACs and the role they play in legislative careers and aspirations for higher office). Some PACs, like BIPAC, formed by the National Association of Manufacturers, tend to be leaders among the PACs, helping others to make contribution decisions and instructing them about how to raise funds. The role of these organizations needs to be explored in some depth. PAC influence in potentially more crucial yet largely "hidden" points in the congressional process, such as effects on subcommittee decision-making, remains unexplored. We also know little about how candidates "use" PACs and pressure the interests, or how "the growth of PACs may have altered the way congressmen allocate their scarce resources, staff and time" (Wright 1985, 412). The "mutual adjustments" of PACs and candidates may obscure what are stronger relationships than those captured in standard empirical tests (Austen-Smith 1987) and worthy of further inquiry. Finally, since the growth of PACs apparently has leveled off and may even have started to decline (Sorauf 1988), it would be useful to know why some organizations have decided to eliminate their PACs.

Perhaps most needed on the future research agenda dealing with groups in the electoral process, however, are more studies on aspects other than PAC behavior (Hershey 1983, 1986; Fowler 1982). For example, the activist farmers, teachers, and members of organized labor who play such an important role in the presidential nomination campaigns in Iowa and New Hampshire have not been systematically studied from the perspective of interest group strategy, nor has the role of organized interests in the writing of party platforms. Group activity in elections reflects more than the impact of money. "In-kind" contributions, from conducting registration drives to lending group staff to campaign organizations, suggest a relationship between candidates and interest groups of a different kind, where groups are actively involved in the strategic decisions of political campaigns. In short, the research agenda on groups in the electoral process is far from complete.

Washington Representatives in the Policy Process

As in the electoral process, assessing the impact of special interests in
the policy process poses major analytical challenges. Researchers are often confronted with decision-makers who claim total freedom from any
outside influences and groups that realize it is in their organizational
interest to exaggerate their claims of impact. To equate "noise" and
activity with impact can be misleading, as can be the tendency to equate
apparent group "silence" and little overt involvement with the absence
of influence. The large number of actors in many decision-making situations, the many access points in the process, and the private or semiprivate aspects of much organized interest activity, all make the task of the
researcher difficult. Faced with such obstacles, it is not surprising that
the traditional method of analysis used to study lobbyist and group impact upon public policy impact has been the case study.

Since the profession has long been interested in public policy, many
studies have potential relevance to interest group scholars, including
much of the literature dealing with congressional, bureaucratic, and judicial decision-making. Still, there is a growing body of literature that
makes the role of groups its primary focus. The findings from this literature, though often narrowly derived and very policy-area specific, tend
both to confirm and challenge much of the previous research and conventional wisdom about groups in the policy process.

As the scope of government has broadened in recent decades, affected societal groups and institutions have flocked to Washington,
causing a tremendous growth in the number of group actors in the policy process. For example, in the decade after 1975, the number of registered lobbyists in the national capital more than doubled, and the
number of attorneys more than tripled (Salisbury 1986). The latest edition of *Washington Representatives* (Close 1988) lists more than twice as
many individuals than did the 1979 edition.

Much of what we know about the universe of Washington representatives and their activities comes from a large data set constructed from
personal interviews of 806 Washington representatives during late
1983 and early 1984 (an extended discussion of the design procedures
is found in Nelson et al. 1987, 194–200). The interviewees were active
in one of four policy domains: agriculture, labor, health, or energy.

As expected, the study found that representatives tend to be well-
educated, male, white, and to have other background characteristics
compatible with the policy domain in which they operate; agriculture
representatives tended to come from the South and West, for example,
and labor and health representatives from northeastern metropolitan
areas (Salisbury 1986). Given the common depiction of lobbyists as ex-
government officials, the researchers surprisingly found that only 56

percent of respondents reported they had prior government experience (45 percent at the federal level), a figure not much changed from Milbrath's study (1963) of 114 lobbyists in 1956 (Salisbury and Johnson 1989).

The representatives were unlikely to be "in-and-outers," moving often between employment in the government and private sectors. Most respondents with government experience had been out of government for a number of years (Salisbury and Johnson 1989), and "continuity" appears to be the norm in representational relationships (the issues represented continuity as well). The core actors in the four policy domains have remained relatively constant over time, and relatively few were "guns for hire," who lobby on an ad hoc basis for contracting organizations. Indeed, over 80 percent of those sampled were employees of the organization which they represented (43 percent were trade association executives), while less than 20 percent were outside lawyers or paid consultants (Salisbury 1986). Even among the external representatives, continuity is more common than ad hoc relationships, with most having served the contracting organization for a number of years (Nelson et al. 1987).

Nor were Washington representatives typically narrow task "specialists." This was especially true of associational executives and public affairs officers, where actual lobbying may be only one of a myriad of activities they must engage in, from securing funds to mobilizing grassroots support to contacting and monitoring policy-makers. While some patterns of substantive focus or agency specialization did appear among the survey respondents, organization representatives "typically distribute their time among a number of substantive fields and contact many government institutions," and "pursue the interest of the client organization, wherever it may take them" (Nelson et al. 1987, 192). Further, outside legal counsel, in contrast to previous eras, serves the client organization more often as a technical specialist than as an adviser on public policy questions (Nelson et al. 1987; Salisbury 1986; Lauman and Heinz 1985).

Another research project, this time at the organizational level, adds additional insight into the activities of Washington representatives (Schlozman and Tierney 1984, 1986). In interviews with 175 members of a range of political organizations based in Washington, these researchers also found that continuity and change are evident in group activities meant to influence government. While organizational representation has admittedly become more sophisticated and professional, groups tend to engage in the same kinds of activities they have always engaged in, ranging from protests or demonstrations (20 percent of groups used this technique) to testimony at hearings (99 percent used this technique). But the level of activity is much elevated, a fact the re-

searchers see as attributable not only to the expansion of government
policies in so many areas but also to changes in Congress since the early
1970s, which have "evoked more pressure activity primarily by multi-
plying the number of access points and expanding the variety of opportunities interested parties have to exert their political will" (Schlozman
and Tierney 1984, 369). Particularly important have been the decentralization of Congress, the turnover in committee membership, and
the expansion and professionalization of congressional staffs.

The two empirical studies described above present a picture of
Washington representatives somewhat different from the journalistic
accounts of "upper-tier," top-echelon lobbyists and consultants like
Charls Walker or ex-Reagan aide Michael Deaver. Differences between
"old-breed" lobbyists and "new-breed" lobbyists may be overdrawn in
more popular accounts (Smith 1988).

Still, our knowledge about the vast number of individuals associated with organized interests in Washington remains at the rudimentary
level. Basic recruitment and career ladder studies, along the lines of
those employed by students of legislative decision-makers (Barber
1965; Schlesinger 1966), should be undertaken. We know little about
what motivates these individuals and their own perceptions of their
jobs, and the linkages between the various background characteristics of
the lobbyists and their effectiveness are yet unknown (do those with
government experience have an advantage?). Finally, although there is
some research on actual lobbying techniques and the circumstances under which they may be effective (Loomis 1983; Wright 1990), this area
has been largely neglected by political scientists. No study could be
found, for example, that examined the use of honoraria, an influence
technique that elicits much press attention.

Organized Interests in the Policy Process

The expanding presence of the federal government in the lives of citizens, the proliferation of organized interests represented in Washington, and the expansion of access points in the policy arena, have not
only changed the number of participants in the policy process but appears to have affected the process itself in fundamental ways. Political
scientists have been forced to rethink their traditional conception of
how public policy is made in the nation's capital.

The subgovernment, or "iron triangle," model of policy-making,
where decisions were essentially made in private among a limited number of congressional, bureaucratic, and interest group spokesman,
tended to be the way many interest group scholars conceptualized the
process until recent years. The metaphor of the iron triangle is one of a
stable system of policy-making impervious to input by or accountability

to those outside the system (including party leaders or the president). Issues both arise and are decided upon by this small group of participants, to the advantage of the organized interests in the triangle. While there are legitimate scholarly questions about how widely applicable the iron triangle metaphor ever was in American politics, it did seem accurately to describe decision-making in a number of individual policy arenas (Maass 1950; Cater 1964; Fritschler 1975; Lawrence 1966; Davidson 1975; Freeman 1965).

By the late 1970s, the context that permitted iron triangles to operate in American politics no longer was present, having been replaced by a much less stable environment characterized by large numbers of groups, intergroup competitiveness within policy sectors, less hegemonic interests, more openness in the decision-making process, and a willingness among partisan officials, including the president, to intervene even in narrow policy arenas (Heclo 1978; Gais, Peterson, and Walker 1984; Pika 1983; Salisbury 1989). Research conducted over the past decade appears to confirm this view, although policy domains differ substantially.

For example, findings from the Salisbury et al. data set of 806 Washington representatives (now supplemented by interviews with 301 officials in the four policy domains) indicate that substantial conflict among interests exists in each domain, with large majorities of respondents able to identify both allies and adversaries (Salisbury et al. 1987). The intensity of conflict varied by domain, being intensely partisan and bipolarized in the labor domain (between business and labor interests), and less so in the health care arena. Regardless, no longer is it possible for groups like the American Medical Association or the American Farm Bureau Federation not to face serious challenges in their policy domains.

Detailed case studies in a number of policy areas further illustrate the open and conflictual nature of the contemporary policy process. The agriculture sector, for example, which at one time witnessed the development of a coherent farm bloc and a rather closed policy-making system among a small number of actors (Hansen 1987), has evolved into a loose configuration of group actors, ranging from the traditional farm groups (AFBF, Farmers Union), which are often at odds, to environmentalists and churches (Browne 1986, 1987). By the 1970s the newer public interest groups had drastically changed farm politics, making it more visible and lengthening the agenda to consider questions such as how farm subsidies affect consumer purchasing power and the effects of various fertilizers, herbicides, and pesticides on public health. Indeed, Browne (1987) identified over two hundred organized interest actors involved in the 1985 farm bill.

Another example can be found in the energy arena, long known for its policy-making favorable to the interests of energy producers and sup-

pliers but now harboring much more conflict, especially on key allocation issues, because of public interest group involvement (Chubb 1983;
Nivola 1986). A variety of other policy domains, including marine research (King and Shannon 1986), health care (Laumann and Knoke
1987), and water resources management (Miller 1985; McCool 1987)
appear to be far more open and competitive than previously, and regulatory policy arenas are anything but closed (J. Wilson 1980; Bosso
1986). Some of the relatively newer policy areas, like food stamps, were
competitive and conflictual right from their inception, not only among
groups, but between liberals and conservatives and Democrats and
Republicans (Berry 1984). And despite some exceptions, group influence in foreign policy-making does not resemble "iron triangle"
politics; rather, it is more reactive than initiating, and groups character-
istically mobilize public opinion and the press to overturn or modify
executive policy (Uslaner 1986; Watanbe 1984).

Interest group domination in the policy process tends most often to
occur in distributive and self-regulatory arenas, typified by concentrated
benefits and widely distributed costs, "because often the only groups
finding it rational to overcome the free rider problem . . . are those
seeking governmental largess" (Hayes 1981, 99). Consensual politics
becomes the norm because losers are either outside the legislative process or unorganized, "perhaps even unaware that they are threatened"
(Hayes 1981, 99).

Although policy-makers seek distributional solutions to policy
problems, such policy arenas may occur less often in contemporary politics. It has become more difficult to practice consensual politics due to
changes in the nature of public policy, structural reforms in the policy
process, and the impact of the public interest movement, which has
brought a number of actors into the process who are willing to utilize
"outsider" strategies and has introduced electoral costs for legislators
unwilling to pay attention to broader interests (Gais, Peterson, and
Walker 1984; McFarland 1983; McCann 1986, 1989; Berry 1989;
Salisbury 1989).

Many issues have been redefined. The period between the Kennedy
and Reagan administrations witnessed a "regulatory and redistributive
revolution in American public policy" (Gais, Peterson, and Walker
1984); and such policies are not characterized by compromise, accommodation, and secrecy. Rather, they involve confrontation, a wider
scope of conflict, and, often, more public scrutiny. Unlike iron triangle
politics, where the final arbiter is a key bureau or subcommittee, the
politics of regulatory and redistributive issues is typified by involvement
of the full Congress, the executive branch, and even the president (Gais,
Peterson, and Walker 1984).

There still can be, of course, relatively closed and narrow policy-making subsystems. Salisbury et al. (1988) find, for example, that veterans' groups report a number of "allies" and no "adversaries" as they operate in the health policy domain. Like the veterans, there may be other groups in society that are "privileged" by circumstance and that draw no stable opposition. For example, who would organize against the disabled? One study (Scotch 1985) finds that decision-making in the area of disabled policy approximates a tightly unified subgovernment, with no effective opposition, in which it became difficult to distinguish between public and private policy actors.

There are also still many areas of policy-making with substantial concentrated benefits for single or small numbers of actors but whose overall costs are small and widely diffused, and draw no opposition groups. In the agriculture policy arena, for example, Browne (1988) suggests that while many of the key issues and major farm bills involved keen organized interest competition, single-purpose groups (such as the Rice Millers Association) "want—and, in agriculture at least, they most often get—elite control over issue representation through their successful occupancy of an issue niche" (28). Using a transaction model as the framework for his analysis, Browne finds that an organized interest seeks a "recognizable identity by defining a highly specific issue niche for itself and fixing its political assets (i.e., recognition and other resources) within that niche" (1988, 28). Over time, groups in the policy domain tend to accommodate each other on such issues, and potential contending groups (like the public interest groups) do not enter the fray because they simply do not have the resources to contest "minor" issues. Browne suggests that aspects of agriculture policy are characterized by "elite pluralism" and are "organized around the accommodation of more and more players than the open and freewheeling discussion of all relevant policy ideas and alternatives" (1988, 30).

Chubb's (1983) analysis of policy-making in the energy area is suggestive of similar arrangements. Energy industries, because of their domination of technical expertise—coupled with the lack of resources of potential challenging groups and their inability to cultivate relationships within the bureaucracy—may totally dominate issue debate in areas like research and development. Even certain aspects of social regulation policy are apparently decided behind closed doors (Harris 1989). The presence of more groups in a sector simply does not automatically translate into greater openness or competitiveness on many policy issues.

Overall, however, it is likely that the trend toward more open and competitive policy areas will continue, at least on major redistributive issues. Even "sacred cow" policies like the Social Security system now face at least token opposition from groups of young taxpayers, and a reexamination of the disabled rights policy arena in the late 1980s might find that those who found compliance with laws costly (for example, universities and public transportation systems) have become more willing to confront rights advocates than in the past, especially during a period of budgetary constraints.

Partisan and ideological factors may enter in as well. The Reagan administration, for example, was quite willing to intervene in subsystems politics and had a major effect on group access to government bureaucrats (Peterson and Walker 1986). In the 1980s, the federal government, which had helped to create a "cozy" subsystem composed of numerous state and local interest groups during the 1960s and 1970s, turned to defunding the intergovernmental lobby, which now was "in a battle for survival rather than expansion" (Levine and Thurber 1986, 210).

A number of political scientists have speculated about the meaning of the newer conflictual and competitive policy-making process (Schlozman and Tierney 1986; Gais, Peterson, and Walker 1984; Salisbury 1983, 1989; Cigler and Loomis 1986; Loomis and Cigler 1986; Berry 1988, 1989). A more open and competitive process may approximate the pluralistic ideal, by broadening the scope of the political agenda and potentially encouraging broad public input and enlightened decision-making. Some policy subsystems, for example, are responsive to executive leadership and the outcomes of congressional elections—even to broad public-opinion preferences—and congressional oversight is relatively effective (Berry 1984).

From the other perspective, however, more groups, more openness, and the possibility of intervention by a large number of elected officials do not necessarily mean better public policy or public policy in the national interest. The policy process has been destabilized, "as the decentralized system of conflict resolution organized about distributive policy issues is displaced by a process characterized by programmatic disputes over mainly redistributive or regulator issues involving more elaborate coalitions of groups" (Gais, Peterson, and Walker 1984, 181). There may be far greater complexity and too many demands for decision-makers to process. The content of demands may be ambiguous and the priorities difficult to set (Loomis and Cigler 1986). Browne (1986, 1987) finds, for example, that within the area of agriculture this is indeed the case, with policy priorities hard to set, leading to an unstable political situation in which programmatic tinkering is routine. The result is that long-term planning is virtually nonexistent, and actual policy decisions often reflect short-term reactions to a series of crises.

Whatever the case, the contemporary policy process poses a challenge to academic researchers. One reason the iron triangle metaphor survived so long was its simplicity and the fact "the subgovernment idea could be communicated easily to students and scholars alike" (Berry 1989, 241). In its place a number of scholars, at least in principle, have adopted Hugh Heclo's (1978, 103) notion of an "issue network, . . . a shared-knowledge group having to do with some aspect . . . of public policy."

Defining issue networks is problematic, because they often are comprised of "a large number of participants with quite variable degrees of mutual commitment or of dependence," who "move in and out of the network constantly," to the point where it is "almost impossible to say where a network leaves off and its environment begins" (Heclo 1978, 102, 103). Unlike the impervious and autonomous iron triangle, with its relatively small number of policy actors, issue networks are "sloppy and unpredictable," and force the researcher to grasp their "complexity and fluidity . . . in highly controversial, and often technical, policy areas" (Cigler and Loomis 1986, 309).

A relatively small number of researchers have attempted to operationalize the issue network concept. Laumann and Knoke (1987) have applied a sophisticated, statistical network model to actor interactions in the health and energy domains. Jeffrey Berry (1988) has attempted to map the telecommunications network through a less formal means; included in his methodology was letting the individual telecommunications lobbyists themselves try to map the issue network. Other researchers, while not dealing with issue networks specifically, have attempted to determine the basis of interest group alliances (Salisbury et al. 1987) and how coalitions are created in unstable and shifting policy environments (Loomis 1986; Costain and Costain 1981b).

Clearly, the task of understanding the role of organized interests in the policy process is both complex and vast. A number of research questions have yet to be explored in any detail, including the linkage between interest group demand aggregation factors such as organizational characteristics and the degree of policy success (Salamon and Siegfried 1977). Few generalizations can be offered from the literature reviewed that seem more than highly tentative or individual-policy domain-specific. While some policy domains (like agriculture) are comparatively well studied from an interest group perspective, others have received minimal or no attention from political scientists. It does not seem unreasonable to conclude that perhaps the most pressing research need in this area is simply more analytically descriptive research on a broader range of policy domains, both of the case-study variety and the analysis of data derived from large data sets across domains.

CONCLUSION

A number of conclusions can be drawn from this review of recent research efforts in the interest group subfield. First, despite the substantial gaps in the literature, if the ultimate test of a subfield's progress lies in the advancement of knowledge about the subject matter, those who study organized interests should feel good about the enterprise. We now know much more about the interest group universe, its complexity, scope, and biases, than we did even a decade ago. The vastness of the task should not detract from the real progress that has been made.

Second, it should also be clear that interest groups, as a subfield, lacks the internal unity and distinctiveness that characterize many other subfields in the profession. Many of the researchers who authored the projects noted herein probably view themselves more as public-choice theorists, policy and legislative specialists, or students of campaigns, elections, and political participation. Theoretical and methodological diversity is the hallmark of the interest group subfield. Modes of analysis found in the works covered range from historiography and immersion in government and group documents, to participant observation, elite interviewing, survey research, and the construction of formal mathematical models.

Subfield diversity can be viewed from a number of perspectives. Although a large number of researchers in the subfield do use explicit or implicit rational-actor or market models as a framework for their analyses (particularly in the collective action, PAC, and policy literature), some might see the lack of an agreed upon paradigm or commonality of methodology as a weakness. Others would see this as a strength. Researchers studying organized interests are not bound by orthodoxies and are free to pursue inquiry by whatever means necessary.

In the future, it is likely that diversity of both subject matter and approaches will continue. Interest group politics is a "catchall" subfield, attracting even those interested in the courts (O'Connor 1980; O'Connor and Epstein 1983; Lee Epstein 1985; Caldeira and Wright 1988) and those concerned with macro-level economic issues (Olson 1982; Brace 1988; Gray and Lowery 1988). No doubt the scope of the subfield will continue to broaden, and no doubt the dependent variable of "interest group impact" will remain elusive.

REFERENCES

Andres, Gary J. 1895. "Business Involvement in Campaign Finance. *PS* 18: 213–20.

Arnold, R. Douglas. 1982. "Overtilled and Undertilled Fields in American Politics." *Political Science Quarterly* 97:91–103.

Austen-Smith, David. 1987. "Interest Groups, Campaign Contributions, and Probablistic Voting." *Public Choice* 53:123–40.

Axelrod, Robert. 1984. *The Evolution of Cooperation*. New York: Basic Books.

Barber, James David. 1965. *The Lawmakers*. New Haven: Yale University Press.

Baumgartner, Frank R., and Jack L. Walker. 1989. "Survey Research and Membership in Voluntary Associations." *American Journal of Political Science* 32:908–28.

Bentley, Arthur F. 1908. *The Process of Government.* Chicago: University of Chicago Press.

Berry, Jeffrey M. 1977. *Lobbying for the People.* Princeton, N.J.: Princeton University Press.

————. 1978. "On the Origins of Interest Groups." *Polity* 10:379–97.

————. 1984. *Feeding Hungry People.* New Brunswick, N.J.: Rutgers University Press.

————. 1988. *The Interest Group Society.* 2d ed. Boston: Scott, Foresman/Little, Brown.

————. 1989. "Subgovernments, Issue Networks, and Political Conflict." In Richard A. Harris and Sidney M. Milkis, eds., *Remaking American Politics.* Boulder, Colo.: Westview Press.

Bibby, John, and Robert J. Huckshorn. 1983. "Parties in State Politics." In Virginia Gray, Herbert Jacob, and Kenneth Vines, eds., *Politics in the American States.* Boston: Little, Brown.

Bosso, Christopher J. 1986. *Pesticides and Policy.* Pittsburgh, Pa.: University of Pittsburgh Press.

Brace, Paul, 1988. "The Political Economy of Collective Action: The Case of the American States." *Polity* 20:1109–27.

Brown, Clyde. 1989. "Explanations of Interest Group Membership Over Time." *American Politics Quarterly* 17:32–53.

Brown, Kirk F. 1983. "Campaign Contributions and Congressional Voting." Paper presented at the annual meeting of the American Political Science Association, Chicago.

Browne, William. 1983. "Mobilizing and Activating Group Demands: The American Agriculture Movement." *Social Science Quarterly* 64:19–34.

————. 1986. "Policy and Interests: Instability and Change in a Classic Issue Subsystem." In Allan J. Cigler and Burdett A. Loomis, eds., *Interest Group Politics.* 2d ed. Washington, D.C.: CQ Press.

————. 1987. *Private Interests, Public Policy, and American Agriculture.* Lawrence: University Press of Kansas.

————. 1988. "Organized Interests and Their Issue Niches." Typeset manuscript, Central Michigan University.

Caldeira, Gregory, and John R. Wright. "Organized Interests and Agenda Setting in the U.S. Supreme Court." *American Political Science Review* 82: 1109–27.

Cater, Douglas. 1964. *Power in Washington.* New York: Vintage Books.

Chappell, Henry. 1982. "Campaign Contributions and Congressional Voting." *Review of Economics and Statistics* 64:77–83.

Chubb, John E. 1983. *Interest Groups and the Bureaucracy*. Stanford, Calif.: Stanford University Press.

Cigler, Allan J. 1985. "Special Interests and the Policy Process." *Policy Studies Journal* 14:318–25.

———. 1986. "From Protest Group to Interest Group: The Making of American Agriculture Movement, Inc." In Allan J. Cigler and Burdett A. Loomis, eds., *Interest Group Politics*. 2d ed. Washington, D.C.: CQ Press.

———, and John Mark Hansen. 1983. "Group Formation through Protest: The American Agriculture Movement." In Allan J. Cigler and Burdett A. Loomis, eds., *Interest Group Politics*. 1st ed. Washington, D.C.: CQ Press.

———, and Burdett A. Loomis. 1986. "Moving On: Interests, Power, and Politics in the 1980s." In Allan J. Cigler and Burdett A. Loomis, eds., *Interest Group Politics*. 2d ed. Washington, D.C.: CQ Press.

Clark, Peter B., and James Q. Wilson. 1961. "Incentive Systems: A Theory of Organizations." *Administrative Science Quarterly* 6:129–66.

Close, Arthur, ed. 1988. *Washington Representatives—1988*. Washington, D.C.: Columbia Books.

Colgate, Gregory, ed. 1982. *National Trade and Professional Associations of the United States 1982*. Washington, D.C.: Columbia Books.

Cook, Constance E. 1984. Participation in Public Interest Groups. *American Politics Quarterly* 12:409–31.

Costain, Douglas W., and Ann N. Costain. 1981a. "Representing Women: The Transition from Social Movement to Interest Group." *Western Political Quarterly* 34:100–13.

———. 1981b. "Interest Groups as Policy Aggregators in the Legislative Process." *Polity* 14:249–71.

Dahl, Robert. 1961. *Who Governs*. New Haven: Yale University Press.

Davidson, Roger H. 1975. "Policy Making in the Manpower Subgovernment." In M. P. Smith, ed., *Politics in America*. New York: Random House.

Delaney, John Thomas, Jack Fiorito, and Marick F. Masters. 1988. "The Effects of Union Organization and Environmental Characteristics on Union Political Action." *American Journal of Political Science* 32:616–43.

Denzau, Arthur T., and Michael C. Munger. 1986. "Legislators and Interest Groups: How Unorganized Interests Get Represented." *American Political Science Review* 80:89–106.

Dunleavy, Patrick. 1988. "Group Identities and Individual Influence: Reconstructing the Theory of Interest Groups." *British Journal of Political Science* 18:21–49.

Eismeier, Theodore J., and Phillip H. Pollack III. 1984. "Political Action Committees: Varieties of Organization and Strategy." In Michael J. Malbin, ed., *Money and Politics in the United States*. Chatham, N.J.: Chatham House.

———. 1986. "Strategy and Choice in Congressional Elections." *American Journal of Political Science* 30:197–213.

Epstein, Lee. 1985. *Conservatives in Court*. Knoxville: University of Tennessee Press.

Epstein, Leon D. 1983. "The Scholarly Commitment to Parties." In Ada W. Finifter, ed., *Political Science: State of the Discipline*. Washington, D.C.: American Political Science Association.

Evans, Diana. 1986. "PAC Contributions and Roll-Call Voting: Conditional Power." In Allan J. Cigler and Burdett A. Loomis, eds., *Interest Group Politics*. 2d ed. Washington, D.C.: CQ Press.

————. 1988. "Oil PACs and Aggressive Contribution Strategies." *The Journal of Politics* 50:1047–56.

Fowler, Linda L. 1982. "How Interest Groups Select Issues for Voting Records of Members of the U.S. Congress." *Legislative Studies Quarterly* 7:401–13.

Frantzich, Stephen E. 1989. *Political Parties in the Technological Age*. New York: Longman.

Freeman, J. Leiper. 1965. *The Political Process*. 2d ed. New York: Random House.

Frendreis, John P., and Richard W. Waterman. 1985. "PAC Contributions and Legislative Behavior: Senate Voting on Trucking Deregulation." *Social Science Quarterly* 66:401–12.

Fritschler, Lee. 1975. *Smoking and Politics*. New York: Appleton-Century-Crofts.

Frohlich, Norman, Joe Oppenheimer, and Oran Young. 1971. *Political Leadership and Collective Goods*. Princeton, N.J.: Princeton University Press.

Frohlich, Norman, and Joe Oppenheimer. 1978. *Modern Political Economy*. Englewood Cliffs, N.J.: Prentice-Hall.

————. 1984. "Beyond Economic Man: Altruism, Egalitarianism, and Difference Maximizing." *Journal of Conflict Resolution* 28:3–24.

Gais, Thomas L., Mark A. Peterson, and Jack L. Walker. 1984. "Interest Groups, Iron Triangles, and Representative Institutions in American National Government." *British Journal of Political Science* 14:161–85.

Garson, G. David. 1978. *Group Theories of Politics*. Beverly Hills, Calif.: Sage Publications.

Gamson, William. 1975. *The Strategy of Social Protest*. Homewood, Ill.: Dorsey Press.

Ginsberg, Benjamin, and John C. Green. 1986. "The Best Congress Money Can Buy: Campaign Contributions and Congressional Behavior." In Benjamin Ginsberg and Alan Stone, eds., *Do Elections Matter?* Armonk, N.Y.: M. E. Sharpe.

Gleiber, Dennis, James King, and H. R. Mahood. 1987. "PAC Contributions, Constituency Interest and Legislative Voting: Gun Control Legislation in the U.S. Senate." Paper presented at the annual meeting of the Midwest Political Science Association, Chicago.

Godwin, R. Kenneth. 1988. *One Billion Dollars of Influence*. Chatham, N.J.: Chatham House.

———, and R. C. Michell. 1982. "Rational Models, Collective Goods, and Non-Electoral Political Behavior." *Western Political Quarterly* 35:160–80.

Gopian, David J. 1984. "What Makes PACs Tick? An Analysis of Allocation Patterns of Economic Interest Groups." *American Journal of Political Science* 28:259–81.

———. 1985. " Change and Continuity in Defense PAC Behavior." *American Politics Quarterly* 13:297–322.

Gray, Virginia, and David Lowery. 1988. "Interest Group Politics and Economic Crunch in the U.S. States." *American Political Science Review* 82: 109–31.

Green, John C., and James L. Guth. 1986. "Big Bucks and Petty Cash: Party and Interest Group Activists in American Politics." In Allan J. Cigler and Burdett E. Loomis, eds., *Interest Group Politics*. 2d ed. Washington, D.C.: CQ Press.

Greenstone, J. David. 1975. "Group Theories." In Fred I. Greenstein and Nelson W. Polsby, eds. *Handbook of Political Science*, vol. 4. Reading, Mass.: Addison-Wesley.

Grenzke, Janet M. 1989. "PACs and the Congressional Supermarket: The Currency Is Complex." *American Journal of Political Science* 33:1–24.

Handler, Edward, and John R. Mulkern. 1982. *Business in Politics*. Lexington, Mass.: Lexington Books/D. C. Heath.

Hansen, John Mark. 1985. "The Political Economy of Group Membership." *American Political Science Review* 79:79–96.

———. 1987. "Choosing Sides: The Creation of the Agricultural Policy Network in Congress, 1919–1932." In Karren Oren and Stephen Skowronek, eds., *Studies in American Political Development*, vol. 2. New Haven: Yale University Press.

Hardin, Russell. 1982a. *Collective Action*. Baltimore: The Johns Hopkins University Press.

———. 1982b. "With Regret: Comment on Rational Models, Collective Goods and Non Electoral Political Behavior." *Western Political Quarterly* 35:181–88.

Harris, Richard A. 1989. "Political Management: The Changing Face of Business in American Politics." In Richard A. Harris and Sidney Milkis, *Remaking American Politics*. Boulder, Colo.: Westview Press.

Hayes, Michael T. 1981. *Lobbyists and Legislators*. New Brunswick, N.J.: Rutgers University Press.

———. 1983. "Interest Groups: Pluralism or Mass Society?" In Allan J. Cigler and Burdett A. Loomis, eds., *Interest Group Politics*. 1st ed. Washington, C.D.: CQ Press.

———. 1986. "The New Group Universe." In Allan J. Cigler and Burdett A. Loomis, eds., *Interest Group Politics*. 2d ed. Washington, D.C.: CQ Press.

Heclo, Hugh. 1978. "Issue Networks and the Executive Establishment." In Anthony King, ed., *The New American Political System*. Washington, D.C.: American Enterprise Institute.

Herrnson, Paul S. 1985. "National Party Organization and Congressional Campaigns: National Parties as Brokers." Paper presented at the annual meeting of the Midwest Political Science Association, Chicago.

Hershey, Marjorie Randon. 1983. "Single-Issue Politics: Prolife Groups and the 1980 Senate Campaign." In Allan J. Cigler and Burdett A. Loomis, eds., *Interest Group Politics*. 1st ed. Washington, D.C.: CQ Press.

———. 1986. "Direct Action and the Abortion Issue: Political Participation of Single-Issue Groups." In Allan J. Cigler and Burdett A. Loomis, eds., *Interest Group Politics*. 2d ed. Washington, D.C.: CQ Press.

Hirschman, Albert O. 1982. *Shifting Involvements*. Princeton, N.J.: Princeton University Press.

Hrebenar, Ronald J., and Clive S. Thomas, eds. 1987. *Interest Group Politics in the American West*. Salt Lake City: University of Utah Press.

Humphries, Craig. 1988. "Corporate Political Behavior at the National Level." Paper presented at the annual meeting of the Southern Political Science Association, Atlanta.

Johnson, Paul E. 1987. "Foresight and Myopia in Organizational Membership." *Journal of Politics* 49:678–703.

———. 1990. "The Unraveling Problem." In Melvin Dubnick and Alan Gitelson, eds., *Public Policy and Economic Institutions*. Greenwood, Conn.: JAI Press.

Kau, James B., and Paul H. Rubin. 1982. *Congressmen, Constituents, and Contributors*. Boston: Martinus Nijhoff.

King, Lauriston R., and W. Wayne Shannon. 1986. "Political Networks in the Policy Process: The Case of the National Sea Grant Program." *Polity* 19: 213–31.

Knoke, David, and James W. Wood. 1981. *Organized for Action*. New Brunswick, N.J.: Rutgers University Press.

Langton, Stuart. 1978. "Citizen Participation in America." In Stuart Langton, ed., *Citizen Participation in America*. Lexington, Mass.: D. C. Heath.

Latham, Earl. 1952. *The Group Basis of Politics*. Ithaca, N.Y.: Cornell University Press.

Latus, Margaret Ann. 1983. "Ideological PACs and Political Action." In Robert R. Leibman and Robert Wuthnow, eds., *The New Christian Right*. New York: Aldine.

———. 1984. "Assessing Ideological PACs: From Outrage to Understanding." In Michael J. Malbin, ed., *Money and Politics in the United States*. Chatham, N.J.: Chatham House.

Laumann, Edward O., and John P. Heinz. 1987. "Washington Lawyers and Others: The Structure of Washington Representation." *Stanford Law Review* 37:465–502.

Laumann, Edward O., and David Knoke. 1987. *The Organization State*. Madison: University of Wisconsin Press.

Lawrence, Samuel A. 1966. *United States Merchant Marine: Policies and Politics*. Washington, D.C.: The Brookings Institution.

Levine, Charles H., and James A. Thurber. 1986. "Reagan and the Intergovernmental Lobby." In Allan J. Cigler and Burdett A. Loomis, eds., *Interest Group Politics*. 2d ed. Washington, D.C.: CQ Press.

Loomis, Burdett A. 1983. "A New Era: Groups and the Grass Roots." In Allan J. Cigler and Burdett A. Loomis, eds., *Interest Group Politics*. 1st ed. Washington, D.C.: CQ Press.

———. 1986. "Coalitions of Interests." In Allan J. Cigler and Burdett A. Loomis, eds., *Interest Group Politics*. 2d ed. Washington, D.C.: CQ Press.

———, and Allan J. Cigler, 1986. "Introduction: The Changing Nature of Interest Group Politics." In Allan J. Cigler and Burdett A. Loomis, eds., *Interest Group Politics*. 2d ed. Washington, D.C.: CQ Press.

Lowi, Theodore J. 1969. *The End of Liberalism*. New York: Norton.

Maass, Arthur. 1950. "Congress and Water Resources." *American Political Science Review* 44:576–93.

McCann, Michael W. 1986. *Taking Reform Seriously*. Ithaca, N.Y.: Cornell University Press.

———. 1988. "Public Interest Liberalism and the Modern Regulatory State." *Polity* 21:373–400.

McCool, Daniel. 1989. *Command of the Waters*. Berkeley: University of California Press.

McFarland, Andrew S. 1976. *Public Interest Lobbies*. Washington, D.C.: American Enterprise Institute.

———. 1984. *Common Cause*. Chatham, N.J.: Chatham House.

Malbin, Michael J. 1984. "Looking Back at the Future of Campaign Finance Reform: Interest Groups and American Elections." In Michael J. Malbin, ed., *Money and Politics in the United States*. Chatham, N.J.: Chatham House.

Margolis, Howard 1984. *Selfishness, Altruism, and Rationality*. Cambridge, Mass.: Cambridge University Press.

Marsh, David, 1976. "On Joining Interest Groups." *British Journal of Political Science* 6:257–72.

Marwell, Gerald, and Ruth E. Ames. 1979. "Experiments on the Provision of Public Goods. I. Resources, Interests, Group Size, and the Free-Rider Problem." *American Journal of Sociology* 84:1335–60.

———. 1980. "Experiments on the Provision of Public Goods. II. Provision

Points, Stakes, Experience, and the Free-Rider Problem." *American Journal of Sociology* 85:927–37.

Milbrath, Lester W. 1963. *The Washington Lobbyists*. Chicago: Rand McNally.

Miller, Tim R. 1985. "Recent Trends in Federal Water Resource Management: Are the 'Iron Triangles' in Retreat?" *Policy Studies Review* 5:395–412.

Mitchell, Robert Cameron. 1979. "National Environmental Lobbies and the Apparent Illogic of Collective Action." In Clifford Russell, ed., *Collective Decision Making*. Baltimore: The Johns Hopkins University Press.

Moe, Terry M. 1980a. *The Organization of Interests*. Chicago: University of Chicago Press.

———. 1980b. "A Calculus of Group Membership." *American Journal of Political Science* 24:593–632.

———. 1981. "Toward A Broader View of Interest Groups." *Journal of Politics* 43:531–43.

Nagel, Jack H. 1987. *Participation*. Englewood Cliffs, N.J.: Prentice-Hall.

Nelson, Robert L., John P. Heinz, Edward O. Laumann, and Robert Salisbury. 1987. "Private Representation in Washington: Surveying the Structure of Influence." *American Bar Foundation Research Journal*, 141–200. Winter.

Nivola, Pietro S. 1986. *The Politics of Energy Conservation*. Washington, D.C.: The Brookings Institution.

O'Connor, Karen. 1980. *Women's Organizations' Use of the Courts*. Lexington, Mass.: Lexington Books/D. C. Heath.

———, and Lee Epstein. 1983. "The Rise of Conservative Interest Group Litigation." *Journal of Politics* 45:478–89.

Olson, Mancur, Jr. 1965. *The Logic of Collective Action*. Cambridge, Mass.: Harvard University Press.

———. 1982. *The Rise and Decline of Nations*. New Haven: Yale University Press.

Peterson, Mark A., and Jack L. Walker. 1986. "Interest Groups and the Reagan White House." In Allan J. Cigler and Burdett A. Loomis, eds., *Interest Group Politics*. 2d ed. Washington, D.C.: CQ Press.

Pika, Joseph. 1983. "Interest Groups and the Executive." In Allan J. Cigler and Burdett A. Loomis, eds., *Interest Group Politics*. 1st ed. Washington, D.C.: CQ Press.

Rothenberg, Larry. 1988a. "Choosing among Public Interest Groups: Membership, Activism and Retention in Political Organizations." *American Political Science Review* 82:1129–52.

———. 1988b. "The Route to Activism Is Through Experience: Contributor Mobilization in Interest Groups." Typeset manuscript, California Institute of Technology.

Ryan, Mike H., Carl L. Swanson, and Rogene A. Buchholz. 1987. *Corporate Strategy, Public Policy and the Fortune 500*. New York: Basil Blackwell.

Sabato, Larry J. 1984. *PAC Power*. New York: Norton.

Salamon, Lester M., and John J. Siegfried. 1977. "Economic Power and Political Influence." *American Political Science Review* 77:1026–43.

Salisbury, Robert H. 1969. "An Exchange Theory of Interest Groups." *Midwest Journal of Political Science* 13:1–32.

———. 1975. "Interest Groups." In Fred I. Greenstein and Nelson Polsby, eds., *Handbook of Political Science*, vol. 4. Reading, Mass.: Addison-Wesley.

———. 1983. "Interest Groups: Toward a New Understanding." In Allan J. Cigler and Burdett A. Loomis, eds., *Interest Group Politics*. 1st ed. Washington, D.C.: CQ Press.

———. 1984. "Interest Representation: The Dominance of Institutions." *American Political Science Review* 87:64–76.

———. 1986. "Washington Lobbyists: A Collective Portrait." In Allan J. Cigler and Burdett A. Loomis, eds., *Interest Group Politics*. 2d ed. Washington, D.C.: CQ Press.

———. 1990. "The Paradox of Interests in Washington, D.C.: More Groups and Less Clout." In Anthony S. King, ed., *The New American Political System*. 2d version. Washington, D.C.: AEI Press.

———, and Paul Johnson. 1989. "Who You Know versus What You Know: The Uses of Government Experience for Washington Lobbyists." *American Journal of Political Science* 33:175–95.

Salisbury, Robert H., John P. Heinz, Edward O. Laumann, and Robert L. Nelson. 1987. "Who Works with Whom? Interest Group Alliances and Opposition." *American Political Science Review* 81:1217–34.

———. 1988. "Iron Triangles: Similarities and Differences among the Legs." Paper presented at the annual meeting of the American Political Science Association, Washington, D.C.

Schattschneider, E. E. 1960. *The Semisovereign People*. New York: Holt, Rinehart, and Winston.

Schlesinger, Joseph A. 1965. *Ambition and Politics*. Chicago: Rand McNally.

Schlozman, Kay Lehman. 1984. "What Accent and Heavenly Chorus? Political Equality and the American Pressure System." *Journal of Politics* 46:1006–32.

———, and John T. Tierney. 1983. "More of the Same: Washington Pressure Group Activity in a Decade of Change." *Journal of Politics* 45:351–77.

———. 1986. *Organized Interests and American Democracy*. New York: Harper & Row.

Schumaker, Paul, Allan J. Cigler, and Howard Faye. 1989. "Bureaucratic Perceptions of the Municipal Group Universe: 1975 and 1986." In Harald Baldersheim, Terry Clark, and Hankan Magnusson, *New Leaders, Parties and Groups in Local Politics*. Bordeaux, France: CERVEL.

Scotch, Richard. 1985. *From Goodwill to Civil Rights: Transforming Federal Disability Policy*. Philadelphia: Temple University Press.

Silberman, Jonathan I., and Garey C. Durden. 1976. "Determining Legislature Preferences on Minimum Wage." *Journal of Political Economy* 84:317–29.

Smith, Hedrick. 1988. *The Power Game: How Washington Works*. New York: Random House.

Smith, Kerry. 1985. "A Theoretical Analysis of the Green Lobby." *American Political Science Review* 79:132–47.

Sorauf, Frank. 1984–85. "Who's In Charge? Accountability in Political Action Committees." *Political Science Quarterly* 99:591–614.

––––––. 1988. *Money in American Politics*. Glenview, Ill.: Scott, Foresman/Little, Brown.

Tillock, Harriet, and Denton Morrison. 1978. "Group Size and Contributions to Collective Action: An Examination of Mancur Olson's Theory Using Data from Zero Population Growth." In Louis Kriesberg, ed., *Research in Social Movements: Conflicts and Change*, vol. 2. Greenwich, Conn.: JAI Press.

Truman, David B. 1951. *The Governmental Process*. New York: Knopf.

Uslaner, Eric M. 1986. "One Nation, Many Voices: Interest Groups in Foreign Policy Making." In Allan J. Cigler and Burdett A. Loomis, eds., *Interest Group Politics*. 2d ed. Washington, D.C.: CQ Press.

Vogel, David. 1978. *Lobbying the Corporation*. New York: Basic Books.

Walker, Jack L. 1983a. "The Mobilization of Political Interests." Paper delivered at the annual meeting of the American Political Science Association, Chicago.

––––––. 1983b. "The Origins and Maintenance of Interest Groups." *American Political Science Review* 77:390–406.

Watanabe, Paul Y. 1984. *Ethnic Groups, Congress, and American Foreign Policy*. Westport, Conn.: Greenwood Press.

Welch, William P. 1982. "Campaign Contributions and Legislative Voting: Milk Money and Dairy Price Supports." *Western Political Quarterly* 35:478–95.

Wilcox, Clyde. 1988. "Political Action Committees of the Christian Right." *Journal for the Scientific Study of Religion* 27:60–71.

Wilson, Graham. 1981. *Interest Groups in the United States*. New York: Oxford University Press.

––––––. 1986. "American Business and Politics." In Allan J. Cigler and Burdett A. Loomis, eds., *Interest Groups Politics*. 2d ed. Washington, D.C.: CQ Press

Wilson, James Q. 1973. *Political Organizations*. New York: Basic Books.

––––––, ed. 1980. *The Politics of Regulation*. New York: Basic Books.

Wright, John R. 1985. "PACs, Contributions, and Roll Calls: An Organizational Perspective." *American Political Science Review* 79:400–14.

––––––. 1990. "Contributions, Lobbying and Committee Voting in the U.S. House of Representatives." *American Political Science Review* 84:417–38.

5

Political Parties:
Issues and Trends

William Crotty

INTRODUCTION: THE CONTEXT

Political parties constitute one of the oldest and one of the more traditional areas of political science inquiry. It is also one of the subfields
with the richest lodes of research works. The variety of efforts is impressive, ranging in style from the constrained and tightly reasoned approaches of relevance to party concerns of William Riker or Joseph
Schlesinger, through the empirical, incrementally developed analyses of
political partisanship and party activists, to the colorful and fictionlike
accounts of Tammany Hall and its sister machines.

Defining the Enterprise

There is a range and scope to the studies that defies simple categorization. There is also little unity of approach, research method, conceptualization, or problems explored: in fact, one of the strengths, and
weaknesses, of the area is the wide diversity of undertakings. The only
common bond is that the research deals in some manner with an aspect
of political parties or a topic of immediate concern to the understanding of party operations. The consequence is that the field—in contrast,
say, to voting behavior or the study of an institution such as the Congress or the presidency—is pretty much what an observer wants to make

I appreciate the comments of John F. Bibby, Joseph A. Schlesinger, and Frank J. Sorauf in
developing this paper.

of it. The boundaries are flexible; the work lacks unity and coherence; the approaches used, the questions asked, and the propositions developed in one emphasis or focus (as examples, party organization at the state level, the electoral evolution of party coalitions, presidential nominations) can have little relation to the concerns of investigators in another corner of the field.

Political parties research, then, is more a uniting of a broad disparity, or at best confederation, of individual studies and research emphases with a tenuous relationship to one another than it is a highly focused, clearly demarcated, or well-integrated subfield of the discipline. The rubric "political parties" is all that holds it together.

To varying degrees, this could be said of many of the subfields in political science. The parties area in this regard may be more akin to research on "comparative politics" or "political economy" or, to take a different tack, such ill-defined areas as "elite studies" or "power" or "conflict studies" than it is to studies with a clear sense of subfield limits and some common analytic and conceptual threads. It is pretty much what the commentator chooses to make it, a point that will be amply evidenced in the following discussion.

Initial Perception

A second concern is with the nature of the way in which an academic concern with political parties has evolved. The initial responses to party developments have colored much of what has followed. The result has been a rather tortuous and ambivalent relationship to the subject matter. The perspective on the parties and the research into their operations have had both a negative quality and a normative aspect that is not easy to dismiss. To this day, it influences the way we look at parties. At different periods, the contest among commentators seems to be on who prizes them the most and what is likely to strengthen them most significantly.

I think the reasons for the psychological mood that surrounds party analysis are explainable. Although related, they can be divided into two categories. First is the popular perception of parties, which harks back to the nation's founding. Political parties were not anticipated by the founders; they were considered acrimonious, divisive, and self-serving, as manifest in Washington's Farewell Address; and they were considered hostile to the general will of the people and the nation's best interest. In the context of the times, this view makes considerable sense. Conflict was considered dysfunctional; social harmony was the objective. The political parties of the day were quarrelsome factions espousing divisive and seemingly minority interests. There was no experience, either in the United States or elsewhere, with broad and competitive popular coalitions intended to further responsive government. The modern concept of parties was unknown. As historian Richard Hofstadter indicates, the Founders "stood at a moment of fecund inconsistency, suspended between their acceptance on one side of political differences and opposition criticism, and on the other their rejection of parties as agencies to organize social conflict and political debate. . . . They did not usually see conflict as functional to society, and above all they could not see how organized and institutionalized party conflict could be made useful, or could be anything other than divisive, distracting, and dangerous" (Hofstadter 1969, ix). This is a position not unfamiliar to many countries attempting to institute more democratic governments in the contemporary era. The result in the United States was, in Hofstadter's terms, "a Constitution against parties" propagated "in a quest of unanimity" (Hofstadter 1969, 40–73, 170–211).

It is difficult to overemphasize how important this strain has been in the national psyche. Its most immediate impact can be seen in the state and local regulations governing party conduct, arguably the most restrictive of any advanced democratic nation.

More broadly, there is the mood of suspicion, distrust, and, on occasion, active hostility to the concept of party. In part, this latter attitude results from a mythologizing of the American experience that emphasizes its exceptionalism and divine mandate. There has been a messianic quality to American political oratory from the nation's inception that contains little accommodation for the concept or, as they worked, the operations of political parties.[1] This strain affects both popular perceptions of the parties and, for academicians, the relatively judgmental—or, more accurately, normative—way in which they are often studied.

If the conception of the public interest is a unitary well-being built on an idealized direct democracy, or town-meeting style of political representation, then parties constitute an unknown quantity, and at worst one that poses a distinct threat to the nation's political harmony and social progress. Theories of political representation built on such assumptions from the time of Rousseau to the present day provide little role or tolerance for political parties (Barber 1984).

Even James Madison, one of the earliest party theorists, saw party factions as based on economic differences and the promotion of self-interest in juxtaposition to a general will or public good. Madison relied on a marketplace regulation of competing demands built into government structure to contain the problem and turn it to the state's advantage. Jane J. Mansbridge contends that this was an acknowledgment of the "adversary democracy" that came to underlie American political representation (1983, 16–17). It is a far cry from the concept of a harmonious public will that many early founders chose to emphasize.

The theme of an unanticipated and unwanted party system grafted onto a political system and often serving other than democratic ends is found in many of the early accounts of the parties' birth (Chambers 1963; Main 1974; Charles 1956; Cunningham, ed. 1969; Ford 1967). This strain was to continue in the observations of writers from de Tocqueville (1845) through Bryce (1891) and Ostrogorski (1902) and up to the present. Early academic assessments of parties provided by Woodrow Wilson and A. Lawrence Lowell (Ranney 1954) incorporated such attitudes in advocating relief. The latter are founding members of a tradition in criticism of parties that has advocated replacing the American parties with something closer to the British model. It is noteworthy that the "responsible party" school remains (to this day) the major criterion judging party performance and the preferred alternative for the American party system among critics (American Political Science Association 1950; Schattschneider 1942; Everson 1980; Ranney 1975, 1954).

Certainly, the popular perception of political parties is as critical as it was in the early years of the Republic. At one level, this is the American heritage (Dennis 1985, 1980, 1975, 1966).

The Relevance of the Inquiry

There is another apparent theme, one more influential among parties specialists in the contemporary period. Virtually all now recognize the contributions parties make to a democratic order and, in fact, the indispensability of a party system to an operating democracy. The list of scholars who concur on this point includes, to my knowledge, everyone who has written on political parties in the modern era: V. O. Key, Jr., Frank J. Sorauf, Leon D. Epstein, E. E. Schattschneider, Avery Leiserson, Giovanni Sartori, Austin Ranney, William J. Keefe, Samuel J. Eldersveld, Walter Dean Burnham, Gerald M. Pomper, and James Mac-Gregor Burns, to name a representative list of prominent scholars. The praise has been fulsome and the warnings as to a politics without parties dire. Without parties, or with a degenerating party system, Burnham believes that "democracy will be progressively emptied of any operational meaning and executive-bureaucratic imperatives [will] come to dominate the political system" (1975, 354).

As L. Sandy Maisel has put the matter, since the parties provide the representation and accountability that elected democracy requires, and since they "already exist, we should get on with the work of making them function more productively" (1987, 283).

Such thoughts are indicative of the intensity of the commitment to and the thinking about the critical significance of the parties to the broader democratic system as well as the need and desire to keep them

strong. With varying degrees of zeal, most parties specialists would sub-
scribe to positions close to those cited.

Parties scholars are not alone in their perceptions. Political theorists
in general reinforce the critical importance of political parties to the
realization of a democratic society. Political parties are linked to, and
are a natural outgrowth of, elections, mass suffrage, broad participation
in political decision-making, the popular control of elected officials,
and, most generally, representative government. All of these are intimately interrelated. Henry B. Mayo states that "the existence of political opposition—by individuals and groups, by the press, and above all,
by organized parties—is the litmus test of democracy. It requires no
subtle definitions, nothing that a child could not apply" (Mayo 1960,
147). Political parties are, in Max Weber's phrasing, "the children of
democracy" (quoted in Mayo 1960, 148). It should be added that Weber was not an uncritical advocate of party development.

J. Roland Pennock, in assessing the evolution of Western political
thought, writes that for "the establishment of a stable democracy, the
development of political parties appears to be of first importance"
(1979, 253). If elections are crucial to democracy, as they are, then the
critical role of parties can be taken as a given. Robert A. Dahl argues that
"the system of organizing the major political conflicts of a society by
allowing one or more opposition parties to compete with the governing
parties for votes in elections and in parliament is not only modern . . .
it is also one of the greatest and most unexpected social discoveries that
man has ever stumbled onto" (1976, 276; see also Dahl 1956, 1971,
1982; see also Spitz 1984, 80, 84).

Another contemporary political theorist writing from a different
perspective and with a different set of objectives, and a not uncritical
observer of contemporary political divisions, C. B. MacPherson contends that for the obtaining and functioning of the type of participatory
democratic system he favors "the most important factor . . . is the existence of political parties" (1977, 192; see also MacPherson 1973).

Contemporary theorists of different persuasions, then, as well as
those who compare and assess democratic performance, assign a major
if not dominating role in democratic representation to political parties
(Lijphart 1984a; Powell 1982a). It would appear, as party theorist E. E.
Schattschneider argued so forcibly, that democracy in the contemporary
age truly is "unthinkable save in terms of the parties" (1942, 1).

A cautionary note should be sounded. It may be that a strong attachment to the subject matter and its importance could evolve into a
commitment to what is and a propagandizing for what should be rather
than an assessment of where things realistically stand. Most theorists
equate party worth, rightly, with the functions served by parties for the
political system. Political parties are assumed to perform these better

than any other social institution, which again appears to be correct. Political parties are in a state of change; the direction and consequences of the transitional period are unclear. It might be worthwhile to keep the broader criteria of party relevance in mind when examining party performance and to allow for and explore alternative agencies and processes in relation to how they may have assumed (or may be assuming) some aspects of the parties' role. A sensitivity to competing avenues of political expression, the ramifications of their significance, and the evaluation of party developments within this broader, less uncritical, and more comparative context might be helpful in future research. There is a challenge here to which I return in what follows.

In the hidden assumptions in any research on party institutions or operations there may be a problem. An uncritical emphasis on party "good," that is, its contributions to a highly preferred system of political representation, may blind us to changes that have taken place in the broader political environment. It may also lead to an ossification or rigidification of the field—that is, to the study of a phenomenon or agency acknowledged to be important to ends sought by virtually all (a democratic system) without an uncritical weighing of its changing role or importance or the quality of its performance of its assigned duties. A party is studied because it is believed to be important. By studying it to the exclusion or, more realistically, (unintentional) deemphasis of other, alternative forms of political representation and communication, we could do ourselves a disservice.

The process may be subconscious, but it has clear ramifications. The study of political parties is suffused with a normative element—a "good-bad" dimension—that has been with it since the first such political organizations attracted any notice. Critical analyses of party changes and, more importantly, a shifting societal role for the parties can draw heated reaction. In some form, the observer is suspected of being "disloyal" to the system—or at least less sensitive to the significance of parties, possibly even of promoting a "weakening" of the parties. The point is that a reification of what is, or has been, can blind us to what "is" at present or what might be happening that will have future consequences. The results would serve no good social science ends.

An assumption of the parties' importance can also lead to a reinforcing of the academic community's perception of their pivotal role, again with somewhat unintended and unhelpful consequences. If one goes into a community to study party operations but does not make allowances for competing forms of political expression for the transmission of political influence or for a potential atrophying of form and weakening of impact, one may well be doing an injustice to his/her own research and to the field in general. The questions may remain, as they have in the past: How do the parties operate? What services do they perform? How are they structured? Who are the professionals that man party positions and what motivates them? And how are issue positions decided and whose views do they reflect? These are not insubstantial concerns. My point is that a second level of inquiry might be added, and one of more immediate concern: How important are the political parties in mobilizing and representing voters? What alternatives does the electorate have and what groups compete (and with what degree of success) with the parties in performing these functions? How has the parties' role changed over time? And what are their contributions today, as compared with the past and or with alternative agencies of representation, in fulfilling the theoretical duties of such importance to democratic operations that they have assumed? These are broader questions and, I would suggest, ones that are much more difficult to answer. They are the ones, however, more likely to frame the research agenda of the future than the less critical, assumedly more value-free approaches of the recent past.

A Reservoir of Assessments

Another factor shapes the discussion of political parties. Unlike many subfields in political science, first-rate recent and comprehensive assessments of parties research are available. The most significant for our purposes is Leon D. Epstein's *Political Parties in the American Mold* (1986). This work, the product of a decade's research and a working lifetime's observation of parties, constitutes a starting point for any understanding of political parties' operation or the nature and quality of research in the area. It covers the core areas and basic research dimensions in a considered and balanced manner.

Two other sources of value, both also by Epstein and both incorporated in varying forms into the above work, are his "The Scholarly Commitment to Parties" (1983) and the overview "Political Parties," which appeared in the *Handbook of Political Science* (1975). These, along with the more elegant longer work, provide a foundation on which to base contemporary evaluations of the direction and potential of future research efforts.

Being, as noted, a traditional subfield of the discipline has its advantages. Periodic assessments of political parties, in volume perhaps disproportionate to the current interest in the field or the number of researchers active in it, are available. In addition to Epstein's contributions, an earlier and intellectually demanding effort at placing parties' concerns in a framework would be Avery Leiserson's *Parties and Politics: An Institutional and Behavioral Approach* (1958). Samuel J. Eldersveld's hardcover textbook (1982) contains, among other things, the most complete assessment of the questions raised in conjunction with the

organizational and motivational forces that underlie party performance. Without beginning to exhaust what is available in recent years,
two other hardcover texts—those by Alan R. Gitelson, M. Margaret
Conway, and Frank B. Feigert (1984) and by Robert J. Huckshorn
(1984)—provide systematic introductions to the topics of concern and
to the knowledge in the area.

Some recent, briefer text treatments have appeared in paperback
editions. These contain a range of perspectives that, while building on a
common research base, allow for more thematic perspectives. Such
works would include those by Maisel (1987), a former congressional
candidate as well as a political scientist who relates the classroom to a
practical and field interest in the subject matter; John Bibby (1987), an
author long concerned with state and national party structural and resource development; David A. Everson's study (1980), which assesses
modern parties in accord with responsible party criteria; Howard L. Reiter's (1987) "opinionated" and "radical" (p. vii) presentation, an approach rare for academicians writing in this subfield, which looks at the
"rightward" swing of 1980 party politics and its economic base; and
Richard L. Kolbe's effort (1985) to view party change from a policy
outcome and public benefits perspective.

Variety exists here. In addition to facts, the interpretative positions
provide contrast as well as comprehensiveness. To these can be added
synthesizing efforts that overlap more conventional party overviews,
such as, for example, Herbert B. Asher's (1988, 4th ed.) emphasis on
the recent strains in party affiliation patterns and the parties' impact on
the vote (as well as nominations, the media, campaigning, and other
areas of interest); Malcolm E. Jewell's and David M. Olson's (1988, 3d
ed.) thorough accounting of the highly differentiated state party systems; and David R. Mayhew's (1986) broad yet empirically generated
exploration of organization within the state and local party systems.

These, in turn, can be added to less recent yet valued assessments of
political parties, such as V. O. Key, Jr.'s *Politics, Parties, and Pressure
Groups* (1942–64, 5 eds.); Austin Ranney and Willmoore Kendall's theoretical and influential *Democracy and the American Party System*
(1956); Hugh A. Bone's multieditioned *American Politics and the Party
System* (1949–71); Edward McChesney Sait's *American Parties and
Elections* (originally published in 1927 and going through many editions); and Charles E. Merriam's *The American Party System* (1922).
These are supplemented by Frank J. Sorauf's more recent *Party Politics
in America* (6th ed., coauthored with Paul A. Beck). The result is a rich
and full series of works that provide in-depth overviews of both party
developments and the intellectual evolution of the thinking of scholars
on party-related questions.

Such works provide a strong resource base and, possibly, even an overabundance of relevant synthesizing efforts. There being no lack of comparable efforts of recent vintage makes the job of evaluating promising avenues of research in the area considerably easier. The previously published overviews allow for the identification, isolation, and examination of potentially significant themes in this paper without arousing fears that other, equally important work has been neglected. Current research efforts should receive their due in one context or another. The emphasis in the following has been selective; the intent, to raise questions and to advance a few ideas and possibilities for future research.

These thoughts, then, provide a background against which to examine a number of areas of active research interest: (1) the search for theory; (2) the party as vote mobilizer; (3) the party as activist; (4) the party as nominator; and (5) the party as organization.

The analysis ends with some thoughts on the current status and future direction of parties research.

THE SEARCH FOR THEORY

There has been no dominant theoretical perspective in the study of political parties, and in fact most of the research is self-consciously empirical and atheoretical. This condition is not likely to change in the foreseeable future. What we can do is acknowledge what is available that is of direct relevance to political parties and, briefly, the assumptions made, most of which are of limited utility given the type of problems treated in the rest of this paper. One perspective, more recent and more intimately related to party concerns—namely, that of Joseph A. Schlesinger (1983, 1985, 1975)—will be treated in more detail.

All of the theoretical approaches should be familiar and most all of them require only passing notice. Among the most common is Anthony Downs's rational modeling approach, in which the party is viewed as "a team seeking to control the governing apparatus by gaining office in a duly constituted election" (1957, 1). Downs's assumptions apply to the electoral party and provide the basis for a theory of party competition. His ideas have had enormous weight in rational-actor perspectives, and his assumptions and team emphasis find voice in many of the political economy approaches. The theme can be found in the party-related analyses of policy outcomes, presidential support patterns, and voter decision-making (Monroe 1984). In a variety of ways, and particularly in terms of assumptions of rationality and identifiable underlying dimensions of explanation, the perspective relates to approaches such as those used by Mancur Olson, Jr. (1965), discussed at different points in this paper, and by Albert O. Hirschman (1970), both of influence, and the work of Morris Fiorina, Benjamin I. Page, and others in their treatment of public-

choice and rational-modeling explanations of opinion formation and
voter influences (Fiorina 1981; Page 1978). Two rational-actor perspective approaches of direct relevance to modeling the prenomination process are discussed later (Aldrich 1980; Bartels 1988).

The "team" concept is not new; in varying contexts, E. E.
Schattschneider (1942) and Joseph A. Schumpeter (1950), among others, employed it. Schattschneider was concerned with arguing for accountable, responsible, and issue-oriented political parties. Schumpeter
defined democracy in terms of process: "the democratic method is that
institutional arrangement for arriving at political decisions in which individuals acquire the power to decide by means of a competitive struggle for the people's vote" (269). The competing teams, indispensable to
the operation of a democratic system, were the rival parties that mobilized and represented the electors.

Both team conceptions have had influence in the study of political
parties. The Schattschneider party-responsibility model (Schattschneider
1942; American Political Science Association 1950) has provided the
principal criteria for critically evaluating the performance of the American parties. Schumpeter's conception (like Schattschneider's) assumes
the lack of need for intraparty democracy within organizations (choice
and democratic control are confined solely to the vote between competitive parties in the general election). This perspective has provided a theoretical point of departure for critics of the recent party reforms and has
been influential in the debate (Crotty 1987, 1980). Many, perhaps most,
party specialists share the Schumpeterian assumptions.

There are competitive schemes for classifying political parties, the
most prominent being Maurice Duverger's (1954) and Giovanni Sartori's (1976). These are useful for the broad purposes of categorization.
They are static, however, and provide few clues to the multiplicity of
party types or the social conditions that give birth to the various party
systems, limitations that restrict their applicability. Such classifications
make no claims to predictive or explanatory force.

An approach deserving attention at present is Joseph A. Schlesinger's application of rational-choice modeling explicitly to the party
organization. It ranks among the most carefully constructed theoretical
reasonings to date and has had significant success in accounting for the
specialization of function and the idiosyncracies in organization that
characterize parties in the United States (1983). It also has proven useful in a field study of local parties (Lawson, Pomper, and Moakley
1986). For his achievements in this regard, Schlesinger's work was recognized by the Political Organizations and Parties Section of the American Political Science Association.

Schlesinger proceeds from two assumptions: first, that in political science there is agreement on a basic framework and a set of propositions

concerning political parties; second, that less developed than theories of political competition, like Downs's, are the theories of party organization. Schlesinger would link the two. He devotes his attention to articulating an understanding of party organization, "since the development of a cumulative theory of party rests upon our views of organization, and since all of the discordant perception of what is happening to American parties today flows around different views of organization" (1983, 373).

The nuances of Schlesinger's theorizing cannot be conveyed; the basics can. He employs Downs's definition of a party. He then develops his model by identifying its characteristics. First, the political party is market-based: its goal is to win public office. The "political market" compared with the economic marketplace is discontinuous (electoral cycles vary) and offers collective (policy) benefits to all, as well as private benefits to a few. The market goal (winning office) dominates decision-making (policy-making is secondary), and internal organizational arrangements and intraorganizational influence are exercised by winning candidates (those who account for market performance and therefore for organizational success). The political marketplace is the key here: "the political market evaluates openly, automatically, externally, and with exquisite numerical precision the output of the political party" (1983, 381). "It is the clarity of the electoral market from the party's standpoint that matters," Schlesinger writes (1983, 380).

Second, organizational output affects organizational maintenance. Political parties produce collective goods. As Olson has argued, the incremental addition to the collective good for the individual is so small in a large organization that it is less than the expenditure of effort the individual must make to join or stay active in a group. Olson's explanation for being active, of course, was side benefits, and this provides an elegant affirmation of what we know about activist motivation within parties. Those who are attracted by broad collective ends (issues, ideology, an individual candidate's attractiveness) to join a political party will be the young, the least experienced, and the least knowledgeable. Because of the frustrations met in achieving or contributing to collective objectives, turnover within the organization will be high. Those who stay do so primarily for personal reasons (friendships, enjoyment of the activities, status, or some type of immediate private gain). The explanations for lack of intraparty democracy and oligarchic tendencies can be found in the ties that bind people to political activity.

Third, organizational compensation is indirect rather than direct; labor is contributed and voluntary rather than paid. This is central to explaining how and why party organizations operate as they do. Those indirectly compensated by an organization have less stake in the group and feel less responsibility to it, and their needs, more than the organization's, shape performance standards.

The party, then, as organization is distinct from other groups. It is market-based, offers collective benefits, compensates its members indirectly and is thus unable to discipline them, and cannot reassess its objectives. It is not a normal business organization. Yet,"from this unique combination of properties flows the peculiar character of the party and its ability to adapt to a changing world" (1983, 389).

Schlesinger's assumptions are a development and extension of his previous work, which emphasized that ambition for electoral office motivated party behavior (Schlesinger 1968, 1965). The model is parsimonious and proceeds from a basic assumption that most would agree is fundamental to the American parties: a party's success is measured by winning elections. The model, as Schlesinger notes, does not say, "how well the parties represent the variety of interests in the society, how well they articulate or moderate conflict, how well they are perceived by the electorate, how successful they are in inducing popular participation, how well they provide effective government, nor how responsible they are in providing realistic alternatives" (1983, 397). Nonetheless, by the criteria assumed in the model, Schlesinger does believe that "the two major parties have never been healthier" (1983, 396).

Schlesinger's model is relatively new and its ultimate impact hard to judge. It provides a perspective, one of the most comprehensive available, for tying together a number of diverse strains in the analysis of political parties. The likelihood is that there will be more such efforts, which is all to the good. The more theoretical applications and conceptual developments that are attempted, the more models generated and explanations advanced, the better it will be for a field that has not been known for the quality or variety of its theorizing.

The overall objective of theorizing was stated by William H. Riker a generation ago: "to rise above the level of wisdom literature . . . to join in the creation of genuine sciences of human behavior" (1962, viii). This is the intention in political parties research, as it is in other areas of the social sciences. At the moment it is just that: a goal to be sought. At present, there is no grand theory of political parties. There are, however, several potentially promising leads; but for the foreseeable future the necessary strategy may be to seek middle-range or weaker, problem-oriented working guides to direct specific research efforts.

THE PARTY AS MOBILIZER OF VOTES

The relationship of the party to its electoral base, curiously, is a tenuous one. On the one hand it could be argued that the link is the key to what the party does. That is, the point where the party intersects with the voter, the way it does, and the behavior enhanced by doing so are among the most important research questions the subfield could explore.

This may be so. However, the relative paucity of studies that concentrate on this interdiction indicate that either it is perceived to be less important than suggested here or, more likely, that it is a particularly difficult relationship to explore. The problems are many, including trying to isolate cause-and-effect relationships, a virtual impossibility in the social sciences, and attempting to pinpoint the boundaries and impact of a traditionally vague and malleable organization by using relatively amorphous mass public tests, which require the most imaginative of research designs. What, of course, can be shown are tendencies and statistical relationships—assuming that reasonably decent indicators of the party organization and its activities can be devised. This is not easy to accomplish. Most studies of the party trace changes in its levels of activity, funding, services offered candidates, organizational growth, and the like, and then presume that, if these have become more significant, then the party per se must be having a greater impact and therefore be of more importance. Much of the party decline/revitalization debate is conducted at this level.

The Party and Its Constituents: Mobilization Activities

One researcher who has consistently explored such elusive questions is Samuel J. Eldersveld (1986, 1982b; Katz and Eldersveld 1961). Most prominent is his classic study of local parties in Detroit/Wayne County (1964). In this, he identified what could be considered the most important ("critical") of party activities—registration, canvassing, and election-day efforts to get voters to the polls—and assessed the extent of local party efforts in these areas. Only 17 percent of the Democratic precinct leaders and 25 percent of the Republican precinct leaders engaged in all three activities. Further, two-thirds of the Democrats engaged in no election-day activities, two-thirds of the Republicans and over one-half of the Democrats did no canvassing. If American parties aspire to be electoral machines concerned with winning elections, the most common depiction of their raison d'être and the explanation usually given for their weak organizational articulation and deemphasis of policy-making, this is an undistinguished performance. Eldersveld extended his research canvass by combining organizational indicators at the precinct level (record-keeping, number of precinct workers, leadership direction) with task performance (i.e., the precinct's investment in critical activities) and ended by classifying only 7 percent of the Democratic precincts and 3 percent of the Republican precincts as "ideal" (i.e., meeting all of these criteria). One-third of the Democratic and three-fourths of the Republican precinct leaders admitted never meeting with their precinct workers (1964, 349–51). Such findings as these raise questions about the organizational efficiency and vote mobilization skills of the parties.

If the party at the local level is presumed to be the strongest and the one most closely in touch with constituents, as it has been argued at least until recent times, then such results raise further questions as to what exactly a party does do and whom it serves. The diplomatic thing to say is that more empirical studies of this nature are needed in order to make any broad judgments about party efficiency and relevance. In reality, the Detroit parties are not only fair indicators of party performance, but it is likely that they are among the better organized and more productive of the local parties (Crotty 1986a). On another level, and difficult to explain, is that Eldersveld's lead in conceptualizing a manageable urban research agenda has not served as the model and basepoint for like-minded investigations in other localities.

Eldersveld himself has extended his original work (1986), analyzing the Detroit precincts at successive elections up to the present. Comparing Detroit party activists with those sampled by Dwaine Marvick in Los Angeles over a similar time span (1986), Eldersveld found that roughly between something less than one-fifth to a maximum of one-third performed all three tasks. Overall, the outcomes were similar or somewhat below those found in Detroit in an earlier period. An application of the same measures to four other cities, three taken to be indicative of the developments in the Sunbelt, shows broadly similar results (Los Angeles, as indicated, Houston, and Nashville). The one exception is Chicago, where the remnants of the Daley machine still produce impressively at both ward and precinct levels (Crotty 1986b). In referring to his earlier findings in Detroit and Marvick's in Los Angeles, Eldersveld writes that "the nature of task performance was, on the one hand, not intensive and, on the other hand, characterized by improvisation and autonomy. Party activists were pretty much left to organize their own operations, and therefore the level of performance was minimal" (1986, 107–8). Little seems to have changed over time.

Others have dealt with related problems, but the number of studies is limited relative to the potential payoff of the research. The example that has been given is an extended one. Similar efforts should be relatively easy to duplicate. The hope is that more studies along these lines will be a priority in the future. The results would help to fill in empirically much of the conjecturing that passes for debate in the area.

There is another link between party and constituency that also holds promise, although its relevance may be more limited in today's political environment. The political machine based its support on its abilities as a service agency for ethnic voters (Erie 1988; Bridges 1984; Gove and Masotti 1982; Rakove 1975, 1979; Gosnell 1968). A constituency service approach—what does the party do for its supporters?—

could hold promise, although perhaps more so in some localities than others. Thomas M. Guterbock (1980) postulated a number of "exchange models" to explain the interactions he observed between a Chicago ward organization and its constituent base. The value and results of this approach are developed elsewhere (Crotty 1986a). It may be that most party units have little to no interaction of this nature with voters, which brings us back to their election-only focus. The service approach could be expanded to investigate the between-election activities of parties that do connect with supporters (Eldersveld 1964; Crotty 1971). Again, the chances are that such efforts are limited.

The point of such research is to explicate the linkage of the party to the voter. Where do they intersect? What does the party do specifically to mobilize voters and to develop electoral support? How comprehensively and how well does it perform such activities? Has its linkage efforts increased or decreased over time? Put more broadly, how intregrated with or isolated from its constituent base is the political party? Efforts to answer such questions would be welcome.

Linkage and Voter Attitude

Limited attention is going to be paid here to party-related voter attitudes and voter decision-making. The judgment is not based on degree of significance—if the preceding discussion has merit, this linkage process is one of the most significant of party ties. American parties have always been cadre parties, composed of a small, self-selected band of activists whose principal concern is campaign activity designed to win elective office. One contribution of the voter decision-making research has been to show the extent of voter loyalty in the electorate and the influence of party identification on the vote decision. A party so conceived has been the single most important factor influencing the vote. Whether this still holds true is a matter of debate, but it remains among the handful of most powerful predictors (Campbell et al. 1960; Nie et al. 1976; Asher 1988; Miller 1987). The research in this area is abundant and among the best executed in the discipline.

Why, then, not treat it in depth? There is some question among party specialists as to whether the voting studies explicitly belong in the area of party research. The newly organized American Political Science Association section, Political Organizations and Parties, has been engaged in a debate about whether to welcome voting researchers as kindred souls, perhaps renaming the organization to reflect their pivotal role, or to define parties more narrowly, discouraging students of mass electorates and focusing attention on organizational and activist concerns. It would appear to be difficult to ignore the best-researched and mostly explicitly developed area of party impact.

The reason for a restricted treatment is not relevance, but the ready availability of assessments of the voting research (see Dennis; and Leege, Lieske, and Wald in these volumes, and the works listed in Asher 1988). It ranks among the most systematically explored and thoroughly reviewed research areas in the social sciences.

The major concern related to political parties is declining voter identification. There is agreement among students of voting behavior that proportionally fewer people (as compared with the stable party period of the 1950s) are identifying with the political parties; that party loyalty is strongest among the oldest cohorts, weakest among the younger and weakest among new entrants to the electorate; that the proportion and influence of independents in the electorate have increased and that many of the new independents do not fit the profile of the marginalized voter of old; that among those who do identify, party loyalty is less intense and less strongly associated with the vote (contributing to such phenomena as split-ticket voting); and that the party is less influential (although still highly significant) in determining the election outcome.

Beyond these basic points there is considerable disagreement over such questions as the correct measurement of party identification (Dennis 1981; Weisberg 1980; Petrocik 1974); the precise impact of party identification on the vote and its relative importance compared to other factors, specifically issue concerns; the most appropriate way to measure how policy, as compared with party, factors influence the vote (Fiorina 1981); the reasons for an atrophying party base, disaffection or disinterest (Wattenberg 1986, 1984; Craig 1985; Stanga et al. 1986); whether party defectors are basically the product of one historical period and whether defection rates have stabilized over the last decade, returning to identification levels comparable to those of a generation ago; and, most significantly, the meaning and implications of all of these for understanding the continuing influence of party in shaping voter attitudes and electoral outcomes (Nie et al. 1976; Miller 1986, 1987; Asher 1988; Burnham 1970, 1975, 1976, 1982).

Each of these questions presents research opportunities, particularly for over-time analyses of importance. For the present, however, it is enough to take what is given: namely, that the mass of voters have had a psychological attachment to the major parties strong enough to preclude space for alternative parties and to confine true independents to a small minority of the electorate, and that both the inclusiveness and the intensity of these forces has weakened significantly in recent decades.

If this is correct, then by itself it means a new era for the parties. In effect, they will approach something approximating the competing teams models, offering candidates and incentives (policy positions) to a relatively unattached (or less attached) and less predictable electorate. One might surmise a greater reliance on money, media, campaign technology, the personal qualities of candidates, and candidate-centered campaigns in elections; in effect, more of exactly what we have. One could also predict a more limited linkage and party impact, no matter how approached or measured, than in the past.

Such developments have broad ramifications. The problem may be more serious than parties' researchers have chosen to assume. Clearly, the parties' role and influence would be reduced. But the implications are broader. In his discussion of the political parties' contributions to "responsiveness and responsibility" in a political system, J. Roland Pennock asks if the party system can survive under the control of a small band of activists within an independent electorate? The question, while unanswerable at present, "may pose a problem for democracy in the United States" (1979, 298).

It is recognized that the consequences of such developments could be substantial. One implication can be pointed out. Roughly 50 percent of the electorate now votes in the high-turnout presidential elections. If party mobilization efforts weaken further and party loyalties continue to erode, it is reasonable to expect little improvement in the levels of participation and the possibility of even further decline. The reasons given for not voting vary from institutional factors and satisfaction with the status quo to apathy, ignorance, and even alienation from the system (Conway, in these volumes; Wolfinger and Rosenstone 1980; Conway 1985). What researchers do agree on is that there is a systematic class bias to turnout: the higher the individual's social status, the more likely he/she is to vote; the lower the social status, the less likely the vote. Political parties have served to mobilize the less affluent in coalition against those with power in the system. A number of party specialists have pointed this out—none more persuasively than Walter Dean Burnham: "Our whole electoral politics rests upon a huge and growing political vacuum at the bottom of the social structure." Burnham attributes this in large part to the absence of relevant policy choices for those at the lower end of the economic order in a limited-option party system. The "debates between the defenders of a confused and degenerate political capitalism on one side and the resurgent advocates of social and economic conservatism on the other are simply irrelevant to a great many of them [non-voters]." Those with "literally no alternatives . . . rationally abstain" (1981, 126–27).

This may be. There are a number of persuasive explanations for different categories of nonparticipants, as Burnham has made clear in his extensive writings (1970, 1965). It is also apparent that a party system that fails to mobilize one-half of the electorate, for whatever reason, creates problems. Party loyalty is a family legacy (Conover, in these volumes). Also, the structural aspects of American electoral politics dictate that only two parties can effectively compete. In practical terms, this means that there is a limit to the depths to which the parties can fall, a cushion is imposed by the system and socialization practices that provides a minimal base of support regardless of circumstances. What the bounds of the system are at present is unclear. Assuming some continuation of present tendencies, questions are raised. What are the implications of the weakening attachments for party vitality and performance? for policy-making? for representation within the society? How effective will a "competing teams" model, likely to emerge from such a downscaling of participation and long advocated by some, be in fulfilling a range of traditional party functions? Such concerns may be moving to the forefront of the research agenda.

THE PARTY AS ACTIVIST

If the party system is evolving in the directions indicated in earlier sections, then of increasing importance will be an understanding of the activists who represent the party in performing its duties. This "subculture with its own peculiar set of norms of behavior, motives, and approved standards," as V. O. Key, Jr., described them, may hold the key to "the puzzle of how democratic regimes manage to function" (1961, 537).

Following this reasoning, the assumption is that the exploration of activists' social status, motivations, and policy and ideological views will accomplish a number of objectives. First, the social and issue commitments of the core stratum most influential in party decision-making indicate the representativeness and the quality and nature of their linkages with broader publics. And, second, changes in these dimensions over time chart the transition in a party's role within the society, the groups and other influences to which it is responding, and the directions in which it is headed.

Traditional approaches to elite analysis focus on social background dimensions; motivations for joining or continuing to work in an organization; and the issue positions, ideological commitments, and democratic values held by the activists (Lawson 1979).

Social-status profiles are a conventional focus of social science research. The depictions and conclusions—activists are recruited disproportionately from higher socioeconomic classes—are too familiar to require further comment.

Party activists are mostly self-starters, self-recruited into politics. Of interest are the motivations that induce them to undertake activity as well as those which sustain their involvement. One answer appears to be that people enter politics for altruistic ideological and policy reasons. They see their efforts as contributions of service to the community. This emphasis appears to be standard; recruits in different sections of the country and over a period of years follow the same general pattern.

There is, of course, turnover in personnel. It results from a number of factors, including, primarily, a reordering of personal priorities or simply burnout, reasons suggested by Marvick's longitudinal analyses of Los Angeles's activists (1987). A changing social base for the parties can also force the replacement of party representatives (Marvick 1986, 125–26).

The emphasis undergoes a transformation for those who remain in party activity. Ideology gives way to social concerns; activists stay predominantly for "solidarity" or "personalized" reasons—they enjoy what they do and the other professionals with whom they work. "After activists have been in the party, they clearly 'learn' to see party work as socially rewarding and personally gratifying in terms of mobility and recognition needs. . . . For those who stay, the party is a rewarding 'social group' " (Marvick 1986, 107; Eldersveld 1986; 1983, 177–79).

The number of studies attempting to illuminate activists' ties to the party organization are limited. The approach would appear to offer rewarding opportunities for further research, including experimentation with more sophisticated measures of individual motivation.

More varied and more common are studies of activists' policy and ideological views. Dwaine Marvick has employed a variant of the "competing teams" approach as a theoretical starting point for an empirical investigation into local parties. In the process, he has given the conception fuller elaboration and more substantive body than is usually found in the often abstract references encountered in the less empirical work.

Marvick writes that "something that can be called *performance symmetry . . .* seems necessary if electoral democracy, by vesting genuine power in the electorate, is to make the election-day outcome open to doubt" (1980, 65). Such a symmetry involves a balancing of commitment with varying mixes of organizational resources by the competing parties to provide a basically open and meaningful choice for elections.

In addition, to make the voter's decision significant, "It is necessary to ask whether the rival parties stand for alternative styles of governing, for alternative programs of public-policy implementation, and for alternative notions of persistence and change. In short, it is necessary to establish in what sense the rival parties are *asymmetrical*" (1980, 65–66).

Marvick examines Los Angeles cadres in terms of their personal characteristics, ideological persuasions, intraparty cohesiveness, and interparty differences, and in relation to the accuracy of their perceptions of the electorate. The last dimension could be expanded to include an evaluation of the strategic choices in campaigns made by party decisionmakers and the weight given ethical concerns in determining tactics (1986, 1980, 1967; Marvick and Nixon 1961). These dimensions are used mostly to develop the "asymmetries" Marvick has outlined. Organizational indicators such as those explored by Eldersveld and others

(Eldersveld 1986; Crotty, ed. 1986; also see below) could be employed to examine the competitive balance between parties in the allocation of strategic resources (Marvick's "symmetry").

A common line of inquiry in relation to political views has been the succession of studies that followed Herbert McClosky and associates' (1960; McClosky 1964) analysis of the competing issue centers of the Republican and Democratic parties. The research focused on the 1956 national convention delegates. The same approach has been repeated by Jeane J. Kirkpatrick, Warren E. Miller, M. Kent Jennings, and John S. Jackson III, among others, to trace the policy commitments or such factors as "professional/amateur" perceptions of, arguably, the most important of activists, those who select their party's presidential nominee and determine its policy priorities.

Kirkpatrick (1976) argued with more vigor than is usual in political science that a new and unrepresentative elite had captured the Democratic party in the wake of the nominating reforms; that the reforms themselves had "significantly weakened" the party; and that the new elite and its attitudes posed significant threats to the party system as it is understood in the United States (see also Kirkpatrick 1973). The attack was broad-ranging and fundamental—again, the type of approach not normally encountered in the discipline. In developing her points, Kirkpatrick wrote: "the assumption that winning elections is the prime goal of political leaders and parties is the foundation of the theory and practice of two-party politics as we have known it" (italics omitted), and that "The assumption that parties will continue to make winning elections their principal goal is the basis of an expectation that American parties will continue to be inclusive, aggregative, pragmatic, responsive, and representative. Any deemphasis on winning elections would profoundly alter the fundamental character of the American parties by removing the 'discipline of the market' " (italics omitted, 1976, 353).

From the examination of the 1972 national convention delegates, and specifically of the McGovern Democrats, Kirkpatrick concluded that "the new presidential elite" held views and represented constituencies antithetical to the traditional operation of the party and severe enough to constitute a direct threat to the entire party system. Among the factors believed to hurt the party were: (1) changing incentives to political participation among activists in presidential politics, notably the presence of significant numbers of delegates for whom support for party was not a significant incentive to political activity; (2) changing attitudes toward organizational maintenance, notably the presence of significant numbers of Democrats with negative attitudes toward those practices generally regarded as necessary to preserving an organization; (3) changing ideological styles, notably the rise of holistic, internally consistent ideologies at both ends of the political spectrum; (4) changing patterns of "group bias" within the presidential parties, notably the rise of "constituencies" based on race, sex, age, and candidate preference and a concomitant decline in the concern for those geographical constituencies that are the traditional units of American politics and the basis of the federal system; and (5) the changing social composition of the political elite, notably a continuing decline in the political role of labor and business and the rise in the political influence of symbol specialists (1976, 351).

Seldom is a condemnation so broad or such emotion generated by a research study. The reaction illustrates a number of points addressed in the introduction to this paper: namely, that political parties are important to those that study them; that a transition is in process and that it is not always welcome (Polsby 1983; Ceaser 1982; Price 1985); and that there is a normative undercurrent of considerable force within parties research, a factor to consider when judging research efforts in the field. Of greater immediate concern, Kirkpatrick's interpretations raised questions that others in the field were forced to address.

John S. Jackson III and associates (1976, 1982; Crotty and Jackson 1985, 103–39) sampled both successive national convention memberships and compared delegate issue positions and politically relevant attitudes to those of state chairs and national committee members (Jackson 1982, 1976). Not surprisingly, this research indicated considerable variability in the social characteristics and policy commitments of cadre representatives in different contexts. American parties are structurally isolated and ideologically pluralistic. They are more resilient than any sampling of one activist subgroup at one point in time could hope to capture. The activists represented at national conventions are more likely to have a greater sensitivity to policy and to be more subject to turnover than activists in other less visible and less important positions (Crotty 1990; Baker et al. 1990; Crotty and Jackson 1985).

Some of the flavor of the continuities and changes in personnel and political perceptions of delegates has been caught in the work of Miller and Jennings who, with a base of five thousand respondents, traced national convention members over three presidential elections (1972, 1976, and 1980). They found, for example, in what they refer to as a "signal contribution," that "the large majority of delegates are hard-core, quadrennial campaign participants. They are not one-timers, drawn only by the uniqueness of a given year. These hard-core activists tend to be the most loyal, the most devout, the most party-oriented, and the most at odds with the opposition party" (1986, 240). The views of party elites change, and "most generally the conversion was in accordance with the secular winds of change sweeping over the party" (1986, 241).

The parties' base in the electorate and their nominating elites responds to much the same electoral and systemic influences. Both parties experience multifactional divisions, and these can be cause for concern. "The schisms within parties—while not as great as those across parties—are deep, pervasive, and less easily handled than the more institutionalized conflict across party lines" (1986, 245).

By the 1980s, the Republican elite was more out-of-touch with its mass base and the public more generally than were Democratic activists. Nevertheless, the party decisively won all three presidential elections held in the decade.

The question of representation through party elites is more complex than many have assumed. Perhaps this is the greatest contribution of such research. The process is subtle, varied, and responsive to immediate or long-term public concerns in often unpredictable ways. "Mass preferences and behavior change with almost glacial slowness over time, . . . seldom at the pace implied by much elite rhetoric . . . in the short run, the different degrees to which the various party factions 'represent' the values and interests of their party's followers are more than consequences of accidental fits or misfits of ideological convictions than they are the product of leaders' anticipatory reactions of their powers as political persuaders," according to Miller and Jennings (1986, 250).

Overall, a more fundamental question is raised by the research than the controversy that spawned it: "At the very least, the repeated evidence of the lack of elite rapport with a mass electoral base reveals a certain looseness or weakness in the institutional linkage that is supposed to ensure representation of mass demands through the workings of the competitive two-party system" (1986, 249). If the linkage is found wanting in this association, then where is it strong? Presumably, nominating processes are the most open and most responsive of the political party's representational channels. Are other party elites better representatives of the mass values? How, exactly, does the representative process operate within the parties? More to the point, how adequate is the process to the demands of a democratic society? These questions are significant, the answers yet to be found.

Miller extended this line of analysis to the 1984 national convention delegates and, in related approaches, Ronald B. Rapoport, Alan I. Abramowitz, John McGlennon and associates (1986) examined the views of seventeen thousand delegates to state presidential nominating conventions in eleven states in 1980. Rapoport et al. have effectively widened the canvass, analyzing the pool of activists in eleven states from which the final national convention delegates were chosen.

The Miller study in 1984 found that, "compared to delegates chosen by the traditional party mechanisms of convention or caucus, delegates chosen by primary election are more representative of the party's rank and file—just as the advocates of primary elections hoped they would be" (1988, 129). The advocates may have hoped, but this finding goes against the popular wisdom in the discipline. The Miller research reemphasizes the impact of parties. "Party as the mobilizer of activists, the guide for activists' decisions, the shaper of the local context for activists' participation, or the goal for activists' efforts does more than candidate loyalty or ideological conviction to preserve the bond between the leaders and the led" (1988, 133).

Rapoport and colleagues address continuing issues in the field when they assert that the research they report shows "contemporary party activists to have more complex motivations, beliefs, and values than previous research had suggested, holding strong views on issues along with strong party loyalties and capable of pursuing ideological goals and electoral success simultaneously" (1986, 6).

One final example: a series of studies by Charles D. Hadley, Robert P. Steed, Lawrence W. Moreland, Harold Stanley, Charles Prysby, Tod A. Baker (1990), and others have looked at southern national convention delegates as indicators of the transformation taking place within southern politics. The change is marked; the parties are cohesive and ideological, one liberal, the other conservative; the defectors from one party to the other are more ideologically comfortable in their new surroundings; blacks have assumed a major role in the Democratic party, none of consequence in the Republican; and, in general, the two parties polarize along contrasting issue lines. Compare these findings with the South of a decade ago or the one depicted in Key's *Southern Politics* (1949). To the extent that presidential activists accurately represent political change more broadly and the transformations within the parties—significant concerns that have already been raised—the South may be further along in its realignment than the rest of the nation and in a further transference of roles may provide the model toward which the party system nationwide may be evolving (Crotty 1990).

As Miller and Jennings indicate, the time frame in their studies is "too brief for the mapping of the dynamics of mass-elite linkages through national party politics" (1986, 249). This could be said for all of the studies and for the research in the field generally. But a productive start has been made. Serious questions have been asked and a debate has been joined. The quality of work is high. It is likely that these particular lines of inquiry will continue and are in little need of encouragement or promotion. The likelihood is, further, that they will be pursued on a more systematic and cumulative basis. If anything, we are likely to see more rather than less attempted, and on an increasingly sophisticated and broader scale. Within this context, some further questions that could be addressed are: How do the various party activists—state and local party officials, public officeholders—link together into some form of collective representative whole? What differentiates the perceptions found in activist subgroups? What serves to explain the differences

found? How representative of broader party elites are the national convention activists? How do the attitudes and policy positions of elite subgroups compare to party supporters and to the public? Should attempts
be made to expand research efforts to incorporate a variety of party
elites, assessed in relation to the symmetrical/asymmetrical competing
teams approach that Marvick advocates or in another context that holds
equal or better promise of being comprehensively structured? And, ultimately, how do representative processes work through party elites? This
last concern can be said to underlie much of the research in the field and
to provide it with its most fundamental significance.

THE PARTY AS NOMINATOR:
THE INSTITUTIONS

The nominating function is widely believed to be the most essential
contribution of a party. It is the critical center of party operations, the
parties' principal gift to democratic governance. Anything that affects
the parties' role in nominating candidates consequently receives extensive academic and public attention.

Two fundamental concerns emphasize the importance of the parties' nominating role and explain why its significance extends well beyond party specialists and party concerns. First is the importance of the
decisions made. Second is the quality of the outcomes. The latter consideration—how you get the best people to govern—underlies much of
the concern over nominating forms from the time of the Constitutional
Convention up through the present.

The debate over identifying the best of candidates evolves into other
issues that command a good deal of attention: concerns about intraparty
democracy versus "peer review," selection by amateurs as opposed to
professionals, broad participation versus mediation through group and
party leaders, the impact of campaign finance practices and the media on
the process, the proper mix of primary and caucus/convention structures, the issue and demographic representativeness of those who participate in the process, and the servicing of party- and coalition-building
needs. The debate on each point is spirited. But the concern over quality
and outcomes is fundamental to debates over the selection process. Quality and outcomes are the most significant of the issues facing students of
the process, and ones to which many of the other issues can be reduced.
These dimensions attract continuing attention from the media, politicians, academicians, private foundations, and ideological and policy oriented groups—virtually anyone seriously interested in the political
system and with a stake in how it operates. When things go wrong (or
appear to), the presidential nominating process is the first object of attack. This is one aspect of party goals whose importance is broadly recog-

nized. "One must always realize that the nomination of candidates for President and other elected offices is and always has been the raison d'être of American political parties, and because the presidential nominating process plays a vital role in determining *who* eventually get elected, such discussion always involves the large questions of governance" (McCorkle and Fleishman 1982, 141).

The process may be even more important than most Americans choose to realize. The presidential candidates are selected, increasingly, by the parties' activist base. The ultimate victor is in reality reduced to the choice between two contenders by the voters in the general election. The crucial choice among a range of contending alternatives is made at the nominating stage. And it is a crucially significant decision. Americans choose the president, but, in effect, they are selecting the "President of the World." The winner commands the greatest military and economic arsenal of any nation. And, unlike in domestic areas, there are lesser restraints on a president in foreign-policy decision-making. The president, literally and without overdramatization, controls the supreme power of war and peace. Presidential campaigns are fought primarily on domestic issues, and yet, to use the words of Ernest R. May, the "American citizens who go to the polls act on behalf of humankind"; they are the "surrogates" for "all the people in other nations with a stake in the outcome" (May 1987, 41, 42; Dahrendorf 1987, 27).

It is unlikely that voters in the United States think of themselves in this manner. On the upside, voters have traditionally favored the reasoned approach and the predictable candidacy to the risk-takers: "Looking back over the whole of American political history, one is struck by the extent to which, in presidential selection, the electorate has seemed to put a premium on prudence. . . . Most of the time . . . the nominating process has winnowed out just about everyone whose approach was not careful, prudent, and risk-minimizing. In instances in any way exceptional, the voters nearly always choose the more prudent-seeming candidate when the general election comes around" (May 1987, 42).

This is a comforting thought. One wonders if it is accurate. Does the "prudent" candidate prevail in the two-party general election? Does the nominating process reward the centrist and discourage the fringe candidate? Is boldness on policy matters a negative in presidential selection? Is such a condition of restraint within the process in and of itself a "good"? These are the types of concerns that ignite never-ending speculation.

The stakes are high. The importance of the office and the power wielded therein, regardless of party concerns, invite attention to the process.

This raises a second major issue, not unrelated to the first, and again one that helps to stimulate a continuing interest in nominations. The

quality of presidential candidates has been a constant point of controversy. After every presidential election the losing party and some of the
public are induced to blame the system: a better process would result in
better candidates and consequently in electoral success, so the equation
runs. The calculation is not quite so straightforward. There are broader
social and political factors at work in any given election that are often
dismissed in simplistic, one-factor explanations. The process may be as
open and receptive to diverse candidacies as it can get without al-
together breaking the constraints of a party-bounded institution (in
fact, this is one point of criticism raised by those displeased with the
present system).

The attacks on nominating processes are not new. Over a century
ago, in his *The American Commonwealth* (1891), James Bryce chose to
explore "Why Great Men Are Not Chosen President." Bisexualizing it,
many might ask the same question today. A main component of the
Progressive Era attacks on the parties was the effort to restructure nominating forms in order to secure more acceptable results. The fascination
with nominating processes is likely to continue, given what is at stake.
Such concerns favor a continuing research interest in the procedures.

It may be, as Bryce claimed, that mediocrities (May's "risk-minimiz-
ers"?) dominate in those selected for the presidency. Some critics tend to
be defensive on the point and, for this and other reasons, look to a parliamentary party arrangement as producing better candidates, possibly offering features or assumptions they would like to see incorporated into
the American nominating process. The principal points along these lines
are that the parliamentary system rewards those who have had extensive
experience in office, are familiar with the issues confronting the nation,
and are skilled in the give-and-take of legislative exchange and policy-
making—all useful qualities for serving as a nation's chief executive. The
American system, in contrast, is said to give prime weight to campaigning abilities, virtually to the exclusion of most others. Of the skills that a
president or prime minister would find useful to give direction to government, an American president is likely to enter with only one: the ability to
mobilize popular support. The American system, writes Richard Rose,
"makes campaign skills not only the be-all of the presidency, but also
threatens to make it the end-all" (Rose 1987, 68; see also DiClerico and
Uslaner 1984, 171–201; Kessel 1988).

The problem may come down to the acceptability of the people
chosen and the criteria used in selection (Hess 1988; Ceaser 1979; Nelson 1987; Keech and Matthews 1976; Aldrich 1987). The question may
be whether any other types of system produce significantly better results. The claim here would be that they do not. Even if the results of
other processes were decisively superior, a further question arises as to
whether it would be feasible to incorporate the procedures needed to

achieve such outcomes into the American system (the answer again is likely to be no). A comparison of the candidates put forth by parliamentary party systems in the European democracies and by the participant-oriented system now in use (or its predecessors) in the United States would indicate that quality (or the lack thereof) is not confined to any one nominating process. Is a Reagan or a Bush significantly better or worse than a Thatcher or a Mitterand? "I see the danger, but cannot discover the remedy," Albert Gallatin once said about problems respecting the electoral college. Others might apply the same reasoning to presidential selection (although most have a fair number of reforms to propose). Debates of this nature are likely to continue unresolved.

At present, and by any measure, the area does not want for research attention. The 1968 presidential election constituted a turning point in renewing academic interest in studying the process. The efforts to democratize nominating procedures spurred an outpouring of work. The focus has been on the causes and consequences of the reform measures adopted in the election's wake. The controversy generated by the redesign of the nominating process raised anew questions about the operation of nominating institutions and the representativeness of presidential-level party activists (a topic treated elsewhere in this paper). Since then, the amount of attention given the reform measures and their impact—and related issues growing out of these concerns—has been extensive (Ranney 1975, 1987; Price 1985; Shafer 1983, 1988; Polsby 1983; Marshall 1981; Kirkpatrick 1973, 1976; Ceaser 1979, 1982; DiClerico and Uslaner 1984; Lengle 1981; Crotty 1978, 1983, 1980; Keeter and Zukin 1983; Pomper 1980; Heard and Nelson 1987; Crotty and Jackson 1985; Miller and Jennings 1986; Miller 1988).

There is little advantage in reviewing what has been written. In point of fact, the debate may be in its closing stages, a product of changing times and social conditions and the tacitly understood need to live with (if not fully accept) what has occurred—the warts, compromises, reallocations of power, intended and unintended consequences, and all the rest (Ranney 1987; Crotty 1987). More useful would be to focus on a limited number of efforts that have attempted to organize the information in the field and to superimpose a sense of order and predictability on an unruly process.

Three such approaches have been chosen to illustrate the type of organizing schema and eventually predictive and explanatory theorizing that is gaining a toehold in the area. These range from the conscientiously developed arguments of a Howard L. Reiter (1985) to the attempts at more formal theorizing put forth by John H. Aldrich (1980) and Larry M. Bartels (1988).

Reiter sets up competing alternative explanations, or what he refers to as "four causal theories," in order to explore systematically what has occurred in presidential nominating practices and the reasons for these. The four explanatory models are not unfamiliar. They are: the "1972 School," the "Party-Decline School," the "1936 School," and the "Static School." Reiter uses these as a basis for a close analysis of both the events that have occurred and the reasoning put forward to explain or critique these. He sets up decision-making rules, or standards, to measure and accept or reject those arguments on behalf of the viability and superiority of the various approaches. He attempts to operationalize and test the contentions with empirical data. Reiter concludes that "the nominating process has evolved since the early 1950s gradually into one in which state and local party leaders can no longer control nominations," and that it is a product of "the long-term decay of party organization in the United States" (1985, 14; italics omitted). The key references are "gradually" and the "long-term decay of party organization."

One does not have to accept Reiter's judgments, or for that matter agree with his critiques of the competing schools of thought, to realize that such a closely reasoned approach, employing the available empirical evidence and developing a clear focus for evaluating the often generalized arguments being made, provides a service to those in the area. It also indicates one approach to organizing the diversity of data sources available and the conflicting claims put forth within a meaningful and comprehensive format.

The Aldrich and Bartels studies can be treated in relation to each other. Both employ formal theory, empirical data, and, in different degrees, statistical modeling to explore concepts that give order and predictability to the process. Aldrich uses rational-actor theory to explain the behavior and the constraints in the decision-making of presidential candidates in the prenomination period. Bartels uses a public-choice model to develop the concept of "momentum" in conditioning choices and outcomes at successive stages of the nomination process. He is more concerned with influences on voter decision-making in the primary elections.

Both efforts, then, are serious attempts at social science theorizing: producing order from the seemingly arbitrary; accounting for and predicting the nonobvious; and combining theory, observation, and empirical data to test and explain propositions. The ends more than the specific explanations advanced give importance to the undertakings; this is the beginning of what is likely to be many such efforts of relevance to this particular field.

Aldrich's intention is "to offer a theory that can explain the actions of candidates in preconvention presidential campaigns" (3). He approaches this objective through rational-choice modeling, the assumption that candidate behavior is purposive, nonemotional, and goal-directed. There are questions concerning the clarity of goals to be articulated and the "utility functions," or the ordering or ranking, of an individual's preferred outcomes; how fully informed actors are or can be in situations of uncertainty; and the impact of roles and institutional arrangements in limiting choice. The problems are substantial but in this context manageable.

Aldrich illustrates how "policy, resource, delegate, and vote gathering strategies are inexorably intertwined." As he notes, "where a candidate competes is a decision made in the light of the campaign" (201). He also assesses the impact of institutional factors, policy positions, timing, financing, background characteristics, and the political climate in which the contests take place in reviewing how candidates decide strategy and what makes for successful candidacies. For example, in targeting the primaries likely to be contested, Aldrich puts forth a series of propositions that in light of both the finite limits imposed on any campaign and practical experience appear reasonable: candidates are more likely (than unlikely) to compete in any given primary; several are more likely to compete in primaries seen as competitive; winner-take-all and the nonproportional allocation of delegate votes discourage all but the likely winners; the more delegates at stake, the greater the probability of competition; and, on days with several primary elections, candidates are more likely to compete in several than one and more likely to compete in one than none (143–44). The rules change as the conditions change. Aldrich believes, overall, in modeling the 1976 races as he did, that the patterns uncovered were not exceptional, but rather that "such dynamics are common to all nomination campaigns" (135). Among the "more refined conclusions" reinforced by Aldrich's research were:

> the instability of preconvention campaigns; the possibility of a stable campaign for one candidate amidst a generally unstable campaign; the importance of an outright victory, preferably early; the importance of subsequent victories in augmenting that first one; the importance of avoiding a failure to meet expectations, especially in key and early states; and the apparent inevitability of momentum or its negative once there has been a significant turn in the candidate's fortunes. (135)

Bartels's concerns are somewhat different. As to his accomplishments, he writes that "In addition to demonstrating the decisive importance of momentum under specific political circumstances, my analysis goes some way toward providing the systematic theory of primary voting across campaign settings . . . [once] considered so unlikely" (1988, 11).

As indicated, prenomination voter decision-making is approached through the perspective of public-choice modeling. Bartels would make two claims for his analysis. First, that traditional public-choice theories—the attempt to "aggregate individual preferences into collective preferences while simultaneously satisfying some minimum conditions of fairness and reasonableness" (296–97)—do not adequately deal with changes in social choice in fluid situations, the example of course being nomination decision-making. The alterations in candidate preferences he observed worked in "systematic, predictable ways" and were "an integral part of the process of choice itself" (307). Second, in shaping individual choices into a collective decision, he suggests that "at least under some circumstances [as in the prenomination campaigns], quite diverse individual preferences can be shaped and modified by social interaction to produce, if not a consensus, at least a genuine majority for a single alternative" (307).

These would be contributions to public-choice theory, providing a more dynamic element to the modeling without actually disputing some of its main assumptions. The points are important, especially when looking at voter decision-making in a volatile situation such as the prenomination cycles, but the evaluation of such considerations is well beyond the bounds of this paper. The main contributions for specialists in parties are: the process through which individual political choices are made and candidate coalitions built; the factors that contribute to these collective decisions; the inherent logic of voter decision-making in primaries; and the nature of the interrelationships and explanatory models that can emerge from the systematic explanation of political processes. It is this last point that both Bartels and Aldrich can be used to illustrate nicely. On these counts, they can serve as examples for future such undertakings.

There is little likelihood that research in this area will fall off to any great degree. The problems to be addressed are intrinsically interesting; a research tradition of consequence has been established that holds promise (as indicated above) of pushing further the limits of social science research; and the institutions addressed are fundamental to the operations of a democratic society. The questions are important, and the forces working to alter both the party and the nominating system over the coming years will demand attention. There is much here to occupy the prospective researcher, and the quality of the work being done suggests that this could be one of the more fruitful areas of parties research.

THE PARTY AS ORGANIZATION

Organization has provided a convenient point of departure for parties researchers concerned with tying together a number of threads of party activity. Organization has served as a key for those who focus on the party as a complex of operations; organization can give it focus, coherence, and meaning. At least, this is the belief of those who chose this approach as the nucleus of their investigations.[2]

Theories of Party Organization

Serious attention has been paid to the role and operations of party organization by a number of prominent writers, from Michels (1962) to Duverger (1954) and Eldersveld (1964) to any of a number of recent scholars. "Democracy is inconceivable without organization," writes Michels, a sentiment that party organizational theorists would applaud. Michels went on to spell out the differentiation of function, the complexity of organizations, the psychology of leadership, and control of resources that led him to declare that "organization implies the tendency to oligarchy" and, most notably, the famous words "Who says organization, says oligarchy." Michels's "iron law" has provided one analytic perspective. The general mechanisms he elaborates that separate the mass from the leadership in an organization and that push toward the inevitable control of organizations by an active minority are undoubtedly true, although the picture may be more complex. Michels's claim may be truer for well-articulated, tightly disciplined organizations with clear reward and advancement structures than they are for the episodic, voluntaristic, and vaguely bounded American party organizations, notable more for their diversity of forms, multiplicity of objectives, and diffuse incentive systems. A first step, then, would be to identify the conditions under which oligarchic tendencies prevail and those under which they are tested. While the "iron law" may identify universal organizational tendencies, it does not necessarily have the same consequences that Michels envisioned.

Second, there is a gap between leaders and led, between those with power and the apathetic mass, as Michels, Pareto, Mosca, and other more recent writers have contended. The focus in such comparative parties research is on the characteristics of parties' elites and the extent to which these reflect a party's base. The perspective is useful and the findings serve to reinforce Michels's insights. Exceptions are rare and the emphasis is on explaining why some party leadership cadres are closer in views and background to their followers than others. The approach in its broadest conceptualization—elite-mass differences and linkages— has been productively applied to American parties, but here its usefulness may be more limited. While the elite-follower comparisons are useful for any one point in time, there is no one elite that regularly controls party decision-making. In comparison with other organizations and other parties, American parties are relatively open; there is turnover in the top echelons of party leaders (national convention delegates, national committee members, the national and state chairs, various party committees, presidential and other candidates for elective office), and the nature of competition for office and the coalitional base of the parties make control of career lines and reward structures difficult to impossible. Replacement and circulation of elite themes seem more profitable foci than any strict applications of Michels's ideas. As Samuel H. Barnes notes in reference to Michels, "if by oligarchy we mean merely that minorities rule, then the law is irrefutable; but it is also trivial and tautological" (1967, 135). If, on the other hand, the implication is that elites promote their own interests in contrast to those of their memberships, or that the elite distorts membership values in significant ways, these questions can be (and have been) researched.

There are other organizational perspectives. Maurice Duverger proposed two. One dealt with electoral arrangements: a plurality vote tends to create a two-party system; proportional representation and a two-ballot election, a multiparty system. It may not be correct to credit this assertion—"the closest to a sociological law" of those found in his *Political Parties* (1954)—with giving rise to the emphasis on the impact of electoral structures in party systems, but it did contribute to a development that emphasized these arrangements, and thus to a continuingly profitable strain of parties research (Duverger 1986; Riker 1986). The clarity of association and the formulations that can be tested make the subarea relevant to parties one that is conceptually tight and systematically explorable (Rae 1971; Rae and Taylor 1970; Riker 1986; Duverger 1954, 1986; Grofman and Lijphart 1986; Lijphart 1984a, 1984b; Satori 1976, 1986; Taagepera and Shugart 1989).

Duverger's second focus has received considerable attention from organizational researchers. In this, he postulated four organizational types and attempted to develop the causes and consequences of each. The categorizations are broad and descriptive and, as Kenneth Janda's research has indicated, require considerable effort to articulate precisely (Janda 1980). The consequence may be classificatory types that add both insight and richness of language to the study of parties but contribute less to comparative empirical work than might have been expected. Duverger's more important accomplishment may be in highlighting relationships between electoral forms and party structures.

Taking another approach, Samuel H. Barnes (1967) has adapted Mancur Olson's "logic of collective action" to study democracy within the Italian Socialist party. It is a provocative application that manages to illustrate the strengths of one well-received rational-actor theory and, as far as I know, is one that has not been duplicated. Olson's theory was intended for interest groups. He stipulated that "rational, self-interested individuals will not act to achieve their common or group interest" in a large organization. In groups that seek collective goods that benefit all, the individual's input would be limited because he is not likely to affect the outcome; yet he profits from whatever group concessions are won. The large group is likely to achieve "suboptimal" collective ends, that is, less than it might attain if its membership were fully mobilized; noncollective group services (friendship, social attributes, status awards) attract group members from "latent" publics; and new, large-scale groups are difficult to organize because of high start-up costs and the prospect of limited collective rewards for the individual.

Barnes's applications of these broadly stated propositions to political parties is imaginative. First, there is the question of the role and utility of the party in seeking collective goods.

> The mass political party is a brilliant invention for mobilizing for collective action politically unsophisticated people in a highly stratified society. . . .
>
> The logic of collective action suggests why. . . . For upper strata with their multiple memberships and high political competence, politics is a by-product of other organizational activity. But for low status groups, the costs of initial organization are prohibitive unless skills can be purchased with specific benefits. Political organization becomes crucial for providing *and* controlling these specific benefits. (Barnes, 111–12)

Some tensions in party operations are not easily explained. How are party activists mobilized or encouraged to continue their efforts if collective rewards are minimal or, in the case of out-parties, if the party's collective goals cannot be met? The answer is now familiar. Barnes writes that "individuals can be tied through socialization and emotional relationships into a political subculture that fulfills most of their needs despite the absence of control over public policy" (113). This is exactly what Eldersveld's research has shown and what Schlesinger, in his adaptation of Olson and rational modeling, has also argued (Eldersveld 1964, 1986; Schlesinger 1985, 1975). The question Barnes believes researchers should ask is "what are the specific noncollective benefits accruing to party participants" (138)? The answer can largely determine the relationship between leadership cadres and followers within a party and the ends and success of the party organization in realizing its collective goals. In the case of the party studied, he concludes that "As the logic of collective action suggests, party democracy . . . was a by-product of different leaders pursuing their individual noncollective benefits" (138). "The lesson to be learned is obvious: it is unreasonable to expect rational people to act counter to their own interests, and if one wishes to maximize the democratic potential of an organization one must find ways to secure specific benefits for those who are willing to oppose the majority" (137).

The potential is there for understanding the parties' mobilization strategies, activist conflicts within the parties, and organizational successes in achieving goals (winning office), in fostering intraparty democracy, or in simply sustaining themselves.

There are other approaches. Better known is Eldersveld's advocacy of "stratarchies," overlapping and competing leadership groups within the parties, as a model for explaining organizational behavior. In part, the approach offers an answer to questions raised by Michels. It goes beyond this, however. Eldersveld posits four "primary structural properties" that distinguish parties. First, there is the party as permeable, flexible, adaptive, and responsive to its environment, the party as an "open accordion"; second, there is the party as a product of "subgroup coalitions" representing differing social and economic interests and the need to integrate, reward (partially), and stabilize these multiple demands, the party as coalition alliance; third, there is the party as a mix of hierarchical relationships, power and decision-making mechanisms, the party as "stratarchy"; and fourth and last, there is the party as a product of the recruitment, advancement, motivation, and turnover of activists, the party as end product of "multiple elite" career patterns. "Our major foci," says Eldersveld, "are . . . the *congruence* of leadership perspectives, the *coherence* of hierarchical relationships, and the *competence* of the group in the fulfillment of social and political functions" (1964, 3).

Eldersveld's "stratarchy model" allows for a broad range of empirical efforts and provides a basis for comparative research. The dimensions are nonobvious and subtle. The model is also general, possibly more so than it first appears, although the application to the Detroit parties should provide a baseline for comparing results. It is also complicated and depends on the skill of the researcher in developing empirical indicators to illustrate its relevance. The model itself has not been actively employed to guide research investigations, perhaps as a result of the obvious nontheoretical approach in the field, or possibly because it is less clear or adaptable than it may first appear.

There are still other theoretical perspectives. Joseph A. Schlesinger has advanced "ambition theory," winning elective office as the goal of parties (Schlesinger 1965, 1966, 1968) and a theory of party organizations discussed earlier (Schlesinger 1983). Party organizations can be approached as "public utilities," as Epstein does in inviting comparisons with other quasi-public regulated agencies (Epstein 1986, 1989); from a political economy or resource allocation or "resource theory" perspective, stressing, as Thomas Ferguson and Joel Rogers (1986) do, the influence that shifting economic elites and their positioning on policy matters has on party priorities; or from a broadly defined "linkage" focus (Lawson 1979). And there are others: the party as an accountable agent of public policy (the party responsibility school); and, less relevant to the American experience, the party as a mass membership organization or the party as an instrument of revolution (Eldersveld 1982).

Each of these approaches has relevance for party organizations. Neither these nor any others, however, have produced to date the unity of focus, the potential for related comparative efforts, or the explanatory power or elegance necessary to be considered a dominating theory of party organization for research purposes. For now, it may be enough to try to answer such questions as: What type of organization relates to what ends? What are the patterns (elite, issue, ideological, communication, decision-making, structural) to be found within the organizations? What factors contribute to what types of organizations? What activities do the organizations engage in, with what degree of success? And how do the organizations compare on these dimensions across levels or across nations? These are not significantly different from the questions that party specialists have been asking for generations.

Adapting to the Terrain

There are fundamental problems to which researchers must adapt. They may be more acute in studying American parties than in some other areas of inquiry.

First, the reason that Epstein refers to parties as public utilities is because of the extensive and, in cross-national comparison, virtually unique manner in which they are regulated by law. The controls exercised by the states resemble those applied to certain types of quasi-public business enterprises. They began in earnest during the Progressive Era and cover everything from financial resources to ballot positions and nominating procedures. The specificity and scope of the regulations vary by state and overall reflect "a civic culture that is broadly hostile to party organizational control" (Epstein 1986, 155–56). In effect, there are two factors here: American culture is antagonistic to political parties generally, as discussed earlier (Dennis 1980), and, more to the point, this strain is evidenced in the state regulation of party structures and activities, a fact of life for which organizational analysts must make allowances. The observation is not new. Sait (1926), Sorauf (1954), and others have made the same point. Yet this is an aspect of party organizational research that distinguishes it from other bureaucratic structures and from political parties in other nations.

Second, political parties were developed to parallel government structure. This evolution makes cohesive organizations difficult and, in the fragmented American political system, more than likely impossible. It means that parties at different levels reflect the needs of the governing unit at that level. Hierarchical decision-making, program development, and organizational articulation are subservient to the demands of political survival that shape any one level of competition. If the usual distribution between legislative and executive or nonlegislative parties is added, the complexity of party research and the failure to develop adequately coherent organizational models becomes more understandable.

There are two (or four, counting the legislative parties) national parties; a hundred state parties; a possible seven thousand county parties (based on 3,600 counties); and "perhaps 200,000 or more precinct, ward and township units" (Eldersveld 1982, 95). These figures alone help to explain why party analysis, much less party organizational research, can be taxing.

The research on organizations reflects these divisions; it traditionally focuses on one set or level of parties—the national (presidential or legislative), state, or local (as an example, see Beck 1974). The demands and characteristics of each level are different. Segmentation by layer provides a manageable way of dealing with the diversity of organizational forms and relationships. Students of parties concentrate either on one level or on a small number of related aspects of organizational performance. To put the point another way: few studies look at party organization from top to bottom, for the very good reason that each organizational level focuses on its own ends. Hierarchical cohesion is a fiction. The ties between party levels are fragile and poorly developed. The overarching connecting linkage may be little more than a claim to membership in the same political community.

The complexity of investigation at the state level alone is indicative of the diversity of political environments in which the parties compete. It is illustrated by the multiplicity of categorizations of party types, approached either in relation to measures of party competition or cross-tabulations of local-state party structures (Jewell and Olson, 3d ed., 1988, 26–27, 64–65). These categorizations of state party organizations are based on the research of Cornelius P. Cotter, James L. Gibson, John F. Bibby, and Robert J. Huckshorn, easily the most comprehensive of its type ever conducted.

The Cotter et al. (1984b, 1984a, 1980; Huckshorn et al. 1986) research compared the state parties in relation to bureaucratic development and service capabilities, impact on the electoral process, relationship to their political environments, and influence on officeholders and public policy. The field research concentrated on a sample of 54 state parties. The other 46 state parties were surveyed through mail questionnaires, as were 560 state chairs who served during the period 1960–78. Although the research was executed in the late 1970s, the data base allowed for some over-time comparisons. The authors write that their analysis shows "the parties are found to have gained in organizational strength over a period when they were generally thought to be in decline" (1984b, 158). They conclude, "It may well be that the changes observed in American party politics in the past few decades are changes which should be expected as a system of episodic voluntary associations gives way to modern institutionalized parties" (1984b, 168). A professionalization and maturation of the state parties may be in progress.

Cotter and associates also examined county parties. They found that these were not well organized bureaucratically, that much of the party-building that characterized the state level had not penetrated to the county parties, and that while state parties did assist county parties, county party strength was independent of state party strength. State party influences appeared to have a modest impact on the county parties.

Most county parties did engage in some activities and, to the extent that organizational strength could be measured against a previous study of 122 counties in 1964, Cotter et al. could conclude that "local party organizations have not become less active or less organized over the past two decades" (1984b, 57). There are indicators in the research that county parties, much like state parties, respond more to the demands of their immediate environment than they do to intraparty hierarchical needs. Gibson et al.'s continuing studies of the county parties reinforce many of these themes. Gibson and associates found that, at a minimum, parties in the counties are active and operate at a level consistent with that of a generation ago.

In comparing a panel of county parties between 1980 and 1984, for example, Gibson et al. found that organizational strength was maintained at the level it had been earlier. Where there was change, while modest, it was in the direction of greater party strength. The research is multifaceted, in part employing a form of Marvick's "performance symmetry" conception (1968a, 1980, 1983b). The authors suggest that Eldersveld's "stratarchy" idea "may well become an anachronism" (Gibson et al. 1989, 86), giving way to a more integrated party presence. (It is a view not shared by Kay Lawson, Gerald Pomper, and Maureen Moakley in their study of party organization and activists in twenty-five New Jersey municipalities [Lawson et al. 1986, 362].) Gibson and associates emphasize the adaptability of county parties and the opportunities for their growth and development.

At the local level, the research of Eldersveld, Marvick, Gibson, and Alan Ware (1985, 1979), among others, provides a necessarily selective and somewhat fragmentary insight into party developments. Comparisons over time or across cities are difficult to make and generalizations hard to come by. Overall, the research output is not as extensive as one might expect. A study by Eldersveld, Marvick, and others of five localities found that, to the extent it could be determined, party activities and organizations have changed little over time. They have not dramatically improved where such change might be expected (the Sunbelt) or deteriorated in the declining industrial cities of the North. Over-time comparisons of urban parties are based primarily on Eldersveld's (1986, 1964) and Marvick's (1986, 1968a, 1979; Marvick and Nixon 1961) continuing studies of Detroit and Los Angeles. Their measures also show little fundamental change. The conclusion could be that party decline has not penetrated to lower-level parties; or that party activity at this level is generally minimal and this has not changed much; or that the revitalization within the national and state parties has not yet permeated the precinct and ward level parties; or that party units at this level march to their own drummer and whatever change does take place, for better or worse, will be in response to pressures generated by community forces.

The area receiving the most attention at present is national party operations. This is where the most substantial recent party development has taken place. The improvements in funding, staffing, organizational expansion, candidate recruitment, media services available, and involvement in campaigns provide the bulk of evidence of party resurgence. The increasing institutionalization of the parties at the national level, and especially that of the Republican party, the model for what has occurred, has led to optimistic assumptions concerning the parties' future. Xandra Kayden, an academician, and Eddie Mahe, Jr., a practitioner, are enthusiastic proponents of the developments they chronicle and their implications for a resurgent party system. They write that "both parties went through a metamorphosis and are now emerging in a far stronger organizational position than they have ever been [in]" (1985, 10). In the process, the American party system has undergone a rebirth.

A. James Reichley, in recounting the expansion of campaign services, funding, and organizational capabilities of the national presidential and congressional parties, concludes that the "effectiveness of the national parties . . . is probably at an all-time high" (1985, 196). Others would agree (Kayden and Mahe 1985; Kayden 1980; Herrnson 1988, 1986; Price 1984; Bibby 1980; Bibby and Huckshorn 1978; Huckshorn and Bibby 1982; Longley 1980a, 1980b, 1980c). Reichley is properly cautious about what can be expected in changing eras and from different administrations but does go on to suggest that "a politics tied more closely to principles and ideals is more appropriate to the current stage of our national life" (197). The perspective is well summed up by Larry J. Sabato's apt phrase "the party's just begun" (1988).

If revitalization is in progress, it is a top-down phenomenon, a new twist in American politics. Previously, the national parties had little power and few resources. The national committees filled a limited role as planning agencies for the quadrennial national conventions. The parties are emerging as more effective service agencies for candidates. Of what core importance they are to congressional campaigns or in influencing broad-based political thinking is difficult to measure. The bet is that in presidential campaigns their importance has probably decreased and their influence over nominations is more restricted. But, as indicated in the introduction, there are no real substitutes for the mass party.

For organizational analysts, questions emerge as to the scope, penetration, and causes of party institutionalization. How do the various party units interrelate? What gives them coherence or provides unity? What has produced the dynamic for growth—or at least a reorientation of concerns—at the national level? Do the changes indicate an evolution in a progressive shift of party organizations toward a more bureaucratized, campaign-effective, and policy-aware institutional development? Are the changes likely to affect all levels of party organization? What are the critical factors in fixing where transformations occur and the type of change that takes place? Are hierarchically structured parties more a future reality (or probability) than a present fact? Or, in fact, are the formal party structures—despite impressive funding and organizational gains—becoming more peripheral to the political enterprise? As for a research perspective, is a bureaucratic, organizational orientation a reasonable synthesizing overview for an integrated research approach to parties—now or in the foreseeable future? Can it serve as a useful jumping-off point to address such concerns? These are open questions at present, not easily answered.

The Party Environment

To complicate matters further, substantial changes have taken place in peripheral institutions and practices that directly impact on party performance. These are well known and have been extensively reported. They include: changes in campaign finance and regulatory practices; the public funding of presidential prenomination and general election races; the creation of the Federal Election Commission to oversee the distribution of public funds and the conduct of federal campaigns; the Supreme Court's, and the judicial system's in general, more active involvement in determining the applicability of statutory limits affecting the parties; the rise in influence and importance of the PACs (Political Action Committees); the dominant role of the media and, more specifically, television in serving as the major means of communication between candidate and voter; the reliance on political consultants to run the candidate-centered campaign; and the emphasis on polls, direct marketing techniques, telephone surveys, and computer-generated voter identification programs in operating a campaign. Add to these, the fundamental restructuring of the presidential nominating process; the dealignment of party affiliations in the electorate; the realignment of the party coalitions and voting blocs taking place in the South; the increasing policy and ideological polarization of the major parties; and a continuingly apathetic and inattentive electorate, and the picture emerges of parties attempting to operate within a social and political culture undergoing redefinition. The rules are changing. Each of these developments should be reflected (and undoubtedly is) in how the parties attempt to do what they do. The attention paid to these developments has been substantial, as befits their importance. To the diversity of social settings and the technological/communications advances of recent years can be added the complications posed by the levels of government problems, the quasi-public regulation of significant elements of party activity, and the parties' state-supported monopolization of electoral power. Party organizations are complex entities under any conditions. At present, the problems implicit in the analysis of parties as organizations are compounded by a party culture in transition.

Measuring Party Organization

Joseph A. Schlesinger has pointed out that parties research has not called on organizational theory to any great extent. The reasons are varied and many of them obvious. As should be clear from the above discussion, political parties are not typical organizations. In 1965, Schlesinger argued that "it is remarkable how little the study of party organization . . . has developed beyond its state at the turn of the century." He attributed the failure principally to "the intractable character of the notion of party which has referred to instruments as different as the Communist Party of the Soviet Union and the Prohibition Party of the United States" (1965, 764). The result has been that "the literature on parties presents a confusion of methods of classification, a compound of descriptive and prescriptive ideas" (1965, 765).

First, if, as has been argued, American party organizations are more attuned to the demands of the level of government at which they compete and are directly influenced by the technological, communications, and electoral changes of the social setting in which they operate, then the complications for orderly bureaucratic behavior are compounded enormously. Second, it is reasonable to assume that with parties, as with other organizations, there is a "correlation between the time in history that a particular type of organization was invented and the social structure of that type which exists at the present time" (Stinchcombe 1965, 143).

American parties are a product of evolutionary development during the nineteenth century, and their forms and structures reflect that parentage. The basic unit of the party is at the state level—the national developments have been more recent—and even then the state units have little communication with or influence on subunits such as county or local party organizations.

These can be taken as reasonable propositions supported by the literature. These points reemphasize the uniqueness of parties as organizations. Still, organizational theory and an organizational perspective may have their uses. A general conceptual framework, borrowed from the organizational theory literature, that lays out the dimensions to be explored may be of help in indicating what can or should be done. Also, a broad typology of parties may have relevance for indicating relationships and resultant structural responses to different social settings, as well as suggesting a developmental framework for organizational change over time (see Anderson 1968).

Typologies of Organizations

A simple classification of the types of information needed to provide a fuller picture of the dimensions of organizational operations would include those shown in table 5.1.

These represent areas susceptible to exploration. They have the virtue of opening the perspective on parties to a number of different factors more common to the study of conventional organizations. For each dimension, there are a series of measures that could be adapted to use in the study of parties.

It should be clear that the party organization will score poorly on many of these measures. One problem is the variety of party forms, all of which are distinctive and none of which conforms to those of traditional bureaucracies. An elaboration of the structural types to be found—or which are put forward as desirable for party operations—could include the "personalistic," familiar in one-party areas and more traditional party cultures; the "pluralistic," reflecting the coalitional alliances and interest-group leadership bargaining of the dominant New Deal system; the "programmatic," an issue-based association of likeminded supporters resembling the party responsibility model, the major reform alternative advocated for the American party system; and the "populist," an approach that would emphasize participation, open decision-making, and intraparty democracy, a model implicit in early reform efforts in the nominating process. Each approach is characterized by a different series of organizational arrangements that provide a clearer indication of the nature of the party system in relation to the articulation of the various units of the party structure (see table 5.2). Conceivably, each could provide a broad model or stage of party development, ranging from the inchoate and rudimentary forms of an unformed system to the more accountable and developed stages suggested by the "programmatic" or "populist" directions in which the American party system may be moving. When each basic type is cross-tabulated with the dimensions suggested for organizational exploration, the elaboration of the parties' bureaucracy and operations should be well advanced over what is now known. Not incidentally, there should be more than enough to occupy research attention.

Table 5.1
A Classificatory Schema for Dimensions of Party Organizations

Category	Indicators
I. Political environment	
Social setting	SES characteristics, census data, income and educational levels; competitive patterns
Attitudinal base	Pro- and anti-party values, political views
Interorganizational relations	(a) Relations with other complimentary or competing organizations (PACs, community groups) and opposition party (b) relationship to other party units—national, state, local
Legal setting	Laws limiting party activity, financing, competition for office, or structural arrangements
II. Organizational structure	
Formal authority	Organizational mandate, charter, rules, by-laws
Decision-making	Power over decision-making—who makes decisions, who influences these—and resources of organization; at what level major decisions are made; enforcement
Communication patterns	Who communicates with whom, on what issues, how open are channels, what effect on organizational decision-making—what types of information are passed on

continued

Cornelius P. Cotter and John F. Bibby, in an unpublished paper on party organization, proceed from the assumption that "Party organization is an especially useful focal point for consideration of ramifying relationships with other actors in the political process" (Cotter and Bibby 1986, 1). This is a view held by many party researchers. An organizational focus can help to integrate within a broad context the many

Table 5.1
continuing

Category	Indicators
Social relations	Informal patterns of communication, influence and friendship patterns within and outside organization—relationship to community groups and external power centers
Division of labor	Structural articulation of organization; specialization; variety of subunits and services; number of specialists
Activities	Duties performed by level during campaign and between campaign periods; electoral, organizational, service activities; specialization and differentiation of activities by unit; policy-formation and enforcement
III. Attitudes	
Organization objectives and values	Perception of organization and organizational aims; loyalty to organization; satisfaction with operations and decision-making; amateur/professional orientations; goal(s) assigned
Role norms	Perception of roles; clarity and precision of role divisions; values, duties, activities associated with the roles
Motivations	Initial attractions to party work; reasons for continuing; satisfactions and frustrations for different levels of cadre; what members enjoy most/least about jobs; ambitions; likelihood to continue in position and reasons why

Source: Developed from Allen H. Barton, *Organizational Measurement* (New York: College Entrance Examination Board, 1961).

subcultures and differing concerns of the party specialist. By focusing on the party per se, this approach devotes less attention to the theoretical significance of parties within the broader political system. But it does not neglect the contributions of the parties to governing. It opens potential avenues for comparative research exploration, and while it is

Table 5.2
Models of Comparative Party Development

Type of Party System

Dimensions	Personalistic	Pluralistic
Characteristics	Extreme decentralization, fluid, often chaotic, built on changing coalitions and personalities	Organized subgroups competing through their leadership for power and policy commitments
Structure	Weak, independent centers of power at county and local levels, poorly articulated, closed	Moderately articulated, quasi-open, dependent on professionals
Decision-making	Elitist, authoritarian	Competitive among subgroup elite leaders
Membership	Limited	Open but effectively powerless; based on group affiliations
Policy orientation	None	Responsive to subgroup agendas
Activities	Virtually none, quiescent	Electioneering activities
Political support	Steady, predictable, small turnout	Moderate turnout, broad support
Clientele base	Small, homogeneous, exclusive	Inclusive, identifiable, built on economic lines, mixed

continued

not totally inclusive (the party-in-the-electorate is not a major contributor to any of the models), it is more comprehensive and integrative than most.

The organizational dimensions and party types are suggestive of research questions and of the varying perspectives that could be pursued. If even selective efforts were made along these lines, the results would sizably expand the agenda of problems addressed and the pool of information available.

Table 5.2
continuing

Type of Party System

Dimensions	Programmatic	Populist
Characteristics	Cohesive, subgroup coalitions, coherent policy standards, party committed to implementation when in office, accountable	Open, democratic decision-making, broad coalitions, weak subgroup structure and weak organization, appeal based on issue stands, responsive to and representative of broad constituencies
Structure	Well-organized, clearly articulated, impartial and objective	Weak organizational emphasis, open, not significant in party's operations
Decision-making	Open, structured, decision-making bodies responsive to clientele groups	Open, democratic, directly responsive to base party's concerns
Membership	Broad and issue-based	Broad and issue-based
Policy orientation	Focus on broad social and national issues	Focus on broad social and national issues
Activities	Program formation, policy decision-making, and electioneering activities	Organizational and policy decision-making, campaign strategy, and candidate nominations all open to broad input; electioneering activities
Political support	Broad support, moderate-to-high turnout	Broad support, high turnout
Clientele base	Inclusive, changing with policy concerns, heterogeneous, broadly cohesive within parties	Inclusive, heterogeneous, fluid

The best place to end any discussion of party organizations, however, is with a word of caution.

> Individuals in organizations are motivated by more than self-interest;
> they are more likely to satisfice than maximize; organizations have
> more than one goal; choice involves a search for goals as well as for
> means; it seldom is possible to find objective probabilities for the alter-
> natives faced by the organization; feedback concerning decisions is
> likely to be vague and incorrect; and the cost of achieving consensus is
> a major part of most organizational decisions. (Palumbo 1975, 361)

Dennis J. Palumbo is talking here of the limits of rational-choice theory in studying organizations in general. The same caution would apply to party organizations.

These are only some of the problems. If their plasticity—the permeable, nonhierarchical, episodic, and voluntaristic nature of parties—is combined with their goal-based fixation on vote-maximization and electoral success and their peculiar need to adapt to contrasting government structures and a variety of political environments, the conclusion is readily drawn that such research ventures are demanding. This may be the lesson of the studies in the area to date. The effort that must be expended, however, may well be worthwhile.

CONCLUSION

This paper has looked at a number of areas of relevance to research on political parties. The topics receiving most attention have been: the continuing quest for a viable and comprehensive theoretical perspective to counter the starkly empirical and often normative outlook on questions of research in the field; continuing developments in the study of party activists; the renewed attention to nominating forms and their consequences during the last two decades; and a focus on party organization as a potential source for an expanded research agenda. More could have been attempted.

Cross-national comparative studies were only indirectly touched upon, one reason being the failure of any one approach or model to supply an adequate perspective for relevant analysis. Much of the work is broad and difficult to integrate, focusing on a variety of concerns such as: the characteristics of party electorates; voter participation and party support patterns; the evolution of, or structural explanations for, competitive divisions and cleavage structures; or social attributes, values, and policy positions (Lawson 1979; Dalton 1988; Converse and Pierce 1986; Merkl 1980; Dalton et al. 1984; Rokkan 1970; Lipset and Rokkan 1967; Allardt 1970). These examples, of course, do not exhaust the range of studies (Epstein 1980; Janda 1980; Harmel and Janda 1982; Castles 1982; Castles and Wildenmann 1986; Jackman 1972; Eldersveld 1982a, 1983, 1979; Eldersveld and Ahmed 1978; Eldersveld and Marvick 1983; Eldersveld, Kooiman, and van der Tak 1981; Lorwin 1974; Lijphart 1984; Powell 1982a, 1982b, 1981; Rose 1984; Merkl and Lawson 1988; Marvick 1976, 1983a; Marvick and Eldersveld 1983), but they do illustrate major thrusts in the research approaches.

The conceptualizing of cross-national studies is difficult (Sartori 1976), and its long-run impact can be disappointing (Duverger 1954). The reasons are not hard to discover. If one looks at one-party systems alone, the variety is daunting. It ranges from the one-party South described by V. O. Key, Jr. (*Southern Politics*, 1949; see also Black and Black 1987; and Lamis 1984), to the PRI of Mexico, the authoritarian parties of developing nations in Africa, Asia, and Latin America, to the one-party systems of Eastern Europe. The failure of conceptual approaches plus the variety of examples contending for attention have resulted in parties research becoming more of an adjunct of area studies and individual nation, or bloc of nations, specialization than a product of comparative investigations (Triska, ed. 1969; Zolberg 1966, 1985; Merkl 1980; Huntington and Moore 1970). The relevance of the parties within societies, as Aristide R. Zolberg says of the nations themselves and their contradictions, "can be grasped intuitively, but it is difficult to express it with conceptual precision" (Zolberg 1966; 1985, 130). This can serve as a fair summation of the problems faced.

There also appears to be a fondness for typologizing, a classifying of individual parties or national party systems in relation to regime types or policy orientations (social democratic or socialistic, most commonly) or in terms of social fragmentation or consensus-building. The questions asked are broad and fundamental, unlike the narrower focus in most American parties research, and the associations drawn can be said to be equally broad. The typologies vary greatly among studies (Sartori 1976, 1966; Powell 1982, 1981; Lijphart 1984a, 1977; Lange and Meadwell 1985; Lorwin 1974). What may be absent in such perspectives is a focus on understanding party performance per se and party differences in operations and impact within, and across, national boundaries.

There are exceptions, of course, to any generalizations. Gøsta Esping-Andersen (1985) employs a political economy approach in describing the contrasting party sensitivities to policy concerns and structural reforms to account for the durability and relative successes of socialist parties in Scandinavia. Adam Przeworski and John Sprague (1986) model the available aggregate and survey data to trace the fate of European socialist parties since the turn of the century and the continuing dilemmas (ideological purity against across-class political compromise) they face in attempting to implement their programs. Of such work, sweeping in scope, thematic and innovative in development, and unlike most of what is done in American politics (except, perhaps, work such as Burnham's), we are likely to see more in cross-national research.

Nor has much attention been given in this paper to policy-making, whether in legislative parties or in the formulation of party positions for campaign purposes. This perspective is a favorite for those concerned with responsibility and accountability. In an electorally-oriented party, it is secondary. Legislative parties are virtually independent entities and, although within the purview of the party specialist, are more often than not treated by legislative specialists. This does not excuse their omission, but at present there may be less of an interest in this area than in others.

Traditionally, studies of legislative parties focus on party support scores and, less frequently, on organizational structure and campaign activities. Of increasing interest is the perspective found in political economy studies that looks at economic relationships between policies and voting or at policy manipulations to influence election outcomes. The problem is that the emphasis is tangential to a focus on political parties, at least as viewed here, and contributes more to an understanding of policy-making, or possibly voter decision-making, than it does to party performance directly.

Closer to party concerns may be work like that of Ian Budge and associates, who correlated the electoral pledges and issue stands of the parties both in the United States and in 18 to 22 other democratic nations, along with the electoral strategies and policies enacted once in office (Budge and Farlie 1983; Budge and Laver 1986; Budge, Robertson, and Heard 1987). The economic consequences of party policy (on inflation, spending, employment) have also been assessed. Generally speaking, such studies have revealed a relationship between party promises and policy directions and thus reaffirm the party's role as a linkage agency of consequence between voter and government. The proportion of party pledges implemented in varying degrees tends to be high. These studies reaffirm that policy differences of significance are associated with the parties and that the parties act on their commitments (Pomper 1968; Rose 1984; Castles 1982; Castles and Wildenmann 1986; Monroe 1984; Hibbs 1977, 1987; Tufte 1978; Ginsberg 1976; Jennings 1979; Lange and Meadwell 1985; Cameron 1984; Budge et al. 1987; Krukones 1984; Ferguson and Rogers 1986).

Also neglected, and among the more promising of developments, is the study of the electoral history of parties (Clubb, Flanigan, and Zingale 1980; Sibley, Bogue, and Flanigan 1978; Dalton, Flanigan, and Beck 1984; Shefter 1976, 1978; Bridges 1984). The quality of researchers contributing to this area and the increasing accessibility of longitudinal empirical data have produced creative efforts that challenge the way we think about party representation. The likelihood is that, with electoral data being collected on presidential and congressional races at the University of Michigan and by Malcolm Jewell and associates on the state-level general election and primary races, the wealth of material available can only increase. With an expanded data base, our understanding of the dynamics that led to the present party system can only improve. A critique of the contributions and future of such analyses deserves a separate paper. For present purposes, it was beyond the bounds of a discussion that centered on a select number of topics.

I have also chosen not to look in any depth at the party-in-the-electorate—supporters who identify or vote with a party for reasons that have little to do with party operations—or at the campaign technology, funding practices, and financial regulations, PACs, or the role the media play in shaping the environment in which the parties compete. Those are major concerns best left to others or to be addressed in another context (Sorauf 1988; Alexander, 3d ed., 1984; Sabato 1984, 1981; Graber, 2d ed., 1984a, 1984b; Arterton 1984; Kessel, 3d ed., 1988; Jamieson 1984; Asher, 4th ed., 1988; Godwin 1988; Salmore and Salmore 1985; Jones 1984, 1981). The focus here, to the extent practicable, has been on the party structures and those who man the party machinery and are influential in its decision-making. These topics, in themselves, provide an ample emphasis for extended discussion.

Parties research is demanding. This much is clear. Any extensions of what is presently being done will entail serious efforts at conceptualization, particularly in comparative work, and more adequate funding than has been available in the past. Such needs alone make the thrust of future work even more problematical than in the past. Whatever the challenges, the likelihood is that the importance attached to a deeper understanding of party operations is likely to increase rather than diminish. We may be entering a promising era, certainly one of great excitement, in the study of political parties. The American parties are undergoing a transformation in response to a changing social and technological order. Abroad, developments are even more enticing; a number of countries—among them Taiwan and Korea—are evolving from authoritarian, one-party systems to more democratic and competitive party structures. Other countries—Chile, Argentina, Uruguay, El Salvador, Brazil, Honduras—are attempting to devise party systems equal to the task of democratic government. One-party states—Mexico and Nicaragua, several African and Asian nations, and, most surprisingly, the Soviet Union and several of its Eastern European neighbors—are contemplating a turn toward a competitive party system. These developments are significant. The challenge is to address them within a social science research context that rises to the demands being made on it.

NOTES

1. The words of the nation's fourth president, James Monroe, articulate the self-perception: "Discord does not belong to our system. . . . The American people . . . constitute one great family with a common interest." And, again, "Never did a government commence under auspices so favorable, nor ever was success so complete. If we look to the history of other nations, ancient or modern, we find no example of growth so rapid, so gigantic, of a people so prosperous and happy. . . . the heart of every citizen must expand with joy when he reflects how near our Government has approached to perfection; that in respect to it we have no essential improvement to make" (quoted in Hofstadter 1969, 197). Apart from their eloquence, these words could be familiar to observers of contemporary politics. According to Monroe and others of like mind then, the nation was blessed with unity, an unlimited future, prosperity, and a governing system close to ideal. And, in reflecting Washington's concerns, Monroe would later argue that changes in the system, through a reliance on such instruments as political parties, would bring discord of sufficient proportions to threaten the American experiment.

2. The concern with party organization was explained by the late Bernard Hennessey:

> We are interested in party organization for two reasons. First, description. Political parties are significant social organizations in every modern state, and in all those communities that are in transition from traditional to modern forms. Significant social organizations need to be described, and all the more when, as in the case with parties, their characteristics are so irregular, amorphous, and ill defined . . . the second reason we are interested in party organization: . . . If we believe that political parties, their organization and processes are related to substantive ends such as democracy, the representation of interests, governmental efficiency, or the distribution of indulgences and deprivations, then we want to investigate those relationships to the extent necessary for understanding, prediction, or manipulation . . . a powerful argument can be made that the organization of the political parties of a modern or transitional state is, in fact, systematically related to the policies of that state. Whether there are certain invariant and/or causal relationships between party organizations and policy outcomes is a question that is, at the moment, as unclear as it is fascinating. (1968, 3)

Hennessey provides the rationale and the linkage function in the governing chain that an exploration of party organization could help to clarify.

REFERENCES

Aldrich, John H. 1980. *Before the Convention*. Chicago: University of Chicago Press.

———. 1990. "Methods and Actors: The Relationship of Processes to Candidates." In Alexander Heard and Michael Nelson, eds., *Presidential Selection*, 155–87. Durham, N.C.: Duke University Press.

Alexander, Herbert. 1984. *Financing Politics: Money, Elections, and Political Reform*. 3d ed. Washington, D.C.: Congressional Quarterly Press.

Allardt, Erik, and Stein Rokkan, eds. 1970. *Mass Politics*. New York: The Free Press.

American Political Science Association. 1950. *Toward a More Responsible Two Party System*. New York: Rinehart.

Anderson, Lee F. 1967. "Organizational Theory and the Study of State and Local Parties." In W. Crotty, ed., *Approaches to the Study of Party Organization*, 105–38. Boston: Allyn and Bacon.

Arterton, F. Christopher. 1984. *Media Politics*. Lexington, Mass.: Lexington Books/D. C. Heath.

Asher, Herbert B. 1988. *Presidential Elections and American Politics*. 4th ed. Chicago: Dorsey Press.

Barber, Benjamin. 1984. *Strong Democracy: Participatory Politics for a New Age*. Berkeley: University of California Press.

Barnes, Samuel H. 1967. "Party Democracy and the Logic of Collective Action." In W. Crotty, ed., *Approaches to the Study of Party Organization*. 105–38. Boston: Allyn and Bacon.

Bartels, Larry M. 1988. *Presidential Primaries and the Dynamics of Public Choice*. Princeton, N.J.: Princeton University Press.

Barton, Allen H. 1961. *Organizational Measurement*. New York: College Entrance Examination Board.

Beck, Paul A. 1974. "Environment and Party: The Impact of Political and Demographic County Characteristics on Party Behavior." *American Political Science Review* 68:1229–44.

Bibby, John F. 1980. "Party Renewal in the National Republican Party." In Gerald M. Pomper, ed., *Party Renewal in America*, 102–15. New York: Praeger.

———. 1987. *Politics, Parties, and Elections in America*. Chicago: Nelson-Hall.

———, and Robert J. Huckshorn. 1978. "The Republican Party in American Politics." In Jeff Fishel, ed., *Parties and Elections in an Anti-Party Age*, 55–64. Bloomington: Indiana University Press.

Black, Earle, and Merle Black. 1987. *Politics and Society in the South*. Cambridge, Mass.: Harvard University Press.

Bone, Hugh A. 1971. *American Politics and the Party System*. 4th ed. New York: McGraw-Hill.

Bridges, Amy. 1984. *A City in the Republic*. Cambridge: Cambridge University Press.

Bryce, James. 1888. *The American Commonwealth*. New York: Macmillan.

———. 1891. *The American Commonwealth*. 2 vols. Chicago: Sergel.

Budge, Ian, and Dennis J. Farlie. 1983. *Explaining and Predicting Elections*. London: George Allen & Unwin.

Budge, Ian, and Michael Laver. 1986. "Policy and Party Distance: Election Programmes in 19 Democracies." *Legislative Studies Quarterly* 4:608–18.

Budge, Ian, David Robertson, and Derek Heard, eds. 1987. *Ideology, Strategy, and Party Change: Spacial Analyses of Post-War Election Programmes in 19 Democracies*. London: Cambridge University Press.

Burnham, Walter Dean. 1965. "The Changing Shape of the American Political Universe." *American Political Science Review* 59:7–28.

———. 1970. *Critical Elections and the Mainsprings of American Politics*. New York: Norton.

———. 1975. "Party Systems and the Political Process." In William Nisbet Chambers and Walter Dean Burham, eds., *The American Party Systems*. 2d ed. New York: Oxford University Press.

———. 1976. "Revitalization and Decay: Looking toward the Third Century of American Electoral Politics." *Journal of Politics* 38:146–72.

———. 1981. "The 1980 Earthquake: Realignment, Reaction, or What?" In Thomas Ferguson and Joel Rogers, eds., *The Hidden Election*, 98–140. New York: Pantheon Books.

———. 1982. *The Current Crisis in American Politics*. New York: Oxford University Press.

Cameron, David R. 1984. "Social Democracy, Corporatism, Labour Quiescence, and the Representation of Economic Interest in Advanced Capitalist Society." In John H. Goldthorpe, ed., *Order and Conflict in Contemporary Capitalism*. Oxford: Clarendon Press.

Campbell, Angus, Philip E. Converse, Warren E. Miller, and Donald E. Stokes. 1960. *The American Voter*. New York: Wiley.

Castles, Francis G., ed. 1982. *The Impact of Parties, Politics and Policies in Democratic Capitalist States*. Beverly Hills, Calif.: Sage Publications.

———, and Rudolph Wildenmann, eds. 1986. *Visions and Realities of Party Government*. Berlin: Walter de Gruyter.

Ceaser, James W. 1979. *Presidential Selection: Theory and Development*. Princeton, N.J.: Princeton University Press.

———. 1982. *Reforming the Reforms*. Cambridge, Mass.: Ballinger.

Chambers, William Nisbet. 1963. *Political Parties in a New Nation*. New York: Oxford University Press.

Charles, Joseph. 1956. *The Origins of the American Party System*. New York: Harper & Row.

Chubb, John E., and Paul E. Peterson, eds. 1985. *The New Direction in American Politics*. Washington, D.C.: Brookings Institution.

Clark, Peter B., and James Q. Wilson. 1961. "Incentive Systems: A Theory of Organizations." *Administrative Science Quarterly* 6:129–66.

Clubb, Jerome, William Flanigan, and Nancy Zingale. 1980. *Partisan Realignment*. Beverly Hills, Calif.: Sage Publications.

Converse, Philip, and Roy Pierce. 1986. *Representation in France*. Cambridge, Mass.: Harvard University Press.

Conway, M. Margaret, and Frank B. Feigert. 1968. "Motivation, Incentive Systems, and the Political Organization." *American Political Science Review* 62:1159–73.

Cotter, Cornelius P., and John F. Bibby. 1980. "Institutional Development of Parties and the Thesis of Party Decline." *Political Science Quarterly* 95:1–27.

Cotter, Cornelius P., James L. Gibson, Robert J. Huckshorn, and John F. Bibby. 1984a. "The Condition of the Party Organizations at the State Level: State-Local Party Integration." Paper read at the Southern Political Science Association, Savannah.

Cotter, Cornelius P., James L. Gibson, John F. Bibby, and Robert J. Huckshorn. 1984b. *Party Organizations in American Politics*. New York: Praeger.

Cotter, Cornelius P., and John F. Bibby. 1986. "A Focus for Research on Party Organizations: Differentiation and Cohesion." Paper read at the annual meeting of the American Political Science Association, Washington, D.C.

Craig, Stephen. 1985. "The Decline of Partisanship in the United States: A Reexamination of the Neutrality Hypothesis." *Political Behavior* 7:57–58.

Crotty, William. 1968. "The Party Organization and Its Activities." In W. Crotty, ed., *Approaches to the Study of Party Organization*, 247–306. Boston: Allyn and Bacon.

———. 1971. "Party Effort and Its Impact on the Vote." *American Political Science Review* 65:439–50.

———. 1978. *Decision for the Democrats*. Baltimore: The Johns Hopkins University Press.

———. 1980. "The Philosophies of Party Reform." In Gerald M. Pomper, ed., *Party Renewal in America*, 31–50. New York: Praeger.

———. 1983. *Party Reform*. New York: Longman.

———. 1984. *American Parties in Decline*. 2d ed. Boston: Little, Brown.

———. 1985. *The Party Game*. New York: W. H. Freeman.

———. 1986a. "An Agenda for Studying Local Parties Comparatively." In W. Crotty, ed., *Political Parties in Local Areas*, 1–38. Knoxville: University of Tennessee Press.

———. 1986b. "Local Parties in Chicago: The Machine in Transition." In W. Crotty, ed., *Political Parties in Local Areas*, 157–95. Knoxville: University of Tennessee Press.

———. 1987. "Party Reform, Nominating Processes, and Democratic Ends." In Kay Lehman Schlozman, ed., *Elections in America*, 63–86. Boston: Allen & Unwin.

———. 1990. "The Study of Southern Party Elites." In Tod A. Baker, Charles

D. Hadley, Robert P. Steed, and Laurence W. Moreland, eds., *The Transformation of Southern Party Coalitions*. New York: Praeger.

———, and John S. Jackson III. 1985. *Presidential Primaries and Nominations*. Washington, D.C.: Congressional Quarterly Press.

Cunningham, Jr., Noble E., ed. 1965. *The Making of the American Party System 1789 to 1809*. Englewood Cliffs, N.J.: Prentice-Hall.

Cutright, Phillips. 1963. "Measuring the Impact of Local Party Activity in the General Election Vote." *Public Opinion Quarterly* 27:372–86.

———. 1963. "Nonpartisan Electoral Systems in American Cities." *Comparative Studies in Society and History* 5:212–26.

———. 1964. "Activities of Precinct Committeemen in Partisan and Nonpartisan Communities." *Western Political Quarterly* 17:93–108.

Dahl, Robert A. 1956. *A Preface to Democratic Theory*. Chicago: University of Chicago Press.

———. 1971. *Polyarchy*. New Haven: Yale University Press.

———. 1976. *Democracy in the United States: Promise and Performance*. 3d ed. Chicago: Rand McNally.

———. 1982. *Dilemmas of Pluralist Democracy*. New Haven: Yale University Press.

Dahrendorf, Ralf. 1987. "Presidential Selection and Continuity in Foreign Policy." In Alexander Heard and Michael Nelson, eds., *Presidential Selection*, 15–31. Durham, N.C.: Duke University Press.

Dalton, Russell J. 1988. *Citizen Politics in Western Democracies*. Chatham, N.J.: Chatham House.

———, Scott Flanagan, and Paul Beck, eds. 1984. *Electoral Change in Advanced Industrial Democracies*. Princeton, N.J.: Princeton University Press.

Dennis, Jack. 1966. "Support for the Party System by the Mass Public." *American Political Science Review* 60:600–615.

———. 1975. "Trends in Public Support for the American Party System." *British Journal of Political Science* 5:187–230.

———. 1980. "Changing Public Support for the American Party System." In W. Crotty, ed., *Paths to Political Reform*. Lexington, Mass.: Lexington Books/D. C. Heath.

———. 1981. "Some Properties of Measures of Partisanship." Paper presented at the annual meeting of the American Political Science Association, New York, September 3–6.

———. 1985. "Public Support for the Party System, 1964–1984." Paper prepared for annual meeting of the American Political Science Association, New Orleans.

deTocqueville, Alexis. 1949. *Democracy in America*. New York: Knopf.

DiClerico, Robert E., and Eric M. Uslaner. 1984. *Few Are Chosen*. New York: McGraw-Hill.

Downs, Anthony. 1957. *An Economic Theory of Democracy*. New York: Harper.

Duverger, Maurice. 1954. *Political Parties*. New York: Wiley.

————. 1986. "Duverger's Law: Forty Years Later." In Bernard Grofman and Arend Lijphart, eds., *Electoral Laws and Their Consequences*, 69–84. New York: Agathon Press.

Eckstein, Harry. 1968. "Party Systems." In *International Encyclopedia of the Social Sciences*, 436–53. New York: Macmillan.

Eldersveld, Samuel J. 1964. *Political Parties: A Behavioral Analysis*. Chicago: Rand McNally.

————. 1979. "Political Elite Linkages in the Dutch Consociational System." In Kay Lawson, ed., *Linkage and Political Parties*, 157–82. New Haven: Yale University Press.

————. 1982a. "Changes in Elite Composition and the Survival of Party Systems: The German Case." In Moshe Czudnowski, ed., *Does Who Governs Matter?*, 68–69. DeKalb: Northern Illinois University Press.

————. 1982b. *Political Parties in American Society*. New York: Basic Books.

————. 1983. "Motivations for Party Activism: Multi-National Uniformities and Differences." *International Political Science Review* 4:57–70.

————. 1984. "The Condition of Party Organization at the Local Level." Paper prepared for annual meeting of the Southern Political Science Association, Savannah.

————. 1986. "The Party Activist in Detroit and Los Angeles: A Longitudinal View, 1956–1980." In W. Crotty, ed., *Political Parties in Local Areas*, 89–119. Knoxville: University of Tennessee Press.

————, and Bashiruddin Ahmed. 1978. *Citizen and Politics: Mass Political Behavior in India*. Chicago: University of Chicago Press.

————, Jan Kooiman, and Theo van der Tak. 1981. *Elite Images of Dutch Politics*. Ann Arbor: University of Michigan Press.

————, and Dwaine Marvick. 1983. "Work on the Origins, Activities, and Attitudes of Party Activists." *International Political Science Review* 4:11–12.

Epstein, Leon D. 1967. *Political Parties in Western Democracies*. New York: Praeger.

————. 1975. "Political Parties." In Fred I. Greenstein and Nelson W. Polsby, eds., *Handbook of Political Science*. Vol. 4, *Nongovernmental Politics*, 229–77. Reading, Mass.: Addison-Wesley.

————. 1980. *Political Parties in Western Democracies*. New Brunswick, N.J.: Transaction Books.

————. 1983. "The Scholarly Commitment to Parties." In Ada Finifter, ed., *Political Science: The State of the Discipline*, 127–54. Washington, D.C.: American Political Science Association.

————. 1986. *Political Parties in the American Mold*. Madison: University of Wisconsin Press.

————. 1989. "Will American Political Parties Be Privatized?" *The Journal of Law and Politics* 2:239–74.

Erie, Steven P. 1988. *Rainbow's End: Irish-Americans and the Dilemmas of Urban Machine Politics, 1840–1985.* Berkeley: University of California Press.

Esping-Andersen, Gøsta. 1989. *Politics Against Markets: The Social Democratic Road to Power.* Princeton, N.J.: Princeton University Press.

Everson, David H. 1980. *American Political Parties.* New York: Franklin Watts.

Ferguson, Thomas, and Joel Rogers. 1986. *Right Turn.* New York: Hill and Wang.

Fiorina, Morris P. 1981. *Retrospective Voting in American National Elections.* New Haven: Yale University Press.

Ford, Henry Jones. 1967. *The Rise and Growth of American Politics.* New York: DeCapo Press. First published in 1898.

Gibson, James L., Cornelius P. Cotter, John F. Bibby, and Robert J. Huckshorn. 1983. "Assessing Party Organizational Strength." *American Journal of Political Science* 27:193–222.

Gibson, James L., and Gregg W. Smith. 1984. "Local Party Organizations and Electoral Outcomes: Linkages between Parties and Elections." Paper prepared for annual meeting of the American Political Science Association, Washington, D.C., September.

Gibson, James L., John P. Frendreis, and Laura L. Vertz. 1989. "Party Dynamics in the 1980s: Changes in County Party Organizational Strength, 1980–1984." *American Journal of Political Science* 33:67–90.

Gibson, James L., Cornelius P. Cotter, John F. Bibby, and Robert J. Huckshorn. 1985. "Whither the Local Parties? A Cross-Sectional and Longitudinal Analysis of the Strength of Party Organizations." *American Journal of Political Science* 29:139–60.

Ginsberg, Benjamin. 1976. "Elections and Public Policy." *American Political Science Review* 70:41–50.

Gitelson, Alan R., M. Margaret Conway, and Frank B. Feigert. 1984. *American Political Parties: Stability and Change.* Boston: Houghton Mifflin.

Godwin, R. Kenneth. 1988. *One Billion Dollars of Influence.* Chatham, N.J.: Chatham House.

Gosnell, Harold. 1968. *Machine Politics: Chicago Model.* Rev. ed. Chicago: University of Chicago Press.

Gove, Samuel K., and Louis H. Masotti, eds. 1982. *After Daley: Chicago Politics in Transition.* Urbana: University of Illinois Press.

Graber, Doris A. 1984a. *Mass Media and American Politics.* 2d ed. Washington, D.C.: Congressional Quarterly Press.

————. 1984b. *Processing the News: How People Tame the Information Tide.* New York: Longman.

Grofman, Bernard, and Arend Lijphart, eds. 1986. *Electoral Laws and Their Political Consequences.* New York: Agathon Press.

Guterbock, Thomas M. 1980. *Machine Politics in Transition: Party and Community in Chicago*. Chicago: University of Chicago Press.

Harmel, Robert, and Kenneth Janda. 1982. *Parties and Their Environments: Limits to Reform?* New York: Longman.

Heard, Alexander, and Michael Nelson, eds. 1987. *Presidential Selection*. Durham, N.C.: Duke University Press.

Hennessey, Bernard. 1968. "On the Study of Party Organization." In W. Crotty, ed., *Approaches to the Study of Party Organization*, 1–44. Boston: Allyn and Bacon.

Herrnson, Paul S. 1986. "Do Parties Make A Difference? The Role of Party Organizations in Congressional Elections." *Journal of Politics* 48: 589–615.

———. 1988. *Party Campaigning in the 1980s*. Cambridge, Mass.: Harvard University Press.

Hess, Stephen. 1988. *The Presidential Campaign*. 3d ed. Washington, D.C.: Brookings Institution.

Hibbs, Douglas A., Jr. 1977. "Political Parties and Macroeconomic Policy." *American Political Science Review* 71:1467–87.

———. 1987. *The Political Economy of Industrial Democracies*. Cambridge, Mass.: Harvard University Press.

Hirschman, Albert O. 1970. *Exit, Voice, and Loyalty*. Cambridge, Mass.: Harvard University Press.

Hoffstetter, C. Richard. 1971. "The Amateur Politician: A Problem in Construct Validation." *Midwest Journal of Political Science* 15:34–50.

Hofstadter, Richard. 1969. *The Idea of a Party System*. Berkeley: University of California Press.

Huckshorn, Robert J. 1976. *Party Leadership in the States*. Amherst: University of Massachusetts Press.

———. 1984. *Political Parties in America*. 2d ed. Monterey, Calif.: Brooks/Cole.

———, and John F. Bibby. 1982. "State Parties in an Era of Political Change." In Joel Fleishman, ed., *The Future of American Political Parties*. Englewood Cliffs, N.J.: Prentice-Hall.

———, James L. Gibson, Cornelius P. Cotter, and John F. Bibby. 1986. "Party Integration and Party Organizational Strength." *Journal of Politics* 48: 976–91.

Huntington, Samuel P., and Clement H. Moore, eds. 1970. *Authoritarian Politics in Modern Society*. New York: Basic Books.

Jackman, Robert. 1972. "Political Parties, Voting, and National Integration." *Comparative Politics* 5:511–36.

Jackson, John S. III, and Robert Hitlin. 1976. "A Comparison of Party Elites." *American Politics Quarterly* 4:441–81.

Jackson, John S. III, Barbara L. Brown, and David A. Bositis. 1982. "Herbert McClosky and Friends Revisited: 1980 Democratic and Republican Party Elites Compared to the Mass Public." *American Politics Quarterly* 10: 158–80.

Jamieson, Kathleen Hall. 1984. *Packaging the Presidency*. New York: Oxford University Press.

Janda, Kenneth. 1980. *Political Parties: A Cross-National Survey*. New York: The Free Press.

Jennings, Edward T. 1979. "Competition, Constituencies, and Welfare Policies in the American States." *American Political Science Review* 73:414–29.

Jewell, Malcolm E., and David M. Olson. 1988. *American State Political Parties and Elections*. 3d ed. Chicago: Dorsey Press.

Jones, Ruth S. 1981. "State Public Campaign Finance: Implications for Partisan Politics." *American Journal of Political Science* 25:342–61.

———. 1984. "Financing State Elections." In Michael J. Malbin, ed., *Money and Politics in the United States*, 172–213. Chatham, N.J.: Chatham House.

Katz, Daniel, and Samuel J. Eldersveld. 1961. "The Impact of Local Party Activity upon the Electorate." *Public Opinion Quarterly* 25:1–24.

Kayden, Xandra. 1980. "The Nationalizing of the Party System." In Michael Malbin, ed., *Parties, Interest Groups, and the Campaign Finance Laws*. Washington, D.C.: American Enterprise Institute.

———, and Eddie Mahe, Jr. 1985. *The Party Goes On: The Persistence of the Two-Party System in the United States*. New York: Basic Books.

Keech, William R., and Donald R. Matthews. 1976. *The Party's Choice*. Washington, D.C.: Brookings Institution.

Keeter, Scott, and Cliff Zukin. 1983. *Uninformed Choice*. New York: Praeger.

Kessel, John H. 1988. *Presidential Campaign Politics*. 3d ed. Homewood, Ill.: Dorsey Press.

Key, V. O., Jr. 1949. *Southern Politics*. New York: Knopf.

———. 1961. *Public Opinion and American Democracy*. New York: Knopf.

———. 1964. *Politics, Parties, and Pressure Groups*, 5th ed. New York: Thomas Y. Crowell.

Kolbe, Richard L. 1985. *American Political Parties: An Uncertain Future*. New York: Harper & Row.

Kirkpatrick, Jeane J. 1973. *Dismantling the Parties*. Washington, D.C.: American Enterprise Institute.

———. 1976. *The New Presidential Elite*. New York: Russell Sage Foundation and Twentieth Century Fund.

Kramer, Gerald H. 1970. "The Effects of Precinct-Level Canvassing on Voter Behavior." *Public Opinion Quarterly* 34:560–72.

Krukones, Michael G. 1984. *Promises and Performance: Presidential Campaigns as Policy Predictor*. Lanham, Md.: University Press of America.

Lamis, Alexander P. 1984. *The Two-Party South*. New York: Oxford University Press.

Lange, Peter, and Hudson Meadwell. 1985. "Typologies of Democratic Systems: From Political Inputs to Political Economy." In Howard J. Wiarda, ed., *New Directions in Comparative Politics*, 80–112. Boulder: Westview Press.

Lawson, Kay, ed. 1979. *Linkage and Political Parties*. New Haven: Yale University Press.

———, Gerald Pomper, and Maureen Moakley. 1986. "Local Party Activists and Electoral Linkage: Middlesex County, N.J." *American Politics Quarterly* 14(4):345–75.

Leiserson, Avery. 1958. *Parties and Politics*. New York: Knopf.

Lengle, James I. 1981. *Representation and Presidential Primaries*. Westport, Conn.: Greenwood Press.

Lijphart, Arend. 1977. *Democracy in Plural Societies: A Comparative Exploration*. New Haven: Yale University Press.

———. 1984a. *Democracies*. New Haven: Yale University Press.

———. 1984b. "Advances in the Comparative Study of Electoral Systems." *World Politics* 36:424–36.

Lipset, S. M., and Stein Rokkan. 1967. *Party Systems and Voter Alignments*. New York: The Free Press.

Longley, Charles H. 1980a. "National Party Renewal." In Gerald M. Pomper, ed., *Party Renewal in America*, 69–86. New York: Praeger.

———. 1980b. "Party Nationalization in America." In W. Crotty, ed., *Paths to Political Reform*, 167–205. Lexington, Mass.: Lexington Books/D. C. Heath.

———. 1980c. "Party Reform and Party Nationalization: The Case of the Democrats." In W. Crotty, ed., *The Party Symbol*, 359–78. San Francisco: W. H. Freeman.

Lorwin, Val R. 1974. "Segmented Pluralism: Ideological Cleavages and Political Cohesion in the Smaller European Democracies." In Kenneth McRae, ed., *Consociational Democracy*, 33–69. Toronto: McClelland and Stewart.

MacPherson, C. B. 1973. *Democratic Theory: Essays in Retrieval*. Oxford: Clarendon Press.

———. 1977. *The Life and Times of Liberal Democracy*. Oxford: Oxford University Press.

Main, Jackson Turner. 1974. *Political Parties before the Constitution*. New York: W. W. Norton.

Maisel, L. Sandy. 1987. *Parties and Elections in America*. New York: Random House.

Mansbridge, Jane J. 1983. *Beyond Adversary Democracy*. Chicago: University of Chicago Press.

Marshall, Thomas R. 1981. *Presidential Nominations in a Reform Age*. New York: Praeger.

Marvick, Dwaine. 1961. "Introduction: Political Decision-Makers in Contrasting Milieus." In D. Marvick, ed., *Political Decision-Makers*, 13–28. New York: The Free Press.

———. 1968a. "The Middlemen of Politics." In W. Crotty, ed., *Approaches to the Study of Party Organization*, 341–74. Boston: Allyn and Bacon.

———. 1968b. "Political Recruitment and Careers." In *International Encyclopedia of the Social Sciences*, 12:273–82. New York: Macmillan.

———. 1976. "Continuities in Recruitment Theory and Research: Toward a New Model." In H. Eulau and M. Czudnowski, eds., *Elite Recruitment in Democratic Politics*, 29–44. Beverly Hills, Calif.: Sage Publications.

———. 1976. "Recruitment Patterns of Campaign Activists in India: Legislative Candidates, Public Notables, and the Organizational Personnel of Rival Parties." In H. Eulau and M. Czudnowski, eds., *Elite Recruitment in Democratic Polities*, 133–62. Beverly Hills, Calif.: Sage Publications.

———. 1979. "Political Linkage Functions of Rival Party Activists in the United States: Los Angeles, 1969–1974." In Kay Lawson, ed., *Linkage and Political Parties*, 100–128. New Haven: Yale University Press.

———. 1980. "Party Organizational Personnel and Electoral Democracy in Los Angeles, 1963–1972." In W. Crotty, ed., *The Party Symbol*, 63–86. San Francisco: W. H. Freeman.

———. 1983a. "Ideological Thinking among Party Activists: Findings from India, Germany, and America." *International Political Science Quarterly* 4: 94–106.

———. 1983b. "Party Activists in Los Angeles, 1963–1978: How Well-Matched Rivals Shape Election Options." In M. Czudnowski, ed., *Political Elites and Social Change*, 64–101. DeKalb: Northern Illinois University Press.

———. 1986. "Stability and Change in the Views of Los Angeles Party Activists, 1968–1980." In W. Crotty, ed., *Political Parties in Local Areas*, 121–55. Knoxville: University of Tennessee Press.

———, and Charles Nixon. 1961. "Recruitment Contrasts in Rival Campaign Groups." In D. Marvick, ed., *Political Decision-Makers*, 193–217. New York: The Free Press.

———, and Samuel J. Eldersveld, eds. 1983. "Party Activists in Comparative Perspective." Symposium in *International Political Science Review* 4:11–12.

May, Ernest R. 1987. "Changing International Stakes in Presidential Selection." In Alexander Heard and Michael Nelson, eds., *Presidential Selection*, 32–52. Durham, N.C.: Duke University Press.

Mayhew, David R. 1986. *Placing Parties in American Politics*. Princeton, N.J.: Princeton University Press.

Mayo, Henry B. 1960. *An Introduction to Democratic Theory*. New York: Oxford University Press.

McClosky, Herbert. 1964. "Consensus and Ideology in American Politics." *American Political Science Review* 58:361–79.

———, Paul J. Hoffman, and Rosemary O'Hara. 1960. "Issue Conflict and Consensus among Party Leaders and Followers." *American Political Science Review* 54:406–27.

McCorkle, Pope, and Joel L. Fleishman. 1982. "Political Parties and Presidential Nominations: The Intellectual Ironies of Reform and Change in the Mass Media Age." In Joel L. Fleishman, ed., *The Future of Political Parties*, 140–68. Englewood Cliffs, N.J.: Prentice-Hall.

Merkl, Peter, ed. 1980. *Western European Party Systems*. New York: The Free Press.

———, and Kay Lawson, eds. 1988. *When Parties Fail*. Princeton, N.J.: Princeton University Press.

Merriam, Charles E. 1922. *The American Party System*. New York: Macmillan.

Merton, Robert K. 1957. *Social Theory and Social Structure*. New York: The Free Press.

Michels, Robert. 1962. *Political Parties*. New York: Crowell-Collier.

Miller, Warren E. 1987a. "The Election of 1984 and the Future of American Politics." In K. L. Schlozman, ed., *Elections in America*, 293–320. Boston: Allen and Unwin.

———. 1987b. "A New Context for Presidential Politics in the United States: The Reagan Legacy." In *After the Storm: American Society a Decade after the Vietnam War*, 181–212. Taipei: Institute of American Culture, Academia Sinica.

———. 1988. *Without Consent: Mass-Elite Linkages in Presidential Politics*. Lexington: University Press of Kentucky.

———, and Kent M. Jennings. 1986. *Party Leadership in Transition*. New York: Russell Sage.

Monroe, Kristen Renwick. 1984. *Presidential Popularity and the Economy*. New York: Praeger.

Nelson, Michael. 1987. "Who Vies for President?" In Alexander Heard and Michael Nelson, eds., *Presidential Selection*, 120–54. Durham, N.C.: Duke University Press..

Nie, Norman H., Sidney Verba, and John R. Petrocik. 1976. *The Changing American Voter*. Cambridge, Mass.: Harvard University Press.

Norrander, Barbara. 1986. "Determinants of Local Party Campaign Activity." *Social Science Quarterly* 67:561–71.

Olson, Mancur. 1965, 1971. *The Logic of Collective Action*. Cambridge, Mass.: Harvard University Press.

Ostrogorski, M. 1902. *Democracy and the Organization of Political Parties*. 2 vols. New York: Macmillan.

Page, Benjamin I. 1978. *Choices and Echoes in Presidential Elections*. Chicago: University of Chicago Press.

Palumbo, Dennis J. 1975. "Organizational Theory and Political Science." In Fred Greenstein and Nelson Polsby, eds., *Handbook of Political Science*. Vol. 2, *Micropolitical Theory*, 319–69. Reading, Mass.: Addison-Wesley.

Pennock, J. Roland. 1979. *Democratic Political Theory*. Princeton, N.J.: Princeton University Press.

Petrocik, John R. 1974. "An Analysis of Intransitivities in the Index of Party Identification." *Political Methodology* 1:31–47.

———. 1981. *Party Coalitions: Realignment and the Decline of the New Deal Party System*. Chicago: University of Chicago Press.

Polsby, Nelson. 1983. *Consequences of Party Reform*. New York: Oxford University Press.

Pomper, Gerald M. 1968. *Elections in America*. New York: Dodd, Mead and Company.

———. 1977. "The Decline of Party in American Elections." *Political Science Quarterly* 92:21–41.

———, ed. 1980. *Party Renewal in America*. New York: Praeger.

Powell, G. Bingham. 1981. "Party Systems and Political Performance: Participation, Stability and Violence in Contemporary Democracies." *American Political Science Review* 75, 4:861–79.

———. 1982. *Contemporary Democracies: Participation, Stability, and Violence*. Cambridge, Mass.: Harvard University Press.

Price, David E. 1984. *Bringing Back the Parties*. Washington, D. C.: Congressional Quarterly Press.

Przeworski, Adam, and John Sprague. 1986. *Paper Stones: A History of Electoral Socialism*. Chicago: University of Chicago Press.

Rae, Douglas W. 1971. *The Political Consequences of Electoral Laws*. Rev. ed. New Haven: Yale University Press.

———, and Michael Taylor. 1970. *The Analysis of Political Cleavages*. New Haven: Yale University Press.

Rakove, Milton. 1975. *Don't Make No Waves, Don't Back No Losers*. Bloomington: Indiana University Press.

———. 1979. *We Don't Want Nobody Nobody Sent*. Bloomington: Indiana University Press.

Ranney, Austin. 1954. *The Doctrine of Responsible Party Government*. Urbana: University of Illinois Press.

———. 1975. *Curing the Mischiefs of Faction: Party Reform in America*. Berkeley: University of California Press.

———. 1987. "Farewell to Reform—Almost." In Kay Lehman Schlozman, ed., *Elections in America*, 87–111. Boston: Allen and Unwin.

————, and Willmoore Kendall. 1956. *Democracy and the American Party System*. New York: Harcourt, Brace.

Rapoport, Ronald B., A. Abramowitz, and J. McGlennon. 1986. *The Life of the Parties: Activists in Presidential Politics*. Lexington: University Press of Kentucky.

Reichley, A. James. 1985. "The Rise of National Parties." In John Chubb and Paul Peterson, eds., *The New Direction in American Politics*, 175–200. Washington, D. C.: Brookings Institution.

Reiter, Howard L. 1985. *Selecting the President: The Nominating Process in Transition*. Philadelphia: University of Pennsylvania Press.

————. 1987. *Parties and Politics in Corporate America*. New York: St. Martin's Press.

Riker, William H. 1962. *The Theory of Political Coalitions*. New Haven: Yale University Press.

————. 1986. "Duverger's Law Revisited." In Bernard Grofman and Arend Lijphart, eds., *Electoral Laws and Their Consequences*, 19–42. New York: Agathon Press.

Rokkan, Stein. 1970. *Citizens Elections Parties*. Olso: Universitetsforlaget.

Rose, Richard. 1984. *Do Parties Make a Difference?* 2d ed. Chatham, N.J.: Chatham House.

————. 1987. "Learning to Govern or Learning to Campaign?" In Alexander Heard and Michael Nelson, eds., *Presidential Selection*, 53–73. Durham, N.C.: Duke University Press.

Rossi, Peter H., and Phillips Cutright. 1958. "Grass Roots Politicians and the Vote." *American Sociological Review* 23:171–79.

Sabato, Larry J. 1981. *The Rise of Political Consultants*. New York: Basic Books

————. 1984. *PAC Power: Inside the World of Political Action Committees*. New York: Norton.

————. 1988. *The Party's Just Begun*. Glenview, Ill.: Scott, Foresman.

Sait, Edward McChesney. 1927. *American Parties and Elections*. New York: Century.

Salmore, Stephen A., and Barbara G. Salmore. 1985. *Candidates, Parties, and Campaigns*. Washington, D.C.: Congressional Quarterly Press.

Sartori, Giovanni. 1966. "European Political Parties: The Case of Polarized Pluralism." In J. LaPalombara and M. Weiner, eds., *Political Parties and Political Development*. Princeton, N.J.: Princeton University Press.

————. 1976. *Parties and Party Systems*. Cambridge and New York: Cambridge University Press.

Schattschneider, E. E. 1942. *Party Government*. New York: Rinehart.

————. 1960. *The Semisovereign People*. New York: Holt, Rinehart and Winston.

Schlesinger, Joseph A. 1965. "Political Party Organization." In James G. March, ed., *Handbook of Organizations*, 764–801. Chicago: Rand McNally.

————. 1966. *Ambition and Politics*. Chicago: Rand McNally.

————. 1968. "Party Units." In *International Encyclopedia of the Social Sciences*, 428–36. New York: Macmillan.

————. 1975. "The Primary Goals of Political Parties: A Clarification of Positive Theory." *American Political Science Review* 69:840–49.

————. 1983. "On the Theory of Party Organization." *Journal of Politics* 46: 369–400.

————. 1985. "The New American Political Party." *American Political Science Review* 79:1152–69.

Schumpeter, Joseph A. 1950. *Capitalism, Socialism and Democracy*. 3d ed. New York: Harper.

Shafer, Bryon E. 1983. *Quiet Revolution: The Struggle for the Democratic Party and the Shaping of Post-Reform Politics*. New York: Russell Sage Foundation.

————. 1988. *Bifurcated Politics: Evolution and Reform in the National Party Convention*. Cambridge, Mass.: Harvard University Press.

Shefter, Martin. 1976. "The Emergence of the Political Machine: An Alternative View." In Willis Hawley, ed., *Theoretical Perspectives on Urban Politics*, 14–44. Englewood Cliffs, N.J.: Prentice-Hall.

————. 1978. "The Electoral Foundations of the Political Machine: New York City, 1884–1897." In Joel H. Sibley, Allan G. Bogue, and William H. Flanigan, eds., *The History of American Electoral Behavior*, 263–98. Princeton, N.J.: Princeton University Press.

Sibley, Joel H., Allan G. Bogue, and William H. Flanigan. 1978. *The History of American Electoral Behavior*. Princeton, N.J.: Princeton University Press.

Sorauf, Frank J. 1954. "Extra-Legal Political Parties in Wisconsin." *American Political Science Review* 48:692–704.

————. 1988. *Money in American Elections*. Glenview, Ill.: Scott Foresman.

————, and Paul A. Beck. 1988. *Party Politics in America*. 6th ed. Boston: Little, Brown.

Spitz, Elaine. 1984. *Majority Rule*. Chatham, N.J.: Chatham House.

Stanga, John, Patrick Kenney, and James Sheffield. 1986. "The Myth of Zero Partisanship: Attitudes toward American Political Parties, 1964–1984." Paper delivered at the annual meeting of the American Political Science Association, Washington, D.C., August 27–31.

Stinchcombe, Arthur. 1965. "Social Structure and Organizations." In James G. March, ed., *Handbook of Organizations*. Chicago: Rand McNally.

Stone, Walter J., and Alan I. Abramowitz. 1983. "Winning May Not Be Everything, But It's More Than We Thought: Presidential Party Activists in 1980." *American Political Science Review* 77:945–56.

Sundquist, James. 1983. *Dynamics of the Party System: Alignment and Realignment of Political Parties in the United States*. Rev. ed. Washington, D.C.: Brookings Institution.

Taagerera, Rein, and Matthew Soberg Shugart. 1989. *Seats and Votes*. New Haven: Yale University Press.

Triska, Jan F., ed. 1969. *Communist Party States*. Indianapolis: Bobbs-Merrill.

Tufte, Edward. 1978. *Political Control of the Economy*. Princeton, N.J.: Princeton University Press.

Vertz, Laura, John Frendreis, and James Gibson. 1987. "Nationalization of the American Electorate: A Multi-Office Perspective." *American Political Science Review* 81:961–66.

Ware, Alan. 1979. *The Logic of Party Democracy*. New York: St. Martin's Press.

———. 1985. *The Breakdown of Democratic Party Organization, 1960–1980*. New York: Oxford University Press.

Wattenberg, Martin P. 1984. *The Decline of American Political Parties, 1952–1980*. Cambridge, Mass.: Harvard University Press.

———. 1986. "Do Voters Really Care about Political Parties Anymore? A Response to Craig." Paper delivered at the annual meeting of the American Political Science Association, Washington, D.C., August 27–31.

Weisberg, Herbert F. 1984. "A Multidimensional Conceptualization of Party Identification." In Richard G. Niemi and Herbert F. Weisberg, eds., *Controversies in Voting Behavior*, 456–78. 2d ed. Washington, D.C.: Congressional Quarterly Press.

Wolfinger, Raymond E. 1963. "The Influence of Precinct Work on Voting Behavior." *Public Opinion Quarterly* 27:387–98.

———. 1972. "Why Political Machines Have Not Withered Away and Other Revisionist Thoughts." *Journal of Politics* 34:365–98.

Zolberg, Aristide R. 1966, 1985. *Creating Political Order: The Party-States of West Africa*. Chicago: University of Chicago Press.

6

Federalism and Intergovernmental Relations: The Centralization versus Decentralization Debate Continues

Susan A. MacManus

The scope of federalism . . . is such that no individual scholar can write authoritatively on all its aspects.

—Donald Smiley, *American Political Science Review* 82 (1988): 285

The meaning of federalism . . . is an issue that is never finally resolved.

—Thomas J. Anton (1989): 2

There has been a rebirth of interest in federalism and intergovernmental relations in the decade of the 1980s.[1] Three major events have prompted this renewal: (1) the fiscal problems of local governments in the late 1970s (New York City's fiscal crisis and California's Proposition 13 movement); (2) the Reagan presidency and its special brand of "New" Federalism; and (3) the nation's bicentennial. Research on federalism and intergovernmental relations among scholars and practitioners during the 1980s reflect reactions to these events.

I wish to thank panelists at the Midwest Political Science Association's annual meeting, David R. Beam, Martha Derthick, John Kincaid, and Kenneth Wong, for their critiques and their outstanding individual contributions to the study of federalism and intergovernmental relations.

The theoretical, substantive, and methodological approaches to the study of federalism and intergovernmental relations (IGR) may have changed throughout history, but the big questions have remained the same. At the center of the debate is the perennial question of which level of government has (or should have) the authority for various functional responsibilities.[2] The question is, of course, central anywhere a federal system of government is in place. Federal systems also spark debates over whether centralization is preferable to decentralization, consolidation is better than fragmentation, larger is better than smaller, and governmentally imposed solutions are preferable to private-sector or market-based solutions. Relatedly, there is always the question of which level of government is most responsive to the needs of its constituents.

Previous research has provided us with many normative theories and prescriptions about what should be the answers to the perennial questions posed above. Only within the past several decades have we begun to approach generating answers in any rigorous, methodical, empirical manner. To a large degree, the development of our subfield has been heavily constrained by an overreliance on case studies and cross-sectional data.[3] Anton (1989, 2) states the dilemma best:

> The thousands of descriptions of "how they did it in Oshkosh" or "what happened in Hoboken" provide marvelously detailed and often valuable information. On the other hand, such information is difficult to place in a general theoretical framework. Because scholars have studied a great many different things, or used different languages to study similar things, we are left with a mountain of details, but no widely accepted theory or theories that allow us to evaluate the significance of those details. *Empirical studies of American federalism, in short, are descriptively strong but theoretically weak.* (author's emphasis)

The very existence of fifty autonomous states with their different political, economic, social, and legal cultures, and the thousands of local governments scattered across the nation present significant challenges to the search for answers to the perennial questions. Likewise, the very nature of the fragmented governmental landscape poses extreme methodological problems.

In rising to meet theoretical and methodological challenges, federalism and intergovernmental relations scholars have made significant contributions to the broader political science discipline. Specifically, they have been the leaders in the discipline's use of public-choice and political economy models (cf. Ostrom, Tiebout, and Warren 1961; E. Ostrom 1972; Cameron 1978; Rich 1980; Jacobs 1981; Gramlich 1982; Kirlin 1982; Chubb 1985a, 1985b, 1985c, 1988; Barrilleaux and Miller 1988; Chubb and Moe, 1988), just as they were instrumental several decades earlier in assimilating the systems model into the discipline (cf. work of Dye 1966; Sharkansky 1969, 1970, 1972).

Researchers in our subfield have also led the discipline in the development of innovation theory (cf. Walker 1969; Gray 1973; Savage 1985) and in the operationalization of the concepts of political culture (cf. Elazar 1966; Savage 1981; Erickson, McIver, and Wright 1987) and community power (cf. Polsby 1980; Stone 1980; Waste 1987). Models of growth and decline of governments and organizations have also been developed by scholars in our subfield (cf. Borcherding 1977; Blair and Nachmias 1979; Lowery and Berry 1983; Dye 1982, 1988b; Rubin 1982; Levine, Rubin, and Wolohojian 1981; Lowery, Brunn, and Webster 1986; Berry and Lowery 1987; Garand 1988; Gray and Lowery 1988). The incorporation of legal constraints into models of political participation, public policy processes, and policy outcomes is another important contribution of intergovernmental scholars (cf. ACIR publications; Lovell et al. 1979; Peterson 1981; MacManus 1981; Sharp 1982; Zimmerman 1983). The fragmented state and local environment affords the best laboratory for empirical tests of many hypotheses because it offers multiple units of analysis.

There are several explanations for federalism and intergovernmental relations being on the cutting edge of this discipline. First, students of federalism and intergovernmental relations tend to be more *interdisciplinary* in their approaches to research. This means they are quicker to incorporate new theories, paradigms, and methodologies developed in other disciplines. Second, students of federalism and intergovernmental relations tend to link this interest to research in other subfields of the political science discipline.

THE INTERACTIVE RESEARCH INTERESTS OF FEDERALISM AND IGR SCHOLARS

As the figures in table 6.1 show, members of the American Political Science Association who belong to the Organized Section on Federalism and Intergovernmental Relations are also likely to belong to at least one other organized section (91 percent), and generally to at least two others (84 percent).[4] The most common combinations are with: policy studies (36 percent); public administration (33 percent); urban politics (28 percent); law, courts, and judicial process (20 percent); legislative studies (18 percent); political parties and organizations (17 percent); presidency (14 percent); and representation and electoral systems (11 percent) (see table 6.2). These combinations are not surprising and, in fact, reflect the basic "rank orderings" of the focus of intergovernmen-

Table 6.1
Level of Participation in ASPA Organized Section: Members of
Federalism and Intergovernmental Relations Section

Number of Organized Sections to Which Member Belongs (n = 20)	Federalism Section Members	
	Number (n = 293)	Percent*
1 (Federalism Section Only)	26	9
2	79	27
3	79	27
4	47	16
5	27	9
6	17	6
7	7	2
8	7	2
9	1	0
10	2	1
17	1	0
Totals	293	99

Source: Calculated from membership lists of American Political Science Association, March 1989.
*Percentages do not add to 100 percent due to rounding.

tal research publications that have appeared since 1980 (see References). These cross-interest rankings also parallel the general development patterns within the broader political science discipline.

The Public Policy Link

The strong linkage between public policy and federalism and IGR is a natural outgrowth of the public policy movement (cf. Henig 1985; Benton and Morgan 1986). "As we direct attention to such concerns as what governments do, why they do it, and what difference it makes, we are immediately struck by the intergovernmental context within which the making, implementation, and impact of public policy is set. . . . The quest to develop sound and accurate theories about public policy . . . has been enhanced in large measure by viewing the policy process from an intergovernmental perspective" (Benton and Morgan 1986, 5–6). The focus of most of the public policy research with an intergovernmental dimension has been on various federally funded programs administered by state and local governments.

Table 6.2
The Interactive Research Interests of Federalism and Intergovernmental Relations Scholars

ASPA Organized Section	Federalism Section Members with Membership in Section	
	Numbers (n = 293)	Percent*
Policy studies	106	36
Public administration	98	33
Urban politics	82	28
Law, courts, judicial process	58	20
Legislative studies	52	18
Political organizations and parties	50	17
Presidency research	40	14
Representation and electoral systems	31	11
Women and politics	25	9
Applied political science	24	8
Conflict processes	24	8
Religion and politics	22	8
Computer users	15	5
Foundations of political theory	15	5
Politics and life sciences	15	5
Science and technology studies	15	5
Political methodology	14	5
Comparative politics	13	4
International security and arms control	7	2
Totals	706	241

Source: Calculated from membership lists of the American Political Science Association, March 1989.
*Percentages do not add to 100 percent due to multiple listings.

The Public Administration Link

The strong linkage between federalism and IGR and public administration parallels important dynamics of change in the federal system. Federal grants have played a key role in promoting professionalism among public-sector employees. They have also mandated professional administration of these programs (cf. Carroll and Campbell 1976; Kettl 1980; Reeves 1981; Shapek 1981; Howitt 1984; Robin and Dodd 1985; Agranoff 1986; O'Toole 1988).

O'Toole describes the scenario as follows:

the *practice* of federalism has come to encompass detailed and continuing involvement by administrative actors and institutions in many of the core activities of the federal system. Mere mention of the grants system as it has evolved, plus allusion to nearly any contemporary policy issue of importance—from urban problems to AIDS to the environment to welfare reform—necessitates some discussion of matters administrative. Efforts to trim the extensive and intensive ties across governments also raise administrative themes and recurring difficulties, as national authorities seek to influence through regulation what they used to seek direct via inducement (e.g., ACIR, 1984). Even a predominantly-judicial focus cannot ignore topics of administration, as the federal courts have become involved over recent decades in a whole array of apparently administrative questions, like the details of busing plans and the management of prisons. (1988, 2)

Interestingly, in spite of this rather strongly worded rationale for the linkage between public administration and federalism and IGR, O'Toole reiterates the complaint expressed five years earlier by Beam, Conlan, and Walker (1983), namely, that the literature on the administrative aspects of federalism remains largely descriptive and atheoretical.

The Urban Politics Link

The strong interrelationship between urban politics and federalism and intergovernmental relations is, of course, predictable in light of the strong linkages already observed between public policy and public administration. Without question, the study of the evolution and impact of the intergovernmental grants system (cf. Anton, Cawley, and Kramer 1980; Break 1980; Bahl 1981; Barfield 1981; Fossett 1983; Anton 1983a, 1983b; Orlebeke 1983; Schmandt, Wendel, and Tomey 1983; Brown, Fossett, and Palmer 1984; Liebschutz 1984; Nathan and Associates 1977, 1983; Dommel and Associates 1980, 1982; Dilger 1989) and the accompanying maze of regulations and mandates (cf. Lovell et al. 1979; Mueller and Fix 1980; Lovell and Tobin 1981; Kettl 1983) either begins or ends with an urban focus (cf. Walker 1980, 1981; Friedland and Wong 1983; Conlan 1984, 1985; Chubb 1985a, 1985b, 1985c).

It has largely been in the urban context that the issues of the relative responsiveness (equity) of federal versus state governments have been examined (cf. Dye and Hurley 1978; Stein 1981a, 1981b; Ward 1981; Nathan, Doolittle, and Associates 1984; Pelissero 1984, 1985; Stein and Hamm 1987). The urban setting has also been the laboratory for tests of the relative efficiency of centralized versus decentralized service delivery systems and decision-making structures (cf. Bish

1971; Ostrom 1972; Ostrom, Bish, and Ostrom 1988). Finally, the retrenchment and devolution mode of the 1980s, in combination with the technological revolution (i.e., computers and readily accessible sophisticated methodological techniques such as econometric modeling) naturally promoted examinations of policy impacts in cities and metropolitan areas where there were sufficient units of analysis for empirical testing of hypotheses.

The Link with Law, Courts, and Judicial Process

The cross-fertilization between federalism and intergovernmental relations and law, courts, and the judicial process has been strong for quite some time. As noted by O'Toole (1988, 2): "The field of federalism for much of its development drew liberally from the traditions of scholarship favoring law-based approaches to understanding the substantive subject matter." However, two of the events noted at the beginning of the article have changed the emphasis somewhat. The first was the Reagan presidency. Many observers have noted that Reagan's judicial appointments were where the real Reagan revolution occurred. Consequently, the decade of the 1980s was characterized by a significant number of studies examining: (1) the impact of the federal judicial appointment process and the courts' ideological, racial, and gender composition on court rulings; and (2) the ability and degree to which state laws and state court rulings "led," "lagged," or "dragged" federal policies (cf. Johnson 1981; Hansen 1980; Johnston and Thompson 1980; Canon and Baum 1981; Haas 1981; Porter and Tarr 1982; Caldeira 1983, 1985; Dalton 1985; Fino 1987; Macedo 1987; Epstein and O'Connor 1988; Farber 1988; Friedelbaum 1988).

The second event that strengthened the linkage between laws, courts, and judicial process and federalism and IGR was the nation's bicentennial. Nice (1987, 2) accurately notes that: "As the bicentennial of the U.S. Constitution approached[d], Americans continue[d] to wrestle with many of the same issues that faced the Philadelphia Convention in 1787. Many of these issues involve[d] the nature of federalism and the conduct of intergovernmental relations."

Reexaminations of the "original intent" of the Founders in creating a federal system and of the current mix of functional responsibilities not only sparked interest in federal constitutional law (cf. Diamond 1964, 1970; Davis 1978; Schreiber 1978, 1980, 1987; Rakove 1979; Crosskey and Jeffrey 1981; Storing 1981; Jillson and Eubanks 1984; Rohr 1986; Benton 1987; Berger 1987; Derthick 1987; Elazar 1987, 1988; Kurland and Lerner 1987; Lutz 1987; Middlekauff 1987; Ostrom 1987; Popcock 1987; Reid 1987; Riker 1987; Sandoz 1987a, 1987b; Whicker, Strickland, and Moore 1987; White 1987) but in state constitutional law as well (cf. Onuf 1982; Curtis 1986; Kincaid 1987, 1988; Advisory Commission on Intergovernmental Relations, 1988). Predictably, the interpretive nature of this research makes this literature's contributions more normative than empirical. Perhaps the most interesting development has been the emergence of greater support for decentralization among judicial and constitutional scholars than was characteristic of their research in the past (Kenyon and Kincaid 1988).

The Link to Political Parties and Organizations

The federalism and intergovernmental relations linkage to the study of political parties and organizations also has a long tradition. The symbiotic relationship with regard to political parties is as follows:

> Federalism affects the operation of political parties by creating numerous forces for disunity and by creating subnational bases where a party can survive when it is out of power nationally. The parties in turn shape the function of the federal system. Competitive, sectionally based parties with regional internal divisions are conducive to subnational autonomy. . . . (Nice 1987, 40)

A similar symbiotic relationship exists with regard to political interest groups:

> A federal system shapes interest group behavior by creating many avenues where groups may pursue their policy goals. At the same time, groups influence the federal system by trying to persuade officials at levels where the groups are most influential to promote group goals and, at times, to encourage officials at other levels of government to do the same. (ibid.)

Wright (1989), in his excellent overview "The Origins, Emergence, and Maturity of Federalism and Intergovernmental Relations: Two Centuries of Territory and Power," reviews the early literature promoting the "party-as-decentralizer" thesis (cf. Truman 1955; Grodzins 1960; Riker 1964; Buchanan 1965; Leach 1970) and the research on the emergence of intergovernmental lobbying groups and organizations (cf. Beer 1976; Farkas 1971; Haider 1974). The thrust of this research continued into the decade of the 1980s. While scholarly support for decentralization increased somewhat in the 1980s in other subfields, the reverse seems to have been true among scholars studying political parties and interest groups (cf. Crotty 1984). The regionalization of political parties and the increasing numbers of special interest groups are generally perceived as negative influences on our federal system rather than positive ones.

The Link with Research on the Presidency

The interaction between scholarly interest in the presidency and federalism and intergovernmental relations is predictable. "Usual practice is to attribute changes in intergovernmental relations to the influence of particular presidents" (Beam and Benton 1986, 204). Each brand of "new" federalism is associated with a particular president. According to Hawkins (1982, 5), "The last six presidents have all raised the issue of federalism." But, as noted earlier, it was Ronald Reagan's "new" federalism and the unprecedented ardor with which he approached intergovernmental reform during his first term in office that gave the study of federalism "unprecedented prominence, ferment, and vitality" in the 1980s (O'Toole 1985, 40).

Ironically, most of the elements of Reagan's New Federalism (federal aid cuts, grant consolidation, a tradeoff among domestic aid programs, regulatory relief, and a balanced budget) had earlier origins (Beam and Benton 1986, 204; Conlan 1988). It is likely that his Republican party affiliation and ideological conservatism, more than his programs, sparked inquiry from an academic discipline noted for its predominantly liberal Democratic composition.[5]

The Link to Representation and Electoral Systems

The wedding of researchers' interest in representation and electoral systems and federalism and intergovernmental relations was also a predictable one. In the decade of the 1980s, the relationship was strengthened by numerous federal court rulings on the fairness of various state and local electoral systems. These rulings followed the extension and revision of the Federal Voting Rights Act in 1982. The most notable Supreme Court case was *Thornburg v. Gingles* 106 S. Ct. 2752 (1986).

The predominant question in this area of research has been, "Does structure make a difference in descriptive representation?" Stated differently, do electoral structures such as at-large elections, majority vote requirements, staggered terms, short terms of office, anti–single-shot voting requirements, and other structures increase minority participation in the political process and election of representatives of their choice? (See Lyons 1978; Karnig and Welch 1980; Morgan and Pelissero 1980; Engstrom and McDonald 1981; Davidson 1984; Foster 1985; Thernstrom 1987; and Bullock and MacManus 1987, for good reviews of this literature.)

There have been a few inquiries into the impact of structures on partisan representation (cf. Grofman 1985). Undoubtedly, this will be one of the major focal points of research in the 1990s, following the 1990 Census and the requisite reapportionments and redistricting.

3   To the Mainstream!

The linkages between research in federalism and intergovernmental relations and other subfields of the political science discipline reinforce the fact that it is inappropriate, and impossible, to treat them as mutually exclusive. (Some would regard this as an argument for recentralization of the profession or the elimination of organized sections!) More significantly, the linkages reflect the fact that the study of federalism and intergovernmental relations is now part of the political science "mainstream." Just twenty years ago Stenberg and Walker (1969, 155) reported that "Academic research in American intergovernmental (Federal-State-Local) relations ha[d] not yet entered the 'mainstream.'" Today many researchers in our subfield are among the profession's leading scholars and associational leaders.

SIGNIFICANT NEW THEORIES AND FINDINGS

Out of the voluminous literature dealing with fiscal federalism, specifically the impact of grants-in-aid, have come several new and interesting ways of conceptualizing how the federal system works.

Analytic Frameworks

One body of work focuses on how better to implement federally formulated policy at the state and local levels. Peterson, Rabe, and Wong (1986), in *When Federalism Works*, have developed what they call "a differentiated theory of federalism." They use this theory to explain the successes (and failures) of federal programs administered at the state and local levels. The theory distinguishes between programs and policies that are developmental (improve the economic position of a government in its competition with other governments) and redistributive (benefit low-income or otherwise especially needy groups within a constituency). The authors conclude with a prescription for what should be the appropriate responsibilities of various levels of government. Specifically, they call for "primary responsibility for redistributive programs at the federal level and primary responsibility for developmental ones at state and local levels" (Peterson, Rabe, and Wong 1986, 230).

Anton (1989), in *American Federalism and Public Policy: How the System Works*, develops a somewhat different conceptual framework for describing how public policy is formulated within a federal system. He refers to it as the "benefit-seeking coalition" framework: "conceptualizing federal politics as patterned interactions among benefit-seeking coalitions, where the products of such interactions are benefits for members (including governments) of victorious coalitions" (Anton 1989, 36). He argues that this framework incorporates the strengths of three other popular analytic frameworks (fiscal federalism, hierarchy, public choice) while avoiding their basic flaw (normative prescriptions about how government policy-making ought to be made) by focusing on the actual behavior of public officials and more clearly operationalizing key concepts.

Findings

One of the most interesting themes to emerge from the huge body of literature examining the impact of Reagan's New Federalism programs is that states are more responsive (and redistributive) than the federal government. In fact, this is not really a new theory. The subfield's leading scholars (Dye 1966; Derthick 1974; Lowi 1979; Elazar 1984; and others) had observed this quite some time ago. But several well-publicized studies presented empirical evidence to support these observations. Nathan, Doolittle, and Associates (1987) investigated the effects of the Reagan budget cuts on state and local governments. They found that, at the national level, programs that are most highly redistributive to politically vulnerable groups among the poor were the most likely to be cut. However, at the state level, they observed that this was not necessarily the case:

> Our initial assumption, and we believe the same assumption was made by officials of the Reagan administration, was that devolutionary measures would aid and abet the administration's overarching domestic commitment to retrenchment in the sphere of social policy. But this was not always the way it worked out. There is evidence from this study and from other sources that Reagan's federalism reforms have stimulated and are continuing to stimulate state governments to increase their efforts to meet domestic needs in the functional areas in which the national government either was cutting grants-in-aid or threatening to do so. (Nathan, Doolittle, and Associates 1987, 8)

Another study of regulatory enforcement procedures in the fifty states concluded that state agencies, with their smaller size and greater flexibility, were more responsive than the federal agency (OSHA) to political and task differences (Scholz and Wei 1986). Numerous other studies also reported that states are no longer the weak half of the federal partnership (cf. Garnett 1980; Sabato 1983; Bowman and Kearney 1986, 1988).

One interesting study of the redistributive nature of state welfare policies (Althaus and Schachter 1983) concluded that too much redistribution could be damaging in the long term if it encouraged middle- and upper-income taxpayers to move to less redistributive states!

In sum, these studies are evidence that decentralization is not inherently inequitable, as much of the earlier, nonempirical work on federalism and intergovernmental relations had inferred. States (and localities) can be equitable and redistributive in their allocational policies without federal mandates dictating such behavior to them.

New findings and theories about the relative efficiency of centralized versus decentralized decision-making systems also emerged from the fiscal federalism literature. (See Dye 1988a for a good review of this literature.) The basic tenet of many of these studies, which tend to use public-choice, market-based theoretical frameworks, is best expressed by Hawkins:

> Apart from the fact that centralized, hierarchical structures have frequently failed to achieve the responsiveness or efficiencies of scale that advocates have attributed to them, they raise a fundamental difficulty that goes to the heart of federalism. In the process of rearranging things, reformers have ignored the crucial relationship between community and political authority. The evidence is now mounting that as authority has been centralized—i.e., taken away from citizens and local communities—legitimacy and social connectedness have also been lost. (1982, 9–10)

A rather impressive literature demonstrating the importance and effectiveness of citizen-contracting and neighborhood organizations reflects this public-choice philosophy (cf. Jones, Greenberg, and Drew 1980; Lipsky 1980; Vedlitz and Durand 1980; Sharp 1982, 1986; Cole and Caputo 1984; Magleby 1984; Williams 1985; Thomas 1986; Desario and Langston 1987; Zisk 1987). The general theme of this literature is that decentralized decision-making structures promote responsiveness and accountability. There is, however, some research that attributes this phenomenon to the cross-cutting citizen participation requirement of federal grants (cf. Browning, Marshall, and Tabb 1984).

The relative efficiency of public versus private service delivery systems has been the focus of an extensive literature on privatization (see Fisk, Kiesling, and Muller 1978; DeHoog 1984; Savas 1987; Morgan and England 1988; Morgan, Hirlinger, and England 1988, for reviews of this literature). The basic conclusion is that for certain functions—namely, those that are priceable—private-sector delivery is more cost-effective than public-sector delivery. But the real determination of this must be made by using longitudinal not cross-sectional data. If the effect of privatization strategies is to create private monopolies, the cost savings will only be temporary. Morgan and England (1988, 979) also warn that "While privatization may improve service delivery efficiency, the desire for cost savings must be balanced against more normative issues that ensure competition and allow active citizen participation."

In sum, the 1980s produced considerably more empirically based research, which concluded that smaller, more decentralized service delivery and decision-making systems are more equitable and efficient than larger, more centralized ones, especially the national government. But will this conclusion endure? Certainly fiscal retrenchment has stimulated the use of privatization as a coping strategy—and a fairly effective one. But there is also evidence that retrenchment has promoted functional consolidations and the transferring upward of certain functional responsibilities. This has occurred where governments are too small and the subsequent diseconomies of scale too large to sustain efficient production (MacManus 1989). City-county consolidation has also reemerged as an alternative for consideration in certain jurisdictions (Halter 1989).

Relatedly, the whole issue of the equity and efficiency of direct democracy devices (referenda, recall, initiatives) is being reexamined in states where their use is rampant (e.g., California). These "new" countercyclical developments are merely exemplary of the dynamic nature of the federal system.

Methodological Challenges and Innovations

The one concrete conclusion about the subfield of federalism and intergovernmental relations is, of course, its dynamic nature. The questions remain the same; it is the answers, and the approaches used to generate them, that change. Scholars in our subfield have made important contributions to political science methodologies. We have had to be innovative because we do not have access to a national state and local election data base or easy access to roll-call votes in either the fifty state legislatures or the thousands of city councils, county commissions, school boards, town councils, or special district and authority boards. Comparative studies, particularly of decision-making processes, are extremely difficult. They are grossly expensive both in terms of time and money.

There is also a size bias in the aggregate-level revenue and expenditure data available for analysis. Census publications are skewed toward large governments (cities over 50,000 population), but the overwhelming majority of all local governments in the United States are well below 50,000 population. Without detailed longitudinal data on smaller jurisdictions, true tests of centralization versus decentralization and fragmentation versus consolidation hypotheses cannot be conducted. Likewise, the equities and efficiencies of public versus private service delivery, and the relative responsiveness of various types of local governments to constituencies, cannot be comprehensively tested without data on smaller jurisdictions.

So what have we done to cope with these methodological challenges? Perhaps the most significant approach has been to rely on decentralized networks of scholars who generate data for similar time frames using a standardized data collection and research format designed by a central research staff. The field network approach which has been relied upon heavily in this decade has been critical to the development of the subfield of federalism and intergovernmental relations. It has contributed significantly not just in terms of methodology, but in theory and substance, particularly with regard to local governments.

The field network evaluation methodology (Hall and MacManus 1982; Nathan 1982) gained prominence through the work of researchers affiliated with studies of the impact of various federal block grant programs (e.g., General Revenue Sharing, CETA, Community Development Block Grant) in state and local governments. These studies were funded by federal agencies and administered through The Brookings Institution under the direction of Richard Nathan and Paul Dommel. This methodology has been particularly effective in generating descriptive models of policy implementation and evaluation processes within the federal framework. It has subsequently been used in studies, conducted by Lester Salamon of the Urban Institute, of the effects of Reagan budget cuts on the nonprofit sector and volunteerism. A new network of U.S. researchers studying rural and smaller governments has also recently been created within the past two years through efforts of Beverly Cigler of Pennsylvania State University at Harrisburg and researchers at the United States Department of Agriculture. The methodology has been adapted to international comparative studies as well. The Urban Fiscal Austerity Project, headed by Terry Nichols Clark of the University of Chicago, links urban scholars in Europe, Asia, Africa, and North and South America who are studying the political and economic effects of fiscal retrenchment.

Research focusing on the American states has also generated some important methodological approaches. The availability of annual data for a variety of variables (political, social, economic, legal) and the relative ease of analyzing fifty units of analysis have made states the ideal testing ground for time series and econometric models. Preeminent have been models of state government growth and decline (noted at the beginning of the article). Also significant have been models testing the impact of federal grants on state taxing and spending policies. The work of Chubb (1985) has been particularly influential in cautioning political scientists too quick to endorse purely economic models that political variables are also important determinants of policy outcomes in a federal system.

In sum, political economy and public-choice approaches to the study of politics first appeared in studies of intergovernmental relations. These approaches are perceived by many scholars as being the new replacements for the systems model that has dominated models of policy-making for several decades. The question is how long these new approaches will be the dominant analytic frameworks.

CRYSTAL BALL GAZING: PREDICTING FUTURE AVENUES OF RESEARCH

If one believes that graduate dissertations are among the better forecasters of trends in the discipline and the subdiscipline, the evidence suggests that studies of government retrenchment are "out" while studies of economic development are "in." Domestic research has taken a back seat to international comparative studies.

The data bases of dissertations completed in 1987 and 1988 are predominantly cross-national in nature. Many deal with economic development issues in developing nations and use political economy-based models as their primary analytic technique. A significant number also study the role of leadership in economic development or contrast elite and mass opinion and behavior. Others focus on the role international political and economic competition play in promoting development. The globalization of the world economy means that comparative studies of federalism and intergovernmental relations will be the focus of research well into the next decade.

The strong interest in decentralization among many of the major non-Western nations (China, Korea, Russia, Nigeria, to name a few) will also have a major impact on the evolution of new theoretical and empirical approaches to the study of federalism and intergovernmental relations. Efforts will center on the determination of optimal size and scale for the delivery of certain services, particularly among small, rural jurisdictions. Interest in this research will be great among scholars and practitioners in developing nations.

The Direction of Research in the United States

Dissertations focusing exclusively on United States governments tend to be noncomparative case studies of specific policy areas (mostly at the state level). Policy areas receiving the bulk of attention among emerging scholars are those which declined at the federal level during the Reagan presidency (environmental, civil rights and civil liberties, racial and ethnic concerns, health). The renewed interest in social issues will dominate intergovernmental policy studies into the next decade, particularly if federal revenues remain scarce due to the deficit. The equity, efficiency, and responsiveness of subnational governments will continue to be the focus of these inquiries.

Closer examinations will be made of the effectiveness of various types of public economic development strategies within the context of the centralization-decentralization debate. Are states better at promoting economic development than the federal government? Are local governments better than the states at such promotions? These questions will be thoroughly examined in the future. The debate has already taken on an international dimension, as mayors, governors, and presidents scramble to secure foreign markets for their constituents' products and compete to attract foreign investors.

One final forecast relates to another avenue of research likely to be well traveled in the early 1990s. Following the release of the 1990 Census results, political geography, and its empirical mapping of political boundaries and public policy outcomes, will emerge as another important technique for modeling certain types of intergovernmental relations. The next "reapportionment revolution" will generate new theoretical and legal interpretations of what is representation and what is a fair representational system. We can expect renewed interest in the concept of proportional representation and a heated debate over the role of the national government (especially the federal courts) in dictating the form of state and local representational systems.

CONCLUSION

To summarize, the study of federalism and intergovernmental relations will focus more on international intergovernmental relations in the next decade. The field network evaluation methodology will be employed to generate comparative data bases, the requisite building blocks of sound empirically-based comparative models. Although it is expected that the political economy model will continue to guide research on the perennial questions associated with federalism and intergovernmental relations, it is probable that, as the focus becomes more international, the political cultural component will ultimately weigh heavier in the model than it currently does.

With regard to expectations regarding models and methodologies for studying the United States system, I shall conclude with the observations of Leach (1989, 402): "Experience teaches us that the federal system is always in a flux. The framers of the Constitution bequeathed us an open-ended system. *We can only be the losers if we try to close it off by adopting permanently any set of theoretical principles, any model, any construct*" (author's emphasis).

This brief review of the evolution of the federalism and intergovernmental relations subfield has demonstrated that no one theory, model, or construct is likely to assume permanency either in the short or long term. Ours is a dynamic, not a static, subfield.

NOTES

1. Scholars differ in how they distinguish between federalism and intergovernmental relations. For example, O'Toole (1985, 2) defines federalism as "a system of authority constitutionally apportioned between central and regional governments"; "intergovernmental relations" is the more comprehensive term, including a full range of federal-state-local relations. Wright (1989, 350) refers to intergovernmental relations as an "altered character of American federalism" inclusive of national-state, interstate, and national-local, regional, and interlocal relationships. Wright goes so far as to state that "there are no *intergovernmental* relations; there are only relations among officials who govern in different roles in diverse and numerous units of government." It is "this 'human' dimension . . . that distinguishes IGR from federalism" (Wright 1989, 350). For an excellent overview of the distinctions between federalism and intergovernmental relations, see Benton and Morgan (1986, 3–4).

2. An alternative viewpoint, as expressed by John Kincaid, is that "it is difficult to find a unifying theme in the literature, in part, because there has been a breakdown in political consensus as to what the American federal system is and should be." In his view, use of the term "level of government" is indicative of a centralization bias that has dominated the work of most political scientists. "There continues to be stubborn adherence to the idea that a federal system organized like a pyramid is a good thing."

3. Indicative of this phenomenon is the proliferation of edited volumes featuring case studies of intergovernmental relations: c.f. Hawkins 1982; Ballard and Jones 1983; Howitt 1984; Gelfand and Neymeyer 1985; Hanf and Toonen 1985; O'Toole 1985; Bender and Stever 1986; Benton and Morgan 1986; Gittell 1986; Nathan, Doolittle, and Associates 1987. The heavy reliance on data from a single point in time and its consequences, particularly in studies with an urban dimension, are spelled out in Tucker (1982) and MacManus (1988).

4. The question raised by one of the panelists is the degree to which federalism and intergovernmental relations is the *central* research area of these "multi-section" members. It was suggested that "many of these people really have a different primary focus and that they only periodically bump into federalism." Nonetheless, the same panelist acknowledged the fact that more political scientists are writing about federalism and intergovernmental relations today.

5. It is my guess, however, that there is more partisan and ideological balance among scholars in the federalism and intergovernmental relations subfield of the political science discipline than in any other subfield.

REFERENCES

Emphasis is on the literature published in the 1980s.

Abney, Glen, and Thomas P. Lauth. 1986. *The Politics of State and City Administration*. Albany: State University of New York.

Advisory Commission on Intergovernmental Relations. 1962. *State Constitutional and Statutory Restrictions upon the Structural, Functional, and Personnel Powers of Local Government*. Washington, D.C.: U.S. Government Printing Office.

————. 1963. *Performance of Urban Functions: Local and Areawide*. Washington, D.C.: The Commission.

————. 1965. *Metropolitan Social and Economic Disparities: Implications for Intergovernmental Relations in Central Cities and Suburbs*. Washington, D.C.: The Commission, January.

————. 1967. *Fiscal Balances in the American Federal System*. Vol. 1. Washington, D.C.: U.S. Goverment Printing Office, October.

————. 1969a. *Urban America in the Federal System*. Washington, D.C.: U.S. Goverment Printing Office.

————. 1969b. *State Aid to Local Governments*. Washington, D.C.: U.S. Government Printing Office.

————. 1971. *Measuring the Fiscal Capacity and Effort of State and Local Areas*. Washington, D.C.: U.S. Government Printing Office.

————. 1972. *Multistate Regionalism*. Washington, D.C.: U.S. Government Printing Office.

————. 1973. *Regional Decision Making: New Strategies for Substate Districts*. Vol. 1 of *Substate Regionalism and the Federal System*. Washington, D.C.: U.S. Government Printing Office.

————. 1974. *The Challenge of Local Government Reorganization*. Washington, D.C.: U.S. Government Printing Office.

————. 1976. *Pragmatic Federalism: The Reassignment of Functional Responsibility*. Washington, D.C.: U.S. Government Printing Office.

————. 1977a. *Block Grants: A Comparative Analysis*. Washington, D.C.: Advisory Commission on Intergovernmental Relations.

————. 1977b. *The Intergovernmental Grant System as Seen by Local, State, and Federal Officials*. Washington, D.C.: U.S. Government Printing Office.

————. 1977c. *Regionalism Revisited: Recent Areawide and Local Responses*. Washington, D.C.: U.S. Government Printing Office.

————. 1977d. *State Limitations on Local Taxes and Expenditures*. Washington, D.C.: U.S. Government Printing Office.

————. 1978a. *Categorical Grants: Their Role and Design*. Washington, D.C.: U.S. Government Printing Office.

————. 1978b. *The Intergovernmental Grant System: Summary and Concluding Observations*. Washington, D.C.: U.S. Government Printing Office.

————. 1978c. *State Mandating of Local Expenditures*. Washington, D.C.: U.S. Government Printing Office.

————. 1979. *Citizen Participation in the American Federal System*. Washington, D.C.: Advisory Commission on Intergovernmental Relations.

————. 1980a. *Awakening the Slumbering Giant: Intergovermental Relations and Federal Grant Law*. Washington, D.C.: U.S. Government Printing Office.

————. 1980b. *Central City-Suburban Fiscal Disparity: City Distress*. Washington, D.C.: U.S. Government Printing Office, Fall.

————. 1980c. *A Crisis of Confidence and Competence: The Federal Role in the Federal System: The Dynamics of Growth*. Washington, D.C.: U.S. Government Printing Office, July.

————. 1980d. *In Brief—The Federal Role in the Federal System: The Dynamics of Growth*. Washington, D.C.: Government Printing Office.

————. 1980e. *State Administrators' Opinions on Administration Change, Federal Aid, Federal Relations*. Prepared by Deil S. Wright. Washington, D.C.: U.S. Government Printing Office.

————. 1981a. *An Agenda for American Federalism: Restoring Confidence and Competence*. Washington, D.C.: U.S. Government Printing Office.

————. 1981b. *The Condition of Contemporary Federalism: Conflicting Theories and Collapsing Constraints*. Washington, D.C.: U.S. Government Printing Office.

————. 1981c. *The Role of the States in Local Governments: Adapting Form to Function*. Washington, D.C.: U.S. Government Printing Office.

————. 1981d. *State and Local Roles in the Federal System*. Washington, D.C.: U.S. Government Printing Office.

————. 1983. *Regional Growth: Interstate Tax Competition*. Washington, D.C.: U.S. Government Printing Office.

————. 1984. *Regulatory Federalism: Policy, Process, Impact, and Reform*. Washington, D.C.: Government Printing Office.

————. 1985. *The Question of State Government Capability*. Washington, D.C.: U.S. Government Printing Office.

————. 1986a. *A Framework for Studying the Controversy Concerning the Federal Courts and Federalism*. Washington, D.C.: Advisory Commission on Intergovernmental Relations.

————. 1986b. *The Question of State Government Capability*. 2d ed. Washington, D.C.: Advisory Commission on Intergovernmental Relations.

————. 1986c. *Reflections on Garcia and Implications for Federalism*. Washington, D.C.: Advisory Commission on Intergovernmental Relations.

————. 1986d. *The Transformation in American Politics: Implications for Federalism*. Washington, D.C.: The Commission, August.

————. 1987a. *Federalism and the Constitution: A Symposium on Garcia*. Washington, D.C.: Advisory Commission on Intergovernmental Relations.

————. 1987b. *Fiscal Discipline in the Federal System: National Reform and the Experience of the States*. Washington, D.C.: Advisory Commission on Intergovernmental Relations.

————. 1987c. *Is Constitutional Reform Necessary to Reinvigorate Federalism? A Roundtable Discussion*. Washington, D.C.: Advisory Commission on Intergovernmental Relations.

————. 1987d. *Measuring State Fiscal Capacity*. Washington, D.C.: Advisory Commission on Intergovernmental Relations.

————. 1987e. *Organization of Local Public Economies*. Washington, D.C.: Advisory Commission on Intergovernmental Relations.

————. 1988a. *Interjurisdictional Competition in the Federal System: A Roundtable Discussion*. Washington, D.C.: Advisory Commission on Intergovernmental Relations, August.

————. 1988b. *State Constitutional Law: Cases and Materials*. Washington, D.C.: Advisory Commission on Intergovernmental Relations, December.

————. 1989. *Hearings on Constitutional Reform of Federalism: Statements by State and Local Government Association Representatives*. Washington, D.C.: Advisory Commission on Intergovernmental Relations, January.

————. Annual. *Changing Public Attitudes on Governments and Taxes*. Washington, D.C.: Advisory Commission on Intergovernmental Relations.

————. Annual. *Significant Features of Fiscal Federalism*. Washington, D.C.: U.S. Government Printing Office.

Agranoff, Robert. 1986. *Intergovernmental Management: Human Services Problem-Solving in Six Metropolitan Areas*. Albany: State University of New York.

Althaus, Paul G., and Joseph Schachler. 1983. "Interstate Migration and the New Federalism." *Social Science Quarterly* 64:34–45.

Anagnoson, J. Theodore. 1982. "Federal Grant Agencies and Congressional Election Campaigns." *American Journal of Political Science* 26:547–61.

Anderson, William. 1946. *Federalism and Intergovernmental Relations: A Budget of Suggestions for Research*. Chicago: Public Administration Service.

————. 1955. *The Nation and the States, Rivals or Partners?* Minneapolis: University of Minnesota Press.

————. 1960. *Intergovernmental Relations in Review*. Minneapolis: University of Minnesota Press.

Anton, Thomas. 1983a. *Federal Aid to Detroit*. Washington, D.C.: Brookings Institution.

————. 1983b. "The Regional Distribution of Federal Expenditures, 1971–1980." *National Tax Journal* 36:429–42.

————. 1984. "Intergovernmental Change in the United States: An Assessment of the Literature." In *Public Sector Performance: A Conceptual Turning Point*, ed. Trudi C. Miller. Baltimore: The John Hopkins University Press.

————. 1987. "Economic Development, Employment and Training Policy, and Federalism." *Policy Studies Review* 3:451.

————. 1989. *American Federalism and Public Policy*. New York: Random House.

————, Jerry P. Cawley, and Kevin L. Kramer. 1980. *Moving Money: An Empirical Analysis of Federal Expenditure Patterns*. Cambridge, Mass.: Oelgeschlager, Gunn, & Hain.

Antunes, George, and John Plumlee. 1977. "The Distribution of an Urban Public Service: Ethnicity, Socioeconomic Status, and Bureaucracy as Determinants of the Quality of Neighborhood Streets." *Urban Affairs Quarterly* 12:313–32.

Austermann, Winnefred M. 1980. *A Legislator's Guide to Oversight of Federal Funds*. Denver, Colo.: National Conference of State Legislators.

Bahl, Roy, ed. 1981. *Urban Government Finance: Emerging Trends*. Beverly Hills, Calif.: Sage Publications.

Baker, Earl, Bernadette A. Stevens, Stephen L. Schechter, and Harlan A. Wright. 1974. *Federal Grants, The National Interest and State Response—A Review of Theory and Research*. Philadelphia: Center for the Study of Federalism, Temple University.

Baldassare, Mark. 1986. *Trouble in Paradise: The Suburban Transformation in America*. New York: Columbia University Press.

Ball, Howard, Dale Krane, and Thomas P. Lauth. 1982. *Compromised Compliance: Implementation of the 1965 Voting Rights Act*. Westport, Conn.: Greenwood Press.

Ballard, Steven C., and Thomas E. James, eds. 1983. *The Future of the Sunbelt: Managing Growth and Change*. New York: Praeger.

Bardach, Eugene. 1977. *The Implementation Game*. Cambridge, Mass.: MIT Press.

Barfield, Claude E. 1981. *Rethinking Federalism: Block Grants and Federal, State and Local Responsibilities*. Washington, D.C.: American Enterprise Institute.

Barrilleaux, Charles J., and Mark E. Miller. 1988. "The Political Economy of State Medicaid Policy." *American Political Science Review* 82:1089–1108.

Barsh, Russell Laurence, and James Youngblood Henderson. 1980. *The Road: Indian Tribes and Political Liberty*. Berkeley: University of California Press.

Barton, Weldon V. 1967. *Interstate Compacts in the Political Process*. Chapel Hill: University of North Carolina Press.

Baum, Lawrence. 1976. "Implementation of Judicial Decisions: An Organizational Analysis." *American Politics Quarterly* 4:86–114.

Beam, David R. 1984. "New Federalism, Old Realities: The Reagan Administration and Intergovernmental Reform." In *The Reagan Presidency and the Governing of America*, ed. Lester M. Salamon and Michael S. Lund. Washington, D.C.: The Urban Institute Press.

————. 1988. "Reinventing Federalism: State-Local Government Roles in the New Economic Order." Paper presented at the annual meeting of the American Political Science Association.

————, and J. Edwin Benton. 1986. "Intergovernmental Relations and Public Policy: Down the Road." In *Intergovernmental Relations and Public Policy*, ed. J. Edwin Benton and David R. Morgan. New York: Greenwood Press.

————, Timothy J. Conlan, and David B. Walker. 1983. "Federalism: The Challenge of Conflicting Theories and Contemporary Practice." In *Political Science: The State of the Discipline*, ed. Ada W. Finifter. Washington, D.C.: APSA.

Beatty, Jerry K. 1972. "State Court Evasion of United States Supreme Court Mandates during the Last Decade of the Warren Court." *Valparaiso University Law Review* 6:260–85.

Beer, Samuel H. 1977. "Political Overload and Federalism." *Policy* 10:5–17.

————. 1978a. "Federalism, Nationalism, and Democracy in America." *American Political Science Review* 72:9–21.

————. 1978b. "In Search of a New Public Philosophy." In *The New American Political System*, ed. Anthony King. Washington, D.C.: American Enterprise Institute.

Beiser, Edward N. 1968. "A Comparative Analysis of State and Federal Judicial Behavior: The Reapportionment Cases." *American Political Science Review* 62:688–95.

Bender, Lewis G., and James A. Stever, eds. 1986. *Administering the New Federalism*. Boulder, Colo.: Westview Press.

Bennett, R. J. 1980. *The Geography of Public Finance: Welfare under Fiscal Federalism and Local Government Finance*. New York: Methuen.

Bennett, Walter Hartwell. 1964. *American Theories of Federalism*. University, Ala.: University of Alabama Press.

Bensel, Richard Franklin. 1984. *Sectionalism and American Political Development, 1880–1980*. Madison: University of Wisconsin Press.

Benson, Charles, and Peter Lund. 1969. *Neighborhood Distribution of Local Public Services*. Berkeley, Calif.: Institute of Governmental Studies.

Benson, George C. S. 1941. *The New Centralization: A Study of Intergovernmental Relations in the United States*. New York: Farrar and Rinehart.

Benton, J. Edwin, and David R. Morgan, eds. 1986. *Intergovernmental Relations and Public Policy*. Westport, Conn.: Greenwood Press.

Benton, Wilbourn E., ed. 1987. *1787: Drafting the U.S. Constitution*. College Station: Texas A&M University Press.

Berger, Raoul. 1987. *Federalism: The Founder's Design*. Norman: University of Oklahoma Press.

Berke, Joel S., Margaret E. Goertz, and Richard J. Coley. 1984. *Politicians, Judges, and City Schools*. New York: Russell Sage Foundation.

Berry, Jeffrey J. 1977. *Lobbying for the People*. Princeton, N.J.: Princeton University Press.

Berry, William D., and David Lowery. 1987. "Explaining the Size of the Public Sector: Responsive and Excessive Government Interpretations." *Journal of Politics* 49:401–40.

Bish, Robert L. 1971. *The Public Economy of Metropolitan Areas*. Chicago: Markham Publishing Co.

Blair, John P., and David Nachmias, eds. 1979. *Fiscal Retrenchment and Urban Policy*. Beverly Hills, Calif.: Sage Publications.

———, and Robert Premus. 1987. "Major Factors in Industrial Location: A Review." *Economic Development Quarterly* 1:84.

Bollens, John C., and Henry J. Schmandt. 1975. *The Metropolis: Its People, Politics, and Economic Life*. 3d ed. New York: Harper & Row.

Borcherding, Thomas E. 1977. *Budgets and Bureaucrats: The Sources of Government Growth*. Durham, N.C.: Duke University Press.

Boulay, Harvey. 1983. *The Twilight of Cities: Political Conflict, Development and Decay in Five Communities*. Port Washington, N.Y.: Associated Faculty Press.

Bowman, Ann, and Richard Kearney. 1986. *The Resurgence of the States*. Englewood Cliffs, N.J.: Prentice-Hall.

Bowman, Ann O'M., and Richard Kearney. 1988. "Dimensions of State Government Capability." *Western Political Quarterly* 41:341–62.

Boyle, John, and David Jacobs. 1982. "The Intracity Distribution of Services: A Multivariate Analysis." *American Political Science Review* 76:371–79.

Boyte, Harry C. 1980. *The Backyard Revolution: Understanding the New Citizen Movement*. Philadelphia: Temple University Press.

Bradbury, Katharine L., Anthony Downs, and Kenneth A. Small. 1982. *Urban Decline and the Future of American Cities*. Washington, D.C.: Brookings Institution.

Break, George F. 1967. *Intergovernmental Fiscal Relations in the U.S.* Washington, D.C.: Brookings Institution.

———. 1980. *Financing Government in a Federal System*. Washington, D.C.: Brookings Institution.

Brecher, Charles, and Raymond D. Horton, eds. 1985. *Setting Municipal Priorities, 1986*. New York: New York University Press.

Brodkin, Evelyn. 1986. *The False Promise of Administrative Reform: Implementing Quality Control in Welfare*. Philadelphia: Temple University Press.

Brown, Lawrence D., James W. Fossett, and Kenneth T. Palmer. 1984. *The Changing Politics of Federal Grants*. Washington, D.C.: Brookings Institution.

Browning, Rufus P., Dale Rogers Marshall, and David H. Tabb. 1984. *Protest Is Not Enough: The Struggle of Blacks and Hispanics for Equality in Urban Politics*. Berkeley: University of California Press.

Brown-John, C. Lloyd. 1988. *Centralizing and Decentralizing Trends in Federal States*. Lanham, Md.: University Press of America.

Bryan, Frank M. 1981. *Politics in the Rural States: People, Parties and Progress*. Boulder, Colo.: Westview Press.

Buchanan, James M., and Gordon Tullock. 1962. *The Calculus of Consent: Logical Foundations of Constitutional Democracy*. Ann Arbor: University of Michigan Press.

Buchanan, William. 1965. "Politics and Federalism: Party or Anti-Party?" *The Annals* 359:107–15.

Bullock, Charles S., III, and Charles M. Lamb, eds. 1984. *Implementation of Civil Rights Policy*. Monterey, Calif.: Brooks/Cole Publishing.

Bullock, Charles S., III, and Susan A. MacManus. 1987. "The Impact of Staggered Terms on Minority Representation." *Journal of Politics* 49:543–52.

Burchell, Robert W., and David Listokin, eds. 1981. *Cities under Stress: The Fiscal Crisis of Urban America*. Piscataway, N.J.: Center for Urban Policy Research.

Caldeira, Gregory A. 1983. "On the Reputation of State Supreme Courts." *Political Behavior* 51:83–108.

———. 1985. "The Transmission of Legal Precedent: A Study of State Supreme Courts." *American Political Science Review* 779:178–93.

Cameron, David R. 1978. "The Expansion of the Public Economy: A Comparative Analysis." *American Political Science Review* 72:1243–61.

Campbell, Alan K., ed. 1970. *The States and the Urban Crisis*. Englewood Cliffs, N.J.: For the American Assembly of Columbia University.

Canon, Bradley C. 1973. "Reactions of State Supreme Courts to a U.S. Supreme Court Civil Liberties Decision." *Law and Society Review* 8:109–34.

———. 1974. "Organizational Contumacy in the Transmission of Judicial Polities: The *Mapp, Escobedo, Miranda,* and *Gault* Cases." *Villanova Law Review* 20:50–79.

———, and Laurence Baum. 1981. "Patterns of Adoption of Tort Law Innovations: An Application of Diffusion Theory to Judicial Doctrines." *American Political Science Review* 75:975–87.

Caputo, David A., and Richard L. Cole. 1974. *Urban Politics and Decentralization: The Case of General Revenue Sharing*. Lexington, Mass.: D. C. Heath/Lexington.

Caraley, Demetrious. 1986. "Changing Conceptions of Federalism." *Political Science Quarterly* 101:289–306.

Carroll, James D., and Richard W. Campbell, eds. 1976. *Intergovernmental Administration: 1976—Eleven Academic and Practitioner Perspectives*. Syracuse, N.Y.: Maxwell School of Citizenship and Public Affairs, Syracuse University.

Chisman, Forrest, and Alan Pifer. 1987. *Government for the People: The Federal Social Role: What It Is: What It Should Be*. New York: W. W. Norton.

Chubb, John E. 1983. *Interest Groups and the Bureacracy*. Stanford, Calif.: Stanford University Press.

———. 1985a. "Excessive Regulation: The Case of Federal Aid to Education." *Political Science Quarterly* 100:287–312.

———. 1985b. "Federalism and the Bias for Centralization." In *The New Direction in American Politics*, ed. John E. Chubb and Paul E. Petersen. Washington, D.C.: Brookings Institution.

———. 1985c. "The Political Economy of Federalism." *American Political Science Review* 79:994–1015.

———. 1988. "Institutions, The Economy, and the Dynamics of State Elections." *American Political Science Review* 82:133–54.

———, and Terry M. Moe. 1988. "Politics, Markets, and the Organization of Schools." *American Political Science Review* 82:1065–88.

Claggett, William, William Flanigan, and Nancy Zingale. 1984. "Nationalization of the American Electorate." *American Political Science Review* 78:77–91.

Clark, Jane Perry. 1938. *The Rise of a New Federalism: Federal-State Cooperation in the United States*. New York: Columbia University Press.

Clark, Terry Nichols, ed. 1981. *Urban Policy Analysis: Directions of Future Research*. Beverly Hills, Calif.: Sage Publications.

Clark, Terry, and Lorna Ferguson. 1983. *City Money: Political Processes, Fiscal Strain and Retrenchment*. New York: Columbia University Press.

Clavel, Pierre. 1986. *The Progressive City Planning and Participation, 1969–1984*. New Brunswick, N.J.: Rutgers University Press.

Clynch, Edward J. 1972. "A Critique of Ira Sharkansky's 'The Utility of Elazar's Political Culture.'" *Polity* 5:139–41.

Cole, Richard L. 1974. *Citizen Participation and the Urban Policy Process*. Lexington, Mass.: Lexington Books/D. C. Heath.

———, and David A. Caputo. 1984. "The Public Hearing as an Effective Citizen Participation Mechanism: A Case Study of the General Revenue Sharing Program." *American Political Science Review* 78:404–16.

Cole, Stephanie, ed. 1976. *Partnership within the States: Local Self-Government in the Federal System*. Urbana, Ill., and Philadelphia: Institute of Public Affairs, University of Illinois, and Center for Study of Federalism, Temple University.

Committee for Economic Development. 1966. *Modernizing Local Government*. New York: Committee for Economic Development, July.

———. 1970. *Reshaping Government in Metropolitan Areas*. New York: Committee for Economic Development.

———. 1986. *Leadership for Dynamic State Economies*. New York: Committee for Economic Development.

Congressional Budget Office. 1979. *Federal Constraints on State and Local Actions*. Washington, D.C.: U.S. Government Printing Office.

Conlan, Timothy J. 1984. "The Politics of Federal Block Grants." *Political Science Quarterly* 99:247–70.

———. 1985. "Federalism and Competing Values in the Reagan Administration." In *American Intergovernmental Relations*, ed. Laurence J. O'Toole, Jr. Washington, D.C.: CQ Press.

———. 1988. *New Federalism: Intergovernmental Reform from Reagan to Nixon*. Washington, D.C.: Brookings Institution.

Copeland, Gary W., and Kenneth J. Meier. 1984. "Pass the Biscuits, Pappy: Congressional Decision-Making and Federal Grants." *American Politics Quarterly* 12:3–22.

Council of State Governments. 1971. *Interstate Compacts, 1783–1970*. Lexington, Ky.: The Council.

Crenson, Matthew A. 1983. *Neighborhood Politics*. Cambridge, Mass.: Harvard University Press.

Crosskey, William Winslow, and William Jeffrey, Jr. 1981. *Politics and the Constitution in the History of the United States*. Vol. 3, *The Political Background of the Federal Convention*. Chicago: University of Chicago Press.

Crotty, William. 1984. *American Parties in Decline*. 2d ed. Boston: Little, Brown.

———, ed. 1986. *Political Parties in Local Areas*. Knoxville: University of Tennessee Press.

Cucitti, Peggy. 1978. *The Role of Equalization in Federal Grants*. Washington, D.C.: U.S. Government Printing Office.

Curtis, Michael Kent. 1986. *No State Shall Abridge: The Fourteenth Amendment and the Bill of Rights*. Durham, N.C.: Duke University Press.

Dalton, Thomas Carlyle. 1985. *The State Politics of Judicial and Congressional Reform: Legalizing Criminal Justice Policies*. Westport, Conn.: Greenwood Press.

Danielson, Michael N., and Jameson W. Doig. 1982. *New York: The Politics of Urban Regional Development*. Berkeley: University of California Press.

Davidson, Chandler, ed. 1984. *Minority Vote Dilution*. Washington, D.C.: Howard University Press.

Davis, Otto A., M. A. H. Dempster, and Aaron Wildavsky. 1974. "Towards a Predictive Theory of Governmental Expenditures." *British Journal of Political Science* 4:419–52.

Davis, Rufus S. 1978. *The Federal Principle: A Journey through Time in Quest of Meaning*. Berkeley: University of California Press.

Dean, Gillian. 1980. "The Study of Political Feedback Using Nonrecursive Causal Models: The Case of State Divorce Politics." *Policy Studies Journal* 8:920–27.

DeHoog, Ruth Hoogsland. 1984. *Contracting Out for Human Services: Economic, Political, and Organization Perspectives*. Albany: State University of New York Press.

Department of Treasury, Office of State and Local Finance. 1985. *Federal-State-Local Fiscal Relations: Report to the President and Congress*. Washington, D.C.: U.S. Government Printing Office.

Delgado, Gary. 1986. *Organizing the Movement: The Roots and Growth of ACORN*. Philadelphia: Temple University Press.

Delonia, Vine, Jr., and Clifford Lytle. 1984. *The Nations Within: The Past and Future of American Indian Sovereignty*. New York: Pantheon Books.

Derthick, Martha. 1964. *Between State and Nation*. Washington, D.C.: Brookings Institution.

———. 1970. *The Influence of Federal Grants: Public Assistance in Massachusetts*. Cambridge, Mass.: Harvard University Press.

———. 1972. *New Towns In-Town: Why a Federal Program Failed*. Washington, D.C.: The Urban Institute.

———. 1974. *Between State and Nation: Regional Organizations of the United States*. Washington, D.C.: Brookings Institution.

———. 1975. *Uncontrollable Spending for Social Services Grants*. Washington, D.C.: Brookings Institution.

———. 1985. "Intergovernmental Relations in the 1970's." In *Changing Patterns in American Federal-State Relations during the 1950's, the 1960's, and the 1970's*, ed. Lawrence E. Gelfand and Robert J. Neymeyer. Iowa City: University of Iowa Press.

———. 1987. "American Federalism: Madison's Middle Ground in the 1980s." *Public Administration Review* 47:66–74.

———, and Paul Quirk. 1985. *The Politics of Deregulation*. Washington, D.C.: Brookings Institution.

DeSario, Jack, and Stuart Langton, eds. 1987. *Citizen Participation in Public Decision Making*. Westport, Conn.: Greenwood Press.

Devine, Donald J. 1972. *The Political Culture of the United States*. Boston: Little, Brown.

DeWitt, John. 1987. *Shifting Responsibilities: Federalism in Economic Development*. Washington, D.C.: National Governors' Association.

Dexter, Lewis Anthony. 1987. *How Organizations Are Represented in Washington*. Lanham, Md.: University Press of America.

Diamond, Martin. 1964. "What the Framers Meant by Federalism." In *A Nation of States*, ed. Robert Goldwin. Chicago: Rand McNally.

———. 1970. *Notes on the Political Theory of the Founding Fathers*. Philadelphia: Center for the Study of Federalism.

Diamond, Paul R. 1985. *Beyond Busing: Inside the Challenge to Urban Segregation*. Ann Arbor: University of Michigan Press.

Dilger, Robert Jay. 1989. *National Intergovernmental Programs*. Englewood Cliffs, N.J.: Prentice-Hall.

————, ed. 1986. *American Intergovernmental Relations Today: Perspectives and Controversies*. Englewood Cliffs, N.J.: Prentice-Hall.

Doddy, Joanne L., and Larry C. Etheridge. 1976. "Federalism before the Court." *Intergovernmental Perspective* 2:6–14.

Dommel, Paul R. 1974. *The Politics of Revenue Sharing*. Bloomington: University of Indiana Press.

————, et al. 1980. *Targeting Community Development*. Washington, D.C.: U.S. Government Printing Office.

————. 1982. *Decentralizing Urban Policy: Case Studies in Community Development*. Washington, D.C.: Brookings Institution.

Downs, Anthony. 1957. *An Economic Theory of Democracy*. New York: Harper & Row.

————. 1981. *Neighborhoods and Urban Development*. Washington, D.C.: Brookings Institution.

Doyle, Denis P., and Terry W. Hartie. 1985. *Excellence in Education: The States Take Charge*. Washington, D.C.: American Enterprise Institute.

Drennan, Matthew P. 1985. *Modeling Metropolitan Economies for Forecasting and Policy Analysis*. New York: New York University Press.

Duchacek, Ivo D. 1970. *Comparative Federalism: The Territorial Dimension of Politics*. New York: Holt, Rinehart, and Winston.

————. 1987. *Comparative Federalism: The Territorial Dimension of Politics*. Lanham, Md.: University Press of America.

Durant, Robert F. 1984. "EPA, TVA, and Pollution Control: Implications for a Theory of Regulatory Policy Implementation." *Public Administration Review* 44:305–15.

Dye, Thomas R. 1966. *Politics, Economics, and the Public: Policy Outcomes in the American States*. Chicago: Rand McNally.

————. 1982. "Taxing, Spending, and Economic Growth in the American States." *Journal of Politics* 42:1085–1107.

————. 1987. "Introduction: Targeting Intergovernmental Aid." *Social Service Quarterly* 68:443–46.

————. 1988a. "Explaining Government Contraction: A Demand Side Model for Education in the States." *Western Political Quarterly* 41:779–90.

————. 1988b. "A Theory of Competitive Federalism." Paper presented at the annual meeting of the Southern Political Science Association, Atlanta, November.

————, and Thomas Hurley. 1978. "The Responsiveness of Federal and State Governments to Urban Problems." *Journal of Politics* 40:196–207.

Earle, V., ed. 1968. *Federalism: Infinite Variety in Theory and Practice*. Itasca, Ill.: F. E. Peacock Publishers.

Elazar, Daniel. 1966. *American Federalism, A View from the States*. New York: Thomas Y. Crowell.

———, ed. 1974a. *The Federal Polity*. New Brunswick, N.J.: Transaction Books.

———. 1974b. "The New Federalism: Can the States Be Trusted?" *The Public Interest* 35:89–103.

———. 1987a. *Exploring Federalism*. University, Ala.: University of Alabama Press.

———. 1987b. *Federalism as Grand Design: Political Philosophers and the Federal Principle*. Lanham, Md.: University Press of America.

———. 1988. *The American Constitutional Tradition*. Lincoln: University of Nebraska Press.

———, R. Bruce Carroll, E. Lester Levine, and Douglas St. Angelo, eds. 1969. *Cooperation and Conflict: Readings in American Federalism*. Itasca, Ill.: F. E. Peacock Publishers.

———, et al. 1969. *Cooperation and Conflict: Readings in American Federalism*. Itasca, Ill.: F. E. Peacock Publishers.

Ellwood, John, ed. 1982. *Reductions in U.S. Domestic Spending*. New Brunswick, N.J.: Transaction Books.

Elmore, Richard F., and Millbrey Wallin McLaughlin. 1982. *Reform and Retrenchment: The Politics of California School Finance Reform*. Cambridge, Mass.: Bellinger.

Engstrom, Richard L., and Michael D. McDonald. 1981. "The Election of Blacks to City Councils: Clarifying the Impact of Electoral Arrangements on the Seats/Population Relationship." *American Political Science Review* 75:344–54.

Epstein, Lee, and Karen O'Connor. 1988. "States and the U.S. Supreme Court: An Examination of Litigation Outcomes." *Social Science Quarterly* 69: 660–74.

Erikson, Robert S., John P. McIver, and Gerald C. Wright, Jr. 1987. "State Political Culture and Public Opinion." *American Political Science Review* 81: 797–813.

Evans, Diana Yiannakis. 1986. "Sunbelt versus Frostbelt: The Evolution of Regional Conflict over Federal Aid to Cities in the House of Representatives." *Social Science Quarterly* 67:108–17.

Farber, Daniel A. 1988. "Conservative Judicial Activism: 'Taking' Liberties." *The New Republic* 198:19–21.

Farkas, Suzanne. 1971. *Urban Lobbying: Mayors in the Federal Arena*. New York: New York University Press.

Feldman, Paul, and James Jondrow. 1984. "Congressional Elections and Local Federal Spending." *American Journal of Political Science* 28:147–64.

Fellman, David. 1978. "The Nationalization of American Civil Liberties." In *Essays on the Constitution of the United States*, ed. Judd Harmon. Port Washington, N.Y.: Kennikat Press.

Ferman, Barbara. 1985. *Governing the Ungovernable City: Political Skill, Leadership, and the Modern Mayor*. Philadelphia: Temple University Press.

Fesler, James W. 1949. *Area and Administration*. University, Ala.: University of Alabama Press.

Fino, Susan P. 1987. *The Role of State Supreme Courts in the New Judicial Federalism*. Westport, Conn.: Greenwood Press.

Fisk, Donald, Herbert Kiesling, and Thomas Muller. 1978. *Private Provision of Public Services: An Overview*. Washington, D.C.: The Urban Institute.

Fix, Michael. 1984. "Transferring Regulatory Authority to the States." In *The Reagan Regulatory Strategy: An Assessment*, ed. George C. Eads and Michael Fix. Washington, D.C.: The Urban Institute.

Florestano, Patricia S. 1974. *Interstate Cooperation Commissions*. Annapolis: Maryland Commission on Intergovernmental Cooperation.

Fossett, James W. 1983. *Federal Aid to Big Cities: The Politics of Dependence*. Washington, D.C.: Brookings Institution.

Foster, Lorn S., ed. 1985. *The Voting Rights Act: Consequences and Implications*. New York: Praeger.

Franck, Thomas M., ed. 1968. *Why Federations Fail: An Inquiry into the Requisites for Successful Federalism*. New York: New York University Press.

Franklin, Grace A., and Randall B. Ripley. 1984. *CETA: Politics and Policy, 1973–1982*. Knoxville: University of Tennessee Press.

Friedelbaum, Stanley H., ed. 1988. *Human Rights in the States: New Directions in Constitutional Policymaking*. Westport, Conn.: Greenwood Press.

Friedland, Roger, and Herbert Wong. 1983. "Congressional Politics, Federal Grants and Local Needs: Who Gets What and Why." In *Municipal Money Chase: The Politics of Local Government Finance*, ed. Alberta M. Sbragia. Boulder, Colo.: Westview Press.

Friedrich, Earl J. 1968. *Trends of Federalism in Theory and Practice*. New York: Praeger.

Fritschler, A. Lee, and Marley Segal. 1972. "Intergovernmental Relations and Contemporary Political Science: Developing an Integrative Typology." *Publius: The Journal of Federalism* 1:95–122.

Garand, James C. 1988. "Explaining Growth in the United States." *American Political Science Review* 82:837–52.

Gardiner, John A., and Theodore R. Lyman. *The Fraud Control Game: State Responses to Fraud and Abuse in AFDC and Medicaid Programs*. Bloomington: Indiana University Press.

Garnett, James L. 1980. *Reorganizing State Government: The Executive Branch*. Boulder, Colo.: Westview Press.

Gelfand, Laurence E., and Robert J. Neymeyer. 1985. *Changing Patterns in American Federal-State Relations during the 1950s, 1960s, and 1970s*. Iowa City: University of Iowa Press.

Gelfand, Mark J. 1975. *A Nation of Cities: The Federal Government and Urban America*. New York: Oxford University Press.

Ginzberg, Eli, Edith M. Davis, and Miriam Ostow. 1985. *Local Health Policy in*

Action: The Municipal Health Services Program. Totawa, N.J.: Rowman & Allanheld.

Gist, John R., and Carter H. Hill. 1981. "The Economics of Choice in the Allocation of Federal Grants." *Public Choice* 36:63–73.

Gittell, Marilyn. 1980. *Limits to Citizen Participation*. Beverly Hills, Calif.: Sage Publications.

———, ed. 1986. *State Politics and the New Federalism: Readings and Commentary*. New York: Longman.

Glendening, Parris N., and Mavis Mann Reeves. 1984. *Pragmatic Federalism: An Intergovernmental View of American Government*. 2d ed. Pacific Palisades, Calif.: Palisades Publishers.

Goggin, Malcolm L. 1987. *Policy Design and the Politics of Implementation: The Case of Health Care in the American States*. Knoxville: University of Tennessee Press.

Goldwin, Robert A., ed. 1964. *A Nation of States*. Chicago: Rand McNally.

———, and William Schambra, eds. 1980. *How Democratic Is the Constitution?* Washington, D.C.: American Enterprise Institute.

Golembiewski, Robert T., and Aaron Wildavsky, eds. 1984. *The Costs of Federalism: Essays in Honor of James W. Fesler*. New Brunswick, N.J.: Transaction Books.

Goodman, Robert. 1979. *The Last Entrepreneurs: America's Regional Wars for Jobs and Dollars*. Boston: South End Press.

Gramlich, Edward M. 1982. "An Econometric Examination of the New Federalism." *Brookings Papers on Economic Activity* 2:327–60.

Graves, W. Brooke. 1964. *American Intergovernmental Relations: Their Origins, Historical Development, and Current Status*. New York: Charles Scribner's Sons.

Gray, Virginia. 1973. "Innovation in the States: A Diffusion Study." *American Political Science Review* 67:1174–93.

———, and David Lowery. 1988. "Interest Group Politics and Economic Growth in the United States." *American Political Science Review* 52: 109–31.

Green, Robert L., ed. 1985. *Metropolitan Desegregation*. New York: Plenum Press.

Greer, Scott, Ronald Hedlund, and James L. Gibson, eds. *Accountability in Urban Society: Public Agencies under Fire*. Beverly Hills, Calif.: Sage Publications.

Grodzins, Morton. 1960. "The Federal System." In *Goals for Americans*. Report of the President's Commission on National Goals. Englewood Cliffs, N.J.: Prentice-Hall.

———. 1966. *The American System: A New View of Government in the United States*, ed. Daniel J. Elazar. Chicago: Rand McNally.

Grofman, Bernard, ed. 1985. "Gerrymandering: Political Science Goes to Court." *PS* 18:538–81.

Grosenick, Leigh E., ed. 1973. *The Administration of the New Federalism: Objectives and Issues*. Washington, D.C.: American Society for Public Administration.

Gruhl, John. 1980. "The Supreme Court's Impact on the Law of Libel: Compliance by Lower Federal Courts." *Western Political Quarterly* 33:501–19.

Guterbock, Thomas M. 1980. *Machine Politics in Transition: Party and Community in Chicago*. Chicago: University of Chicago Press.

Haas, Kenneth C. 1981. "The 'New Federalism' and Prisoners' Rights: State Supreme Courts in Comparative Perspective." *Western Political Quarterly* 34:552–71.

Haider, Donald H. 1974. *When Governments Come to Washington: Governors, Mayors, and Intergovernmental Lobbying*. New York: The Free Press.

Hale, George, and Marian Lief Palley. 1981. *The Politics of Federal Grants*. Washington, D.C.: Congressional Quarterly Press.

Hall, John S., and Susan A. MacManus. 1982. "Tracking Decisions and Consequences: The Field Network Evaluation Approach." In *Studying Implementation: Methodological and Administrative Issues*, ed. Walter Williams et al. Chatham, N.J.: Chatham House.

Hamilton, Alexander, John Jay, and James Madison. n.d. *The Federalist*. New York: The Modern Library. Originally published in 1788.

Hamilton, Howard D. 1978. *Electing the Cincinnati City Council: An Examination of Alternative Electoral-Representation Systems*. Cincinnati, Ohio: Stephen H. Wilder Foundation.

Hanadle, Beth. 1983. *Public Administration in Rural Areas and Small Jurisdictions: A Guide to the Literature*. New York: Garland.

Hanf, Kenneth, and Theo A. J. Toonen, eds. 1985. *Policy Implementation in Federal and Unitary Systems: Questions of Analysis and Design*. Dordrecht: Martinus Nijhoff.

Hansen, Susan B. 1980. "State Implementation of Supreme Court Decisions: Abortion Rates Since Roe v. Wade." *Journal of Politics* 42:372–95.

Hanson, Russell L. 1983. "The Intergovernmental Setting of State Politics." In *Politics in the American States: A Comparative Analysis*, ed. Virginia Gray et al. 4th ed. Boston: Little, Brown.

Hanus, Jerome J., ed. 1981. *The Nationalization of State Government*. Lexington, Mass.: Lexington Books/D. C. Heath.

Harrigan, John. 1985. *Political Change in the Metropolis*. 3d ed. Boston: Little, Brown.

Harris, Charles W. 1970. *Regional COGs and the Central City*. Detroit: Metropolitan Fund.

Hawkins, Robert B., Jr. 1988. "Rebalancing the Federal Budget and the Federal System." *Intergovernmental Perspectives* 14:13–17.

————, ed. 1982. *American Federalism: A New Partnership for the Republic*. San Francisco: Institute for Contemporary Studies.

Hays, R. Allen. 1985. *The Federal Government and Urban Housing*. Albany: State University of New York Press.

Henig, Jeffrey R. 1982. *Neighborhood Mobilization: Redevelopment and Response*. New Brunswick, N.J.: Rutgers University Press.

————. 1985. *Public Policy and Federalism: Issues in State and Local Politics*. New York: St. Martin's Press.

Herson, Lawrence J. R. 1957. "The Lost World of Municipal Government." *American Political Science Review* 51:330–45.

Hill, Richard Child. 1974. "Separate and Unequal: Government Inequality in the Metropolis." *American Political Science Review* 68:1557–68.

Hobbes, Thomas. 1960. *Leviathan, or the Matter, Forme, and Power of a Commonwealth Ecclesiasticall and Civil*, ed. Michael Oakeshott. Oxford: Basil Blackwell. Originally published in 1651.

Hochschild, Jennifer L. 1984. *The New American Dilemma: Liberal Democracy and School Integration*. New Haven: Yale University Press.

Hofferbert, Richard I. 1971. "The Nationalization of State Politics." In *State and Urban Politics*, ed. R. I. Hofferbert and Ira Sharkansky. Boston: Little, Brown.

Hollingsworth, J. Rogers, and Ellen Jane Hollingsworth. 1979. *Dimensions in Urban History: Historical and Social Science Perspectives on Middle-Size American Cities*. Madison: University of Wisconsin Press.

Howard, Philip K. 1974. "Lower Court Disavowal of Supreme Court Precedent." *Virginia Law Review* 60:494–539.

Howitt, Arnold M. 1984. *Managing Federalism: Studies in Intergovernmental Relations*. Washington, D.C.: Governmental Quarterly.

Hubell, L. Kenneth, ed. 1979. *Fiscal Crisis in American Cities, The Federal Response*. Cambridge, Mass.: Ballinger Publishing Company.

Hull, Elizabeth. 1985. *Without Justice for All: The Constitutional Rights of Aliens*. Westport, Conn.: Greenwood Press.

Humberger, Edward. 1983. *Business Location Decisions and Cities*. Washington, D.C.: Public Technology, Inc.

Ingram, Helen. 1977. "Policy Implementation through Bargaining: The Case of Federal Grants-in-Aid." *Public Policy* 25:499–526.

Jacob, Herbert, and Kenneth N. Vines, eds. 1976. *Politics in the American States: A Comparative Analysis*. Boston: Little, Brown.

Jacobs, Bruce. 1981. *The Political Economy of Organizational Change: Urban Institutional Responses to the War on Poverty*. New York: Academic Press.

Jennings, Edward T. 1979. "Competition, Constituencies, and Welfare Policies in American States." *American Political Science Review* 73:414–29.

————, Dale Krane, Alex N. Pattakos, and B. J. Reed, eds. 1986. *From Nation to*

States: The Small Cities Community Development Block Grant Program. Albany: State University of New York Press.

Jewell, Malcolm E. 1982a. "The Neglected World of State Politics." *Journal of Politics* 44:638–57.

Jewell, Malcolm E. 1982b. *Representation in State Legislatures.* Lexington: University Press of Kentucky.

Jillson, Calvin C. 1981. "Constitution-making: Alignment and Realignment in the Federal Convention of 1787." *American Political Science Review* 75: 598–612.

———, and Cecil L. Eubanks. 1984. "The Political Structure of Constitution Making: The Federal Convention of 1787." *American Journal of Political Science* 28:435–58.

Johnson, Charles A. 1976. "Political Culture in American States: Elazar's Formulation Examined." *American Journal of Political Science* 20:491–509.

———. 1979. "Lower Court Reactions to Supreme Court Decisions: A Quantitative Examination." *American Journal of Political Science* 23:792–804.

———. 1981. "Do Lower Courts Anticipate Changes in Supreme Court Policies? A Few Empirical Notes." *Law and Policy Quarterly* 3:55–68.

Johnson, Gerald, and John G. Heilmon. 1987. "Metapolicy Transition and Policy Implementation: New Federalism and Privatization." *Public Administration Review* 47:468–78.

Johnson, Richard E. 1969. *The Effect of Judicial Review on Federal-State-Relations in Australia, Canada, and the United States.* Baton Rouge: Louisiana State University Press.

———, and John T. Thompson. 1980. "The Burger Court and Federalism: A Revolution in 1976?" *Western Political Quarterly* 33:197–216.

Jones, Bryan D., Saadia Greenberg, and Joseph Drew. 1980. *Service Delivery in the City: Citizen Demand and Bureaucratic Response.* New York: Longman.

Jones, Charles, A., and Robert D. Thomas, eds. 1976. *Public Policy Making in a Federal System.* Vol. 3. Sage Yearbooks in Politics and Public Policy. Beverly Hills, Calif.: Sage Publications.

Judd, Dennis R. 1988. *The Politics of American Cities: Private Power and Public Policy.* 3d ed. Glenview, Ill.: Scott, Foresman.

———, and David Brian Robertson. 1989. "Urban Revitalization in the United States: Prisoner of the Federal System." In *Regenerating the Cities*, ed. Michael Parkinson et al. Glenview, Ill.: Scott, Foresman.

Juster, F. Thomas, ed. 1976. *The Economic and Political Impact of General Revenue Sharing.* Washington, D.C.: U.S. Government Printing Office.

Kann, Mark E. 1986. *Middle Class Radicalism in Santa Monica.* Philadelphia: Temple University Press.

Kantor, Paul, with Stephen Davis. 1988. *The Dependent City.* Glenview, Ill.: Scott, Foresman.

Karnig, Albert K., and Susan Welch. 1980. *Black Representation and Urban Policy*. Chicago: University of Chicago Press.

Kemp, Kathleen A. 1978. "Nationalization of the American States: A Test of the Thesis." *American Politics Quarterly* 6:237–47.

Kenyon, Daphne A., and John Kincaid. 1988. "Rethinking Interjurisdictional Competition." *Multistate Tax Commission*, 1988:12–14.

Kettl, Donald F. 1980. *Managing Community Development in the New Federalism*. New York: Praeger.

———. 1983. *The Regulation of American Federalism*. Baton Rouge: Louisiana State University Press.

Key, V. O., Jr. 1937. *The Administration of Federal Grants to States*. Chicago: Public Administration Service.

Kincaid, John. 1987. "The State of American Federalism—1986." *Publius: The Journal of Federalism* 17:1–6.

———, ed. 1988a. "State Constitutions in a Federal System." *The Annals of the American Academy of Political and Social Science* 496 (March).

———. 1988b. "The State of American Federalism—1987." *Publius: The Journal of Federalism* 18:1–5.

Kirlin, John J. 1982. *The Political Economy of Fiscal Limits*. Lexington, Mass.: D. C. Heath.

Kiser, Larry L., and Elinor Ostrom. 1982. "The Three Worlds of Action: A Metatheoretical Synthesis of Institutional Approaches." In *Strategies of Political Inquiry*, ed. Elinor Ostrom. Beverly Hills, Calif.: Sage Publications.

Kline, John M. 1983. *State Government Influence in U.S. International Economic Policy*. Lexington, Mass.: D. C. Heath.

Klingman, David, and William W. Lammers. 1984. "The 'General Policy Liberalism' Factor in American State Politics." *American Journal of Political Science* 28:598–610.

Kotler, Milton. 1969. *Neighborhood Government: The Local Foundations of Community Life*. Indianapolis, Ind.: Bobbs-Merrill.

Kotter, John E. P., and Paul R. Lawrence. 1974. *Mayors in Action: Five Approaches to Urban Governance*. New York: Wiley.

Kraynak, Robert P. 1987. "Tocqueville's Constitutionalism." *American Political Science Review* 81:1175–97.

Krislov, Samuel, and David H. Rosenbloom. 1981. *Representative Bureacracy and the American Political System*. New York: Praeger.

Kurland, Philip B., and Ralph Lerner, eds. 1987. *The Founder's Constitution*. Chicago: University of Chicago Press.

Kweit, Mary Grisez, and Robert W. Kweit. 1981. *Implementing Citizen Participation in a Bureaucratic Society: A Contingency Approach*. New York: Praeger.

Landau, Martin. 1969. "Redundancy, Rationality, and the Problem of Duplication and Overlap." *Public Administration Review* 29:346–58.

———. 1973. "Federalism, Redundancy, and System Reliability." *Publius: The Journal of Federalism* 3:173–96.

Larkey, P. 1979. *Evaluating Public Programs: The Impact of General Revenue Sharing on Municipal Government.* Princeton, N.J.: Princeton University Press.

———, Chandler Stolp, and Mark Winer. 1981. "Theorizing about the Growth of Government: A Research Assessment." *Journal of Public Policy* 1: 157–220.

Laski, Harold J. 1939. "The Obsolescence of Federalism." *The New Republic* 98: 362–69.

Leach, Richard H. 1970. *American Federalism.* New York: W. W. Norton.

———. 1989. "Federalism and Intergovernmental Relations: Theories, Ideas, and Concepts." In *Handbook of Public Administration*, ed. Jack Rabin, W. Bartley Hildreth, and Gerald J. Miller. New York: Marcel Dekker.

———, ed. 1983. *Intergovernmental Relations in the 1980s.* New York: Marcel Dekker.

Levin, Martin A., and Barbara Ferman. 1985. *The Political Hand: Policy Implementation and Youth Employment Programs.* New York: Pergamon.

Levine, Charles H., ed. 1980. *Managing Fiscal Stress: The Crisis in the Public Sector.* Chatham, N.J.: Chatham House Publishers.

———, and Irene Rubin, eds. 1980. *Fiscal Stress and Public Policy.* Beverly Hills, Calif.: Sage Publications.

———, and Paul L. Posner. 1981. "Austerity and the Intergovernmental System." *Political Science Quarterly* 96:67–86.

———, Irene S. Rubin, and George Wolohojian. 1981. *The Politics of Retrenchment: How Local Governments Manage Fiscal Stress.* Beverly Hills, Calif.: Sage Publications.

Levy, Frank, Arnold Meltsner, and Aaron Wildavsky. 1974. *Urban Outcomes: Schools, Streets, and Libraries.* Berkeley: University of California Press.

Lewis-Beck, Michael S., and Tom W. Rice. 1985. "Government Growth in the United States." *Journal of Politics* 47:2–30.

Liebert, Roland. 1976. *Disintegration and Political Action.* New York: Academic Press.

Liebschutz, Sarah. 1984. *Federal Aid to Rochester.* Washington, D.C.: Brookings Institution.

Lienesch, Michael. 1983a. "In Defense of the Anti-Federalists." *History of Political Thought* 4:65–87.

———. 1983b. "Interpreting Experience: History, Philosophy, and Science in the American Constitutional Debates." *American Politics Quarterly* 11: 379–401.

Light, Alfred R. 1978. "State Agency Perspectives on Federalism." *Social Science Quarterly* 59:284–94.

Lineberry, Robert. 1977. *Equality and Urban Policy*. Beverly Hills, Calif.: Sage Publications.

Lipsky, Michael. 1971. "Street-Level Bureaucracy and the Analysis of Urban Reform." *Urban Affairs Quarterly* 6:391–409.

———. 1980. *Street-Level Bureaucracy: Dilemmas of the Individual in Public Services*. New York: Russell Sage Foundation.

Long, Norton. 1958. "The Local Community as an Ecology of Games." *American Journal of Sociology* 64:251–61.

Lovell, Catherine. 1981. "Evolving Local Government Dependency." *Public Administrative Review* 41:189–202.

——— et al. 1979. *Federal and State Mandating on Local Governments: An Exploration of Issues and Impacts*. Final Report to the National Science Foundation. Riverside: Graduate School of Administration, University of California.

———, and Charles Tobin. 1981. "The Mandate Issue." *Public Administration Review* 41:318–31.

Lowery, David, and Lee Sigelman. 1981. "Understanding the Tax Revolt: Eight Explanations." *American Political Science Review* 75:963–74.

———, and William D. Berry. 1983. "The Growth of Government in the United States: An Empirical Assessment of Competing Explanations." *American Journal of Political Science* 27:664–94.

———, Stanley D. Brunn, and Gerald Webster. 1986. "From Stable Disparity to Dynamic Equity: The Spatial Distribution of Federal Expenditures, 1971–1983." *Social Science Quarterly* 67:98–107.

Lowi, Theodore. 1978. "The Europeanization of America? From United States to United State." In *Nationalizing Government: Public Policies in America*, ed. Theodore J. Lowi and Alan Stone. Beverly Hills, Calif.: Sage Publications.

———. 1979. *The End of Liberalism: The Second Republic of the United States*. New York: Norton.

Luce, Thomas, and Janet Rothenberg Pack. 1984. "State Support under the New Federalism." *Journal of Policy Analysis and Management* 3:339–58.

Luttbeg, Norman R. 1971. "Classifying the American States: An Empirical Attempt to Identify Internal Variations." *Midwest Journal of Political Science* 15:703–21.

Lutz, Donald S. 1987. "The Changing View of the Founding and a New Perspective on American Political Theory." *Social Science Quarterly* 68:669–86.

Lyons, William E., and David Lowery. 1986. "The Organization of Political Space and Citizen Responses to Dissatisfaction in Urban Communities: An Integrative Model." *Journal of Politics* 48:321–46.

Lyons, William. 1978. "Reform and Response in American Cities: Structure and Policy Reconsidered." *Social Science Quarterly* 59:118–32.

———, and Michael R. Fitzgerald. 1987. "Intergovernmental Aid and Ratio Measurement." *Social Science Quarterly* 68:487–90.

———. 1987. "Measurement and Theory in Urban Policy Research: A Reply." *Social Science Quarterly* 68:491–93.

McBreath, Gerald A., and Thomas A. Morehouse. 1980. *The Dynamics of Alaska Native Self-Government*. Lanham, Md.: University Press of America.

McClelland, Peter D., and Alan L. Magdovitz. 1981. *Crisis in the Making: The Political Economy of New York State since 1945*. New York: Cambridge University Press.

McClure, Charles E., Jr., and Peter Mieszkowski, eds. 1983. *Fiscal Federalism and the Taxation of Natural Resources*. Lexington, Mass.: D. C. Heath.

McFeeley, Neil D. 1978. "The Supreme Court and the Federal System: Federalism from Warren to Burger." *Publius: The Journal of Federalism* 8:5–36.

McKay, David. 1985. "Theory and Practice in Public Policy: The Case of the New Federalism." *Political Studies* 33:181–202.

MacMahon, Arthur W., ed. 1955. *Federalism Mature and Emergent*. New York: Doubleday.

———. 1972. *Administering Federalism in a Democracy*. New York: Oxford University Press.

MacManus, Susan A. 1981. "The Impact of Functional Responsibility and State Legal Constraints on the 'Revenue-Debt' Packages of U.S. Central Cities." *International Journal of Public Administration* 3:67–111.

———. 1983a. *Federal Aid to Houston*. Washington, D.C.: Brookings Institution.

———. 1983b. "State Government: The Overseer of Municipal Finance." In *The Municipal Money Chase: The Politics of Local Government Finance*, ed. Alberta Sbragia. Boulder, Colo.: Westview Press.

———. 1986. "Using Federal Budget Cuts for Administrative Reform: CDBG Cutbacks in a City Marginally Dependent upon Federal Funds." In *Administering the New Federalism*, ed. Lewis G. Bender and James A. Stever. Boulder, Colo.: Westview Press.

———. 1988. "Comment: The Missing Element: An Examination of Analytic Time Frames." *Urban Affairs Quarterly* 24:39–45.

———. 1989a. "Decentralizing Expenditures and Responsibilities." In *Decentralization, Local Governments and Markets: Towards a Post-Welfare Agenda?*, ed. Robert Bennett. London: Oxford University Press.

———. 1989b. *Local Government Revenue Diversification: A Comparison of High Growth v. Low Growth Rural Jurisdictions in Florida*. Report prepared for the U.S. Advisory Commission on Intergovernmental Relations, January.

———, Robert M. Stein, and V. Howard Savage. 1986. "The Texas Response to Reagan's New Federalism Program: The Early Years." In *Administering the*

New Federalism, ed. Lewis G. Bender and James A. Stever. Boulder, Colo.: Westview Press.

Macedo, Stephen. 1987. *The New Right v. the Constitution*. Washington, D.C.: The Cato Institute.

Magleby, David B. 1984. *Direct Legislation: Voting on Ballot Propositions in the United States*. Baltimore: The Johns Hopkins University Press.

Maitland, Ian. 1985. "Interest Groups and Economic Growth Rates." *Journal of Politics* 47:44–58.

Marando, Vincent, and Robert Thomas. 1977. *The Forgotten Government*. Gainesville: The University Presses of Florida.

Markusen, Ann R., and Jerry Fastrup. 1978. "The Regional War for Federal Aid." *The Public Interest* 53:87–99.

Markusen, Ann R., Annalee Saxenian, and Marc A. Weiss. 1981. "Who Benefits from Intergovernmental Transfers?" *Publius: The Journal of Federalism* 11:5–35.

Marquez, Camilo. 1972. *Municipal Expenditures by Neighborhood*. New York: Office of the Mayor, City of New York.

Marshall, Dale Rogers, ed. 1979. *Urban Policy Making*. Beverly Hills, Calif.: Sage Publications.

Martin, Roscoe C. 1957. *Grass Roots*. University, Ala.: University of Alabama Press.

———. 1963. *Metropolis in Transition: Local Government Adaptation to Changing Urban Needs*. Washington, D.C.: Housing and Home Finance Agency.

———. 1965. *The Cities and the Federal System*. New York: Atherton Press.

Mashaw, Jerry L., and Susan Rose-Ackerman. 1984. "Federalism and Regulations." In *The Reagan Regulatory Strategy: An Assessment*, ed. George C. Eads and Michael Fix. Washington, D.C.: The Urban Institute.

May, R. J. 1969. *Federalism and Fiscal Adjustment*. London: Oxford University Press.

Meese, Edwin, III. 1985. "The Attorney General's View of the Supreme Court: Toward a Jurisprudence of Original Intention." *Public Administration Review* 45:701–4.

Melnick, R. Shep. 1985. "The Politics of Partnership." *Public Administration Review* 45:656–57.

Merget, Astrid, and William Wolff, Jr. 1976. "The Law and Municipal Services: Implementing Equity." *Public Management* 58:2–8.

Middlekauff, Robert. 1987. "The Assumptions of the Founders in 1787." *Social Science Quarterly* 68:656–68.

Mieszkowski, Peter, and William H. Oakland, eds. 1979. *Fiscal Federalism and Grants-in-Aid*. Washington, D.C.: The Urban Institute.

Miller, Gary J. 1981. *Cities by Contract: The Politics of Municipal Incorporation*. Cambridge, Mass.: MIT Press.

————, and Terry M. Moe. 1983. "Bureaucrats, Legislators, and the Size of Government." *American Political Science Review* 77:297–322.

Miller, Warren E. 1981. "The Role of Research in the Unification of a Discipline." *American Political Science Review* 75:9–16.

Mirengoff, William, and Lester Rindler. 1978. *CETA: Manpower Programs under Local Control*. Washington, D.C.: National Academy of Sciences.

Mladenka, Kenneth, and Kim Hill. 1978a. "The Distribution of Benefits in an Urban Environment: Parks and Libraries in Houston." *Urban Affairs Quarterly* 13:2–8.

————. 1978b. "The Distribution of Urban Police Services." *Journal of Politics* 40:112–33.

Moe, Terry M. 1980. *The Organization of Interests*. Chicago: University of Chicago Press.

Mogi, Sobei. 1931. *The Problem of Federalism: A Study in the History of Political Theory*. 2 vols. London: George Allen and Unwin.

Mogulof, Melvin B. 1971. *Governing Metropolitan Areas: A Critical Review of Council of Governments and the Federal Role*. Washington, D.C.: The Urban Institute.

Mollenkopf, John H. 1983. *The Contested City*. Princeton, N.J.: Princeton University Press.

Monroe, Alan D. 1977. "Operationalizing Political Culture: The Illinois Case." *Publius: The Journal of Federalism* 7:107–20.

Monypenny, Philip. 1960. "Federal Grants-in-Aid to State Governments: A Political Analysis." *National Tax Journal* 13:1–16.

————. 1965. "Interstate Relations—Some Emergent Trends." *Annals of the American Academy of Political and Social Science* 359:54, 56.

Monti, Daniel J. 1985. *A Semblance of Justice: St. Louis School Desegregation and Order in Urban America*. Columbia: University of Missouri Press.

Morgan, David R., and John P. Pelissero. 1980. "Urban Policy: Does Political Structure Matter?" *American Political Science Review* 74:999–1006.

Morgan, David R., and Robert E. England. 1984. "State Aid to Cities: A Causal Inquiry." *Publius: The Journal of Federalism* 14:67–82.

————. 1988. "The Two Faces of Privatization." *Public Administration Review* 48:979–87.

Morgan, David R., Michael W. Hirlinger, and Robert E. England. 1988. "The Decision to Contract Out City Services: A Further Explanation." *Western Political Quarterly* 41:363–72.

Morgan, Robert J. 1981. "Madison's Analysis of the Sources of Political Authority." *American Political Science Review* 75:613–25.

Mosher, Frederick C. 1980. "The Changing Responsibilities and Tactics of the Federal Government." *Public Administration Review* 60:541–48.

Mueller, Dennis C., ed. 1983. *The Political Economy of Growth*. New Haven: Yale University Press.

Muller, Thomas, and Michael Fix. 1980. "Federal Solicitude, Local Costs: The Impact of Federal Regulation on Municipal Finances." *Regulation* 4: 29–36.

Murphy, Thomas P., and John Rehfuss. 1976. *Urban Politics in the Suburban Era*. Homewood, Ill.: The Dorsey Press.

Murphy, Walter F. 1959. "Lower Court Checks on Supreme Court Power." *American Political Science Review* 53:1017–31.

Mushkin, Selma J., and John F. Cotton. 1968. *Functional Federalism: Grants-in-Aid and PPB Systems*. Washington, D.C.: State-Local Finances Project of the George Washington University.

Nakamura, Robert, and Frank Smallwood. 1980. *The Politics of Policy Implementation*. New York: St. Martin's Press.

Nathan, Richard P. 1975. "Federalism and the Shifting Nature of Fiscal Relations." *The Annals of the American Academy of Political and Social Science* 419:120–29.

———. 1982. The Methodology for Field Network Evaluation Studies." In *Studying Implementation: Methodological and Administrative Issues*, ed. Walter Williams et al. Chatham, N.J.: Chatham House.

———. 1983. "State and Local Governments under Federal Grants: Toward a Predictive Theory." *Political Science Quarterly* 98:47–57.

———, et al. 1976. "Decentralizing Community Development." Washington, D.C.: Brookings Institution.

———, and Associates. 1977. *Block Grants for Community Development*. Washington, D.C.: U.S. Government Printing Office.

———, and Associates. 1981. "Public Service Employment: A Field Evaluation." Washington, D.C.: Brookings Institution.

———, Charles F. Adams, Jr., and Associates. 1977. *Revenue Sharing: The Second Round*. Washington, D.C.: Brookings Institution.

———, and Fred Doolittle. 1983. *The Consequences of Cuts: The Effects of the Reagan Domestic Program on State and Local Governments*. Princeton, N.J.: Princeton Urban and Regional Research Center.

———. 1985. "Federal Grants: Giving and Taking Away." *Political Science Quarterly* 100:53–74.

———. 1987. *Reagan and the States*. Princeton, N.J.: Princeton University Press.

———, Fred Doolittle, and Associates. 1983. *The Consequences of Cuts*. Princeton, N.J.: Princeton University Research Council.

National Academy for Public Administration and U.S. Advisory Commission on Intergovernmental Relations. 1981. *The States and Distressed Communities: The 1980 Annual Report*. Washington, D.C.: U.S. Government Printing Office.

National Civic League. 1988. "Panel Assesses New Federalism." *Civic Action* 1:3.

Neuborne, Burt. 1977. "The Myth of Parity." *Harvard Law Review* 90: 1105–31.

Nice, David C. 1983. "An Intergovernmental Perspective on Urban Fragmentation." *Social Science Quarterly* 64:111–18.

———. 1987. *Federalism: The Politics of Intergovernmental Relations.* New York: St. Martin's Press.

Niskanen, William A. 1971. *Bureaucracy and Representative Government.* Chicago: Aldine-Atherton.

Oates, Wallace E. 1972. *Fiscal Federalism.* New York: Harcourt Brace Jovanovich.

Odum, Howard W., and Harry Estell Moore. 1938. *American Regionalism: A Cultural-Historical Approach to National Integration.* New York: Henry Holt.

Olson, Mancur, J. 1969. "The Principle of 'Fiscal Equivalence': The Division of Responsibilities among Different Levels of Government." *American Economic Review* 59:479–87.

———. 1965. *The Logic of Collective Action.* Cambridge, Mass.: Harvard University Press.

Onuf, Peter S. 1982. "From Colony to Territory: Changing Concepts of Statehood in Revolutionary America." *Political Science Quarterly* 97:447–60.

Orfield, Gary. 1978. *Must We Bus? Segregated Schools and National Policy.* Washington, D.C.: Brookings Institution.

Orlebeke, Charles J. 1983. *Federal Aid to Chicago.* Washington, D.C.: Brookings Institution.

Osborne, David. 1988. *Laboratories of Democracy: A New Breed of Governor Creates Models for National Growth.* Boston: Harvard Business School Press.

Ostrom, Eleanor. 1972. "Metropolitan Reform: Proposition Derived from Two Traditions." *Social Science Quarterly* 53:474–93.

Ostrom, Vincent. 1971a. *Institutional Arrangements for Water Resource Development.* PB 207 314. Springfield, Va.: National Technical Information Service.

———. 1971b. *The Political Theory of a Compound Republic: A Reconstruction of the Logical Foundations of an American Democracy as Presented in "The Federalist."* Blacksburg, Va.: Public Choice VIP & SU.

———. 1974. *The Intellectual Crisis in American Public Administration.* University, Ala.: University of Alabama Press.

———. 1987. *The Political Theory of a Compound Republic: Designing the American Experiment.* 2d ed. Lincoln: University of Nebraska Press.

———, Charles Tiebout, and Robert Warren. 1961. "The Organization of Government in Metropolitan Areas: A Theoretical Inquiry." *American Political Science Review* 60:831–42.

————, Robert Bish, and Elinor Ostrom. 1988. *Local Government in the United States*. San Francisco: Institute for Contemporary Studies.

O'Toole, Laurence J., Jr. 1983. "Interorganizational Co-operation and the Implementation of Labour Market Training Policies: Sweden and the Federal Republic of Germany." *Organizational Studies* 4:129–50.

————. 1988a. "Multiorganizational Implementation: A Comparative Analysis for Wastewater Treatment." Unpublished MS.

————. 1988b. "Public Administration and the Theory of American Federalism." Paper presented at the annual meeting of the American Political Science Association, Washington, D.C.

————. 1988c. "Strategies for Intergovernmental Management: Implementing Programs in Interorganizational Networks." *International Journal of Public Administration* 11:417–41.

————, ed. 1985. *American Intergovernmental Relations: Foundations, Perspectives, and Issues*. Washington, D.C.: U.S. Government Printing Office.

————, and Robert S. Montjoy. 1984. "Interorganizational Policy Implementation: A Theoretical Perspective." *Public Administration Review* 44: 491–503.

Palmer, John L., and Isabel V. Sawhill, eds. 1982. *The Reagan Experiment*. Washington, D.C.: The Urban Institute.

Parkinson, Michael, Bernard Foley, and Dennis R. Judd, eds. 1989. *Regenerating the Cities: The UK Crisis and the U.S. Experience*. Glenview, Ill.: Scott, Foresman.

Patton, Simon N. 1890. "Decay of State and Local Government." *The Annals of the American Academy of Political and Social Science*, Vol. 1.

Pelissero, John. 1984. "State Aid and City Needs." *Journal of Politics* 46: 916–35.

————. 1985. "Welfare and Education Aid to Cities: An Analysis of State Responsiveness to Needs." *Social Science Quarterly* 66:444–52.

————, and David R. Morgan. 1987a. "Intergovernmental Aid for Cities and Schools: A Comment on Research Methods." *Social Science Quarterly* 68: 487–90.

————. 1987b. "State Aid for Public Schools: An Analysis of State Responsiveness to School District Needs." *Social Science Quarterly* 68:466–77.

Peterson, George. 1984. "Federalism and the States." In *The Reagan Record*, ed. John L. Palmer and Isabel Sawhill. Cambridge, Mass.: Bellinger.

————, et al. 1986. *The Reagan Block Grants: What Have We Learned?* Washington, D.C.: The Urban Institute.

————, and Carol W. Lewis, eds. 1986. *Reagan and the Cities*. Washington, D.C.: Urban Institute.

Peterson, Paul E. 1981. *City Limits*. Chicago: University of Chicago Press.

————, and Kenneth K. Wong. 1985. "Toward a Differentiated Theory of Federalism." *Research in Urban Policy* 1:301–24.

———, Barry G. Rabe, and Kenneth K. Wong. 1986. *When Federalism Works*. Washington, D.C.: Brookings Institution.

Polsby, Nelson W. 1980. *Community Power and Political Theory: A Further Look at Problems of Evidence and Inference*. Rev. ed. New Haven: Yale University Press.

———. 1984. *Political Innovation in America: The Politics of Policy Initiation*. New Haven: Yale University Press.

Poole, Robert W., ed. 1985. *Unnatural Monopolies: The Case for Deregulating Public Utilities*. Lexington, Mass.: D. C. Heath.

Popcock, J. G. A. 1987. "States, Republics, and Empires: The American Founding in Early Modern Perspective." *Social Science Quarterly* 68:703–23.

Porter, David O. 1976. "Federalism, Revenue Sharing and Local Government." In *Public Policy-Making in the Federal System*, ed. Charles Jones and Robert Thomas. Beverly Hills, Calif.: Sage Publications.

Porter, David R. 1975. "Responsiveness to Citizen-Consumers in a Federal System." *Publius: The Journal of Federalism* 5:51–78.

Porter, Mary Cornelia, and G. Alan Tarr, eds. 1982. *State Supreme Courts: Policymakers in the Federal System*. Westport, Conn.: Greenwood Press.

Posner, Paul L., and Stephen M. Sorett. 1979. "A Crisis in the Fiscal Commons: The Impact of Federal Expenditures on State and Local Governments." *Public Contract Law Journal* 15:341–78.

Pressman, Jeffrey L. 1975. *Federal Programs and City Politics: The Dynamics of the Aid Process in Oakland*. Berkeley: University of California Press.

———, and Aaron Wildavsky. 1984. *Implementation*. 3d ed. Berkeley: University of California Press.

Pride, Richard A., and J. David Woodward. 1985. *The Burden of Busing: The Politics of Desegregation in Nashville, Tennessee*. Knoxville: University of Tennessee Press.

Quigley, John M., and Daniel Rubinfeld, eds. 1985. *American Domestic Priorities: An Economic Appraisal*. Berkeley: University of California Press.

Rabin, Jack, and Don Dodd, eds. 1985. *State and Local Government Administration*. New York: Marcel Dekker.

Rabushka, Alvin, and Pauline Ryan. 1982. *The Tax Revolt*. Stanford, Calif.: Hoover Institution.

Rakove, Jack N. 1979. *The Beginnings of National Politics: An Interpretive History of the Continental Congress*. New York: Knopf.

Reagan, Michael D. 1972. *The New Federalism*. New York: Oxford University Press.

———. 1987. *Regulation: The Politics of Policy*. Boston: Little, Brown.

———, and John Y. Sanzone. 1981. *The New Federalism*. 2d ed. New York: Oxford University Press.

Rebell, Michael A., and Arthur R. Block. 1985. *Equality and Education: Federal*

Civil Rights Enforcement in the New York City School System. Princeton, N.J.: Princeton University Press.

Reeves, Mavis Mann. 1981. "Galloping Intergovernmentalism as a Factor in State Management." *State Government* 54:102–8.

————, and Parris N. Glendening. 1972. *Controversies of State and Local Political Systems*. Boston: Allyn and Bacon.

Reid, John Phillip. 1987. "Originalism and Subjectivism in the Bicentennial Year." *Social Science Quarterly* 68:687–702.

Report of the Kestnbaum Commission on Intergovernmental Relations. 1953. Washington, D.C.: U.S. Government Printing Office.

Rich, Richard C. 1980. "A Political Economy Approach to the Study of Neighborhood Organizations." *American Journal of Political Science* 24:559–92.

Ridgeway, Marion E. 1971. *Interstate Compacts: A Question of Federalism*. Carbondale: Southern Illinois University Press.

Riker, William H. 1964. *Federalism: Origin, Operation, Significance*. Boston: Little, Brown.

————. 1987. *The Development of American Federalism*. Boston: Kluwer Academic.

Ritt, Leonard G. 1974. "Political Cultures and Political Reform: A Research Note." *Publius: The Journal of Federalism* 4:127–33.

————. 1976. "Committee Position, Seniority, and the Distribution of Government Expenditures." *Public Policy* 24:463–89.

Rodwin, Lloyd. 1970. *Nations and Cities, A Comparison of Strategies for Urban Growth*. Boston: Houghton Mifflin.

Rogers, Everett M. 1983. *Diffusion of Innovations*. 3d ed. New York: The Free Press.

Rohr, John A. 1986. *To Run a Constitution: The Legitimacy of the Administrative State*. Lawrence: University Press of Kansas.

Romans, Neil T. 1974. "The Role of State Supreme Courts in Judicial Policy Making: *Escobedo, Miranda* and the Use of Judicial Impact Analysis." *Western Political Quarterly* 27:38–59.

Rose, Douglas D. 1973. "National and Local Forces in State Politics: The Implications of Multi-Level Policy Analysis." *American Political Science Review* 67:1162–73.

Rose-Ackerman, Susan. 1983. "Beyond Tiebout: Modeling the Political Economy of Local Government." In *Local Provision of Public Services: The Tiebout Model after Twenty-Five Years*, ed. George R. Zodrow. New York: Academic Press.

Rosener, Judy B. 1978. "Citizen Participation: Can We Measure Its Effectiveness?" *Public Administration Review* 38:457–63.

Rosenthal, Alan, and Maureen Moakley, eds. 1984. *The Political Life of the American States*. New York: Praeger.

Rosenthal, Donald B. 1979. *Sticking-Points and Ploys in Federal Local Relations.* Philadelphia: Center for the Study of Federalism, Temple University.

———. 1980. *Urban Revitalization.* Beverly Hills, Calif.: Sage Publications.

Rosentraub, Mark S., ed. 1986. *Urban Policy Problems: Federal Policy and Institutional Change.* New York: Praeger.

Rubin, Irene S. 1982. *Running in the Red: The Political Dynamics of Urban Stress.* Albany: State University of New York Press.

Rundquist, Barry S. 1980. *Political Benefits.* Lexington, Mass.: Lexington Books/D. C. Heath.

Sabatier, Paul A. "Top-Down and Bottom-Up Approaches to Implementation Research: A Critical Analysis and Suggested Synthesis." *Journal of Public Policy* 6:21–48.

Sabato, Larry. 1983. *Goodbye to Goodtime Charlie.* 2d ed. Washington, D.C.: Congressional Quarterly Press.

Sachs, Seymour, and Robert Harris. 1964. "The Determinants of State and Local Government Expenditures and Intergovernmental Flow of Funds." *National Tax Journal* 17:75–85.

Saltzstein, Alan. 1977. "Federal Categorical Aid to Cities." *Western Political Quarterly* 30:377–83.

Sandoz, Ellis. 1987a. "The American Constitutional Order after Two Centuries: Concluding Reflections." *Social Science Quarterly* 68:724–44.

———. 1987b. "The New Face of the American Founding." *Social Science Quarterly* 68:653–55.

Sanford, Terry. 1967. *Storm Over the States.* New York: McGraw-Hill.

Savage, Robert L. 1973. "Patterns of Multilinear Evolution in the American States." *Publius: The Journal of Federalism* 3:75–108.

Savage, Robert L. 1975. "The Distribution and Development of Policy Values in the American States." In *The Ecology of American Political Cultures: Readings*, ed. Daniel J. Elazar and Joseph Zikmund II. New York: Thomas Y. Crowell.

———. 1981. "Looking for Political Subcultures: A Critique of the Rummage-Sale Approach." *Western Political Quarterly* 34:331–36.

———. 1985. "Diffusion Research Traditions and the Spread of Policy Innovations in a Federal System." *Publius: The Journal of Federalism* 15:1–27.

———, and Richard J. Gallagher. 1977. "Politicocultural Regions in a Southern State: An Empirical Typology of Arkansas Counties." *Publius: The Journal of Federalism* 7:91–105.

Savas, E. S. 1987. *Privatizing: The Key to Better Government.* Chatham, N.J.: Chatham House.

Savitch, H. V. 1979. *Urban Policy and the Exterior City: Federal, State, and Corporate Impacts upon Major Cities.* New York: Pergamon Press.

Sbragia, Alberta, ed. 1983. *The Municipal Money Chase: The Politics of Local Government Finance*. Boulder, Colo.: Westview Press.

Schechter, Stephen L. 1981. "On the Compatibility of Federalism and Intergovernmental Management." *Publius: The Journal of Federalism* 11: 127–41.

Scheiber, Harry N. 1978. "American Federalism and the Diffusion of Power: Historical and Contemporary Perspectives." *University of Toledo Law Review* 9:619–80.

———. 1980. "Federalism and Legal Process: Historical and Contemporary Analysis of the American System." *Law and Society Review* 14:663–722.

———, ed. 1987. *Perspectives on Federalism: Papers from the First Berkeley Seminar on Federalism*. Berkeley: Institute of Governmental Studies, University of California.

Schmandt, Henry J., George D. Wendel, and E. Allan Tomey. 1983. *Federal Aid to St. Louis*. Washington, D.C.: Brookings Institution.

Schmidhauser, John R. 1958. *The Supreme Court as Final Arbiter in Federal-State Relations: 1789–1957*. Chapel Hill: University of North Carolina Press.

Schneider, Mark. Forthcoming. *The Local Market for Public Goods: The Political Economy of Intermunicipal Competition*. Pittsburgh, Pa.: University of Pittsburgh Press.

Scholz, John T., and Feng Heng Wei. 1986. "Regulatory Enforcement in a Federalist System." *American Political Science Review* 80:1249–70.

Schuck, Peter H., and Robert M. Smith. 1985. *Citizenship without Consent: Illegal Aliens in the American Polity*. New Haven: Yale University Press.

Scott, Stanley, and John C. Bollens. 1968. *Governing a Metropolitan Region: The San Francisco Bay Area*. Berkeley: Institute for Governmental Studies, University of California.

Sears, David O., and Jack Citrin. 1982. *Tax Revolt: Something for Nothing in California*. Cambridge, Mass.: Harvard University Press.

Seroka, Jim, ed. 1986. *Rural Public Administration: Problems and Prospects*. Westport, Conn.: Greenwood Press.

Shapek, Raymond A. 1981. *Managing Federalism: Evolution and Development of the Grant-in-Aid System*. Charlottesville, Va.: Community Collaborators.

Sharkansky, Ira. 1969. "The Utility of Elazar's Political Culture: A Research Note." *Polity* 2:66–83.

———. 1970. *Regionalism in American Politics*. Indianapolis: Bobbs-Merrill.

———. 1972. *The Maligned States*. New York: McGraw-Hill.

Sharp, Elaine B. 1982. "Citizen-Initiated Contacting of Government Officials and Socioeconomic Status: Determining the Relationship and Accounting for It." *American Political Science Review* 76:109–15.

———. 1986a. *Citizen Demand-Making in the Urban Context*. University, Ala.: University of Alabama Press.

———. 1986b. "The Politics and Economics of the New City Debt." *American Political Science Review* 80:1271–88.

Shefter, Martin. 1985. *Political Crisis/Fiscal Crisis: The Collapse and Revival of New York City*. New York: Basic Books.

Siena, James V., ed. 1982. *Antitrust and Local Government: Perspectives on the Boulder Decision*. Cabin John, Md.: Seven Locks Press.

Sigelman, Lee. 1976. "The Curious Case of Women in State and Local Government." *Social Science Quarterly* 56:591–604.

Skok, James E. 1980. "Federal Funds and State Legislatures: Executive-Legislative Conflict in State Government." *Public Administration Review* 40: 561–67.

Smith, Michael P. 1979. *The City and Social Theory*. New York: St. Martin's Press.

Sprague, John D. 1968. *Voting Patterns of the United States Supreme Court: Cases in Federalism, 1889–1959*. Indianapolis: Bobbs-Merrill.

Stein, Robert M. 1981a. "The Allocation of Federal Aid Monies." *American Political Science Review* 75:334–43.

———. 1981b. "The Targeting of State Aid: A Comparison of Grant Delivery Systems." *Urban Interest*, Special Issue.

———. 1982. "The Political Economy of Municipal Functional Responsibility." *Social Science Quarterly* 63:530–48.

———, and Keith E. Hamm. 1987. "A Comparative Analysis of the Targeting Capacity of State and Federal Intergovernmental Aid Allocations: 1977, 1982." *Social Science Quarterly* 68:447–65.

Stenberg, Carl W., and David B. Walker. 1969. "Federalism and the Academic Community: A Brief Survey." *PS* (Spring), 155–67.

Stephens, G. Ross. 1974. "State Centralization and the Erosion of Local Autonomy." *Journal of Politics* 36:44–76.

Stewart, William H. 1984. *Concepts of Federalism*. Lanham, Md.: University Press of America.

Stone, Clarence N. 1980. "Systemic Power in Community Decision-Making: A Restatement of Stratification Theory." *American Political Science Review* 74:978–90.

Stonecash, Jeff. 1981a. "Centralization in State-Local Fiscal Relationships." *Western Political Quarterly* 34:301–9.

———. 1981b. "State Policies Regarding Local Resource Acquisition: Disorder, Compensatory Adjustment, or Coherent Restraint?" *American Politics Quarterly* 9:401–25.

Storing, Herbert J. 1981. *What the Anti-Federalists Were For*. Chicago: University of Chicago Press.

Strouse, James, and Phillippe Jones. 1974. "Federal Aid: The Forgotten Variable in State Policy Research." *Journal of Politics* 36:200–207.

Subcommittee on the City, House Committee on Banking, Finance, and Urban Affairs. 1978. *City Need and the Responsiveness of Federal Grant Programs.* Washington, D.C.: U.S. Government Printing Office.

Sundquist, James, with David W. Davis. 1969. *Making Federalism Work: A Study of Program Coordination at the Community Level.* Washington, D.C.: Brookings Institution.

Sundquist, James L. 1986. "Has America Lost Its Social Conscience—And How Will We Get it Back?" *Political Science Quarterly* 101:513–34.

Tabb, William K. 1982. *The Long-Default: New York City and the Urban Fiscal Crisis.* New York: Monthly Review Press.

Tarr, G. Alan, and Mary Cornelia Aldis Porter. 1988. *State Supreme Courts in State and Nation.* New Haven: Yale University Press.

Taub, Richard P., D. Garth Taylor, and Jan D. Dunham. 1984. *Paths of Neighborhood Change: Race and Crime in Urban America.* Chicago: University of Chicago Press.

Taylor, Theodore W. 1984. *The Bureau of Indian Affairs.* Boulder, Colo.: Westview Press.

Teaford, John. 1979. *City and Suburb: The Political Fragmentation of Metropolitan America, 1850–1970.* Baltimore: The Johns Hopkins University Press.

Thernstrom, Abigail M. 1987. *Whose Vote Counts? Affirmative Action and Minority Voting Rights.* Cambridge, Mass.: Harvard University Press.

Thomas, John Clayton. 1986. *Between Citizen and City: Neighborhood Organization and Urban Politics in Cincinnati.* Laurence: University Press of Kansas.

Thomas, Robert D. 1986. "Cities as Partners in the Federal System." *Political Science Quarterly* 101:49–64.

Thompson, Frank J., and Michael Schicchitano. 1985. "State Implementation Effort and Federal Regulatory Policy: The Case of Occupational Safety and Health." *Journal of Politics* 47:687–703.

Thornton, Grant. 1987. *General Manufacturing Climates of the Forty-Eight Contiguous States.* Chicago: Grant Thornton.

Tiebout, Charles M. 1956. "A Pure Theory of Local Expenditures." *Journal of Political Economy* 64:416–24.

Tobin, Gary A., ed. 1979. *The Changing Structure of the City: What Happened to the Urban Crisis.* Beverly Hills, Calif.: Sage Publications.

Tomasic, Roman, and Malcolm Feeley, eds. 1982. *Neighborhood Justice: Assessment of an Emerging Idea.* New York: Longman.

Treadway, Jack. 1985. *Public Policymaking in the American States.* New York: Praeger.

Truman, David B. 1955. "Federalism and the Party System." In *Federalism Mature and Emergent*, ed. Arthur Macmahon. Garden City, N.Y.: Doubleday.

Tucker, Harvey J. 1982. "It's About Time: The Use of Time in Cross-Sectional State Policy Analysis." *American Journal of Political Science* 26:176–96.

————. 1984. "The Nationalization of State Policy Revisited." *Western Political Quarterly* 37:435–42.

————, and Eric B. Herzik. 1988. "The Persisting Problem of Region in American State Policy Research." *Social Science Quarterly* 67:84–97.

U.S. Office of Management and Budget. 1980. *Managing Federal Assistance in the 1980s.* Washington, D.C.: U.S. Government Printing Office, March.

Van Horn, Carl E. 1979. *Policy Implementation in the Federal System.* Lexington, Mass.: Lexington Books/D. C. Heath.

Vedlitz, Arnold, James A. Dyer, and Roger Durand. 1980. "Citizen Contacts with Local Governments: A Comparative View." *American Journal of Political Science* 24:50–67.

Vertz, Laura C., John P. Frendreis, and James L. Gibson. 1987. "Nationalization of the Electorate in the United States." *American Political Science Review* 81:961–72.

Vines, Kenneth N. 1965. "Southern State Supreme Courts and Race Relations." *Western Political Quarterly* 18:5–18.

Wagner, Richard E. 1976. "Revenue Structure, Fiscal Illusion, and Budgetary Choice." *Public Choice* 25:45–61.

Walker, David B. 1980. "Constitutional Revision, Incremental Retrenchments, or Real Reform: An Analysis of Current Efforts to Curb Federal Growth." *The Bureaucrat* 9:35–47.

————. 1981. *Toward a Functioning Federalism.* Cambridge, Mass.: Winthrop Publishers.

Walker, Jack L. 1969. "The Diffusion of Innovations among the American States." *American Political Science Review* 63:880–89.

Ward, Peter D. 1981. "The Measurement of Federal and State Responsiveness to Urban Problems." *Journal of Politics* 43:83–101.

Warner, Paul D. 1987. "Business Climate, Taxes, and Economic Development." *Economic Development Quarterly* 1:389.

Warren, Charles R. 1980. *The States and Urban Strategies: A Comparative Analysis.* Washington, D.C.: National Academy of Public Administration.

————. 1981. *The State and Urban Strategies: A Comparative Analysis.* Washington, D.C.: U.S. Government Printing Office. National Academy of Public Administration and Department of Housing and Urban Development.

Warren, Robert. 1966. *Government in Metropolitan Regions: A Reappraisal of Fractionated Political Organizations.* Davis: University of California, Institute of Governmental Affairs.

Wasby, Stephen L. 1970. *The Impact of the United States Supreme Court.* Homewood, Ill.: Dorsey.

Waste, Robert J. 1987. *Power and Pluralism in American Cities: Researching the Urban Laboratory.* Westport, Conn.: Greenwood Press.

Waugh, William L., Jr. 1988. "States, Counties, and the Questions of Trust and Capacity." *Publius: The Journal of Federalism* 18:189–98.

————, and Ronald John Hy. 1988. "The Administrative, Fiscal, and Political Capacities of County Governments." *State and Local Government Review* (Winter), 28–31.

Weber, Ronald E., and William R. Shaffer. 1972. "Public Opinion and American State Policy-Making." *Midwest Journal of Political Science* 16:683–99.

Weidner, Edward W. 1960. *Intergovernmental Relations as Seen by Public Officials*. Minneapolis: University of Minnesota Press.

Weimer, David Leo. 1980. *Improving Prosecution? The Inducement and Implementation of Innovations for Prosecution Management*. Westport, Conn.: Greenwood Press.

Welch, Susan, and Kay Thompson. 1980. "The Impact of Federal Incentives on State Policy Innovation." *American Journal of Political Science* 24:715–29.

Whicker, Marcia Lynn, Ruth Ann Strickland, and Raymond A. Moore. 1987. *The Constitution under Pressure: A Time for Change*. New York: Praeger.

White, John Kenneth. 1983. *The Fractured Electorate: Political Parties and Social Change in Southern New England*. Hanover, N.H.: University Presses of New England.

White, Leonard D. 1953. *The States and the Nation*. Baton Rouge: Louisiana State University Press.

White, Morton. 1987. *Philosophy, "The Federalist," and the Constitution*. New York: Oxford University Press.

Wickstrom, Nelson. 1977. *Councils of Governments: A Study of Political Incrementalism*. Chicago: Nelson-Hall.

Williams, Walter. 1980. *The Implementation Perspective*. Berkeley: University of California Press.

Williams, Michael R. 1985. *Neighborhood Organizations: Seeds of a New Urban Life*. Westport, Conn.: Greenwood Press.

Williamson, Richard S. 1983. "The 1982 New Federalism Negotiations." *Publius: The Journal of Federalism* 13:11–32.

Wills, Gary. 1981. *Explaining America: The Federalist*. Garden City, N.Y.: Doubleday.

Wirt, Frederick. 1980. "Does Control Follow the Dollar? Value Analysis, School Policy, and State-Local Linkages." *Publius: The Journal of Federalism* 10:69–88.

————. 1985. "The Dependent City? External Influences upon Local Control." *Journal of Politics* 47:83–112.

Wolfe, Christopher. 1981. "A Theory of U.S. Constitutional History." *Journal of Politics* 43:292–316.

Wood, Gordon. 1969. *The Creation of the American Republic, 1776-1787*. Chapel Hill: University of North Carolina Press.

Wood, Robert. 1961. *1400 Governments: The Political Economy of the New York Metropolitan Region*. Cambridge, Mass.: Harvard University Press.

Wood, Robert C. 1970. "Needs and Prospects for Research in Intergovernmental Relations." *Public Administration Review* 30:265–68.

Wright, Deil S. 1968. *Federal Grants-in-Aid: Perspectives and Alternatives.* Washington, D.C.: American Enterprise Institute for Public Policy Research.

————. 1987. "A Century of the Intergovernmental Administrative State: Wilson's Federalism, New Deal Intergovernmental Relations, and Contemporary Intergovernmental Management." In *Centennial History of the American Administrative State*, ed. Ralph C. Chandler. New York: Macmillan.

————. 1988. *Understanding Intergovernmental Relations.* 3d ed. Monterey, Calif.: Brooks/Cole.

————. 1989. "The Origins, Emergence, and Maturity of Federalism and Intergovernmental Relations: Two Centuries of Territory and Power." In *Handbook of Public Administration*, ed. Jack Rabin, W. Bartley Hildreth, and Gerald J. Miller. New York: Marcel Dekker.

————, and Harvey L. White, eds. 1984. *Federalism and Intergovernmental Relations.* Washington, D.C.: The American Society for Public Administration.

Yates, Douglas. 1977. *The Ungovernable City: The Politics of Urban Problems and Policy Making.* Cambridge, Mass.: MIT Press.

Yin, Robert K., and Douglas Yates. 1975. *Street Level Governments.* Lexington, Mass.: Lexington Books/D. C. Heath.

Zimmerman, Joseph F. 1972. *The Federated City: Community Control in Large Cities.* New York: St. Martin's Press.

————. 1983. *State-Local Relations: A Partnership Approach.* New York: Praeger.

Zisk, Betty H. 1987. *Money, Media, and the Grass Roots: State Ballot Issues and the Electoral Process.* Newbury Park, Calif.: Sage Publications.

7

The Study of State and Local Politics: A Preliminary Exploration of Its Contributions to Empirical Political Theory

Ronald E. Weber

The study of the field of United States state and local politics has advanced remarkably during the past twenty-five years or so during which I have been involved with political science. We have moved from a period when the study of roll-call voting and party cohesion in individual state legislatures was considered seminal work to one where it is possible to examine state legislative elections and behavior across both time and space. Methodological advances have enabled us to progress from an era when statistics like Spearman's Rho and Chi Square were considered the bread-and-butter techniques in this field to one in which two-stage, generalized, least-squares regression and probit analysis techniques are highly likely to be the most appropriate ones to explore the research questions of the field.

By no stretch of the imagination can the state and local politics field be considered a "backwater" of political science, as it has sometimes been characterized by colleagues in other fields of the discipline. As was true twenty-five years ago when I began to dabble in political science, the field today is one that offers opportunities for any scholar to pursue the development and testing of empirical theories of politics (Jewell

1982a). No other field has a comparable number of cases, the richness of data, or the needed variation across variables requisite to successful development and testing of empirical theories. The fact that we work with fifty states, some 250 major urban areas, and thousands of counties (parishes) and school districts gives us a myriad of settings in which to pursue our empirical studies. Since our main focus as political scientists should be on developing theories and explanatory models for the behavior of political actors operating within political and governmental institutions, the field of state and local politics is an ideal one for the fulfillment of this responsibility.

The purpose of this essay is to examine the leading studies of state and local politics to determine the contributions the field has made to empirical theories of politics. I shall focus in particular on contributions made to empirical theories of political participation, vote choice, recruitment, representation, decision-making, and policy-making. In taking this approach, I am consciously choosing to exclude a lot of the work in the field that does not involve these topics, even though that work may be very valuable in helping us to understand the workings of state and local politics and policy-making, or in providing us with the needed examples to illustrate our pedagogical lectures. I have also chosen to focus only on studies that involve state and local institutions, excluding, for example, studies of elections for national offices, even when the states or localities were the unit of analysis. On the other hand, I have included some national-level studies in which state or local variables served as principal contextual variables for the analyses.

POLITICAL PARTICIPATION

Political participation in general and voting turnout in particular have long been topics for research by scholars in the field of state and local politics. The field has contributed much to the development and testing of empirical theories of participation and voting turnout because of the fact that the rules which govern electoral participation in the United States are devised by the states and carried out by local election officials. In essence, one cannot fruitfully look at participation and voting turnout in the U.S. without considering the state and local contexts in which participation and voting occur. Thus, even the seminal studies of voting turnout in U.S. presidential elections invariably include variables meant to capture the state and local contexts in which presidential voting takes place.

Studies of participation and voting turnout in state and local elections can be characterized as adopting one or the other of two approaches. First, there are studies based on the analysis of aggregate data, usually at the state, county, community, or electoral district level. These studies have tended to dominate the field until recently, when scholars began to conduct studies involving a second approach that involves the study of participation and voting turnout based on survey rather than aggregate data. The survey data bases are national, state, or local in scope and permit the researcher to bring to bear individual-level variables that had not been included in the aggregate data studies. The most comprehensive of the studies employing this second approach augment their survey data bases with the types of contextual data typically used in the aggregate data approach and, consequently, have available a data base that permits the analysis of both individual and systemic factors that may affect participation and voting turnout.

Although it is difficult to document the first use of aggregate data to study participation and voter turnout in the states and localities, V. O. Key, Jr. (1949, 1956), in his path-breaking studies of state politics, employed aggregate data to examine gubernatorial primary election turnout in the states. He documented differences in turnout across the states and tried to understand the reasons for the differences. Later aggregate studies of voting turnout seem to have taken the work of Key as a starting point. Students of Key, like Price (1957) and Sindler (1956) as well as Fenton and Vines (1957), examined voter registration and turnout in southern states at the county/parish level to find factors associated with variation in registration and turnout. Matthews and Prothro (1963a, 1963b, 1966) used an aggregate data approach to examine the impact of socioeconomic and political factors upon black voter registration in the South prior to the enactment of the Voting Rights Act of 1965. Since the publication of the work of Matthews and Prothro, studies by Keech (1968), Cassell (1979), Stanley (1987), and Stern (1987) have all employed aggregate data to document the changes in voter registration and voting turnout in the South.

The aggregate data approach has also been employed to study voter turnout in gubernatorial elections. Kenney (1983b), in a study of gubernatorial primaries, found that competitiveness of the contest is associated with higher levels of turnout. Wright (1989), in the only systematic study of voter turnout in runoff primaries, concluded that runoff primaries produce lower levels of turnout generally than do first primaries, and that competitiveness has no significant impact on turnout decline from the first to the runoff primary. Gray (1976b), in a research note on gubernatorial general election turnout, found that electoral competition and turnout were strongly related in cross-sectional analyses but only weakly related across time for a majority of states. Patterson and Caldeira (1983), who examined turnout in gubernatorial general elections employing a cross-sectional design, determined that political mobilization factors like competitiveness and campaign spending are strongly associated with higher levels of turnout and that socioeconomic factors like income, education, and age had little to contribute independently to explaining variation in turnout.

Participation and voting turnout have been rarely studied in state legislative elections. This is undoubtedly due to the fact that it is difficult to measure turnout within legislative districts without some measure of the district voting age population and to the absence of joint returns for top-of-ticket offices needed to determine roll-off in voter turnout (Weber 1980). Caldeira and Patterson (1982b) and Tucker (1986) have conducted the only studies of turnout in legislative elections. Both studies, in different state settings, revealed that electoral competitiveness and campaign spending have positive effects on voting turnout for legislative offices.

Other types of participation and voting turnout studies using the aggregate data approach have included judicial elections (DuBois 1980), local elections (Alford and Lee 1968; Hamilton 1971), and referenda elections (Everson 1981; Magleby 1984; Zisk 1987; Vanderleeuw and Engstrom 1987). These studies have all documented that voting turnout is lower in these elections than in elections for statewide offices, and that roll-off in voting occurs in these elections when contests for more important offices are held at the same time.

Since the purely aggregate data approach to studying state and local turnout has many shortcomings, a second approach has emerged that is based primarily on survey data. The survey data are then augmented with state and local contextual data to measure some of the systemic factors that were found to be of importance in the aggregate data studies. This approach permits the examination of both individual and systemic factors and their relationship to participation and voting turnout.

Matthews and Prothro (1966) were among the pioneers of this second approach. In their study of black political participation in the South, they revealed that community structure and political system variables have an impact on individual attitudes toward participation, which then affect black registration and voter turnout. Kim et al. (1975), in the first national study of the impact of individual and systemic factors on voter turnout, found that state registration laws and practices explained a good deal of variation in voter turnout in the states. Rosenstone and Wolfinger (1978) and Wolfinger and Rosenstone (1980), in a more comprehensive study, determined that particular registration provisions had an impact on voter turnout. They found, after controlling for individual factors, that longer registration closing dates before elections depressed turnout, as did irregular registration office hours, no evening or Saturday registration hours, and no provisions for absentee registration. They also reported that gubernatorial elections held concurrently with national elections tended to increase voting turnout.

In a more recent study using the same approach as those of Kim et al. (1975), Rosenstone and Wolfinger (1978), and Wolfinger and Rosenstone (1980), Squire et al. (1987) reported that the mobility of certain groups of voters works in conjunction with registration laws to depress voter turnout after other potential variables that could influence turnout are controlled. Finally, the recent studies of Boyd (1986, 1989) found that frequent scheduling of elections reduces general election turnout, while the attractiveness of statewide elections increases it.

VOTE CHOICE

Research on theories of vote choice in the state and local field is newly emergent. Whereas this topic has long been the province of study by specialists in national politics, there is growing evidence of research on vote choice using elections for state and local office. This type of research has been stimulated by increased interest in assessing how national politics impacts upon politics at the subnational level as well as by a continuing interest in the study of state and local elections.

Studies of vote choice in the state and local field can be broken down into two main types: those which look primarily at state or local factors as determinants of the vote and those which look at a combination of both national and state-local factors as they jointly impact on vote choice. The former type dominates the literature, while the latter type is quickly emerging to the forefront of the field and promises to make major contributions to empirical theories of vote choice.

The literature that examines vote choice within the state or local context has concentrated on an assessment of the relative importance of one or more factors—political party strength, incumbency, officeholder performance, mobilization, and electoral structure—on electoral outcomes. Political party strength has been found to be an important determinant of vote choice in the gubernatorial election studies of Jacobson (1975), Piereson (1977), Patterson (1982), and Cotter et al. (1984), and in the legislative election studies of Caldeira and Patterson (1982a), Giles and Pritchard (1985), and Tucker and Weber (1987). Incumbency has been determined to be an important factor in gubernatorial elections in the studies of Turett (1971), Cowart (1973), Wright (1974), Piereson (1977), Jewell and Olson (1982), Tompkins (1984a), Kenney and Rice (1984), and Rice (1985); in the legislative election studies of Standing and Robinson (1958), Jewell (1960, 1982b), Welch (1976), Calvert (1979), Grau (1981), and Jewell and Breaux (1988); and in the local election studies of Eulau and Prewitt (1973) and Heilig and

Mundt (1984). There have also been some studies of how officeholder performance may operate in models of state and local vote choice. Pomper's (1980) influential work on this question indicated that a governor's taxing and spending policies did not have much effect on gubernatorial election outcomes. But the more recent studies of Eismeier (1979, 1983), Jewell and Olson (1982), Tompkins and Smith (1982), and Sabato (1983) all found that proposals or enactments of increased taxes tend to work against the incumbent party in gubernatorial elections. Mobilization factors such as campaign spending have also been found to be important in the gubernatorial election studies of Jacobson (1975), Patterson (1982), Beyle (1983), and Jewell (1983); in the legislative election studies of Glantz et al. (1976), Welch (1976), Owens and Olson (1977), Caldeira and Patterson (1982a), Giles and Pritchard (1985), and Tucker and Weber (1987); and in the local election study of Heilig and Mundt (1984). Electoral structure factors such as scheduling of elections (Jewell and Olson 1982), ballot forms (Hecock and Bain 1957; Walker 1966; Weber 1980), and districting schemes (Jewell 1982b, 1982c; Grofman et al. 1986) all have been found to have some influence on vote choice.

The research on vote choice in state and local elections employing a combination of national as well as state and local factors is less extensive than the research that looks solely at state and local determinants of vote choice. This emerging literature has been concerned with bringing three types of factors to bear in modeling vote choice in state and local elections. The first of these is presidential coattails and popularity, while the second is midterm elections as referenda on the popularity of a rational administration, and the third is performance of the national economy.

The studies of the impact of presidential coattails and popularity on gubernatorial elections have produced mixed findings. Holbrook-Provow (1987) and Chubb (1988) found no impact of presidential coattails in aggregate data studies, while Simon (1989) detected that presidential popularity has a strong impact on gubernatorial vote choice in a survey research study. Campbell (1986) and Chubb (1988) both reported that presidential popularity has a positive influence in state legislative elections, with the party winning the presidency having the advantage. Research on the impact of midterm elections as referenda on the popularity of national administrations demonstrated that gubernatorial and legislative candidates of the incumbent president are disadvantaged in those elections (Campbell 1986; Holbrook-Provow 1987; Chubb 1988). Only modest evidence exists on the impact of the performance of the national and state economies on vote choice in state and local elections. Tompkins (1984b), Holbrook-Provow (1987), Peltzman (1987), and Chubb (1988) all found that changes in national economic conditions are related to changes in the fortunes of gubernatorial and legislative candidates, with the impact benefiting Democrats and candidates of the nonincumbent party in bad times and Republicans and candidates of the incumbent party in good times. Kenny (1983a) reported no impact of adverse state economic conditions on incumbent party vote shares in gubernatorial elections.

RECRUITMENT

Recruitment to political office, like participation, has been the subject of many studies by scholars in the state and local politics field. Research on recruitment has focused on who gets chosen for office, the structure of opportunities for elected offices, the motives, incentives, and goals of those who seek political office, the processes of recruitment, and the development of political careers. In each of these subject areas, studies from the state and local field have made contributions toward the development and testing of empirical theories of recruitment.

Research on the question of who is recruited for political office in the states and localities has centered on two issues: who is overrepresented and who is underrepresented. Dahl (1961) and Prewitt (1970) suggested that individuals of the higher social strata were more likely to be recruited to local office than individuals of the lower social strata. Studies of state officeholders, in particular legislators, revealed a similar pattern of overrepresentation from the higher social strata (Wahlke et al. 1962; Sorauf 1963; Barber 1965; Seligman et al. 1974) and also that lawyers, specifically, have been overrepresented (Eulau and Sprague 1964; Hain and Piereson 1975).

While the early studies of who is recruited to political office were devoted to determining which social groups and occupations were overrepresented in state and local offices, the more recent studies have focused on who is missing from political offices. This body of research indicated that women (Werner 1968; Stewart 1980; Darcy et al. 1987; Bullock and MacManus 1991), blacks (Campbell and Feagin 1975; Welch and Karnig 1980; Engstrom and McDonald 1981; Vedlitz and Johnson 1982; Alozie 1988, 1990; Zax 1990; Welch 1990), and Hispanics (Taebel 1978; Karnig and Welch 1979; Fraga et al. 1986; Alozie 1990; Zax 1990; Welch 1990) have been underrepresented in state and local offices. Explanations for why these groups are missing from state and local offices have also been advanced in the studies of Kirkpatrick (1974), Dubeck (1976), Mezey (1978), Merritt (1977), Welch (1978), Darcy et al. (1987), Alozie (1990), and Bullock and MacManus (1991) on women; Robinson and Dye (1978), MacManus (1978), Karnig (1979), Welch and Karnig (1980), Engstrom and McDonald (1981), Vedlitz and Johnson (1982), Alozie (1988, 1990), Zax (1990), and

Welch (1990) on blacks; and Taebel (1978), Karnig and Welch (1979), Fraga et al. (1986), Alozie (1990), Zax (1990), and Welch (1990) on Hispanics. The most common explanations for why women, blacks, and Hispanics are not recruited to political office as frequently as are other groups focus upon structural factors as barriers to the recruitment of minorities.

The question of how the structure of opportunities for political office impacts upon recruitment to state and local offices has been the subject of only one major study (Schlesinger 1966). Schlesinger demonstrates that state and local offices are highly transitory in comparison to national offices, and that the structures of opportunity for many state and local offices definitely influence recruitment patterns for those offices. Since the principal focus of Schlesinger's study was upon statewide offices, we do not know much about the structure of opportunities for state legislative or city council offices.

Most of the research on the motives, incentives, and goals of those who seek political office in the United States has been conducted in the state and local field until very recently. The pathbreaking studies of Clark and Wilson (1961) and Wilson (1962) on recruitment incentives were conducted in local settings using party elites. Barber (1965) examined motivations for seeking legislative office and tied those motivations to the legislative behavior of those who are elected. The work of Schlesinger (1966) on an ambition theory of politics has been a major contribution to the study of motivations, incentives, and goals of political officeholders. His work has stimulated studies of political ambition among state executives (Swinerton 1968) and in the local government arena (Black 1970; Black 1972). Given the interest in rational-goal-seeking theories in political science, it is surprising that little has been done with ambition theory in studies of the recruitment of state legislators.

Research on the processes of recruitment is abundant in the field of state and local politics. This research has identified the steps or stages in recruitment (Seligman et al. 1974; Prewitt 1970) and the various groups involved in recruiting candidates. In some states political parties have been identified as the principal groups involved in the process of recruitment (Sorauf 1963; Tobin 1975; Tobin and Keynes 1975; Thurber 1976; Keynes et al. 1979; Cotter et al. 1984). Typically, state or local political parties have been the recruiting agents. However, considering the importance of state governorships and legislatures in the congressional redistricting process, there has been evidence of national party involvement in recruitment for these state offices (Bibby 1979; Jewell 1985). On the other hand, in states where political parties have traditionally been unimportant, other groups have been identified as the principal recruiting agents (Seligman et al. 1974). And in local nonpartisan settings, of course, groups other than political parties dominate the recruitment process (Prewitt 1970).

The research on the development of political careers by students of state and local politics has focused almost exclusively on turnover in political offices. The studies by Rosenthal (1974), Ray (1974), and Shin and Jackson (1979) of state legislative turnover have documented changes in career opportunities in those institutions. Wiggins and Bernick (1977), Oxendale (1979), and Niemi and Winsky (1987) have examined factors that may be associated with levels of membership turnover in state legislatures. The evidence from these studies is that institutionalization is occurring in some legislatures, and that consequently more members are pursuing legislative careers rather than leaving the legislature.

Although the study of recruitment has long been one of the major subjects of state and local politics, I do not see much exciting or innovative work presently going on in our field that relates to this topic.

REPRESENTATION

Representation has long been one of the focal points of research in state and local politics. The representation literature has centered on the issues of bias, styles, allocation and service aspects, and policy responsiveness.

Research on biases in representation in state and local politics has taken three forms: (1) studies concerned with districting mechanisms that did not represent persons, voters, or groups fairly; (2) studies focused on determining what other biases continued to exist after representation was based fairly on population equality; and (3) studies interested in determining whether or not certain electoral structures were responsible for biases in the representation of groups. Studies of the first type were primarily interested in assessing representation in terms of "one-person, one-vote" criteria (Schubert and Press 1964) and in terms of representational equity (Cole 1974; Jones 1976; Karnig 1976; Robinson and Dye 1978; MacManus 1978; Taebel 1978; Welch and Karnig 1978; Karnig 1979; Latimer 1979; Engstrom and McDonald 1981; Robinson and England 1981; Davidson and Korbel 1981; Engstrom and McDonald 1982; Mundt and Heilig 1982; Vedlitz and Johnson 1982; Heilig and Mundt 1984; Robinson, England, and Meier, 1985; Alozie 1988, 1990; Zax 1990; and Welch 1990). The second type of studies was undertaken after the reapportionment revolution of the 1960s to determine whether or not the equalization of populations in districting left any partisan biases. This literature (Erikson 1971; Uslaner and Weber 1977b; and Scarrow 1983) concluded

that partisanship has been pervasive in redistricting, resulting in districting plans with definite partisan biases. The third type of literature on
biases in representation determined that the use of multimember districts for electing state legislators may work to underrepresent racial minorities (Grofman et al. 1986), while at the same time enhancing the
electoral fortunes of women (Darcey et al. 1985) and producing higher
rates of membership turnover (Niemi and Winsky 1987). The evidence
about the impact of multimember districting on partisan minorities is
mixed, however, with Jewell (1982b, 1982c) finding that multimember
districts underrepresent them, while Niemi et al. (1985) report that
such districts fairly represent them. At the local level, all of the research
(Cole 1974; Jones 1976; Karnig 1976; Robinson and Dye 1978; Mac-
Manus 1978; Taebel 1978; Welch and Karnig 1978; Karnig 1979; Latimer 1979; Engstrom and McDonald 1981; Robinson and England
1981; Davidson and Korbel 1981; Engstrom and McDonald 1982;
Mundt and Heilig 1982; Vedlitz and Johnson 1982; Heilig and Mundt
1984; Robinson, England, and Meier 1985, and Zax 1990), except that
of Welch (1990), found that single-member districting plans tend to
facilitate minority representation on city councils and school boards.
Welch (1990) reported on the basis of recent data that there are negligi-
ble differences between at-large and single-member district schemes in
representing minorities on city councils.

Styles of representation have received a great deal of attention in
research on state and local politics. This research has focused almost
exclusively on the role orientations of state legislators and the relationships they have with their constituencies. The Wahlke et al. (1962)
study of four state legislatures was the first systematically to employ the
role concept in research on state and local politics. The researchers
found that legislators could be readily classified on the basis of role orientations and that several types of representational styles were related to
each other. Their work spawned a number of additional role orientation
studies and had a profound impact on the study of representation by
state and local scholars. The aim of most of these state and local studies
was to identify the types of role orientations in each state and to examine factors associated with variation in representational roles (Sorauf
1963; Bell and Price 1975).

There has been very little research in the state and local field on the
relationship between legislators and constituents. Whereas this question has been extensively explored in the congressional literature, only
the work of Jewell (1982b) has been directed toward examining this
relationship. He found, in a study of representation in nine states, that
state legislators employ many of the same mechanisms as members of
Congress do to communicate with constituents. On the other hand, he
was unable to report that state legislators were as sophisticated as mem-

bers of Congress in perceiving their constituencies in terms of multiple levels of support, as has been documented in the congressional literature.

Just as there has been little research in the state and local politics field of the "home style" of state legislators, so the literature is generally silent on the study of the allocation and service aspects of representation. Again I must turn to the work of Jewell (1982b) for evidence on this dimension of representation. He established that legislators work hard to obtain specific benefits for their districts, while at the same time giving varying emphasis to constituency service activities. He also found that constituency service activities were related to the availability of staff resources to provide them and to single-member districting.

Whereas the allocation and service aspects of representation have been understudied by the state and local field, policy responsiveness as representation has received a little more attention. In these studies the focus has been upon congruence, defined as agreement between constituency preferences, however measured, and state legislative voting. The body of research focused at the constituency-legislator level (Crane 1960; Kuklinski 1978; McCrone and Kuklinski 1979) revealed that responsiveness was high on salient issues but lower on more routine issues, and that responsiveness was fostered by delegate role orientations. In a four-state study of congruence between state opinion and legislator opinion, Ingram et al. (1980) found that congruence was the highest on issues that could be characterized as ideological or partisan in character.

Although representation has been one of the most fruitful areas of empirical theory pursued by state and local politics scholars, this brief survey of the field's contributions indicates that there are significant gaps in the way this field has contributed to the development and testing of empirical theories of representation.

DECISION-MAKING

Research on decision-making by state and local institutions has centered on those institutions that make collective decisions. Thus, the overwhelming majority of decision-making studies have used state and local legislatures and courts as the foci for research. The concern in this body of literature has been on development and testing of theories of decision-making by those institutions, or subcomponents of them. This work can be differentiated from the more general work on policy-making in that decision-making studies focus on single institutions, whereas the policy-making literature has been concerned with explaining the actions of governments as a whole rather than those of single institutions like legislatures or courts.

The state and local politics literature on decision-making includes research of two types—that which focuses on individual decision-making within the institution and that which is concerned with the collective result of those individual decisions. I shall begin by examining the literature on collective decision-making and then turn to the research on individual decision-making. I do so because in the state and local politics field research on the former seems to predate the work on the latter. Many of the early works on state legislatures, for example, were designed and executed in a period when the state and local field was dominated by persons enamored of the idea of responsible party government. This view of democracy has a bias toward thinking of legislatures as collectives rather than as institutions made up of individuals, and hence these early studies of legislatures centered upon collective decisions rather than individual ones.

In the early studies of collective decision-making by state legislatures, the research was conducted for single states in an attempt to determine the degree of intraparty cohesion and interparty conflict from roll-call votes (Keefe 1954; Derge 1958; Flinn 1960; Buchanan 1963; Sorauf 1963; Wiggins 1967; Bryan 1968) or for several states in order to assess possible reasons for cross-state differences in intraparty cohesion and interparty conflict (Zeller 1954; Jewell 1955; Keefe 1956; Lockard 1959; LeBlanc 1969). This literature as it developed documented rather clearly that there was considerable variation across the states studied in terms of intraparty cohesion and interparty conflict (Jewell 1966, 1969). Later additions to the cohesion and conflict literature focused on weak or one-party systems (Patterson 1962; Broach 1972; Welch and Carlson 1973) or on alternatives to party as the basis for agreement or disagreement in legislatures (Keith 1981).

Although this literature had great potential for contributing to the development of empirical theories of collective decision-making, it did not do so. Either because of the methodological criticisms raised against the use of roll calls to measure legislative behavior or because of the difficulty of collecting such data across states and time, these types of studies of collective decision-making by state legislatures are no longer being conducted. Whereas research on collective decision-making by the Congress using roll-call data has blossomed—in particular, studies exploring dimensionality in collective behavior—the study of state legislatures has virtually abandoned the use of roll-call data and the opportunity to develop within the state and local politics field theories of collective decision-making based on dimensionality in voting. The notable exceptions that explored dimensionality in state legislatures are Patterson (1962), Broach (1972), Welch and Carlson (1973), and LeLoup (1976).

Since the demise of the roll-call studies, research on collective decision-making by state legislatures has taken a different turn. Survey research studies such as those of Francis (1967, 1985, 1989) and Uslaner and Weber (1977a) attempted to collect data to permit collective decision-making analyses based on state legislator responses. Francis (1967) found that levels of partisan, interest-group, factional, and regional conflict in state legislatures over key issues varied considerably across the states and attempted to explain the reasons for such differences. Francis and Weber (1980) employed the Uslaner and Weber data to examine the change in issue content considered collectively by state legislatures between the early 1960s and the early 1970s. The Francis survey data sets have also been used to determine the locus for decision-making in state legislatures (Francis 1967, 1982, 1985, 1989; Francis and Riddlesberger 1982), with the latest research suggesting the importance of committees and subcommittees in collective decision-making by state legislatures.

Collective decision-making by state judges of appellate courts has received considerable attention from judicial politics and behavior specialists. The studies of Canon and Jaros (1970) and Jaros and Canon (1971) were among the first to undertake comparative analyses of collective decision-making by state supreme courts. They developed an index of dissent for each state supreme court and then examined the factors associated with dissenting collective behavior. They found that higher rates of dissent were found in states with greater socioeconomic diversity and high degrees of partisan political competition, and that some of the variation in dissent rates could be explained by the individual characteristics of judges. Atkins and Glick (1974, 1976) took a different approach to the collective decision-making of state supreme courts and classified data on cases heard by the courts into types of issue categories. They then used these data to create measures of appellant success (1974) and issue type (1976). In their studies they found no relationship between formal recruitment systems and appellant success but discovered that environmental variables were important predictors of the types of issues resolved by state supreme courts. The recent work of Hall and Brace (1989) and Brace and Hall (1990) reexamined factors associated with dissent rates in state supreme courts and found that decision rules and institutional arrangements were more important than environmental factors in explaining variation in dissent.

These comparative state studies of collective judicial decision-making represent almost all of the studies completed that focus on courts rather than judges as the units of analysis. One recent exception is a study by Dubois (1988) on California intermediate courts of appeal. In this study Dubois found that significant variations in the outcomes of intermediate appellate court decisions could be explained by the partisan composition of the appellate panel and the party affiliation of the judge who wrote the majority opinion. This finding is highly consistent with the judicial behavior literature that has focused on individual decision-making by both trial and appellate judges in the states.

Research on individual decision-making by state legislatures dates from the roll-call study of MacRae (1952). His research, which was later to stimulate a number of studies of individual decision-making in state legislatures, focused on the party loyalty of individual legislators and examined the relationship of constituency type to party loyalty. Replications of the MacRae analysis of individual decision-making in legislatures were conducted by Dye (1961), Patterson (1961, 1962), Parsons (1962), Pesonen (1963), Flinn (1964), and LeBlanc (1969).

Another type of research on individual decision-making by state legislators has examined influences other than party on legislative voting. Francis (1962) and Best (1971) have looked at interest groups and their influence in single-state legislatures. Uslaner and Weber (1977a) have looked at multiple actors in the legislative process and have attempted to determine the relative importance of these actors in giving cues to state legislators as they make decisions. And McCally (1966), Hadley (1977), and Bernick (1978) have explored the role of governors as influencers of decision-making in state legislatures.

Within the state legislative setting, there has also been some research on the role of committees in decision-making. Hamm (1980, 1986) has investigated decision-making in committees to determine whether different settings affect decision-making and whether subgovernments focused within committees are influential in state legislatures. These analyses of Hamm (1982, 1986) and Hamm and Moncrief (1982) have also centered upon the success of committees in obtaining floor approval for their recommendations on legislation.

Finally, some studies of individual decision-making in state legislatures have concentrated on the possible role constituency influence plays in individual decision-making. The studies that have attempted to measure, directly or indirectly, constituency preferences and then to relate them to legislative decisions include the work of Crane (1960), Hedlund and Friesema (1972), Jones (1973), Erikson et al. (1975), Kuklinski (1977a, 1977b, 1978), Kuklinski and Elling (1977), McCrone and Kuklinski (1979), and Kuklinski and McCrone (1980).

Although a number of alternative models for explaining individual decision-making by legislators have been developed and tested in the congressional literature, these models have not been fully explored in state legislative studies. The closest we have come in the state legislative literature has been in conducting some tests of the electoral-incentive model in the constituency influence studies noted above and examining the cue-taking model in the work of Uslaner and Weber (1977a). State legislative studies still have much to contribute to the development and testing of alternative individual decision-making models and theories.

POLICY-MAKING

The study of policy-making is probably the one area of research that has benefited the most from state and local politics studies during the past twenty-five years or so. The area of state and local policy research has developed from one in the early days in which exceedingly simple theories, models, data sets, and methods were dominant to one in which currently the theories are rich, the models sophisticated, the data sets complex, and the methods employed highly advanced. So much progress has been made that rarely do we see cross-sectional studies any more. Instead, the emphasis is on the creation of data sets amenable to time and space analyses and on the testing of theories that have both temporal and spatial aspects. The cross-sectional studies that do continue can be characterized as being so strong in theoretical development as to overcome any concerns with the cross-sectional character of the empirical test of the theories.

The previous state and local research on policy-making can be categorized into several major types: (1) state and local revenue and expenditure determinant studies that focus on attempting to sort out the factors that explain varying levels of state and local revenue raising and expenditures; (2) studies of redistribution policies that usually center around a "politics versus economics" paradigm; (3) studies of the impact of state and local structures upon state and local policies; (4) studies of the state and local delivery of public services; and (5) studies of state and local regulatory policies. While some studies may overlap from one category to another, I will attempt in my appraisal of this literature to place each study into the category where I believe it contributes the most to empirical theories of policy-making.

Research on the determinants of state and local revenue and expenditure policy has been extensive, with most of the effort going into the study of expenditure rather than revenue policies. In the few studies of revenue policies that exist, Dye (1966), Bingham et al. (1978), Portney (1980), and Hansen (1983) all examine the impact of levels of partisanship on state revenue policy outputs, with only Portney and Hansen reporting some influence between partisanship and variations in revenue policies. Hansen (1983, 154–56) indicates that state party control by Democrats is linked to tax adoptions, while Portney (1980) suggests that states were more likely to adopt personal or corporate income taxes as a first choice over sales taxes under conditions of one-party control rather than under the circumstances of party competition. Conversely,

Dye (1966) and Bingham et al. (1978), in cross-sectional analyses, report no impact between level of partisanship and reliance of the states on various tax sources.

In the expenditure studies, most of the cross-sectional work has pointed to the importance of socioeconomic variables as strong determinants of expenditure policies (Dye 1966; Sharkansky 1968; Treadway 1985). The literature on longitudinal studies of expenditures has revealed two principal types of findings. First, incrementalism may be a strong determinant of spending patterns (Lowery et al. 1984); and second, changes in partisan control of institutions may be associated with nonincremental spending change (Jones 1974; Dye 1984; Garand 1985).

My second category of state and local policy studies is that of redistribution policies that usually center around a "politics versus economics" paradigm. Beginning from the work of Key (1949), in which he elaborated a theory of "have versus have-not" policy-making, this field has been concerned with attempts to test this theory empirically. The studies of Dawson and Robinson (1963), Dye (1966), Hofferbert (1966), Sharkansky and Hofferbert (1969), Cnudde and McCrone (1969), Fry and Winters (1970), Sullivan (1972), Booms and Halldorson (1973), Uslaner and Weber (1975), Wright (1975), Winters (1976), Gray (1976a), Lewis-Beck (1977), Jennings (1979), Stonecash and Hayes (1981), Hanson (1983, 1984), Plotnick and Winters (1985), and Barrilleaux and Miller (1988) all examine various aspects of redistribution policy employing some version of the "politics versus economics" paradigm. In contrast to the literature on expenditure policy, this literature tends to point to a number of political factors that are associated with redistributive policies in the states.

My third category of state and local policy studies focuses on the impact state and local structures have upon policy-making. A number of structures have been of major concern in this type of policy studies. There have been studies of the impact of malapportionment (Jacob 1964; Pulsipher and Weatherby 1968) and then reapportionment (Frederickson and Cho 1974; Feig 1978, 1985) on policy-making. The impact of legislative structure and capability has been of concern (Ritt 1973; Carmines 1974; Karnig and Sigelman 1975; LeLoup 1978; Roeder 1979), with most of the studies reporting a relationship between legislative capability and policy-making. And there has been some interest in determining whether executive branch structures have had an impact on policy-making (Dye 1969; Meier 1980).

My fourth category of state and local policy studies are those on state and local delivery of public services. This literature is sparse, despite the fundamental importance of service delivery in policy studies. Sharkansky (1968) first explored the question of whether or not there is any relationship between spending for services and service delivery and confirmed that there is. He then proceeded to examine various factors that, in addition to spending, could account for differences in service delivery. The same type of analysis was pursued in the studies of Wenner (1972) and Dean and Peroff (1977).

The final category of state and local policy studies includes those which I characterize as studies of state and local regulatory policies. The research I place here primarily involves studies of nonexpenditure policy and the factors associated with the making of such policies. This research includes the path-breaking work of Walker (1969), Gray (1973, 1974), and Eyestone (1977) on the diffusion of innovations; studies of dimensions in policy-making (Hopkins and Weber 1976); studies of public opinion and policy-making (Weber and Shaffer 1972; Shaffer and Weber 1974; Sutton 1973; Hopkins 1974; Wright et al. 1987; Lowery et al. 1989; Erikson et al. 1989); and studies of public utility regulation (Gormley 1983).

CONCLUSION

The field of state and local politics is rich in tradition and in potential. The development by Malcolm Jewell and others of data repositories, now under way, to make comparative examinations of primary and general elections within and across states, the consistent quality of the aggregate data available, and the increasing availability of relevant survey information all provide the tools needed to engage in qualitatively fine research. The diversity of forms, settings, and institutional arrangements affords a context in which empirical theories of significance can be developed that will be useful for explaining political behavior at any level. The research to date has shown the way. The challenge is to take advantage of what is now available to us.

REFERENCES

Alford, R. P., and E. C. Lee. 1968. "Voting Turnout in American Cities." *American Political Science Review* 62 (September): 796–813.

Alozie, N. O. 1988. "Black Representation on State Judiciaries." *Social Science Quarterly* 69 (December): 979–86.

———. 1990. "Distribution of Women and Minority Judges: The Effects of Judicial Selection Methods." *Social Science Quarterly* 71 (June): 315–25.

Atkins, B. M., and H. R. Glick. 1974. "Formal Judicial Recruitment and State Supreme Court Decisions." *American Politics Quarterly* 2 (October): 427–49.

————. 1976. "Environmental and Structural Variables as Determinants of Issues in State Courts of Last Resort." *American Journal of Political Science* 20 (February): 97–115.

Barber, J. D. 1965. *The Lawmakers*. New Haven: Yale University Press.

Barrilleaux, C. J., and M. E. Miller. 1988. "The Political Economy of State Medicaid Policy." *American Political Science Review* 82 (December): 1089–107.

Bell, C. G., and C. M. Price. 1975. *The First Term: A Study of Legislative Socialization*. Beverly Hills, Calif.: Sage Publications.

Bernick, E. L. 1978. "The Impact of U.S. Governors on Party Voting in One-Party Dominated Legislatures." *Legislative Studies Quarterly* 3 (August): 431–44.

Best, J. J. 1971. "Influence in the Washington House of Representatives." *Midwest Journal of Political Science* 15 (August): 547–62.

Beyle, T. L. 1983. "The Cost of Becoming Governor." *State Government* 56 (Summer): 74–84.

Bibby, J. F. 1979. "Political Parties and Federalism: The Republican National Committee Involvement in Gubernatorial and Legislative Elections." *Publius: The Journal of Federalism* 9 (Winter): 229–36.

Bingham, R. D., B. W. Hawkins, and F. T. Hebert. 1978. *The Politics of Raising State and Local Revenues*. New York: Praeger.

Black, G. 1970. "A Theory of Professionalization in Politics." *American Political Science Review* 64 (September): 865–78.

————. 1972. "A Theory of Political Ambition: Career Choice and the Role of Structural Incentives." *American Political Science Review* 66 (March): 144–59.

Booms, B. H., and J. R. Halldorson. 1973. "The Politics of Redistribution: Towards a Model of the Policy-Making Process in the American States." *American Political Science Review* 68 (September): 924–33.

Boyd, R. W. 1986. "Election Calendars and Voter Turnout." *American Politics Quarterly* 14 (January): 89–104.

————. 1989. "The Effects of Primaries and Statewide Races on Voter Turnout." *Journal of Politics* 51 (August): 730–39.

Brace, P., and M. G. Hall. 1990. "Neo-Institutionalism and Dissent in State Supreme Courts." *Journal of Politics* 52 (February): 54–70.

Broach, G. T. 1972. "A Comparative Dimensional Analysis of Partisan and Rural Voting in State Legislatures." *Journal of Politics* 34 (November): 905–21.

Bryan, F. M. 1968. "The Metamorphosis of a Rural Legislature." *Polity* 1 (Winter): 191–212.

Buchanan, W. 1963. *Legislative Partisanship*. Berkeley: University of California Press.

Bullock, C. S., III, and S. A. MacManus. 1990. "Municipal Electoral Structure and the Election of Councilwomen." *Journal of Politics* 53 (February): forthcoming.

Caldeira, G., and S. C. Patterson. 1982a. "Bringing Home the Votes: Electoral Outcomes in State Legislative Races." *Political Behavior* 4:33–67.

———. 1982b. "Contextual Influences on Participation in U.S. State Legislative Elections." *Legislative Studies Quarterly* 7 (August): 359–81.

Calvert, J. 1979. "Revolving Doors: Volunteerism in State Legislatures." *State Government* 52 (Autumn): 174–81.

Campbell, D., and J. R. Feagin. 1975. "Black Politics in the South: A Descriptive Analysis." *Journal of Politics* 37 (February): 129–59.

Campbell, J. E. 1986. "Presidential Coattails and Midterm Losses in State Legislative Elections." *American Political Science Review* 80 (March): 45–63.

Canon, B. C., and D. Jaros. 1970. "External Variables, Institutional Structure, and Dissent on State Supreme Courts." *Polity* 3 (Winter): 175–200.

Carmines, E. G. 1974. "The Mediating Influence of State Legislatures on the Linkage between Interparty Competition and Welfare Policies." *American Political Science Review* 68 (September): 1118–24.

Cassell, C. A. 1979. "Change in Electoral Participation in the South." *Journal of Politics* 41 (November): 907–17.

Chubb, J. E. 1988. "Institutions, the Economy, and the Dynamics of State Elections." *American Political Science Review* 82 (March): 133–54.

Clark, P. B., and J. Q. Wilson. 1961. "Incentive Systems: A Theory of Organizations." *Administrative Sciences Quarterly* 6 (September): 129–66.

Cnudde, C. F., and D. J. McCrone. 1969. "Party Competition and Welfare Policies in the American States." *American Political Science Review* 63 (September): 858–66.

Cole, L. A. 1974. "Electing Blacks to Municipal Office: Structural and Social Determinants." *Urban Affairs Quarterly* 10 (September): 17–39.

Cotter, C. P., J. L. Gibson, J. F. Bibby, and R. J. Huckshorn. 1984. *Party Organizations in American Politics*. New York: Praeger.

Cowart, A. T. 1973. "Electoral Choice in the American States: Incumbency Effects, Partisan Forces, and Divergent Partisan Majorities." *American Political Science Review* 67 (September): 835–53.

Crane, W. 1960. "Do Representatives Represent?" *Journal of Politics* 22 (May): 295–99.

Dahl, R. A. 1961. *Who Governs? Democracy and Power in an American City*. New Haven: Yale University Press.

Darcy, R., S. Welch, and J. Clark. 1985. "Women Candidates in Single- and Multi-Member Districts: American State Legislative Races." *Social Science Quarterly* 66 (December): 945–53.

———. 1987. *Women, Elections, and Representation*. New York: Longman.

Davidson, C., and G. Korbel. 1981. "At-Large Elections and Minority Group

Representation: A Re-Examination of Historical and Contemporary Evidence." *Journal of Politics* 43 (November): 982–1005.

Dawson, R. E., and J. A. Robinson. 1963. "Inter-party Competition, Economic Variables, and Welfare Policies in the American States." *Journal of Politics* 25 (May): 265–89.

Dean, G., and K. Peroff. 1977. "The Spending-Service Cliché: An Empirical Evaluation." *American Politics Quarterly* 5 (October): 501–16.

Derge, D. R. 1958. "Metropolitan and Outstate Alignments in Illinois and Missouri Delegations." *American Political Science Review* 52 (December): 1051–65.

Dubeck, P. J. 1976. "Women and Access to Political Office: A Comparison of Female and Male State Legislators." *Sociological Quarterly* 17:42–52.

Dubois, P. L. 1980. *From Ballot to Bench: Judicial Elections and the Quest for Accountability*. Austin: University of Texas Press.

———. 1988. "The Illusion of Judicial Consensus Revisited: Partisan Conflict on an Intermediate State Court of Appeals." *American Journal of Political Science* 32 (November): 946–67.

Dye, T. R. 1961. "A Comparison of Constituency Influences in the Upper and Lower Chambers of a State Legislature." *Western Political Quarterly* 14 (June): 473–81.

———. 1966. *Politics, Economics, and the Public*. Chicago: Rand McNally.

———. 1969. "Executive Power and Public Policy in the States." *Western Political Quarterly* 22 (December): 926–39.

———. 1984. "Party and Policy in the States." *Journal of Politics* 46 (November): 1097–116.

Eismeier, T. J. 1979. "Budgets and Ballots: The Political Consequences of Fiscal Choice." In D. W. Rae and T. J. Eismeier, eds., *Public Policy and Fiscal Choice*, 121–45. Beverly Hills, Calif.: Sage Publications.

———. 1983. "Votes and Taxes: The Political Economy of the American Governorship." *Polity* 15 (Spring): 368–79.

Engstrom, R. L., and M. D. McDonald. 1981. "The Election of Blacks to City Councils." *American Political Science Review* 75 (June): 344–54.

———. 1982. "The Underrepresentation of Blacks on City Councils: Comparing the Structural and Socioeconomic Explanations for South/Non-South Differences." *Journal of Politics* 44 (November): 1088–99.

Erikson, R. S. 1971. "The Partisan Impact of Reapportionment." *Midwest Journal of Political Science* 57 (Spring): 57–71.

———, N. R. Luttbeg, and W. V. Holloway. 1975. "Knowing One's District: How Legislators Predict Referendum Voting." *American Journal of Political Science* 19 (May): 231–46.

———, G. C. Wright, and J. P. McIver. 1989. "Political Parties, Public Opinion, and State Policy in the United States." *American Political Science Review* 83 (September): 729–50.

Eulau, H., and K. Prewitt. 1973. *Labyrinths of Democracy: Adaptations, Linkages, Representation, and Policies in Urban Politics.* Indianapolis: Bobbs-Merrill.

Eulau, H., and J. D. Sprague. 1964. *Lawyers in Politics: A Study in Professional Convergence.* Indianapolis: Bobbs-Merrill.

Everson, D. H. 1981. "The Effects of Initiatives on Voter Turnout: A Comparative State Analysis." *Western Political Quarterly* 34 (September): 415–25.

Eyestone, R. 1977. "Confusion, Diffusion, and Innovation." *American Political Science Review* 71 (June): 441–47.

Feig, D. G. 1978. "Expenditures in the American States: The Impact of Court-Ordered Legislative Reapportionment." *American Politics Quarterly* 6 (July): 309–24.

———. 1985. "Looking at Supreme Court Impact in Context: The Case of Reapportionment and State Spending." *American Politics Quarterly* 13 (April): 167–87.

Fenton, J. H., and K. N. Vines. 1957. "Negro Registration in Louisiana." *American Political Science Review* 51 (September): 704–13.

Flinn, T. 1960. "The Outline of Ohio Politics." *Western Political Quarterly* 13 (September): 702–21.

———. 1964. "Party Responsibility in the States: Some Causal Factors." *American Political Science Review* 58 (March): 60–71.

Fraga, L. R., K. J. Meier, and R. E. England. 1986. "Hispanic Americans and Educational Policy: Limits to Equal Access." *Journal of Politics* 48 (November): 850–76.

Francis, W. L. 1962. "Influence and Interaction in a State Legislative Body." *American Political Science Review* 56 (December): 953–60.

———. 1967. *Legislative Issues in the Fifty States.* Chicago: Rand McNally.

———. 1982. "Legislative Committee Systems, Optimal Committee Size, and the Costs of Decision Making." *Journal of Politics* 44 (November): 822–37.

———. 1985. "Leadership, Party Caucuses, and Committees in U.S. State Legislatures." *Legislative Studies Quarterly* 10 (May): 243–57.

———. 1989. *The Legislative Committee Game: A Comparative Analysis of Fifty States.* Columbus: Ohio State University Press.

———, and J. W. Riddlesberger. 1982. "U.S. State Legislative Committees: Structure, Procedural Efficiency, and Party Control." *Legislative Studies Quarterly* 7 (August): 453–71.

———, and R. E. Weber. 1980. "Legislative Issues in the 50 States: Measuring Complexity through Classification." *Legislative Studies Quarterly* 5 (August): 407–21.

Frederickson, H. G., and Y. H. Cho. 1974. "Legislative Apportionment and Fiscal Policy in the American States." *Western Political Quarterly* 17 (March): 5–37.

Fry, B. R., and R. F. Winters. 1970. "The Politics of Redistribution." *American Political Science Review* 64 (June): 508–22.

Garand, J. C. 1985. "Partisan Change and Shifting Expenditure Priorities in the American States, 1945–1978." *American Politics Quarterly* 13 (October): 355–91.

Giles, M. W., and A. Pritchard. 1985. "Campaign Spending and Legislative Elections in Florida." *Legislative Studies Quarterly* 10 (February): 71–88.

Glantz, S., A. Abramowitz, and M. Burkart. 1976. "Election Outcomes: Whose Money Matters?" *Journal of Politics* 38 (November): 1033–38.

Gormley, W. T., Jr. 1983. "Policy, Politics, and Public Utility Regulation." *American Journal of Political Science* 27 (February): 86–105.

Grau, C. H. 1981. "Competition in State Legislative Primaries." *Legislative Studies Quarterly* 6 (February): 35–54.

Gray, V. 1973. "Innovation in the States: A Diffusion Model." *American Political Science Review* 67 (December): 1174–93.

———. 1974. "Expenditures and Innovation as Dimensions of 'Progressivism': A Note on the American States." *American Journal of Political Science* 18 (November): 693–99.

———. 1976a. "Models of Comparative State Politics: A Comparison of Cross-sectional and Time Series Analyses." *American Journal of Political Science* 20 (May): 235–56.

———. 1976b. "A Note on Competition and Turnout in the American States." *Journal of Politics* 38 (February): 153–58.

Grofman, B., M. Migalski, and N. Noviello. 1986. "Effects of Multimember Districts on Black Representation in State Legislatures." *Review of Black Political Economy* 14 (Spring): 65–78.

Hadley, D. J. 1977. "Legislative Role Orientations and Support for Party and Chief Executive in the Indiana House." *Legislative Studies Quarterly* 2 (May): 309–36.

Hain, P. L., and J. E. Piereson. 1975. "Lawyers and Politics Revisited: Structural Advantages of Lawyers-Politicians." *American Journal of Political Science* 19 (February): 41–51.

Hall, M. G., and P. Brace. 1989. "Order in the Courts: A Neo-Institutional Approach to Judicial Consensus." *Western Political Quarterly* 42 (September): 391–407.

Hamilton, H. D. 1971. "The Municipal Voter: Voting and Non-Voting in City Elections." *American Political Science Review* 65 (December): 1135–140.

Hamm, K. E. 1980. "U.S. State Legislative Committee Decisions: Similar Results in Different Settings." *Legislative Studies Quarterly* 5 (February): 31–54.

———. 1982. "Consistency between Committee and Floor Voting in U.S. State Legislatures." *Legislative Studies Quarterly* 7 (November): 473–90.

———. 1986. "The Role of 'Subgovernments' in U.S. State Policy Making:

An Exploratory Analysis." *Legislative Studies Quarterly* 11 (August): 321–51.

———, and G. Moncrief. 1982. "Effects of Structural Change in Legislative Committee Systems on Their Performance in U.S. States." *Legislative Studies Quarterly* 7 (August): 383–400.

Hansen, S. B. 1983. *The Politics of Taxation: Revenue without Representation*. New York: Praeger.

Hanson, R. L. 1983. "The 'Content' of Welfare Policy: The States and Aid to Families with Dependent Children." *Journal of Politics* 45 (August): 771–85.

———. 1984. "Medicaid and the Politics of Redistribution." *American Journal of Political Science* 28 (May): 313–39.

Hecock, D. S., and H. M. Bain, Jr. 1957. *Ballot Position and Voter's Choice*. Detroit: Wayne State University Press.

Hedlund, R. D., and H. P. Friesema. 1972. "Representatives' Perceptions of Constituency Opinion." *Journal of Politics* 34 (August): 730–52.

Heilig, P., and R. J. Mundt. 1984. *Your Voice at City Hall: The Politics, Procedures, and Policies of District Representation*. Albany, N.Y.: SUNY Press.

Hofferbert, R. I. 1966. "The Relationship between Public Policy and Some Structural and Environmental Variables in the American States." *American Political Science Review* 60 (March): 73–82.

Holbrook-Provow, T. 1987. "National Factors in Gubernatorial Elections." *American Politics Quarterly* 15 (October): 471–83.

Hopkins, A. H. 1974. "Opinion Publics and Support for Public Policy in the American States." *American Journal of Political Science* 18 (February): 167–77.

———, and R. E. Weber. 1976. "Dimensions of Public Policies in the American States." *Polity* 8 (Spring): 475–89.

Ingram, H. M., N. K. Laney, and J. R. McCain. 1980. *A Policy Approach to Representation: Lessons from the Four Corners States*. Baltimore: The Johns Hopkins Press.

Jacob, H. 1964. "The Consequences of Malapportionment: A Note of Caution." *Social Forces* 43 (December): 256–61.

Jacobson, G. C. 1975. "The Impact of Broadcast Campaigning on Electoral Outcomes." *Journal of Politics* 37 (August): 769–93.

Jaros, D., and B. C. Canon. 1971. "Dissent on State Supreme Courts: The Differential Significance of Characteristics of Judges." *Midwest Journal of Political Science* 15 (May): 322–46.

Jennings, E. T. 1979. "Competition, Constituencies and Welfare Policies in the American States." *American Political Science Review* 73 (June): 414–29.

Jewell, M. E. 1955. "Party Voting in American State Legislatures." *American Political Science Review* 49 (September): 773–91.

————. 1960. "Party and Primary Competition in Kentucky State Legislative Races." *Kentucky Law Journal* 48:517–35.

————. 1966. "The Political Settings." In A. Heard, ed., *State Legislatures in American Politics*, 70–97. Englewood Cliffs, N.J.: Prentice-Hall.

————. 1969. *The State Legislature*. 2d ed. New York: Random House.

————. 1982a. "The Neglected World of State Politics." *Journal of Politics* 44 (August): 638–75.

————. 1982b. *Representation in State Legislatures*. Lexington: University Press of Kentucky.

————. 1982c. "The Consequences of Single- and Multi-member Districting." In B. Grofman, A. Lijphart, R. B. McKay, and H. A. Scarrow, eds., *Representation and Redistricting Issues*. Lexington, Mass.: Lexington Books/ D. C. Heath.

————. 1983. "Political Money and Gubernatorial Primaries." *State Government* 56 (Summer): 69–73.

————. 1985. "The Prospects for Nationalizing State Legislative Elections." *Election Politics* 2 (Summer): 12–15.

————, and D. Breaux. 1988. "The Effect of Incumbency in State Legislative Elections." *Legislative Studies Quarterly* 13 (November): 495–514.

————, and D. M. Olson. 1982. *American State Political Parties and Elections*. Rev. ed. Homewood, Ill.: Dorsey Press.

Jones, B. D. 1973. "Competitiveness, Role Orientations, and Legislative Responsiveness." *Journal of Politics* 35 (November): 924–47.

Jones, C. B. 1976. "The Impact of Local Election Systems on Black Political Representation." *Urban Affairs Quarterly* 11 (March): 345–56.

Jones, E. T. 1974. "Political Change and Spending Shifts in the American States." *American Politics Quarterly* 2 (April): 159–78.

Karnig, A. D. 1976. "Black Representation on City Councils: The Impact of District Elections and Socioeconomic Factors." *Urban Affairs Quarterly* 12 (December): 223–41.

————. 1979. "Black Resources and City Council Representation." *Journal of Politics* 41 (February): 134–49.

————, and L. Sigelman. 1975. "State Legislative Reform and Public Policy: Another Look." *Western Political Quarterly* 28 (September): 548–52.

————, and S. Welch. 1979. "Sex and Ethnic Differences in Municipal Representation." *Social Science Quarterly* 60 (December): 465–81.

Keech, W. R. 1968. *The Impact of Negro Voting*. Chicago: Rand McNally.

Keefe, W. J. 1954. "Parties, Partisanship, and Public Policy in the Pennsylvania Legislature." *American Political Science Review* 48 (June): 450–64.

————. 1956. "Comparative Study of the Role of Political Parties in State Legislatures." *Western Political Quarterly* 9 (September): 726–42.

Keith, G. 1981. "Comparing Legislative Studies Groups in Three States." *Legislative Studies Quarterly* 6 (February): 69–86.

Kenney, P. J. 1983a. "The Effect of State Economic Conditions on the Vote for Governor." *Social Science Quarterly* 64 (March): 154–62.

———. 1983b. "Explaining Turnout in Gubernatorial Primaries." *American Politics Quarterly* 11 (July): 315–26.

———, and T. W. Rice. 1984. "The Effect of Primary Divisiveness in Gubernatorial and Senatorial Elections." *Journal of Politics* 46 (August): 904–15.

Key, V. O., Jr. 1949. *Southern Politics in State and Nation*. New York: Knopf.

———. 1956. *American State Politics: An Introduction*. New York: Knopf.

Keynes, E., R. J. Tobin, and R. Danziger. 1979. "Institutional Effects on Elite Recruitment: The Case of State Nominating Systems." *American Politics Quarterly* 7 (April): 283–302.

Kim, J., J. R. Petrocik, and S. N. Enokson. 1975. "Voter Turnout among the American States: Systemic and Individual Components." *American Political Science Review* 69 (March): 107–23.

Kirkpatrick, J. J. 1974. *Political Women*. New York: Basic Books.

Kuklinski, J. H. 1977a. "Constituency Opinion: A Test of the Surrogate Model." *Public Opinion Quarterly* 41 (Spring): 34–40.

———. 1977b. "District Competitiveness and Legislative Roll-Call Behavior: A Reassessment of the Marginality Hypothesis." *American Journal of Political Science* 21 (August): 627–38.

———. 1978. "Representativeness and Elections: A Policy Analysis." *American Political Science Review* 72 (March): 165–77.

———, and R. C. Elling. 1977. "Representational Role, Constituency Opinion, and Legislative Roll-Call Behavior." *American Journal of Political Science* 21 (February): 135–47.

———, and D. J. McCrone. 1980. "Policy Salience and the Causal Structure of Representation." *American Politics Quarterly* 8 (January): 139–65.

Latimer, M. 1979. "Black Political Representation in Southern Cities." *Urban Affairs Quarterly* 15 (September): 65–86.

LeBlanc, H. L. 1969. "Voting in State Senates: Party and Constituency Influences." *Midwest Journal of Political Science* 13 (February): 33–57.

LeLoup, L. T. 1976. "Policy, Party, and Voting in U.S. State Legislatures: A Test of the Content-Process Linkage." *Legislative Studies Quarterly* 1 (May): 213–30.

———. 1978. "Reassessing the Mediating Impact of Legislative Capability." *American Political Science Review* 72 (June): 616–21.

Lewis-Beck, M. 1977. "The Relative Importance of Socioeconomic and Political Variables in Public Policy." *American Political Science Review* 71 (June): 559–66.

Lockard, D. 1959. *New England State Politics*. Princeton, N.J.: Princeton University Press.

Lowery, D., V. Gray, and G. Hager. 1989. "Public Opinion and Policy Change in the American States." *American Politics Quarterly* 17 (January): 3–31.

Lowery, D., T. Konda, and J. C. Garand. 1984. "Spending in the States: A Test of Six Models." *Western Political Quarterly* 37 (March): 48–66.

McCally, S. P. 1966. "The Governor and His Legislative Party." *American Political Science Review* 60 (December): 923–42.

McCrone, D. J., and J. H. Kuklinski. 1979. "The Delegate Theory of Representation." *American Journal of Political Science* 23 (May): 278–300.

MacManus, S. A. 1978. "City Council Election Procedures and Minority Representation: Are They Related?" *Social Science Quarterly* 59 (June): 153–61.

MacRae, D., Jr. 1952. "The Relation between Roll-Call Votes and Constituencies in the Massachusetts House of Representatives." *American Political Science Review* 46 (December): 1046–55.

Magleby, D. 1984. *Direct Legislation: Voting on Ballot Propositions in the United States*. Baltimore: The Johns Hopkins University Press.

Matthews, D. R., and J. W. Prothro. 1963a. "Social and Economic Factors and Negro Voter Registration in the South." *American Political Science Review* 57 (March): 24–44.

———. 1963b. "Political Factors and Negro Voter Registration in the South." *American Political Science Review* 57 (June): 355–67.

———. 1966. *Negroes and the New Southern Politics*. New York: Harcourt, Brace and World.

Meier, K. J. 1980. "Executive Reorganization of Government: Impact on Employment and Expenditures." *American Journal of Political Science* 24 (August): 396–412.

Merritt, S. 1977. "Winners and Losers: Sex Differences in Municipal Elections." *American Journal of Political Science* 21 (August): 731–43.

Mezey, S. G. 1978. "Does Sex Make a Difference? A Case Study of Women in Politics." *Western Political Quarterly* 31 (June): 492–501.

Mundt, R. J., and P. Heilig. 1982. "District Representation: Demands and Effects in the Urban South." *Journal of Politics* 44 (November): 1035–48.

Niemi, R. G., and L. R. Winsky. 1987. "Membership Turnover in U.S. State Legislatures: Trends and Effects of Districting." *Legislative Studies Quarterly* 12 (February): 115–24.

Niemi, R. G., J. S. Hill, and B. Grofman. 1985. "The Impact of Multimember Districts on Party Representation in U.S. State Legislatures." *Legislative Studies Quarterly* 10 (November): 441–55.

Owens, J., and E. Olson. 1977. "Campaign Spending and the Electoral Process in California, 1977–1974." *Western Political Quarterly* 30 (December): 493–512.

Oxendale, J. R., Jr. 1979. "Compensation and Turnover in State Legislative Lower Chambers." *State and Local Government Review* 11:60–63.

Parsons, M. B. 1962. "Quasi-Partisan Conflict in a One-Party Legislative System: The Florida Senate, 1947–1961." *American Political Science Review* 56 (September): 605–14.

Patterson, S. C. 1961. "The Role of the Deviant in the State Legislative System: The Wisconsin Assembly." *Western Political Quarterly* 14 (June): 460–73.

———. 1962. "Dimensions of Voting Behavior in a One-Party State Legislature." *Public Opinion Quarterly* 26 (Spring): 185–201.

———. 1982. "Campaign Spending in Contests for Governor." *Western Political Quarterly* 35 (December): 257–77.

———, and G. A. Caldeira. 1983. "Getting Out the Vote: Participation in Gubernatorial Elections." *American Political Science Review* 77 (September): 675–89.

Peltzman, S. 1987. "Economic Conditions and Gubernatorial Elections." *American Economic Association Papers and Proceedings* 7 (May): 293–97.

Pesonen, P. 1963. "Close and Safe Elections in Massachusetts." *Midwest Journal of Political Science* 7 (February): 54–70.

Piereson, J. E. 1975. "Presidential Popularity and Midterm Voting at Different Electoral Levels." *American Journal of Political Science* 19 (November): 683–94.

———. 1977. "Sources of Candidate Success in Gubernatorial Elections, 1910–1970." *Journal of Politics* 39 (November): 939–58.

Plotnick, R. D., and R. F. Winters. 1985. "A Politicoeconomic Theory of Income Redistribution." *American Political Science Review* 79 (June): 458–73.

Pomper, G. M. 1980. "Governors, Money, and Votes." In G. M. Pomper with S. S. Lederman, eds., 108–27. *Elections in America*. 2d ed. New York: Longman.

Portney, K. E. 1980. "State Tax Preference Orderings and Partisan Control of Government." In W. J. Samuels and L. L. Wade, eds., *Taxing and Spending Policy*. Lexington, Mass.: Lexington Books/D. C. Heath.

Prewitt, K. 1970. *The Recruitment of Political Leaders: A Study of Citizen-Politicians*. Indianapolis: Bobbs-Merrill.

Price, H. D. 1957. *The Negro and Southern Politics: A Chapter of Florida History*. New York: New York University Press.

Pulsipher, A., and J. L. Weatherby. 1968. "Malapportionment, Party Competition, and the Functional Distribution of Government Expenditures." *American Political Science Review* 62 (December): 1207–19.

Ray, D. 1974. "Membership Stability in Three State Legislatures." *American Political Science Review* 68 (March): 106–12.

Rice, T. W. 1985. "Gubernatorial and Senatorial Primary Elections: Determinants of Competition." *American Politics Quarterly* 13 (October): 427–46.

Ritt, L. G. 1973. "State Legislative Reform: Does It Matter?" *American Politics Quarterly* 1 (October): 499–510.

Robinson, T. P., and T. R. Dye. 1978. "Reformism and Black Representation on City Councils." *Social Science Quarterly* 59 (June): 133–41.

Robinson, T. P., and R. E. England. 1981. "Black Representation on Central City School Boards Revisited." *Social Science Quarterly* 62 (September): 493–502.

Robinson, T. P., R. E. England, and K. J. Meier. 1985. "Black Resources and Black School Board Representation: Does Political Structure Matter?" *Social Science Quarterly* 66 (December): 976–82.

Roeder, P. W. 1979. "State Legislative Reform: Determinants and Policy Consequences." *American Politics Quarterly* 7 (January): 51–69.

Rosenstone, S. J., and R. E. Wolfinger. 1978. "The Effect of Registration Laws on Voter Turnout." *American Political Science Review* 72 (March): 22–45.

Rosenthal, A. 1974. "Turnover in State Legislatures." *American Journal of Political Science* 18 (August): 609–16.

Sabato, L. 1983. *Goodbye to Goodtime Charlie: The American Governorship Transformed*. 2d ed. Washington, D.C.: Congressional Quarterly Press.

Scarrow, H. A. 1983. *Parties, Elections, and Representation in the State of New York*. New York: New York University Press.

Schlesinger, J. A. 1966. *Ambition and Politics: Political Careers in the United States*. Chicago: Rand McNally.

Schubert, G., and C. Press. 1964. "Measuring Malapportionment." *American Political Science Review* 58 (June): 302–27.

Seligman, L. G., M. King, C. L. Kim, and R. Smith. 1974. *Patterns of Recruitment: A State Chooses Its Lawmakers*. Chicago: Rand McNally.

Shaffer, W. R., and R. E. Weber. 1974. *Policy Responsiveness in the American States*. Beverly Hills, Calif.: Sage Publications.

Sharkansky, I. 1968. *Spending in the American States*. Chicago: Rand McNally.

———, and R. I. Hofferbert. 1969. "Dimensions of State Politics, Economics, and Public Policy." *American Political Science Review* 63 (September): 867–69.

Shin, K. S., and J. S. Jackson III. 1979. "Membership Turnover in U.S. State Legislatures: 1931–1976." *Legislative Studies Quarterly* 4 (February): 95–104.

Simon, D. M. 1989. "Presidents, Governors, and Electoral Accountability." *Journal of Politics* 51 (May): 286–304.

Sindler, A. P. 1956. *Huey Long's Louisiana*. Baltimore: The John Hopkins University Press.

Sorauf, F. J. 1963. *Party and Representation*. New York: Atherton Press.

Squire, P., R. E. Wolfinger, and D. P. Glass. 1987. "Residential Mobility and Voter Turnout." *American Political Science Review* 81 (March): 45–66.

Standing, W. H., and J. A. Robinson. 1958. "Inter-Party Competition and Primary Standing: The Case of Indiana." *American Political Science Review* 52 (December): 1066–77.

Stanley, H. W. 1987. *Voter Mobilization and the Politics of Race: The South and Universal Suffrage, 1952–1984*. New York: Praeger.

Stern, M. 1987. "Black Voter Registration in the South: Hypotheses and Occurrences." In Lawrence W. Moreland, Robert P. Steed, and Tod A. Baker, eds., *Blacks in Southern Politics*. New York: Praeger.

Stewart, D. W., ed. 1980. *Women in Local Politics*. Metuchen, N.J.: Scarecrow Press.

Stonecash, J., and S. W. Hayes. 1981. "The Sources of Public Policy: Welfare Policy in the American States." *Policy Studies Journal* 9 (Spring): 681–98.

Sullivan, J. L. 1972. "A Note on Redistributive Politics." *American Political Science Review* 66 (December): 1301–5.

Sutton, R. L. 1973. "The States and the People: Measuring and Accounting for 'State Representativeness.'" *Polity* 5 (Summer): 451–76.

Swinerton, E. N. 1968. "Ambition and American State Executives." *Midwest Journal of Political Science* 12 (May): 538–49.

Taebel, D. 1978. "Minority Representation on City Councils: The Impact of Electoral Structure on Blacks and Hispanics." *Social Science Quarterly* 59 (June): 142–52.

Thurber, J. A. 1976. "The Impact of Party Recruitment Activity upon Legislative Role Orientations: A Path Analysis." *Legislative Studies Quarterly* 1 (November): 533–50.

Tobin, R. J. 1975. "The Influences of Nominating Systems on the Political Experiences of State Legislators." *Western Political Quarterly* 28 (June): 553–66.

———, and E. Keynes. 1975. "Institutional Differences in the Recruitment Process: A Four-State Study." *American Journal of Political Science* 19 (August): 667–82.

Tompkins, M. E. 1981. "Changing the Terms: Gubernatorial Election Reform in the Modern Era." Paper delivered at the annual meeting of the Southern Political Science Association, Memphis, Tenn.

———. 1984a. "The Electoral Fortunes of Gubernatorial Incumbents: 1947–1981." *Journal of Politics* 46 (May): 520–43.

———. 1984b. "Assembling the Puzzle: The Determinants of Gubernatorial Elections." Paper delivered at the annual meeting of the American Political Science Association, Washington, D.C.

———, and S. K. Smith. 1982. "Governors and the Electoral-Economic Cycle." Paper delivered at the annual meeting of the American Political Science Association, Denver.

Treadway, J. M. 1985. *Public Policy-Making in the American States*. New York: Praeger.

Tucker, H. J. 1986. "Contextual Models of Participation in U.S. State Legislative Elections." *Western Political Quarterly* 39 (March): 67–78.

———, and R. E. Weber. 1987. "State Legislative Election Outcomes: Contextual Effects and Legislative Performance Effects." *Legislative Studies Quarterly* 12 (November): 537–53.

Turett, J. S. 1971. "The Vulnerability of American Governors, 1900–1969." *Midwest Journal of Political Science* 15 (February): 108–32.

Uslaner, E. M., and R. E. Weber. 1975. "The 'Politics' of Redistribution: Towards a Model of the Policy-Making Process in the American States." *American Politics Quarterly* 3 (April): 130–70.

———. 1977a. *Patterns of Decision-Making in State Legislatures.* New York: Praeger.

———. 1977b. "Reapportionment, Gerrymandering, and Change in the Partisan Balance of Power in the American States." Paper delivered at the annual meeting of the American Political Science Association, Washington, D.C.

Vanderleeuw, J. M., and R. S. Engstrom. 1987. "Race, Referendums, and Roll-Off." *Journal of Politics* 49 (November): 1081–92.

Vedlitz, A., and C. A. Johnson. 1982. "Community Residential Segregation, Electoral Structure, and Minority Representation." *Social Science Quarterly* 63 (December): 729–36.

Wahlke, J. C., H. Eulau, W. Buchanan, and L. C. Ferguson. 1962. *The Legislative System: Explorations in Legislative Behavior.* New York: Wiley.

Walker, J. L. 1966. "Ballot Forms and Voter Fatigue: An Analysis of the Office Block and Party Column Ballots." *Midwest Journal of Political Science* 10 (November): 448–63.

———. 1969. "The Diffusion of Innovations among the American States." *American Political Science Review* 63 (September): 880–99.

Weber, R. E. 1980. "Gubernatorial Coattails: A Vanishing Phenomenon?" *State Government* 53 (Summer): 153–56.

———, and W. R. Shaffer. 1972. "Public Opinion and American State Policy-Making." *Midwest Journal of Political Science* 16 (November): 683–99.

Welch, S. 1978. "Recruitment of Women to Public Office: A Discriminant Analysis." *Western Political Quarterly* 31 (June): 372–80.

———. 1990. "Impact of At-Large Elections on Blacks and Hispanics." *Journal of Politics* 52 (November): 1050–76.

———, and E. H. Carlson. 1973. "The Impact of Party on Voting Behavior in a Nonpartisan Legislature." *American Political Science Review* 67 (September): 854–67.

———, and A. Karnig. 1978. "Representation of Blacks on Big City School Boards." *Social Science Quarterly* 59 (June): 162–71.

———. 1980. *Black Representation and Urban Policy.* Chicago: University of Chicago Press.

Welch, W. P. 1976. "The Effectiveness of Expenditures in State Legislative Races." *American Politics Quarterly* 4 (July): 333–56.

Wenner, L. M. 1972. "Enforcement of Water Pollution Control Law." *Law and Society Review* 6 (May): 481–507.

Werner, E. E. 1968. "Women in State Legislatures." *Western Political Quarterly* 21 (March): 40–50.

Wiggins, C. W. 1967. "Party Politics in the Iowa Legislature." *Midwest Journal of Political Science* 11 (February): 86–97.

———, and E. L. Bernick. 1977. "Legislative Turnover Reconsidered." *Policy Studies Journal* 5 (Winter): 419–24.

Wilson, J. Q. 1962. *The Amateur Democrat: Club Politics in Three Cities*. Chicago: University of Chicago Press.

Winters, R. F. 1976. "Party Control and Policy Change." *American Journal of Political Science* 20 (November): 597–636.

Wolfinger, R. E., and S. J. Rosenstone. 1980. *Who Votes?* New Haven: Yale University Press.

Wright, G. C. 1974. *Electoral Choice in America*. Chapel Hill: Institute for Research in Social Science, University of North Carolina.

———. 1975. "Interparty Competition and State Social Welfare Policy: When a Difference Makes a Difference." *Journal of Politics* 37 (August): 796–803.

———, R. S. Erikson, and J. P. McIver. 1987. "Public Opinion and Policy Liberalism in the American States." *American Journal of Political Science* 31 (November): 980–1001.

Wright, S. G. 1989. "Voter Turnout in Runoff Elections." *Journal of Politics* 51 (May): 385–96.

Zax, J. S. 1990. "Election Methods and Black and Hispanic City Council Membership." *Social Science Quarterly* 71 (June): 339–55.

Zeller, B. 1954. *American State Legislatures*. New York: Crowell-Collier.

Zisk, B. H. 1987. *Money, Media, and the Grass Roots: State Ballot Issues and the Electoral Process*. Newbury Park, Calif.: Sage Publications.

8

Urban Politics and Political Science

Kenneth R. Mladenka
and
Bryan D. Jones

There are two ways of looking at the current state of urban scholarship. The first sees the urban field as characterized by diversity and creativity. Approaches are innovative and the focus is interdisciplinary. Scholars are keenly aware of the importance of theory. It is a dynamic field with an extraordinarily bright future and considerable significance for the larger discipline. If the field has made less of an impact on the broader discipline of political science, it is because of the narrow, conventional approaches of mainstream scholars.

The second perspective is less charitable. Urban scholarship is in trouble. Urban scholars conduct too many case studies, engage in far too little rigorous empirical work, write too many books expounding grand theories, and too eagerly and uncritically accept new ideas. Its outputs are not taken very seriously by the rest of the discipline because its scholarship does not meet the accepted standards of scientific evidence as often as it might.

One point is not open to debate. Urban scholarship does not fare well in the pages of the major political science journals. On the average, during the period 1980–85 the six major journals—*American Political Science Review, Journal of Politics, Polity, Western Political Quarterly, American Journal of Political Science*, and *American Politics Quarterly*—published only one urban article *every other year*. The discipline's major

287

journals published a total of only twenty-two urban articles in six years. The number of urban articles in *American Political Science Review* declined from nine in 1970–75 to only five in 1980–85, while the number in the *Journal of Politics* and *Western Political Quarterly* fell from four to two and five to three, respectively (Burt and Mladenka 1986).

Urbanists are also notably absent from the editorial boards of major journals. Until very recently, none of the members of the American Political Science Review Board listed urban as a major field, or even a secondary area of interest. At the *Journal of Politics*, only one of the fifty-one editorial board members mentions urban as a major field, while only one of the nineteen members of the *Polity* board lists urban as an area of interest. Neither do urbanists get much in the way of grant money to support scholarship. Urban is not even identified as a separate field for granting and accounting purposes by the National Science Foundation. Instead, urbanists are thrown into the "policy" category. Urbanists submit only a few grant proposals each year, and even fewer are funded. Finally, the premier urban journal, the *Urban Affairs Quarterly*, is rated by political scientists at about the same level as the *Legislative Studies Quarterly*—but 49 percent are familiar with *LSQ* and only 30 percent with *UAQ* (Giles, Mizell, and Patterson 1989). By any measure, then, urban analysis has little influence on the broader discipline.

These indicators suggest that the study of urban politics is not well integrated into mainstream political science. Why? The question is a particularly significant one, because we believe that urbanists have a great deal to offer. First, the study of urban politics represents a hallowed research tradition. Research on the American city spawned seminal works on community power, political institutions, racial conflict, and public policy.

The trilogy of theoretical case studies that launched serious study of the city—Banfield's *Political Influence*, Dahl's *Who Governs?* and Sayre and Kaufman's *Governing New York City*—forged the link between careful empiricism and the pluralist school of thought in political science. Moreover, whatever one thinks of the community power debate, it was based in solid empiricism. The work of Lineberry and Fowler (1967) initiated a cottage industry in the quantitative effects of institutions. Vincent and Elinor Ostrom and their collaborators looked, not at single cities, but at the full metropolitan political economy, developing models with supporting data that challenged a half-century of governmental reform assumptions (see Ostrom, Bish, and Ostrom 1989). A vigorous debate emerged in the 1970s over the issue of bureaucratic discretion and the impact of organizational procedures on policy distribution (Lipsky 1980; Jones 1978; Mladenka 1978). Browning, Marshall, and Tabb (1984) rigorously analyzed the effects of governing arrangements on the incorporation of minorities into governing coalitions. Students of the New York fiscal crisis developed explicitly cyclical theories of political change before they came into vogue in other circles (see Shefter 1985; Kantor and David 1987). As important as this and other urban research is, it has not been well incorporated into the main body of political science.

Second, it is at the local level that the impact of extraordinary change is most closely and directly experienced. Further, urbanists are generally more sophisticated than other political scientists in their recognition of and sensitivity to the profound effects of outside forces upon political outcomes. Students of Congress and the courts can perhaps afford to assume that their unit of analysis exists in a steady state; students of the city cannot. That fact immensely complicates the urban research agenda. In the process urbanists have learned a valuable lesson that should be shared with others. For example, we were among the first to recognize the significance of a political economy perspective (see Elkin 1987).

Third, the large number of local governments and their incredible diversity offer great scientific leverage, as well as much intrinsic interest. There is only one Congress, one Supreme Court, and one president. There are thousands of cities and urban counties. The large number of cases and variables provides a unique opportunity to test a variety of competing models.

So why are urbanists not making a larger impact on the discipline? Below we suggest several factors that may account for the incomplete integration of urban politics into the discipline of political science.

1. There is a mismatch between urban theory and the supporting data. Once the study of urban politics consisted of collecting facts about municipal governments. Today, the tables have been turned. There is a pronounced tendency to try to study it all—economics, politics, culture. To accommodate these overarching concerns, theories have become increasingly abstract. But this level of abstraction, while sufficiently broad to permit a consideration of the huge number of factors affecting the behavior of the city, defies the operationalization essential to rigorous empirical testing. As a consequence, scientific progress is limited. It is appropriate to study the city at the level of competing ideas, arguments, and conceptualizations. But without parallel careful empiricism, differing theories can be evaluated only on their plausibility, not their empirical validity. Today we have a book with a "new perspective," tomorrow another with a "compelling and refreshing argument," and next week still another with "a powerful and creative synthesis of conflicting ideas." We are all for new and interesting ideas. But as long as this debate seldom rises above the level of competing perspectives, approaches, and concepts, we shall not get very far.

One might cite the work of the Political Economy Workshop at Indiana University as a counterexample. Under the influence of Vincent and Elinor Ostrom, a set of theories has been developed, and rigorous studies and analyses to shed light on those theories conducted. The results have been controversial but attacked mostly in rhetoric. Now, however, careful empirical work is emerging that questions some of the results reported by the Political Economy Workshop (Lowery and Lyons 1989). With sound empirical work on both sides of the issue, the possibility of a creative synthesis presents itself.

2. Too little rigorous empirical work is being produced. The scientific method requires both ideas and numbers. Or, more appropriately and precisely, it requires both theory and quantification. Quantification does not always require vast data sets and elaborate statistical models. But it does require precision in definition, systematic evaluation of evidence, and careful attention to the issues of validity and reliability.

The crunching of numbers in the absence of theory is an essentially sterile and futile enterprise. However, fewer of us recognize that theorizing without subsequent empirical testing is a similarly limited undertaking. It may make us think, and it may generate useful insights. But it will not systematically advance our level of knowledge of the city. Certainly, much social science is inferior social science. But condemnation should be reserved for the individual case in particular rather than the scientific method in general. The purpose of theory is to guide empirical work. The task of empirical work is to test, refine, and revise theory. To claim that one is superior to the other is unfounded: they are both essential.

Theory without empirical testing is a guarantee of opportunity squandered. Paul Peterson's book *City Limits* (1981) illustrates the point. Few would deny that Peterson's argument is a significant one. But for all the debate his perspective has generated, little empirical work has resulted. This outcome is all the more remarkable considering that the opportunities for empirically testing his theoretical formulations across a large and diverse group of cities are immense. Fortunately, some such work is now emerging (Schneider 1989). It remains to be seen how well theorists will incorporate such rigorous empiricism into their approaches. If they pay serious attention, we could be treated to a refined and more powerful model specifying the role of economic forces in the life of the city. If not, we shall continue to contend over the plausibility of theoretical arguments, blissfully ignorant of relevant empirical work.

The beauty of good theory is that it does not really matter so much whether the original theory is ultimately proven to be right or wrong. What is significant is that the perspective on reality incorporated in the model is compelling. If it stimulates empirical work that generates new knowledge, then the theory has made a contribution. Unfortunately, some have claimed that the really interesting ideas cannot be operationalized. They argue that quantification represents a lower order of intellectual activity and that only trivial concepts are amenable to measurement and testing. It is certainly the case that developing operational measures of complex variables frequently represents a major challenge. However, even an inferior or inadequate operational indicator is generally preferable to no measure at all. Unsatisfactory operational definitions can be criticized, revised, and improved. Invisible ones are beyond reproach. They defy criticism and refinement because they resist precision in definition. Vagueness and abstraction in our writing ensures that constructing theories about urban politics can never proceed in an orderly, rigorous, and systematic way.

We sorely lack those careful analyses essential to a rigorous test of theoretical formulations. When such efforts are undertaken, they pay substantial dividends and are recognized in the larger discipline (Browning, Marshall, Tabb 1984; Lineberry 1967; Jones 1978). Unfortunately, these research projects require a great deal of time and money. Until we develop an incentive structure that rewards empirically supported theory, we are unlikely to see very much work in this vein.

3. The interdisciplinary approach has succeeded too well. The urban field is an empty vessel into which many pour: Marxists, social critics, normative theorists, geographers, political economists, historians, political scientists, planners, anthropologists, and sociologists. Many celebrate this rich diversity. Our interdisciplinary sophistication implies willingness to recognize the value of theories, perspectives, and approaches developed in other fields. The city is our common bond and all comers are welcome.

There is certainly something to be said for diversity. But a sensitivity to the importance of competing interdisciplinary claims also imposes significant costs. Increasingly, however, fewer and fewer urban political scientists are primarily interested in the study of city politics. Instead, their focus is on economics, culture, growth, geography, sociology. We can easily recognize that these forces ultimately exert an impact upon the political life of the city. However, the causal linkages are exceedingly difficult to disentangle. In the process of trying we have lost sight of traditional political issues—interest groups, participation, institutions, political processes, policy outcomes. While an appreciation for the complex of powerful factors that influence the city is commendable, where does one draw the line? At some point, urban political scientists will have to define a body of scholarly concerns that is conceptually distinct from those emphasized by other disciplines. If not, we run the risk of blurring our focus and distorting our agenda and priorities. We have eventually to decide who we are: students of the city or students of urban politics.

It is not a given that it is better to be comprehensive and abstract rather than focused and precise. In our rush to develop holistic models, we have given scanty attention to a number of distinctly important political concerns: authority, legitimacy, participation, equity, representation, responsiveness, accountability, agenda setting. These are decidedly worthwhile pursuits and deserve much more emphasis than they have recently received.

4. Urbanists are prone to an infatuation with the latest scholarly fad. The political economy approach is the dominant perspective in the study of urban politics today. But it is almost certainly the case that in a few years the economic development focus will no longer lay claim to the same share of the attention and energies of urbanists. Instead, some issue not yet on the horizon will take over as the latest scholarly rage. Those who argue that political economy will prove to be the exception to the rule need only reflect on the experience of the past twenty years to realize the extent to which scholarly loyalties are fickle and attention spans limited. Urbanists, in particular, react to a constantly shifting landscape of prominent issues. Our interest darts from community power, to federal urban programs, to urban violence, to the ungovernable city, to the fiscal crisis, to economic growth. Before we have taken the time to carefully develop rigorous empirical theories in a particular area, we rush off to chart new ground.

Why is the urban intellectual agenda so reactive? Unlike the case for students of Congress or the courts, the focus of our research is both extraordinarily complex and subject to the intense and continuous impact of powerful outside forces. Students of legislatures and the judiciary can count roll-call votes and cases with little concern for the federal and state roles. They do not have to worry about competition with other local governments, the struggle for economic growth, the erosion of the tax base, or the changing racial, economic, and social composition of the city. Urban scholars are caught in a dilemma. Because they are keenly aware of the dynamic nature of the city, they are frustrated by the inadequacy of static models. They recognize that the city is in a state of constant and frequently rapid flux. At the same time, they are unable to develop theories that effectively model change itself. (Who *has* been able to develop such models in any field?) Consequently, urbanists are constantly in search of new and better theories to replace existing ones. These new theories are generally tied to the latest urban crisis. It is no coincidence that each crisis spawns a fresh batch of perspectives on the city—urban decay, ghetto violence, crime, fiscal stress, economic change and decline. Whatever crisis holds the city in its grip represents a focal point of change, and draws the attention of those urbanists seeking holistic explanations.

Unfortunately, there is no easy way out of the dilemma. When we jump from one crisis to another in search of new and more satisfactory theoretical formulations, we lose the opportunity to develop a dominant paradigm. In the absence of such a paradigm no rigorous, systematic empirical work is possible. By hopping from one crisis to another, we successively dismiss various theories without ever having given them the chance to be evaluated—and accepted or rejected—on the basis of accumulated evidence. Without a sound theoretical foundation that is conducive to careful and incremental empirical testing, urbanists will be unlikely to have much impact on the larger discipline. This is unfortunate, as the narrow institutional focus of the mainstream discipline misses much of what is important in politics.

As difficult as it may be, we suggest that urbanists should control their collective urges to chase the latest crisis. At present, we lack the theoretical and methodological tools essential to the task of building holistic models that are sensitive to change. We should fashion our own research agenda rather than continue in a reactive mode. We should set our sights at a more modest level. There is nothing wrong with striving to develop a theoretically informed and empirically supported body of literature that is sensitive to traditional political science concerns. But by rejecting the scientific approach in favor of abstract models and case studies, we have thrown a good part of the baby out with the bathwater. In our impatience with our ability to remain abreast of the powerful forces buffeting the city, we have discarded our empirical models and opted for grand theorizing.

It is almost certainly the case that if the central cities were to explode into violence tomorrow, many urbanists would drop the political economy perspective currently in vogue and rush to study race relations in the city (the next round of violence will almost certainly be race-related). The urban research agenda would sustain a fundamental transformation. We would experience an outpouring of case studies on the topic purporting to provide theoretical explanations for the riots. But it is also true that we would not be able to explain why the violence occurred, or what its impact might be, or whether the riots would happen again. We would not be able to do any of these things very well because the tedious empirical groundwork that should have been accomplished years ago was never done. We were off chasing change. And, as usual, we missed it.

CONCLUSION

During the last thirty years, the study of urban politics has moved from a focus on evaluating the economy and efficiency of municipal government to something else. That something else has promised much— theories of urban politics, an understanding of city dynamics, an inte-

gration of all the social sciences around urban concerns, policy prescriptions for urban problems. Urbanists, however, have been unable to
deliver on most of these promises.

This gap between promise and performance is cause for concern.
On the bright side, it is probably safe to say that never before in the
history of the study of urban politics have so many scholars taken the
city as their focus of research. With that many bright and dedicated people at work, there is reason to be optimistic about the future. Moreover,
urbanists carry on an honorable tradition of scholarship that has made
substantial contributions to the discipline of political science. It was
work on the city that produced pioneering efforts on community
power, bureaucracy, intergovernmental relations, equity, public policy,
and political institutions. Urbanists, moreover, have become sensitive
to the need for theory—no trivial accomplishment, given the origins of
the field. If we urbanists can only control our urge toward abstraction,
and can tie theoretical impulses to the available array of methodological
tools, we can accomplish work of much significance.

This considerable potential, however, has yet to be realized. We are
dismayed by the absence of urban research from the pages of the major
journals, and the remarks of some urbanists who characterize these journals as unworthy of our best efforts because they publish unintelligible
articles replete with complex statistical models that ensure the continuing narrowness of these outlets. According to this perspective, urbanists
should be little concerned with publishing in mainstream political science journals, instead, finding their true audience among other
urbanists. Since many and even most of these urbanists are not political
scientists, this course of action will take us further and further away
from vigorous participation in the discipline of political science.

Urban political scientists ought to be students of urban politics first
rather than students of the city. For reasons already discussed, we do not
think it is presently possible to develop empirically supported theories
of urbanism. However, it is possible to develop empirically supported
theories of urban politics.

The city provides a rich opportunity to study a number of important and distinctly political concerns. There is much that we need to
know about political participation and its impact, about public decision-making, about authority and legitimacy, about policy outcomes,
about citizen demand and government response, and about representation. One of the fascinating questions about city politics is the way in
which equity and productivity concerns alternate in their domination of
the public agenda. The cyclical nature of this process structures the political debate and creates an environment in which some policy choices
are more likely than others. The larger issue is the way in which the
public agenda is set. In fact, this issue is of decisive importance to an

effective understanding of the urban political process. Who controls the public agenda? How? What strategies are employed? To what extent do internal actors as opposed to external forces influence the control, setting, and scheduling of the public agenda? What is the relationship between the political agenda and policy choices and outcomes? How does the control of the public agenda vary across a large and diverse number of cities? Who wins and who loses as a result?

The list of significant questions that we could ask about the public agenda is long indeed. However, they are important questions to ask, because the urban agenda exerts a major impact upon the structure and process of political life in the city. Whether equity or productivity concerns dominate is, in part, a function of who controls and sets the agenda. In fact, a systematic and rigorous analysis of the public agenda may eventually point the way toward getting a conceptual grip on the process of urban change itself.

In the rush to examine the impact of economic imperatives upon the city, urbanists have ignored a rich array of vital political concerns and issues. We have become convinced that developmental interests overwhelm political ones, and that economics enjoys primacy over politics. It is said that cities are under immense pressure to pursue developmental policies and avoid redistributive ones. All of this may be true. But in our urgency to become political economists we have lost our bearings as political scientists. The politics of the city is as significant as the economics of the city. To argue that important political decisions are only by-products of economic imperatives is to defy the rich and compelling evidence arrayed before our very eyes. We already have urbanists who are doing the empirically rigorous and theoretically informed work that needs to be accomplished (Browning, Marshall, and Tabb 1984; Wong 1988; Stone 1988). The study of urban politics needs much more of the same if it is to realize its rich potential.

REFERENCES

Banfield, Edward. 1961. *Political Influence*. Glencoe, Ill.: The Free Press.

Browning, Rufus P., Dale Rogers Marshall, and David H. Tabb. 1984. *Protest Is Not Enough*. Berkeley: University of California Press.

Burt, Barbara, and Ken Mladenka. 1986. "Even If We Do the Research, Can We Get It Published?" *Urban Politics Newsletter* 1:4–6.

Dahl, Robert. 1960. *Who Governs?* New Haven: Yale University Press.

Elkin, Stephen. 1987. *City and Regime in the American Republic*. Chicago: University of Chicago Press.

Giles, Michael, Francie Mizell, and David Patterson. 1989. "Political Scientists' Journal Evaluation Revisited." *PS* (September): 613–27.

Jones, Bryan. 1978. "Service Delivery Rules and the Distribution of Local Government Services." *Journal of Politics* 40:332–68.

Kantor, Paul, and Stephen David. 1983. "The Political Economy of Change in Urban Budgetary Politics." *British Journal of Political Science* 13:251–74.

Lineberry, Robert L., and Edmund P. Fowler. 1967. "Reformism and Public Policy in American Cities." *American Political Science Review* 61:701–16.

Lipsky, Michael. 1980. *Street-Level Bureaucracy*. New York: Russell Sage Publications.

Lowery, David, and William Lyons. 1989. "The Impact of Jurisdictional Boundaries." *Journal of Politics* 51:73–97.

Mladenka, Kenneth. 1978. "Rules, Service Equity, and Distributional Decisions. *Social Science Quarterly* 59:192–202.

Ostrom, Vincent, Robert Bish, and Elinor Ostrom. 1989. *Local Government in the United States*. San Francisco: Institute for Contemporary Studies.

Peterson, Paul E. 1981. *City Limits*. Chicago: University of Chicago Press.

Sayre, Wallace, and Herbert Kaufman. 1965. *Governing New York City*. New York: Norton.

Schneider, Mark. 1989. *The Competitive City*. Pittsburgh, Pa.: University of Pittsburgh Press.

Shefter, Martin. 1985. *Political Crisis, Fiscal Crisis*. New York: Basic Books.

Stone, Clarence N. 1988. "Preemptive Power: Floyd Hunter's 'Community Power Structure' Reconsidered." *American Journal of Political Science* 22: 82–104.

Wong, Kenneth K. 1988. "Economic Constraint and Political Choice in Urban Policymaking." *American Journal of Political Science* 22:1–18.

Notes on Contributors

Allan J. Cigler teaches political science at the University of Kansas. He received his Ph.D. from Indiana University in 1972. His most recent interest group publications include *U.S. Agricultural Groups* (1990) and the third edition of *Interest Group Politics* (1991).

William Crotty is professor of political science at Northwestern University. He received his Ph.D. from the University of North Carolina at Chapel Hill in 1964. His areas of interest include political parties and election processes, policy-making, and American and comparative governing institutions. He has served as president of the Political Organizations and Parties Section of the American Political Science Organization, the Midwest Political Science Association, and the Policy Studies Organization. He is the author of a number of articles and books, including *Decision for the Democrats* (1978), *Party Reform* (1983), *The Party Game* (1985), *American Parties in Decline* (coauthor, 1980, 1984), *Presidential Primaries and Nominations* (coauthor, 1985), and *Political Parties in Local Areas* (coauthor, 1987). Professor Crotty has been the recipient of an American Political Science Association Fellowship to study the national political parties and he has served as a member of a number of commissions invited to observe elections and democratic processes in Latin America.

Roger H. Davidson teaches political science at the University of Maryland. He received his Ph.D. from Columbia University in 1963. From 1980 to 1987, he served as senior specialist for the Congressional Research Service. He has written several books, including *Congress and Its Members* (3rd ed., 1989) and *Congress Against Itself* (1977).

Bryan D. Jones is professor and head of the Department of Political Science, Texas A&M University. He has authored or coauthored *Service Delivery in the City, Governing Urban America, Governing Buildings and Building Government*, and *The Sustaining Hand*, and has edited *Leadership in Politics*. In addition, he has published articles in the *American Political Science Review*, the *Journal of Politics*, the *Urban Affairs Quarterly*, and other scholarly journals.

Susan A. MacManus is professor and chair of the Department of Government and International Affairs at the University of South Florida, Tampa. She has published articles on intergovernmental relations, public budgeting and finance, urban and minority politics, and public policy analysis in a number of leading journals, including *The American Journal of Political Science*, the *Journal of Politics, Publius, The Annals of the American Academy of Political and Social Science, The International Journal of Public Administration*, and others. Among her books are *Revenue Patterns in U.S. Cities and Suburbs, Federal Aid to Houston, Governing a Changing America* (with Charles S. Bullock III and Donald M.

Freeman), and *Visions for the Future: Creating New Institutional Relationships among Academia, Business, Government, and Community* (with Francis T. Borkowski). Dr. MacManus serves on the Florida Governor's Council of Economic Advisors and on the Research Advisory Board of the James Madison Institute for Public Policy Studies. She is a consultant to many national, state, and local governments and public and private research foundations.

Kenneth R. Mladenka teaches political science at Texas A&M University. He received his Ph.D. from Rice University in 1975. He has published scholarly articles in the *American Political Science Review*, the *Journal of Politics*, *American Journal of Political Science*, *Social Science Quarterly*, and *Urban Affairs Quarterly*. He is the founder and first president of the Urban Politics Section, American Political Science Association.

Paul J. Quirk teaches political science at the University of Illinois, Urbana-Champaign, and has a research appointment in the Institute of Government and Public Affairs, University of Illinois. He received his Ph.D. from Harvard University in 1978. His books are *Industry Influence in Federal Regulatory Agencies* (1981) and *The Politics of Deregulation* (1985), winner of the Louis Brownlow Book Award of the National Academy of Public Administration. He has published in the *American Political Science Review*, the *Journal of Politics*, and other journals, and has served on the editorial board of the *American Journal of Political Science*. He has published several essays about presidential politics and decision-making.

Elliot E. Slotnick is an associate professor in the Department of Political Science at The Ohio State University, where he has taught since 1977. He received his Ph.D. from the University of Minnesota. His published work focuses on several facets of judicial politics and constitutional interpretation and has appeared in numerous journals, including the *American Journal of Political Science*, the *Journal of Politics*, *American Politics Quarterly*, the *Western Political Quarterly*, *Polity*, the *Yale Law and Policy Review*, *Justice System Journal*, *Judicature*, and the *Law and Politics Quarterly*. He is the coeditor of *Readings in American Government and Politics* (1989). In 1980 he was the recipient of the Outstanding Teaching Award at Ohio State.

Ronald E. Weber is the Wilder Crane Professor of Government at the University of Wisconsin, Milwaukee, and coeditor of *The Journal of Politics*. He received his Ph.D. from Syracuse University in 1969 and previously taught at Indiana University and Louisiana State University. He has written several books, including *Patterns of Decision-Making in State Legislatures* (1977) and *Public Policy Preferences in the States* (1971), as well as numerous scholarly articles in journals such as the *American Political Science Review*, the *Journal of Politics*, *Public Opinion Quarterly*, *Legislative Studies Quarterly*, and *Political Methodology*. He has been active in the work of several professional associations, including service on the executive councils of the American Political Science Association, Southern Political Science Association, and Southwestern Political Science Association. He was a Fulbright Senior Lecturer in American Studies at Hiroshima University, Japan, in 1982–83 and has served as a consultant to federal, state, and local governments.